PROFITING THE CROWN

In 1971 the government of Canada recognized the contribution of Polymer Corporation by putting a picture of it on the back of the $10 bill.

Profiting the Crown

*Canada's Polymer Corporation
1942–1990*

MATTHEW J. BELLAMY

McGill-Queen's University Press
Montreal & Kingston · London · Ithaca

© McGill-Queen's University Press 2005
ISBN 978-0-7735-2815-4 (cloth)
ISBN 978-0-7735-3201-4 (paper)

Legal deposit first quarter 2005
Bibliothèque nationale du Québec

Printed in Canada on acid-free paper that is 100% ancient forest free
(100% post-consumer recycled), processed chlorine free.
Reprinted 2006
First paperback edition 2006
Reprinted 2012

This book was first published with the help of a grant from the Canadian
Federation for the Humanities and Social Sciences, through the Aid to
Scholarly Publications Program, using funds provided by the Social
Sciences and Humanities Research Council of Canada. Funding was also
received from Bayer Inc.

McGill-Queen's University Press acknowledges the support of the Canada
Council for the Arts for our publishing program. We also acknowledge the
financial support of the Government of Canada through the Canada Book
Fund for our publishing activities.

Library and Archives Canada Cataloguing in Publication

Bellamy, Matthew J., 1967-
    Profiting the Crown: Canada's Polymer Corporation, 1942-1990/
Matthew J. Bellamy.

Includes bibliographical references and index.
ISBN 978-0-7735-2815-4 (bnd)
ISBN 978-0-7735-3201-4 (pbk)

1. Polymer Corporation – History. 2. Corporations, Government – Canada –
Case studies. 3. Government business enterprises – Canada – Case studies.
I. Title.

HD4005.B44 2005   338.7'67872'0971   C2004-903560-6

This book was typeset by Interscript Inc. in 10/12 Baskerville.

*To Annette, Heather,
Simon, and John*

Contents

Illustrations

Preface

Crown corporations have long been present on the Canadian landscape. Since 1841, they have been dexterously implemented and hotly debated as instruments of public policy. Yet they have fallen out of favour of late. Today, many view the "Crown" as lazy, inefficient, and ineffective forms of enterprise. To be sure, a number of Crown corporations have failed to realize their objectives. Polymer Corporation Ltd was not one of them. What follows is the history of one of Canada's most successful Crown corporations and the play of public policy and commercial enterprise upon it.

Polymer came into existence in 1942 in response to the Japanese invasion of Southeast Asia, which, as of December 1941, cut off the Allied rubber supply. Before then, over 90 percent of the world's rubber had come from the plantations of the Far East. Rubber was indispensable to modern warfare and wartime industry: most military items used it in one form or another, because its malleable properties minimized mechanical wear and tear. Without an alternative source, the Allied war machine would have come to a grinding halt. Because it lacked the time and climatic conditions that were necessary for cultivating a source of natural rubber, Ottawa embarked upon an experimental project to produce a synthetic substitute. The risky program was designed to produce enough synthetic rubber to meet all Canada's wartime requirements and, therefore, to keep the country in the war. To oversee the construction and operation of its first synthetic rubber plant, Ottawa created Polymer Corporation. As one of twenty-eight Crown corporations set up by the federal government during the war, Polymer was expected to fulfill a public-policy purpose. Despite various obstacles, it managed to achieve its objective. By war's end the nation no longer depended on foreign supplies of rubber.

After the war, Polymer was one of a handful of Crown corporations retained by the Crown. The task assigned to it by the dynamic minister of reconstruction, C.D. Howe, was to act as an industrial polymath. Howe was convinced that by functioning as a commercial enterprise on the free market, it would attract other petrochemical companies to the Sarnia region. It would thus be the cornerstone of a "chemical valley". With its mandate clearly defined, Polymer became a model of state-owned industrial success. How it did so is the subject of this book.

In Canada, Crown corporations have always been expected to perform both policy and commercial roles. Polymer was unique in that for most of its existence, the emphasis was on the commercial role. Making money was its raison d'être. In the process of turning a profit, however, Polymer incidentally served a public purpose – initially winning the war and latterly giving Canada a leading-edge presence in the global synthetic rubber industry. The going was not always easy, of course. Over its history, Polymer faced many challenges. This book identifies those challenges and its response to them. It explores its strategies and structures in the context of international business developments, the role of science and technology in the growth of the firm, the relationship between profits and innovation, and the dynamics of corporate decision making.

Drawing on the rich Polymer/Polysar collection at the National Archives of Canada and the informed comments and reflections of the men who led the corporation over a period of fifty years, the book concludes that, contrary to neoconservative rhetoric, Crown corporations can be both effective instruments of public policy and dynamic and profitable commercial enterprises.

A number of people have helped to make this book possible, and I am pleased to acknowledge their assistance. First and foremost I would like to thank my dear friend Dr Duncan McDowall. This project would not have been possible without his assistance. He brought the topic to my attention in the first place and thereafter faithfully guided me through the ups and downs of academic research. I would also like to thank Bruce Doern, Stephen Azzi, Michael Bliss, Robin Neill, and Peter Fitzgerald for their insights and support. I am especially indebted to Dr E.J. Buckler. His ability to reflect on Polymer's past with humour and acumen made the task of researching and writing this book much less difficult than it would otherwise have been. That said, where errors and omissions exist, they are solely my responsibility. Messrs Bill Pursell, Firm Bentley, Bob Adams, Robert Dudley, and Roger Hatch, all of Polymer Corporation, facilitated my research in Sarnia and were most generous with their time and insights. I owe my gratitude to Ron

Huizingh, Erin McNaughton, and Tina DeMars, of Bayer Polymers, Bayer Inc., Sarnia Site, for allowing me access to the firm's historical documents and aiding in the publication of this book; to my colleagues and friends in the economics and history departments at Carleton University for creating a wonderful environment in which to work; to all those people who helped transform this work from a thesis to a book, especially Aurèle Parisien, Joanne Pisano, Joan McGilvray, Dorothy Beaven, and Ron Curtis. Finally, I would like to thank the members of my family for their tireless and unwavering support.

Introduction

In an article entitled "O Canada, Our Land of Crown Corporations," published in 1929, historian Frank Underhill argued that what made us distinctly Canadian was not our geography or our political culture or even the fact that we were made up primarily of two linguistic peoples.[1] Rather, according to Underhill, our national identity lay in how we handled the economic question. Unlike in the United States – a land that Underhill maintained was defined by an unrelieved capitalistic individualism – in Canada the body politic embraced state-run enterprise and accepted the virtues of the public ownership and operation of various crucial economic institutions. "In such enterprises as Ontario Hydro, the Canadian National Railways, and the provincial telephone systems of the West," argued Underhill in that bugle of contrary thought, the *Canadian Forum*, "we have experimented in another method of providing public services than that of trusting to the private capitalists in search of a profit."[2] At a time when Canadians were struggling to distinguish themselves from their neighbours south of the border, Underhill claimed to have located the quintessential Canadian identity in the nation's innovative use of its Crown corporations.

In the decades that followed, the Crown corporation became an increasingly energetic force in the Canadian marketplace. The need for proactive government in an open and export-driven economy legitimized the idea of public ownership. Added to this, the Great Depression of the 1930s called out for unorthodox solutions. Eventually, in 1935, even Prime Minister R.B. Bennett, stymied by his initial instinct not to tinker with orthodoxy, would acknowledge that the old order was gone and that state intervention should be the new orthodoxy. "I am for reform," he boldly told Canadians. "And, in my mind, reform means Government intervention."[3] Amongst the thin ranks of Canadian academics and public servants, the writings of John Maynard

Keynes and the spread of progressive concepts from the United States
further justified the use of Crown corporations. Isolated scholars began suggesting that managerial innovations from the private sector
could be emulated within the public sector. Political economist J.A.
Corry at Queen's University, for example, spoke about "the fusion of
government and business in the independent public corporation."[4]
He saw the Crown corporation as a progressive force capable of meeting various socioeconomic challenges.

Thereafter the "Crowns" – as they were soon warmly referred to –
were used to fulfill a number of commercial and public-policy functions. Some, like the Canadian Radio and Broadcasting Commission,
which was initially created by R.B. Bennett in 1932 and made a full-
blooded Crown enterprise by Mackenzie King in 1936, were employed
to promote cultural and political cohesion.[5] About the same time, the
federal government reestablished the Canadian Wheat Board, which
had been briefly given life during the First World War, to stabilize prices
in the face of declining world demand. In 1937, a rising force within
the Liberal Party, an engineer-turned-politician named C.D. Howe, created Trans-Canada Airlines to provide a national air transportation service.[6] If the privately managed Canadian Pacific Railway had linked the
coasts in the nineteenth century, a publicly owned airline would mimic
the feat with new technology in the twentieth century. After the outbreak of the war in 1939, Howe showed similar pragmatism in setting
up twenty-eight Crown corporations to coordinate the production of
munitions and supplies. For his efforts, he has frequently been cast in
the role of the "great man" of public enterprise in this country.[7] The
"Howe boys," it was said, won Canada's economic war. During the postwar period, such Crown corporations as Ocean Falls and Sydney Steel
were used by provincial governments to protect jobs. Others still, like
the Industrial Development Bank, were established to stimulate underdeveloped sectors of the economy.[8] Airplane producers like De Havilland were "saved" by Ottawa. The Crown corporation had thus become
laced into the fabric of the postwar boom. Then came a wave of economic nationalism in the 1970s, when various Crown corporations
were established to "take back" control of the Canadian economy. Both
Petro-Canada and the Canada Development Corporation were established for nationalist reasons.[9] Finally, there were those long-lived
Crown corporations, like the Liquor Control Board of Ontario, which
were used to regulate and distribute commodities deemed to have a serious "social cost" and thereby govern Canadians' moral demeanour.
Thus, in the seventy years or so since Underhill dared to suggest Canada's predilection for Crown enterprise, the Crowns were artfully employed to achieve an number of policy objectives.

The extensive use of Crown corporations since the 1930s is evidence of the deep-rooted propensity in Canada toward state intervention. Canada's vast geography, sparse population, and relative lack of technology, capital, and markets have led successive governments to take an active role in the development of the Canadian economy. So widespread has state activism been that political scientist Alexander Brady has concluded that "the role of the state in the economic life of Canada is really the modern history of Canada."[10] Economic historian Hugh Aitken has reached a similar conclusion. In his classic 1959 article, "Defensive Expansionism: The State and Economic Growth in Canada," Aitken argues that government intervention in Canada has been prolific and creative. According to Aitken, the political urgency of protecting the westward-moving Canadian frontier against the threat of American encroachment, as well as the economic necessity of mobilizing scarce resources to promote investment, prompted the government to lend its support to nearly every economic endeavour. The fact that the federal government was the driving force behind the creation of the transcontinental railway in the 1880s led Aitken to conclude that Canada was as much a *political* as an economic achievement.[11] Other economic historians have traced this activism back further still, to the road-building and canal era of the early nineteenth century.[12] The colonial state used its resources to define early Ontario. As early as the 1790s, Yonge Street was pushed north from the lakefront, thereby opening Toronto's future hinterland using military surveys and military labour. Aitken himself has written extensively about the factors that first induced the colonial government to get involved in the construction of the Welland Canal, which by 1841 was wholly state-owned.[13] Thus, Aitken was part of a generation of postwar academics who generally viewed state intervention as a positive force.

The climate is radically different today. The tendency is no longer toward, but rather away from, state intervention and the use of Crown corporations. The faith in the positivist state has passed, and it is now considered "pragmatic" for governments to let the "invisible hand" of market forces determine economic outcomes. The late-twentieth-century failures of such government-sponsored enterprises as Bricklin, Churchill Forest Industries, Deuterium, Consolidated Computer Limited, Skeena Cellulose, and Sydney Steel have led a majority of Canadians to conclude that the state has no place in the boardrooms of the nation. The massive accumulation of debt at Ontario Hydro over its history, particularly during the years 1915–30, 1961–69, 1980–90, and 1994–2002, has reinforced that sentiment. Today the popular consensus is closer to the opinion of journalist Walter Stewart than to the judgment of Frank Underhill. The Crown corporation has become a

favourite whipping boy of critics of Canada's mixed economy. According to Stewart, the Crown corporation is a "gross, ugly, wrong-headed
brute of a thing."[14] Viewed as burdened by political meddling, bureaucratic barriers, mixed and sometimes contradictory objectives, and un-
inspired management, the Crown corporation is now stereotypically
considered an inefficient and ineffectual form of enterprise. The general perception is that private industry can do a better job at achieving
national economic objectives. Our fin de siècle experience was thus
generally one of expelling the state from the business of runnign the
economy; Air Canada and Canadian National offered two telling examples of privatization. Pressured by neoconservative forces such as
the Reform Party in the 1990s, the Liberal Party in Ottawa embraced
this antistatism, which led it, at least in the short term, to deficit reduction and success at the polls. Crown corporations have come to be seen
as incapable of innovation, entrepreneurship, and profit-seeking behaviour. Politicians promise that there will be no more costly "bail
outs."[15] This chorus has persisted into the early twenty-first century,
and across the land federal, provincial, and even municipal governments continue to cast a skeptical eye on public enterprise.

But at least one prominent example contradicts this politically correct mantra and the current widespread belief that Crown corporations are lethargic, unproductive, and disorganized forms of economic
enterprise. Polymer Corporation, a maker of synthetic rubber for war
and peace, was a resourceful state-owned and state-controlled company that played a dynamic, agile, and profitable role in the economy.
Through it, the state forced the pace of the development of a new synthetic rubber industry and in so doing, helped the nation overcome its
innate deficiency in natural rubber. For close to fifty years, from 1942
to 1990, this corporation led the world in synthetic rubber production
and development. Always sensitive to the imperatives of the marketplace, Polymer practised innovation and entrepreneurship in pursuit
of profit. It implemented a series of market-smart strategies and structures in response to a succession of internal and external opportunities and threats. By so doing, Polymer profited the Crown.

How Polymer grew, made money, and confounded the neoconservative critics of state enterprise is the subject of this book. In her classic
study, *The Theory of the Growth of the Firm*, Edith Penrose argues that
growth is an evolutionary process based on a complicated interaction of
a company's resources, capabilities, goals, and market opportunities.[16]
The pace and direction of growth is determined by the company's technical and managerial capabilities, as well as by developments in the
marketplace. But the direction and pace of corporate growth changes
over time, although not in a random way. Rather, it depends on prior

judgments, fixed investments, and changes during the life cycle of the firm. It is thus a historical phenomenon. The forte of the marketplace is that it constantly transmits economic impulses to enterprise; enterprises that adjust to these signals survive.

Theorists of economic evolution have long accepted this conclusion. Following the Austrian economic philosopher Joseph Schumpeter, they provide a model of the process of firm growth, analyzing the ways in which firms transform themselves and their environments. Rather than treating the firm as a passive agent responding to exogenously given technology, consumer demand, and information structures, these economic commentators allow the firm true agency.[17] Harvard's eminent business historian Alfred Chandler, for example, argues that when successful, a firm expands the output of its standard product line and restlessly introduces new sorts of products. All the while, it adjusts its organizational structure to the challenge of serving the market. Structure follows strategy, Chandler famously observes. Sometimes expansion requires vertical integration (to secure raw inputs or broaden market shares) or horizontal integration (to stabilize prices and markets or combine resources for investment). Thereafter, growth entails investment in new products and new geographical markets, often through the acquisition of plant and organizational talent abroad.[18] Thus, firms constantly shed their original skins and pass through a number of stages of development. This is arguably true not only of private corporations but also of successful public corporations.[19] The unique central dilemma for Crown corporations operating in a commercial setting, however, is whether they can evolve and thrive as the initial political exigencies of their creation recede or whether they will succumb to the lethargy of a politically imposed mandate that is never adjusted to the progression of the marketplace. Polymer's history suggests that under certain conditions a Crown corporation can remain alive to the impulses of the market.

The trigger or triggers that cause the firm to move from one stage to another are the result of environmental disturbances of sufficient magnitude. All firms can succumb to inertia. Change occurs only in response to some dramatic opportunity or threat. These disturbances cause the firm to react and change its strategy and structure to cope with the new set of circumstances.[20] "How well a company responds to the key business problems of a given period is the primary determinant of its survival and success," argue business historians Davis Dyer and David Sicilia.[21]

This was to be Polymer's experience and the chapters that follow are organized to capture this contention. Although the treatment herein is largely chronological, the basic logic of this book reflects the notion that a successful company incessantly grows and changes in response to opportunities and threats. Most Crown corporations get stuck in the initial strategy and structure because their *political* purpose (e.g., the development of the A-bomb, stopping the invasion of American commercial radio into Canada, and so on) overrides any ability to sense new challenges and opportunities. When this rigidity sets in, many Crown corporations become chronically unprofitable. Polymer was different because it shed its initial political auspices and was constantly exposed to the invigoration of the marketplace. The organizing principle of this history, therefore, is perpetual challenge and strategic response. Polymer did not invariably make the right decisions in this give and take: in the 1970s it would make several costly strategic decisions. But the key to Polymer's success as a Crown corporation – indeed its uniqueness – was that it constantly engaged this process. Polymer obliged the Crown purpose to align its imperatives with those of the marketplace. Each chapter of this book thus deals with Polymer's growth and change in response to specific historical challenges.

Chapter 1 is dedicated to the period before Polymer's creation. It sets the global stage for Canada's leap into large-scale synthetic rubber production during the war and describes the enormous technical and commercial challenges that had to be overcome in order to transform the experimental dream of synthetic rubber production into an industrial reality. Before the war no synthetic rubber had been produced outside the laboratory in North America, and the art of synthetic rubber production, such as it was, was confined to a small group of largely European private firms.

Chapter 2 details how these tremendous prewar obstacles were finally overcome and why Polymer was created. It explores the precision with which C.D. Howe and his "boys" adeptly brought business and science together under the umbrella of a Crown corporation. The challenges of the period were made all the more difficult because of the agonizing circumstances of war. Critical raw materials were in short supply, and time was of the essence. Canada needed a synthetic rubber plant within months if it was going to continue to wage an effective war.

Ironically, Polymer's success at achieving its wartime task created a new set of challenges that became evident in the postwar period. These challenges, which are the subject of chapter 3, arose from the fact that Polymer's plant had the capacity to produce fifty thousand tons of rubber per year, yet after the war Canadians needed about one-third that amount. Polymer was thus without a postwar market for roughly two-thirds of its operating capacity. In addition, the corporation was designed to accommodate the tightly regulated imperatives of wartime production rather than to compete aggressively in a free market economy. It was a structurally truncated enterprise. Unlike the successful prewar private petrochemical enterprises, Polymer lacked a sales division and a department of research and development, crucial organizational elements for any free-market industrial success. Polymer also lacked a natural market for much of its output, a corporate strategy for postwar survival, and the necessary organizational structure for successful operation in a consumer-oriented economy. In short, it lacked the vital ingredients that Alfred Chandler argues are necessary for any industrial enterprise's success.[22] How these challenges were overcome is thus the topic of the third chapter of this book.

The wisdom of Polymer's immediate postwar strategy became evident during the 1951–57 period. These years are the focus of chapter 4. The company's earlier decision to "go global," to diversify its product line and improve its research and development efforts, positioned it to take advantage of the international economic boom of the 1950s. It was thus creating a template for an efficient new definition of the state presence in the national and international economy. Critical to this whole adjustment was Ottawa's willingness to lengthen Polymer's political leash, to let its managers manage according to the dictates of the market and not those of the ballot box. There was no lazy, deficit-prone Crown corporation here. So prosperous were the years 1951–57 for Polymer that its president, J.D. Barrington, felt no need for any change in corporate strategy. Once its structure was brought into line with its existing strategy, the company was set to seize the opportunities that accompanied an age of mass consumerism and the "great god – Car."

The challenge of the succeeding period, 1958–66, was to maintain this level of prosperity in the face of increasing global competition. Chapter 5 therefore chronicles Polymer's response to the new competitive challenge. The global petrochemical industry had always been highly competitive, but after 1960 the competition became cut-throat. The prosperity of the previous period brought a rush of new competitors into the petrochemical field, principally in Europe and Asia. Many private companies attempted to copy Polymer's prior success. Large American companies aggressively attacked existing markets. European companies, like Bayer and Royal Dutch Shell, ICI and BASF, did likewise. With its established market thus under siege from all sides, Polymer aggressively responded by formulating a new strategy and structure for growth. But in order to see the strategy implemented, its managerial cabal would have to persuade the federal government to widen yet again the parameters of its mission. The challenges of this period therefore had both an economic and political dimension. At one level this book explores the politics of state intervention and the political dimension of corporate decision making at a state-owned enterprise. Ironically, it does so only to show how little politics ultimately came into play in the growth of this firm.

During the period 1967-77, which is the focus of chapter 6, the increasing number of firms entering the synthetic rubber industry led to global overcapacity, intense competition, price cutting, and shrinking profit margins. In addition, the pace of innovation was slowing. To make matters worse, Polymer had to contend with inflationary pressures. Salaries and wages, particularly in Canada, were rising faster than corresponding gains in productivity, leading to higher labour costs. As a result the company embraced a strategy of diversification. It also began to pressure the federal government to privatize the firm. Unfortunately, the corporation lacked the patience, leadership, and insight that it needed to succeed at diversification. This, then, was the company's decade of discord.

The challenge of Polymer's final phase, 1978–90, was to put the mistakes of the previous period behind it and return to profitability. To do this the corporation went back to doing what it did best, or, in the parlance of the early 1980s, "sticking to the knitting." By getting "back to basics," Polymer achieved its goal of once again becoming "a profitable international company of significant standing in the petrochemical industry."[23] By successfully meeting the challenges of the period, Polymer inadvertently made itself a target for takeover. During the 1980s, ownership twice changed hands. Chapter 7 chronicles the 1988 purchase of Polymer by Bob Blair's Nova Corporation and the subsequent ownership flip to the German petrochemical giant, Bayer.

While Polymer's postwar corporate strategy changed periodically, one aspect remained constant. Product innovation continued to play a defining role in Polymer's growth and prosperity. At a time when science-based growth was an enigma to most in Canadian industry, Polymer embraced research and development as part of its corporate strategy. The final focus of this book is on how science and innovation led to the growth of the firm.

Here, too, challenges had to be overcome. The limited size of the domestic market, the general lack of indigenous managerial skills and technology, the shortage of investment capital, and the branch-plant nature of the Canadian economy, all combined to make technological innovation in Canada more problematic than in the United States. In addition, Polymer faced the disadvantages of being a medium-sized (in global terms), government-owned firm operating in the same arena as privately owned petrochemical giants.

Long neglected by academic researchers, the petrochemical industry has recently become the subject of several important books.[24] As these works have demonstrated, the industry has been unusually dynamic: change has been rapid, constant, and expensive. Since the late nineteenth century, it has arguably been more diversified, technology-dependent, capital-intensive, and global than any other industry in its development of modern corporate strategies and management techniques. Perhaps it is not too much to suggest, therefore, that the chemical industry was to the twentieth-century corporation what the rail road was to its nineteenth-century forebears: a wellspring of managerial and technological innovation.

Every successful competitor in the world chemical industry has had to be fast on its feet. Those firms – like Du Pont and ICI – that were among Chandler's "first movers" acquired powerful competitive advantages; they knew how to meet customers' special needs and to provide demonstrations, consumer credit, and installation and after-sales repair and maintenance. In the more technologically complex industries, like the petrochemical industry, these firms were habitually the first to become fully aware of the attributes and intricacies of new products and processes.[25] Polymer, the medium-sized Canadian competitor, had to be especially nimble. In contrast to larger companies such as Esso and Du Pont in the United States, ICI in the United Kingdom, or any of the great triumvirate in Germany – Bayer, BASF, and Hoechst – Polymer rarely enjoyed a commanding position in major product markets. As a result, it was obliged to choose its opportunities and weigh investments with unusual care and to reorient itself quickly in response to changing market conditions. At times in its history, Polymer was a "first mover." At other times it was a challenger. This book chronicles how this medium-sized firm, on the edge of the international trading system, embraced science to innovate, survive, and excel.

What is remarkable about Polymer is how well it responded to the opportunities and challenges of producing petrochemicals in the second half of the twentieth century. It seldom conformed to the stereotype of a slothful, spendthrift Crown corporation that so often emerges from the neoconservative attack on the place of the state in Canadian enterprise. To be sure, this Crown corporation made its share of mistakes, but when all was said and done, its success outweighed its failures. As a result, Polymer was one of Canada's most successful modern corporations. For almost fifty years, the company produced top-quality synthetic rubber for a world-wide market; it was innovative, efficient, and prosperous. As such, Canadians may take pride in it and instruction from it.

PROFITING THE CROWN

Poor by Nature:
Rubber, Industry, and the Seeds
of Polymer Science to 1939

On an unusually warm autumn morning in 1770, the English natural philosopher Joseph Priestly sat hunched over his desk in the cluttered study of his cottage in Leeds. He was engaged in writing *The Theory and Practice of Perspective*. The task was proving to be difficult. His philosophical prose, laboriously pencilled out in longhand, did not flow effortlessly. Phrases often eluded perfection. Corrections were thus numerous and onerous. Remarkably, however, Priestly's manuscript did not exhibit the usual marks of endless corrections. Somewhere he had obtained a bit of an odd, dense, black doughy substance that had been brought as a curiosity to Europe from tropics of the New World. To Priestly's credit, he found that this material could be used to rub out pencil marks. This use gave it the name "rubber."

The early history of rubber is intertwined with economic imperialism, commercial revolution, and technological innovation. During the period from first European contact with the New World to the eve of the Second World War, rubber moved from being a curiosity used to erase pencil marks from paper, to an essential industrial input that was employed in everything from conveyor belts to truck tires. Throughout this period, natural rubber dominated markets. Only after the onset of the Second World War did synthetic rubber come into widespread use. Until that time, Canada remained totally dependent on foreign sources of natural rubber.

Natural rubber was first discovered by Europeans in the New World at the dawn of the age of classical imperialism. In the late fifteenth and early sixteenth century, European explorers found natural rubber in the tropical regions of Central and South America. On his second voyage to the region in 1493, Christopher Columbus witnessed the inhabitants of the New World playing a game using balls prepared from the

milky sap of the rubber tree. The balls behaved "as if they were alive."
Columbus was impressed by the novel qualities of rubber, but could
envision few, if any, additional uses for the substance. In this era of bul-
lionism, Columbus focused on obtaining precious metals from the
New World. A nation's power was determined by its wealth, and a nation's wealth was, in turn, determined by the amount of gold and silver
it possessed. Hence the attraction of the New World. Rubber was therefore of little interest. It would take over two centuries for it to become
widely used in Europe.

Nevertheless, in the New World rubber was used for far more than
simply playing games. After the Spanish conquest of Mexico in 1521,
Spanish conquistadors found rubber in use in southern Mexico. The
Aztecs and the Mayas, who inhabited the Yucatan Peninsula and Gua-
temala, used rubber in various ways: for example, to make bottles,
crude enema syringes, quivers, and shoes. The Aztecs were particularly
innovative. Taking advantage of its plastic and impermeable properties, they lined hemp and linen bags with rubber, enabling them to
carry mercury from the mines. In addition, they impregnated many
different materials with rubber latex and from them made cloaks,
shoes, and outside coverings for many articles. Thus, from the earliest
times rubber proved to be a remarkably exploitable natural substance.

Over two hundred years later the French astronomer and naturalist
Charles de la Condamine found the natives in the tropical rain forest
of the Amazon Valley using rubber to make crude articles of clothing,
shoes, headgear, torches, and other useful items. They made waterproof boots, for example, by dipping their legs and feet repeatedly in
the sap of the rubber tree, thereby fabricating a crudely layered boot.
La Condamine was fascinated by this practice, writing in his diary that
the boots were impervious to water and, when smoked, looked like real
leather.[1] Rubber was a unique natural material with a promising commercial future, since it was water resistant and could be moulded into
almost any form, although this fact was lost on the Western world before the mid-1800s.

The "civilized" world was slow in learning how to make use of rubber. For more than two centuries after it was first brought to the attention of Europeans, it was given no serious commercial consideration.
As late as 1791, James Anderson lamented in an article for the *Edinburgh Bee* that rubber was one of the most underappreciated natural
substances. "It is easy to see that the uses to which this substance might
be applied in arts and manufactures are innumerable, and as such can
be effected by no other known substance in nature. Yet so blind has
mankind hitherto been to these advantages ... all that has been done is
to cut it to pieces for the purposes of effacing marks made upon paper

by a black lead pencil, or that of idly amusing children by stretching it out and observing how perfectly it again recovers its pristine form."[2]

The Old World was slow to acknowledge rubber's enormous potential, in part because other natural substances, many of which came from the New World, dominated European markets before the mid-1800s. After roughly 1550, Europeans came to realize that the New World had more than just gold and silver to offer. Fur, for example, came from the beavers that inhabited the river systems of the Canadian Shield. Beaver pelts were in high demand in Europe for use in broad-brimmed hats – a fashion that dominated Europe during the seventeenth and eighteenth centuries. Fur engaged human vanity in a way that rubber did not, and the short-barbed undercoat of the beaver's fur provided the best properties for holding the shape of the broad brims. For most of the sixteenth century, Russia was the traditional supplier of beaver pelts for the European fur industry. But by the mid-1600s, not enough beavers were left in Russia to meet European demand and attention turned to the New World.

It is a familiar story. While the hope of finding an alternative and more efficient route to the Far East initially brought European explorers to North America's shores, the vast natural wealth of the continent kept them coming back. To be sure the principal attraction of the New World was its gold and silver. At a time when the wealth of nations was conceived of in bullionist terms, the imperial powers of Europe were drawn to the mines of America. But increasingly there were other attractions, especially for England and France. After 1600, these two imperial powers looked upon the New World as a source of raw materials: fish, fur, and timber, and then wheat. Each nation established colonies and conducted a "triangle trade" to exploit the natural wealth of North America. The English were particularly successful.

The fur trade had begun as a by-product of the fishing industry off the coast of Newfoundland. So bountiful was the cod – or "beef of the sea" as it was then termed – that a seasoned fisherman could catch as many as four hundred fish a day with nothing more than a line and hook. Cured cod was shipped back to the fish-hungry markets of Europe. Spain was a particularly heavy consumer of Newfoundland cod. Its predominantly Catholic population was required by the Church to eat fish up to 166 days a year. As a result, Spain traded its gold and silver to England in return for Newfoundland cod. For this reason, the Newfoundland fishery has often been referred to as England's gold mine. Europeans were quickly gaining an appetite for the natural products of the New World.

Fish and furs were the first in a long line of North American staple products that were transported to Europe in return for capital and technology. In the eighteenth and nineteenth centuries, timber and wheat were added to the list. The rich natural resources of colonial British North America stimulated the early economic and political development of the region. Indeed, supporters of the staple theory of economic development argue that the export of one or two staple-based products set the pace of Canadian economic growth.[3] As a young country lacking capital, markets, and technology, Canada traded in products in which it had a comparative advantage. These products were nearly always land intensive; that is, they were natural resources needing relatively few labour inputs. As the nations of Europe industrialized after 1750, they turned to the New World for the raw materials required to fuel the process. European manufactured goods, like ploughs, shovels, stoves, kettles, and blankets, were traded for Canadian lumber, cereal, potash, fish and fur, and, later, pulp and paper, oil and gas, uranium, nickel, and various other mineral products. "Canada," as one commentator noted, "was rich by nature."[4]

While unquestionably blessed by the earth, Canada did not possess all the natural resources required by a developing nation. For all its vast natural wealth, it lacked an indigenous supply of rubber – a product that was as essential to turn-of-the-century industrial life as steel, steam, and rail. Since Charles Goodyear's 1839 discovery of vulcanization (i.e., the process of mixing rubber with sulphur and applying heat to make it resistant to temperature changes) rubber had been in general use in the Western world.[5] Before Goodyear's discovery the rubber industry had been small and precarious. Rubber had been used principally because it was flexible and waterproof; it could be plasticized and moulded, but only by impairing other important properties. Useful and marketable goods could not be produced, because the rubber became unmanageably stiff in winter, while the heat of summer converted it to a sticky mess. The discovery of vulcanization removed these limitations. Now the rubber manufacturer could produce rubber goods that were suited to nearly every purpose.

Rubber's versatility and elastic properties ultimately made it a substance of mass consumption. On the eve of the First World War, rubber was utilized by people of all sorts and descriptions for such unrelated products as surgical gloves, electrical insulation, pneumatic rafts, footwear, parachutes, telephone receivers, mattresses and cushions, adhesive tape, golf balls, life-preserver vests, crash-pad linings, girdles, raincoats, ash trays, hockey pucks, pacifiers, and an endless array of products that were at the heart of modern life. In 1928, *Chatelaine* magazine celebrated the versatility of rubber in an article entitled "The Rubber Band Domesticated."[6] Canadian women were informed of the numerous household uses for the rubber band, everything from holding back curtains to canning food. "You will daily find use for the little time saver – the rubber band."[7] These varied uses caused another observer to note in 1939 that "rubber was the fluxing material without which modern living would be either impossible or tremendously restricted."[8] Rubber had come a long way from the days when it was used simply to rub out pencil marks.

While Canadian women were using rubber in the home, Canadian men were using it in the factory: it was essential to making Canada's factories hum. When manufactured into transmission belts, hoses, conveyor belts, and v-belt drives, rubber made production lines move more quickly, more quietly, and more reliably. It dampened, connected, and stretched any number of industrial processes, causing one commentator to conclude that it was "an industrial sinew of democracy."[9] Without it the wheels of industry would have come to a jarring halt.

But its uses did not end there. At a time when mobility was the outstanding characteristic of modern warfare, rubber was essential to motorized transport and combat effectiveness. It crucially enhanced reliability by reducing vibration – machinery's worst enemy. In addition, it made for silence and stealth on the battlefield. In 1942, *Business Week* pointed out that without rubber, the Allied armed forces would be unable to wage war in Europe.[10] No military vehicle could operate without rubber parts, and rubber was in fact used in nearly every military item. A medium-sized tank, for example, used 1,750 pounds of rubber. It took 3,700 pounds to manufacture a 10-ton pontoon bridge; a carriage for a 75-millimetre gun called for 175 pounds; a B-17 Flying Fortress bomber 500 pounds; and a battleship more than 75 tons. During the First World War, thirty-two pounds of rubber was used per person in the military service; the next time the world went to war, six times that amount was needed.[11] Rubber was thus critical to combat effectiveness.

These varied uses all bore witness to rubber's pliable properties and valuable qualities. Rubber was crucial to civilian and military life. The fact that it retained its shape after having been stretched, squeezed, twisted, and distorted made it like no other natural material. And yet Canada, with its abundance of natural wealth, had no domestic supply.

The Canadian climate was ill-suited to the cultivation of the natural rubber tree *Hevea brasiliensis*, which required a tropical climate. Temperatures needed to be consistently high, winds light, and rainfall well-distributed and considerable. None of these conditions occurred regularly enough in Canada to support the cultivation of the rubber tree. In this rare case, therefore, Canada was poor, not rich, by nature. Canadian manufacturers were therefore forced to import their natural rubber from places where the necessary tropical conditions prevailed.

For much of the nineteenth century, this meant Latin America. In the wilds of the Amazon Basin *Hevea brasiliensis* grew like wheat on the Canadian prairie. In the bark of the tree could be found a juice that looked like milk. To allow the substance to flow, the natives made a diagonal incision in the bark. A coconut or cup was tied to the tree at the lowest point of the incision to receive the flow of the milky sap. After three days in the hot climate, the sap became dark grey-brown and solid. It was then collected by the aboriginal inhabitants and taken by canoe down tributaries to the broad, slow-moving Amazon River, where it was purchased by local middlemen.

Just as Montreal had been the coordinating metropolis of the fur trade, Manaus, in Brazil, was the hub of the commerce in rubber in the late nineteenth century. It was shipped from there in huge, ungainly balls to London, Europe, or New York. Manufacturers like Gutta Percha of Toronto purchased supplies through brokers or dealers who graded the rubber by its origin and quality. This haphazard supply line was sorely taxed, however, in the late 1800s. Commercial demand was on the rise. While Brazilian exports jumped to seventy-four hundred tons in 1870, they still failed to keep pace with burgeoning demand. Nevertheless, for most of the nineteenth century, the rain forest of the Amazon Basin was the dominant source of natural rubber.

But that dominance was eroded after 1876 as a result of the cunning exploits of a young English planter. That year, Henry Wickham illegally collected seventy thousand *Hevea brasiliensis* seeds and smuggled them out of Brazil on the British steamer *Amazonas*.[12] Most of the seeds survived the long ocean voyage from the mouth of the Amazon River to the port at Liverpool and were subsequently germinated in the hothouses of the Royal Botanical Gardens at Kew. In the years that followed, the young rubber plants were used to propagate plantations in the tropical regions of the Eastern hemisphere – Malaya, British Borneo and Sarawak (forming what is present-day Malaysia), the Netherland Indies (which is now Indonesia), and Indochina (modern-day Vietnam and Cambodia). These locations, as the English ethnographer Albert Bickmore noted in his *Travels in the East Indian Archipelago* (1868), fell within a narrow belt extending seven hundred miles on either side of the equator. Like Marco Polo before him, Bickmore was taken by the natural beauty of the region. "Here, the water reflects the light, as from a polished mirror, and the islands appear like gigantic emeralds set in a sea of silver."[13] If Bickmore had been thinking in such terms, he would have pointed out that the climate of the region was ideal for the cultivation of *Hevea*.

The climate, combined with the availability of cheap labour and the successful development of a plantation culture, resulted in the meteoric rise of the Southeast Asian rubber industry after 1915. Concomitantly, the Amazonian wild rubber trade went into decline.[14] At the turn of the century, the Brazilian rubber industry had accounted for over 80 percent of world rubber production. Forty years later it had virtually disappeared. In contrast, the plantations of the Far East, which had produced just 5 tons of rubber in 1899, were producing 550,000 tons per year after 1925. These numbers caused one Canadian commentator to note that the "beginning of the rubber culture [in the Far East] about fifteen years before the mass production of automobiles seems almost providential, if we may assume Providence to have an interest in automobiles."[15] By 1939, the plantations of the Far East were supplying over 90 percent of world rubber requirements. Nearly all of Canada's rubber came from this foreign source.

On the eve of the Second World War, Canada was a voracious consumer of rubber, ranking sixth in the world – behind Japan, France, Germany, the United Kingdom, and the United States. Canadian consumption had increased exponentially since 1910, when Canadians annually consumed roughly 1,500 tons. Ten years later they were consuming almost ten times that amount. During the "roaring twenties" consumption tripled. While rubber consumption declined during the first few years of the Great Depression, it bounced back after 1935, reaching a prewar high of 43,100 tons in 1938. The rise in Canadian consumption was both a cause and a consequence of the growth of the Canadian rubber industry.

In Canada rubber manufacturing began when the world industry was still gathering momentum for the spectacular advance that was to take place after the First World War. Most early rubber manufacturing was in footwear and clothing. Population growth and the rising standard of living had opened new consumer markets for these products. In 1854 the first Canadian rubber factory had been erected at the corner of Monarque and St Mary's Street in Montreal. The factory later became part of the powerful Dominion Rubber Company.[16] During the nineteenth century, Montreal was not only the commercial but also the industrial capital of Canada as well. Toronto, however, was making inroads. The widespread adoption and improvement of Goodyear's vulcanization process after 1850, coupled with the growing use of steam and electrical power, widened the market for rubber mechanical devices (e.g., belting and hoses). In 1883, Gutta Percha built a factory in Toronto to meet the new demand. A decade later, Dunlop Tire and Rubber Goods Company established operations in Toronto. At the turn of the century there were twelve rubber-producing establishments in Canada.

Gutta Percha Rubber Company's exhibition stand at the Made in Canada Fair, September 1905. National Archives of Canada.

Following a world-wide trend, the Canadian rubber industry experienced rapid growth and concentration in the first two decades of the twentieth century during the Laurier boom, when the Combines Investigation Act did not exist, when self-dealing and stock watering were widespread, when massive infrastructure construction was attracting large amounts of investment capital, and when free trade with the United States was a matter of passionate debate. During these years flamboyant venture capitalists like Max Aitken made fortunes by creating integrated industrial structures that could dominate their markets.[17] Aitken, for instance, built a shady reputation as a home-spun robber baron by manipulating the emergence of industrial giants such as Stelco and Canadian Cement. Another such structure was the Canadian Consolidated Rubber Company, which Aitken founded in 1906 through the amalgamation of the six leading rubber plants in Canada.

The company, however, did not remain in Aitken's hand for long. Aitken, it was widely alleged, was interested only in the profits of promotion, not the labour of management. The following year, the United States Rubber Company, the first American tire manufacturer to move abroad, acquired approximately two-thirds of the outstanding capital stock in Canadian Consolidated Rubber.[18] Over the next twenty years, all the major American rubber companies – which had become large by building integrated business organizations – established branch plants in Canada. They brought foreign technology and managerial expertise with them.[19] The American presence continued to grow throughout the period, eventually accounting for two-thirds of all rubber goods manufactured in the Dominion.[20] With increasing regularity, these American firms established Canadian subsidiaries to hurdle the tariff wall.

Tariff protection was a defining feature of the "national policy," with which the federal government sought to encourage industrial expansion by using tariffs to protect the domestic market for Canadian manufacturers and promote industrialization, which was seen as a step towards material prosperity, economic self-sufficiency, and national strength. Industrialization was equated with nationalism. In 1876, John A. Macdonald stated his intention to "afford encouragement and protection to the struggling manufacturers" with tariffs that would make Canada "a union in interest, a union in trade, and a union in feeling."[21] Tariffs would provide Canadians with their own national markets, thus reducing their dependency on the United States, whose policies fluctuated between protectionism and free trade. The resulting stability would ensure a more orderly process of national growth. Tariff protection for Canadian manufacturers would remain a dominant feature of industrial policy.

In the longer term, after it came into effect in 1879, the tariff had the effect of creating a "branch plant" economy, as American companies established Canadian subsidiaries in an effort to avoid paying it. The rubber companies were among the largest American enterprises to do so. In 1916 Goodyear Tire and Rubber Company created a subsidiary "to handle Canadian and such other foreign business as can be shipped advantageously from Canada rather than from the United States owing to tariff conditions."[22] Built or acquired by takeover in response to stiff Canadian rubber tariffs that were upwards of 25 percent, the American-owned rubber plants were located largely in the major markets of southern Ontario and southwestern Quebec. This pattern continued well into the twentieth century. In 1939 less than 8 percent of Canadian rubber manufacturers were situated outside central Canada. Mirroring what was taking place across a number of industries, the Canadian rubber industry had become increasingly centralized and consolidated during the first two decades of the twentieth century. It was also becoming increasingly foreign-owned and controlled.

Nevertheless, by 1939 the rubber industry had become an essential part of Canada's industrial structure. In terms of value added by manufacture, it stood sixth in importance among Canadian firms. Despite the continued dominance of the big six foreign rubber producers, smaller firms were able to enter the market. Indeed, on the eve of the Second World War there were fifty-three rubber establishments in Canada, all but four of which were located in Ontario and Quebec. The factories in Ontario produced over 80 percent of the entire output of rubber manufacturers and employed over 82 percent of the capital and 72 percent of the persons engaged in the industry. By 1939 the Canadian rubber industry represented a total capital investment of over $38 million in land, buildings and equipment and almost $27 million in working capital, or a total of $65 million. In addition, it furnished employment to 12,879 persons, who received almost $15 million in salaries and wages. It was thus a critical part of Canada's industrial structure.[23]

Nowhere was this more evident than in its all-important relation with the automobile industry. While that industry had been on the rise since 1895, before the 1920s cars were really playthings for the rich. Perhaps nothing captured this fact more than an advertisement of the Canada Cycle and Motor Company. Its car, the Russel, "was made up to a standard – not down to a price." Such patrician cars were for the upper class. Price was no object. To be sure, there were exceptions. The Model T Ford – or Tin Lizzie, as it was termed, because of its lightweight metal body – was relatively cheap to buy (three hundred dollars in 1908) and to maintain. But even so, few ordinary Canadians owned a car before the end of the First World War.

In 1903, for example, there were only 220 cars on Ontario roads. Ten years later, there was still only 1 car in Canada for every 335 people. However, after the First World War, in 1918, 275,000 automobiles were registered in Canada. By 1923 that number had doubled, in spite of the postwar recession. Even the depression of the 1930s could not fully curb the demand for cars. In 1939 over 1.1 million passenger cars were registered in Canada. Half of them were in Ontario. Likewise, the demand for trucks grew rapidly during the period. In 1926 there were approximately 88,000 trucks on Canadian roads. On the eve of the Second World War that number had jumped to over 250,000.[24] Society was indeed travelling "down the asphalt path."[25]

The rapid development of the automobile industry brought growth and prosperity to the Canadian rubber industry. The fortunes of each industry were inextricably intertwined. The typical prewar car needed over two hundred rubber parts. Windshield wipers, mouldings, fan belts, radiator hoses, seat cushions, running-board covers, floor mats, and engine mountings were all made primarily, if not exclusively, of rubber, as were tires. On the eve of the Second World War, about three-quarters of the world's consumption of rubber was absorbed in the manufacture of tires. The earliest-known pneumatic tire (i.e., a tire

Dunlop Rubber Company, at the corner of Queen Street and Booth Avenue, Toronto, Ontario (ca. 1929). National Archives of Canada.

supported by air, as opposed to earlier solid rubber tires) had been patented in England in 1845, but it was not a commercial success. Forty years later, John Boyd Dunlop designed his own air-filled tire, which proved infinitely superior to the old solid rubber type. It was lighter, more shock resistant, and showed no signs of wear after use.[26] Dunlop's invention marked a truly historic moment. Having patented his discovery in 1888, a year later he organized the Pneumatic Tire Company in Dublin, which later grew into the worldwide Dunlop Tire organization. It set up operations in Canada in the late 1800s and produced Canada's first pneumatic tire in 1895. On the eve of the Second World War, Dunlop battled with Firestone, Goodyear, and General Tire for control of the Canadian tire and inner tube market – a market that was worth over $60 million per year.[27]

The mushroom growth of the automobile industry during the first part of the twentieth century created unprecedented demand for rubber. Natural rubber supplies had to be transported long distances from foreign plantations at considerable cost. Logically, therefore, Western scientists began looking for possible substitutes. While there were advances in synthetic rubber research and development before the outbreak of the Second World War, the story was generally one of experimentation and frustration.

The quest for synthetic rubber began in 1826 when the English physicist and chemist Michael Faraday broke down natural rubber to its basic elements and found it to be composed largely of hydrocarbon – five parts carbon to eight parts hydrogen. Later, in 1860, another English chemist, Charles Hanson Greville Williams, who was carrying out extensive pyrolysis studies at the University of London, determined that the long coils in natural rubber were actually made up of simpler units of a light hydrocarbon that was later identified as isoprene. Having reduced rubber to individual molecules, Williams produced a colourless liquid that had the same structural formula as natural rubber. Unfortunately, Williams was unable to reconstitute the isoprene into rubber at the time.[28] Nevertheless, Williams' accomplishment was enough to stimulate additional research. Over the next forty years, enterprising chemists made various attempts to convert isoprene into rubber.

Chemistry was at the heart of the second industrial revolution.[29] Through chemistry, innovative scientists like Williams sought to bring new items into productive use, particularly in Britain, Germany, France, and the United States. Britain had taken an early lead. In 1823 the British entrepreneur James Muspratt developed a process to mass-produce soda ash, which was needed to manufacture soap and glass. About the same time, another British entrepreneur, Charles Mackintosh, began mass-producing lightweight waterproof garments made of rubberized fabrics. Mackintosh was chiefly known for the improvements he had brought about in manufacturing dyes and bleaching powder and in the treatment of steel. His discovery of a rubberized fabric, however, was entirely accidental. At his factory in Glasgow he had begun to manufacture cudbear – a violet-coloured powder that gave strength and brilliance to blue dyes. Requiring a fairly large and steady supply of ammonia, Mackintosh contracted with the Glasgow gasworks to receive their waste tar and ammoniacal water. After the separation of the ammonia in the conversion of the tar into pitch, Mackintosh was able to produce naphtha – a volatile oil. It was then that he accidentally exposed a piece of raw rubber to the naphtha. The mix created a rubber-based varnish that, when placed between two layers of fabric, had a waterproofing effect. In 1825, Charles Mackintosh & Company began manufacturing waterproof articles. They were an immediate success. Most eagerly sought after were the company's waterproof overcoats, which quickly became known as "mackintoshes" or "macks." Innovations such as these kept Britain at the forefront of the industrial revolution.

During the same period, other British scientists perfected the method for the production of caustic soda, bleaching powder, and sulphuric and nitric acids. Not only did these endeavours lead to the diversification of British industry, but they also allowed Britain to dominate world markets for these and other heavy chemicals. Towards the end of the century, however, Britain's industrial supremacy was increasingly challenged by the creative chemistry that was being done on the continent. In Germany, for example, companies such as Balische Anilin, Hoechst, AGFA, and Bayer began manufacturing a variety of chemically engineered products. In 1869 the chemists Graebe and Liebermann started producing alizarin, the first artificial dye to replace a natural colourant. In 1897 Bayer first synthesized acetylsalicylic acid in a chemically pure and stable form. Marketed under the brand name Aspirin, it subsequently became the world's favourite pain killer.

These scientific discoveries were stimulated, in part, by nationalistic measures of the German government. Eager to see the development of domestic industry, Germany shaped its tariff and patent laws to sponsor a program of industrial chemistry. (Similar protective measures were later adopted in Canada to stimulate the growth of domestic manufacturing.) German chemists were quick to take advantage of the government's incentives. At Bonn University, Otto Wallach tried to convert isoprene into rubber. He had some success, managing to produce a synthetic, laboratory rubber by treating pure isoprene with hydrochloric acid. In 1884, British scientist Sir William Tilden repeated the feat, but with isoprene that was not obtained from the pyrolysis of natural rubber.[30] The second industrial revolution, with its emphasis on industrial science and developmental technology, inspired research and development in the synthetic rubber field.

After the turn of the century Russian chemists joined in the effort to produce a commercially viable synthetic rubber. They eventually found that other hydrocarbons could also be made into rubber-like products. In 1910, for instance, S.V. Lebedev succeeded in polymerizing butadiene (a colourless, highly flammable gaseous hydrocarbon, C_4H_6, obtained from petroleum or alcohol) into a rubber-like polymer. Despite Lebedev's success in the laboratory, no commercial-scale production of synthetic rubber resulted at that time. There was neither the economic nor the political incentive to find a natural rubber substitute.

That situation changed during the First World War. Cut off by a British blockade, Germany turned its attention to developing a domestic supply of rubber. The project was only moderately successful, however. While a synthetic substance known as methyl rubber was produced by the slow, spontaneous polymerization of dimethylbutadiene from acetylene, it proved to be greatly inferior to natural rubber. Its strength and resistance to abrasion and age deterioration were poor compared to its natural counterpart. Above all else, this problem would plague the embryonic industry for years to come.[31] Indeed, it caused many people to conclude that synthetic rubber of any kind could be only a very inferior substitute for natural rubber. It also set the pattern whereby synthetic rubber was destined to be a child of strategic expediency, its perfection coming at junctures when war or economic crisis made its natural progenitor scarce or unobtainable.

After the First World War, research on synthetic rubber was sporadically carried out on a small scale for several years. The increasing demand for automobiles caused recurring shortages of rubber, as well as provoking wide fluctuations in its price, which was enough to stimulate new research in industrialized nations. During the 1920s, synthetic-rubber research was given a helping hand by discoveries taking place in organic chemistry and particularly by the work of the German scientist Hermann Staudinger. In a series of published papers, Staudinger, who many consider to be the "grandfather" of modern polymer science, argued that polymers were huge molecules with chain-like structures arising from the chemical reaction of a large number of raw material compounds.[32] In the individual molecules of any organic polymer, Staudinger maintained, thousands of atoms were bonded together according to the simple principles that governed all inorganic molecules. High polymers – of which rubber was one – were not linked in blocks, rings, or networks, as had been previously thought, but in enormously long chains, or "macromolecules." Thus, during the first attempts to produce a man-made substitute for natural rubber, the large number of C_5H_8 molecules were being linked together like a chain of safety pins. The formation of one macromolecule by linking together many smaller components was given the name "polymerization." Staudinger's discovery markedly accelerated the development of synthetic rubber during the 1920s and 1930s.[33]

At the time of his discovery, Staudinger had little more than logical assertion to support his concept of long-chained molecules. In 1926, however, his long-chain theory received its first confirmation. At a prominent symposium in Germany, Herman Mark, a Viennese trained in Berlin, announced the results of his structural analysis of long-chained cellulose molecules carried out using the new technique of x-ray crystallography. Although Staudinger's academic opponents continued to complain that Mark's results proved nothing, the imperatives of commerce triumphed in 1927, when the German chemical company, IG Farben, hired Mark to begin systematically exploring synthetic organic polymers along the lines of Staudinger's theory. These initiatives moved artificial rubber to the threshold of commercial production.

Over the next five years, Mark worked assiduously for IG Farben, directing profitable development of such synthetic materials as polystyrene, polyvinyl chloride, and polymethyl methacrylate. But the insidious Nazi rise to power in 1933 led the company to dismiss him because of his Jewish ancestry. Determined to continue developing Staudinger's ideas, Mark returned to Vienna and eventually fled to America. Once there, he found himself welcomed by a scientific community that was already familiar with Staudinger's thinking and eager to develop polymer science further.[34] At a time when scientists were enthusiastically sharing their preliminary discoveries, Mark spent long hours informally discussing theory and method with fellow scientists like William Wiegand and G.S. Whitby. During the Second World War, Whitby – who later edited the first comprehensive study of synthetic rubber chemistry[35] – would act as a consultant on the Canadian synthetic-rubber project.

During the 1930s, Herman Mark went to work at Du Pont in the United States, where he was introduced to Wallace Hume Carothers, a brilliant young scientist. Carothers had made his name in organic chemistry. In 1928, he became the first American to confirm Staudinger's long-chain theory. At the age of thirty-two, in 1929, Carothers left his teaching post at Harvard to head Du Pont's new pure-research laboratory – or Purity Hall, as the cynics dubbed it – at Wilmington, Delaware. Since the turn of the century, Du Pont, along with such firms as General Electric, AT&T, and Kodak, had played a pioneering role in creating formal research organizations that served strategic and corporate goals while maintaining the air, and to a significant extent the reality, of autonomy from the immediate demands of production.[36] Like other formal research organizations springing up across North America at that time, Purity Hall was established as a corporate reaction to competitive threats that could be countered only through the control of deeper and more systematic scientific knowledge.

At Purity Hall, Carothers and his small group of associates made a number of critical contributions to synthetic rubber research and development. In 1929 Carothers, drawing on the lifetime of pure research done by Julius Nieuland, a chemist at the University of Notre Dame, found that vinyl acetylene could be reacted with hydrochloric acid to produce chloroprene. The substance displayed the ability to join hands with its neighbours to form long chains. The resulting product had rubber-like properties. The Du Pont company first called it duprene and later, neoprene.[37] While this synthetic rubber was more expensive than its natural counterpart to produce, it was more resistant to attack by gasoline, air, and sunlight and therefore proved an ideal material for use in gas hoses and gas tank linings.[38]

Du Pont's neoprene was the first man-made rubber that was superior to natural rubber when it was put to a specific use. It was, however, more expensive. First introduced in 1932, neoprene sold at $1.05 per pound. In the same year, the maximum price for a "first quality ribbed smoked sheet" of natural rubber was less than 5¢ per pound. It would take another world war and a conjunction of historical developments before synthetic rubber could appeal to consumers on the basis of both quality and price.[39] During the 1930s, however, neoprene met a specific industrial demand, specifically, for auto parts. As a result, it was soon being produced at a profit for Du Pont, even in the midst of the depression.

Du Pont's success with neoprene had several repercussions. First, it confirmed to American corporations that science could be the driving force behind innovation and that investment in science could pay large dividends. Canada, however, lagged behind the United States in terms of expenditures on research and development. Due to the branch-plant nature of the economy, most research and development continued to be done south of the border or in Europe. The results were then shipped to Canada for productive implementation. This pattern would continue to be a defining feature of Canadian business. Second, Du Pont's work demonstrated to rubber producers that there was in fact a ready market for synthetic rubbers that could meet specific needs. As a result, in the years that followed, petrochemical companies began tailoring their products by applying science to specific consumer requirements. In 1937, William J. Sparks and Robert M. Thomas, two chemists working for the Standard Oil Development Company, one of the world's largest industrial research organizations, did just that. They discovered that the co-polymerization of a small portion of butadiene (2 percent) with isobutylene (98 percent) – a cheap, readily available refinery by-product – produced an artificial rubber with superior resistance to tear, flexing, and ageing.[40] Their product, butyl rubber, was also less permeable than natural rubber to air, gas and water. Thus, it was ideal for use in inner tubes for tires, and in gas masks, waterproof footwear, ground sheets, and fire hoses.

Butyl rubber and neoprene constituted one of two basic categories of man-made rubber – they had specialized uses. A second category was made up of synthetics that were designed to serve more general purposes. While Carothers and his associates at Purity Hall were busy developing rubber for specific uses, two scientists working at IG Farben's university-style research laboratory near Cologne were attempting to perfect the first general-purpose synthetic rubber.

Walter Bock and Edward Tschunkur had been working on the project for several months when they tried co-polymerizing a second monomer – styrene – with butadiene. The combination proved magical. The mix produced a rubber that was far superior to the methyl

rubber developed in Germany during the First World War. Admittedly
it was still inferior to natural rubber in terms of strength and resistance. Nevertheless, the discovery represented another step forward.
The butadiene-styrene co-polymer, which subsequently became the
principal general-purpose rubber produced in Canada during the war,
was designated buna-s and patented in Germany in 1929.

Executives at IG Farben were excited about the potential of their
new product. However, they realized that if it, or any other general
purpose synthetic rubber, was ever to supersede natural rubber, its production cost would have to be significantly reduced. At no time during
its short history did estimates of synthetic rubber's cost come within
hailing distance of natural rubber prices. Even when the natural rubber cartel, the International Rubber Regulation Commission, occasionally manipulated prices to unreasonably high levels, there did not
appear to be any real prospect that the world would move to synthetics.[41] The only other – albeit intangible – variable in synthetic rubber's
cost was the security of the national rubber supply, which in the 1930s
was not in question.

During the 1930s, German scientists experimented with new raw
material bases such as oil, rather than coal tar derivatives, in an effort
to make synthetic rubber more cost competitive. Before the product
could be commercially tested, however, the bottom dropped out of the
natural rubber market, and IG Farben virtually suspended its synthetic
rubber operation. When the National Socialist government came to
power in Germany in 1933, IG Farben's buna operation was minimal.
But shortly thereafter the German synthetic rubber industry was given
a boost when Hitler's government adopted a Four Year Plan to rebuild
the German economy and achieve the maximum degree of national
self-sufficiency. Because of its importance, both from a military and an
economic standpoint, synthetic rubber became one of the strategic pil-
lars of the German program. Germany had been experiencing chronic
difficulties in trying to correct its negative balance of trade. Because
the annual bill for crude rubber imports created one of the nation's
worst foreign exchange problems, the production of synthetic rubber
became a part of the German program, with the government financing
and directing its development. Experimental production of buna rubber was therefore continued and increased. The Germans were thus
the first to realize and pursue the strategic and economic possibilities
of artificial rubber. Elsewhere, the initiative remained in private, corporate hands and, given the effects of the depression, there was little
incentive for hurried development of synthetic rubber. Only in Germany did the imperatives for forced development of artificial rubber
exist.

With renewed German political interest in artificial rubber came new scientific discoveries. Another copolymer, made from butadiene and acrylonitrile rather than styrene, was manufactured by IG Farben under the name buna-N. Like neoprene, buna-N synthetic rubber exhibited good resistance to chemicals and oils. While the Germans made butadiene from oil and coal tar derivatives, other raw materials could be utilized. In 1938 the Russians made fifty thousand tons of rubber from ethyl alcohol, which could itself be made from either potatoes, grains, sugar, or molasses. The debate over the appropriate raw material for manufacturing synthetic rubber would have a long life, especially in Canada, where regional and agrarian interests had strong representation in government.

IG Farben's success in producing buna-N and buna-S rubber inspired Hitler to announce to the world at the seventh Nazi Party congress in Nuremberg, held on 11 September 1935, that "the problem of producing synthetic rubber can now be regarded as definitely solved."[42] Hitler, of course, was overstating the case. Synthetic rubber was still in its infancy. The substance was inferior in terms of elasticity and tackiness, and it cost far more than natural rubber to produce. But the Nazis had instinctively sensed the strategic qualities of synthetic rubber: its production could be made secure, whereas natural rubber remained at the mercy of geopolitics.

The basic scientific and technological groundwork had now been laid for the rapid development of synthetic rubber research and production, which would occur during the Second World War.[43] The most important development from Canada's point of view was a transfer of scientific and technical knowledge from Germany to the United States. Throughout the 1930s, American scientists experienced little success developing a general-purpose synthetic rubber. They were finding it particularly difficult to duplicate IG Farben's accomplishment of producing a man-made rubber that could be used to manufacture airplane and automobile tires. While IG Farben was unwilling to share its synthetic rubber technology, it was willing to cooperate with American firms in other fields, such as fossil fuel development and processing. Ironically, it was the co-operation in this area that allowed Americans to get their hands on Germany's synthetic rubber technology.

In 1929, IG Farben entered into an agreement with Standard Oil of New Jersey to develop a process of hydrogenation of coal and oil. Under the contract, Standard Oil was given unrestricted access to scientific work undertaken in Germany. In 1930, Standard Oil and IG Farben established the Joint American Study Company (JASCO) as a vehicle for the commercial testing and licensing of the new processes developed by either of the two companies. It also became the corporate shell for holding IG Farben's u.s. patents, including its buna rubber patents. In 1939, with war clouds gathering over Europe and IG Farben in need of immediate hard currency, Standard Oil bought out IG Farben's interest in JASCO, which gave Standard Oil absolute patent rights to manufacture and license buna-s synthetic rubber in the Western hemisphere, as well as in the British and French Empires and Iraq. With the transfer of these patent rights from the Rhine to the Cuyahoga, Standard Oil acquired the scientific knowledge and technological know-how to produce the main types of synthetic rubber. During the Second World War, Standard Oil would thus be in a position to share its knowledge with Canada's Polymer Corporation, helping the corporation get off the ground.

Despite the consequential legal and scientific developments taking place in the private sector, the American and Canadian governments showed little awareness of the potential of synthetic rubber until 1939 and did not become partners in its evolution until two years later. The pressures behind Hitler's synthetic-rubber drive simply did not obtain in North America. Unaided by the exigencies of war and without government assistance, synthetic rubber production remained negligible. In 1940, almost one million tons of rubber was consumed by the North American public, but less than 1 percent of it was in synthetic form. In fact, only a meager eighty-five hundred tons of synthetic rubber was produced on the continent that year.[44] Before the outbreak of the Second World War, therefore, large-scale synthetic rubber production was an experimental dream. It would take the enterprising and expedient actions of the federal government and the people at Polymer Corporation to make the dream an industrial reality.

When Priestly had finished *The Theory and Practice of Perspective* in 1770, it was free of imperfections. Any mistake had been rubbed out. For several decades after the publication of the treatise, the Old World remained ignorant of rubber's potential as a revolutionary product. As James Anderson had stated in 1791, mankind hitherto had been "blind" to rubber's advantages.

But that situation began to change during the commercial revolution. One technological innovation after another called for the use of an elastic, malleable, or impermeable material. Rubber was the only natural substance to fit the bill. During the first half of the twentieth century, its uses expanded to include a fantastic array of goods. Enterprising inventors had stretched rubber's possibilities to new extremes. On the eve of the Second World War it was used in approximately fifty thousand items. It had thus become indispensable to the modern way of life.

What was unnerving, although Canadians did not realize it at the time, was the fact that Canada was completely dependent on foreign sources of supply, mainly the British-controlled plantations of the Far East. It would prove to be a dangerous dependency. To make matters worse, Canada could not overcome this dependency in the laboratory, since, to the extent that it existed, the necessary science and technology was in the hands of a few American and German companies that were reluctant to share their industrial secrets. Furthermore, the existing science and technology was anyway at best limited. After one hundred years, synthetic rubber research and development was still in its infancy. To be sure, advances had been made. The imperatives of war and national self-sufficiency had forced the development of both specific- and general-purpose rubber in Germany, but it was far inferior to natural rubber in terms of price and quality. In North America the same imperatives did not apply. As a result, synthetic rubber was rarely used and rarely developed.

That situation would change profoundly, however, during the Second World War. Cut off from the natural rubber plantations of the Far East, North America would turn its attention to developing a man-made substitute for natural rubber. The effort would be of epic proportions. Numerous hurdles would have to be cleared: science and technology would have to be pooled and improved; scarce resources would have to be efficiently allocated; and business, government, and labour would have to demonstrate unprecedented cooperation. But the alternative was unthinkable. Ultimately, it would take the exigencies of the Second World War to turn the experimental dream of synthetic rubber production into an industrial reality.

"Almost a Miracle": The Birth of the Canadian Synthetic Rubber Industry – from Experimental Dream to Industrial Reality, 1942–1945

I have never undertaken a war project which has caused me as much worry and concern as did that of synthetic rubber. At the time we undertook the project no synthetic rubber had been made on the continent outside of laboratories. We were very much in the dark as to costs and we were not at all sure that sufficient engineering data was available to allow us to work out the process ... it was ... a race against time with the possibility of disaster if the project did not turn out well.

C.D. Howe (1944)[1]

On 7 December 1941, in a coordinated strike without equal in the annals of war, the Japanese almost simultaneously wrought havoc on units of the United States Pacific Fleet in a surprise attack on Pearl Harbor, invaded the Philippines and Hong Kong, assumed control of Saigon and the rest of French Indo-China, accepted the capitulation of the Siamese government under Marshal Pibul Songgram, started preparations for the invasion of Burma, landed invading forces at two points in southern Siam and at Kota Bharu on the northeast coast of Malaya, and bombed Singapore, all in one day. Other units headed for key invasion points in Sarawak, North Borneo, and the Dutch East Indies. Using bicycles as their principal means of transport through the Malayan rubber plantations, the Japanese advanced swiftly and silently, outwitting and outdistancing the British, Australian, and Indian defenders. On 10 December, one week before the fall of Penang, the capital warships *Prince of Wales* and *Repulse* were sunk off the east coast of Malaya. These coordinated attacks gave Japan control of the Indian Ocean and severed the artery of the Allied rubber supply.

No other loss of an imported commodity caused as much apprehension on both the war and the home front as did the loss of this strategically important material. "Rubber alone," stated Alan H. Williamson, a one-time Bay Street investment dealer who, following the fall of Penang, was put in charge of regulating the use of rubber in Canada, "constitutes one of the gravest and most ominous problems in our history."[2] The loss of the plantations in the Far East, he declared, "has placed the whole Allied war program in jeopardy."[3]

To be sure, the war brought shortages of other critical materials. Steel, timber, and electricity all became scarce. But these commodities were produced in Canada and shortages could therefore be overcome by increasing production and rationing available supplies. Rubber, on the other hand, was a strategically vulnerable commodity of which, as mentioned, about 90 percent of the world's supply came from Java, Sumatra, Indochina, the Malay peninsula, and the East Indies – a region that as of mid-December 1941 was in Japanese hands. "With Malaya and the Netherlands East Indies out of the picture, due to their subjection by the Japanese," C.E. Beland at the Wartime Bureau of Technical Personnel in Ottawa noted with the coolness of a statistician, "the remaining source of crude rubber will scarcely be able to supply 8 percent of the world requirements ... Consequently, we are confronted with a serious problem."[4]

Ottawa chose to handle it by giving birth to a whole new industry, a synthetic rubber industry that was to prove to be the most effective combination of government, industry, and academia ever assembled to that point in Canadian history and probably to the present time. Never before had synthetic rubber been produced outside the laboratory. For that reason alone the idea was risky. In addition, in order to produce the required amount, an enormous state-of-the-art plant would have to be built. Nothing of its kind had ever been undertaken. Plans called for the construction of an industrial village capable of producing approximately 7 million pounds of synthetic rubber each month, which was equivalent to the output of 14.4 million rubber trees covering 120,000 acres in the South Pacific – more than enough to meet Canada's wartime needs. The huge industrial complex was to have eight acres of permanent buildings, six miles of sewers, five miles of roads, and a complicated mosaic of pipes, conduits, spheres, and towers. Ten factories would produce butadiene, styrene, and isobutylene, as well as both types of synthetic rubber – buna-s (or GR-S, as it was renamed in Canada and the United States) and butyl rubber. It was estimated that the construction of the plant would take the better part of two years to complete, at a cost of close to fifty million dollars. The task was Herculean, and some observers, even within the federal govern-

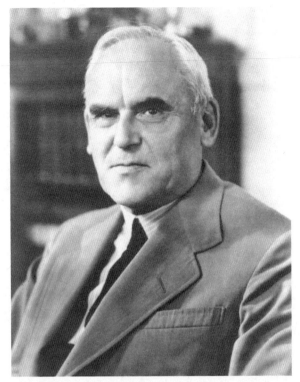

The Right Honourable C.D. Howe, 1947. National Archives of Canada.

ment, worried that the objective would not be achieved. "Frankly," Alan Williamson stated in the summer of 1942, "I believe it will require almost a miracle to provide the plants to produce synthetic rubber on schedule in Canada."[5]

But expediency would prove to be the mother of considerable invention. Of the fifty thousand tons of rubber consumed in Canada in 1941, none was synthetic. By comparison, at the end of the war over 90 percent of all rubber consumed was synthetic. During the war, the federal government forced the development of a new industry and, in so doing, overcame Canada's dependency on foreign rubber.

Of all the remarkable people involved in the birth of this wartime industry, Clarence Decatur Howe, the dynamic minister of munitions and supply, was at the top of the list. He had the courage to say "go ahead" when the words needed to be said. More than anyone else, Howe was responsible for making Canada self-sufficient in rubber.

Howe was an American by birth. Born 15 January 1886 in Waltham, Massachusetts, he was a distant relative of Joseph Howe – the Liberal premier and lieutenant governor of Nova Scotia during the 1860s. From an early age Howe had demonstrated the ability to grasp facts quickly and synthesize information. His high school classmates remembered him as "very bright" and "hard working." Having graduated from Waltham High in 1903, Howe headed off to the Massachusetts Institute of Technology (MIT). It was an exciting time to be there. MIT was being transformed into one of the world's greatest centres of science and engineering. It was also becoming a recruiting ground for big business, as corporations sought to harness science to achieve business goals. It was no accident that one of MIT's turn-of-the-century graduating classes contained four bright young men who would go on to be chief executives of four of the world's largest corporations: General Motors, General Electric, Du Pont, and Goodyear. Engineers in the early 1900s were on the verge of becoming the new ruling elite in American industry – something that the radical American philosopher Thorstein Veblen wrote about at length.[6] Howe would become one of them, but not in his country of birth.

At MIT, Howe gained a deep appreciation for the progressive power of science and technology. Like many engineers of his generation, he believed in the prospect of better living through technology and science. By applying science, humankind could alter matter and bring new items into productive use; it could control the natural environment. In this sense, science and technology had a revolutionary potential. This belief would never leave Howe. The values inculcated at MIT would remain with him for the rest of his life.

Howe had come to Canada shortly after graduation. He would only sporadically return to the United States. Initially he taught civil engineering at Dalhousie University, but after five years of teaching, Howe became restless. His boundless energy was ill suited to the sedentary university life, and when the opportunity arose that year to advise an old friend on the construction of grain elevators, he left the university. In the spring of 1913, he resigned his university position and prepared to move west to join the Board of Grain Commissioners. At the end of the Laurier boom, the federal government had established the board to supervise the grain business and oversee the construction of grain elevators. It provided Howe's first experience with government intervention, and it would leave a good taste in his mouth.

Howe proved tremendously successful at building grain elevators, and in 1916 he created his own firm of consulting engineers, the C.D. Howe Company, which became the foremost grain elevator builder of its day. The company built elevators all over the country, from Port

Arthur to Vancouver and did so faster and more cheaply than anybody. Howe brought this ability to get things done on cost and on time to public life when he entered the House of Commons in 1935. During the election of that year, he ran as a Liberal for Port Arthur, and following his victory, he was quickly recognized as a rising star within the party. Over the next twenty years he held a succession of key portfolios in the King and then the Louis St Laurent cabinets. In fact he held so many cabinet posts – sometimes two or three at a time – that he later became known as the "minister of everything." In 1935, in his freshman year, he was named minister of railways and the marine, a portfolio he retained when his departments were merged into the Department of Transport in 1936. To a great extent Howe brought the business values and standards of his earlier life to his position as minister of transport. He put a premium on efficiency and good management and dealt with things in a matter of fact way.

In April of 1940, as the "phoney war" in Europe began to be overtaken by the reality of total warfare, Mackenzie King moved Howe to the Department of Munitions and Supply. King wanted his most able people in charge of the most important government departments. Howe was among the most able, and the Department of Munitions and Supply was second in importance only to the Department of Defence itself. With the move to Munitions and Supply, C.D. Howe became the central planner in what was to become a planned wartime economy.

Various statutes reintroduced or ratified during the war, such as the 1914 War Measures Act and the 1939 Munitions and Supply Act, gave Howe tremendous powers to control the levels of production and consumption. He could buy, sell, mobilize, construct, requisition, and ration anything he felt was necessary for the production of wartime material. In addition, he could establish Crown corporations without reference to parliament by simply obtaining letters patent under the Companies Act. There was seemingly no barrier to his power, not even a constitutional one, for in wartime the provinces were forced to concede jurisdiction over their resources to the central government. Howe thus had carte blanche to produce what he thought was needed, when and how he wanted, for the prosecution of total war.

This mandate would lead Howe to implement an elaborate system of controls, incentives, and direct interventions that reflected his innate pragmatism and foreshadowed the birth of the mixed economy that would be the abiding postwar legacy of the wartime economy. The market mechanism, faintly at work as it was in Canada in 1940, was suspended by Howe, who was faced with the immediate and daunting task of mobilizing, conserving, and coordinating the economic and industrial facilities of the country. As a crucial initial step in this process, on

24 June 1940 Howe set up the War Industries Control Board to regulate essential sectors of the economy and ensure that his supplies got through. With the overseers of wage and price controls, the War Industries Control Board formed an economic control mechanism unprecedented in Canadian history. As a result of Howe's measures, Canadian firms ceased to function in a laissez-faire environment, setting prices and establishing product lines as they saw fit. Through its controllers, Ottawa pressured each major industry to develop and implement plans for industrial expansion. Even such a Gladstonian free marketer as Sir James Dunn, head of the mighty Algoma Steel Corporation, was forced to cede much of his firm's sovereignty to Howe and his Department of Munitions and Supply. "On all sides," notes the business historian Duncan McDowall, Algoma was the "apparent captive of the federal government."[7] During the war, Algoma, like Alcan, Eldorado and MacMillan and Bloedel – to name but a few other Canadian companies – became cogs in C.D. Howe's wartime wheel of production.[8]

As Canada's economic overlord, Howe's task was to ensure that the nation's war industries had a sufficient supply of essential raw materials. The rubber problem was therefore his problem, and he chose to handle it in two ways. First, he embarked upon a program of conservation of all supplies. Second, he ordered his "boys" to develop alternative sources of rubber.

The philosophy behind these measures was not complex: in order to meet wartime rubber requirements, which had intensified demand beyond its peacetime pattern, it would be necessary to continue expanding sources of supply while curtailing civilian demand. Canada would need approximately fifty thousand tons of rubber per year. The depression had dampened consumer demand for cars and had obliged politicians to skimp on defence budgets. In the 1930s rubber's potential in the marketplace was evident, but demand was depressed. War changed this lethargy into surging demand. In 1942 Canadians were consuming twice as much rubber as they had just three years earlier.[9]

To oversee the process of conservation, Howe appointed Alan Williamson to the position of rubber controller, one of nineteen control officers that he hurriedly appointed during the first few years of the war to regulate the wartime economy. Faced with a rapidly deteriorating rubber supply in Canada, as the war intensified, Ottawa empowered Williamson to conserve existing supplies and to shift the composition of aggregate consumption patterns from civilian to military ends. With that objective in mind, Williamson issued a series of drastic consumption curtailment orders prohibiting the production of such "nonessential" rubber items as ash trays, car mats, garden hoses, rubber bands, erasers, toilet seats, picture screens, combs, arch-supports, buttons, dish drainers, and ink wells.[10] By every indication Williamson's measures were going to have a profound effect on the civilian way of life. "More than any war-born shortage to date," one pained observer noted in the winter of 1942, "the rubber squeeze is going to reach down into every bureau drawer and corner cupboard."[11] Nevertheless the Department of Munitions and Supply maintained that the measures were necessary. Rubber was needed to keep the war machine turning. In January 1942, in an effort to make Williamson's orders more palatable, Howe addressed his fellow Canadians, assuring them that any material discomfort that might result from his department's actions would not be in vain. "Every dollar saved, every purchase delayed, every ounce of material saved," he promised them, "will go to increase the fighting power of those in the forefront of the battle."[12]

The department's conservation policy was guided, in part, by the recommendations of the Rubber Conservation Committee, a body established in December 1941 to advise Ottawa on rubber conservation and suggest alternative sources for crude rubber. The committee was made up of some of the most influential men in the rubber business: Paul Jones of Dominion Rubber, James Simpson of Dunlop, Harold Ireland of Canadian General Rubber, William Funston of Firestone, George W. Sawin of B.F. Goodrich, and Godfrey Smith of the Federal Wire and Cable Company. This caucus of business officials met frequently during the war to tackle the primary task set for it by Howe, namely, "to confer with and advise the Rubber Controller with respect to rubber and rubber products."[13] It was on the advice of the Rubber Conservation Committee that in April 1942 C.D. Howe set up a national scrap rubber division to further bridge the gulf between demand and the available supplies of crude rubber. As in the United States, the program proved productive, although there were some problems. Over time, the elastic quality of the recycled rubber was progressively reduced, and it eventually lost all its "bounce." In addition, the supply was finite and likely to dry up as the war progressed. Conservation and recycling alone, therefore, would not be enough to meet the nation's need for rubber.

These problems caused some individuals to begin investigating the unlikely and desperate possibility of cultivating a domestic source of natural rubber. In the critical, rubber-short environment of 1942, all potential sources of domestically grown natural rubber were examined carefully. Canadian climatic conditions ruled out planting *Hevea brasiliensis*, the conventional rubber tree, but other, more suitable rubber-bearing shrubs and plants, like milkweed and the Russian dandelion, *Kok-saghyz*, were considered. In early 1942, the Dominion Department of Agriculture invited scientists interested in the issue to meet in Ottawa. As a result, a cooperative program was organized to investigate native plants for their rubber content and to study possible production problems.[14] The botany division of the Department of Agriculture, in cooperation with the Experimental Farm, agreed to undertake a systematic survey of Canadian plants to determine which, if any, were "suitably rubber-bearing."[15] The department of botany at the University of Toronto, on the other hand, agreed to investigate some of the fundamental aspects of production, while the National Research Council (NRC) accepted responsibility for the development of extraction methods and for the compounding and physical testing of the rubber obtained.[16] While these efforts offered a tantalizing measure of encouragement, it was apparent that a viable domestic source of crude rubber was at least several years away. The rubber problem demanded a much more immediate solution.

Despite some success at curtailing civilian demand and augmenting raw rubber supplies, it was painfully evident to Howe and his advisors by the spring of 1942 that these measures were at best stop-gaps.[17] True, for the moment they were slowing the deterioration of the rubber supply, but these measures alone would not be enough to halt the alarming shortages that loomed on the horizon. In May 1942, Howe's deputy controller of supplies, J.R. Nicholson, wrote to Dr G.H. Duff, of the Department of Botany at the University of Toronto, advising him that Ottawa was looking for a more immediate solution to the rubber problem than the one he proposed for cultivating native rubber-bearing plants. Among his many tasks, it was Nicholson's job to examine any scheme – however "ivory-towered" it appeared at first glance – that might produce a domestic rubber supply. Following the loss of the plantations in the Far East, Howe had put Nicholson in charge of solving the rubber problem. "It's your job to get rubber," Howe had instructed him with characteristic brevity at the end of 1941. "Go get it."[18] With that objective in mind, Nicholson established communications and functional links with scientists and engineers in the university and at the NRC in Ottawa and the Rubber Reserve Corporation (RRC) in the United States.

Like many of his compatriots, Nicholson believed that scientific expertise was essential to the effective prosecution of the war.[19] Nicholson realized that the second global conflict of the twentieth century was shaping up to be a war of science, a war in which military supremacy would be determined by the ability to invent and develop new materials and devices, and beginning in the winter of 1942 he developed formal and personal relationships with a number of Canadian and American scientists. From the information they provided, he had de-

A rare picture of the vigorous J.R. Nicholson, general manager of Polymer Corporation Ltd (June 1943), sitting at his desk. National Archives of Canada.

termined that the chances of obtaining any appreciable amount of rubber in Canada from an investigation such as Duff was suggesting were "very remote."[20] Instead, he had formulated a far more radical answer to the rubber problem. "The solution of the rubber shortage," Nicholson wrote Duff, "lies in the speedy production of a large quantity of synthetic rubber."[21] This rubber was in no way related to botanical endowment.

It was a radical statement given that on the eve of the Second World War there was still much confusion surrounding production methods and compounding procedures.[22] The manufacturing process was cutting-edge and extremely complicated – as was pointed out by one contemporary observer. "The actual manufacture of synthetic rubber," *Maclean's* magazine stated in 1944, "would present complications to even such deft broth blenders as Shakespeare's three witches."[23] To this day, the manufacture of butyl rubber remains one of the most complicated commercial processes known to humankind. As late as March 1944 there was still confusion about which base – alcohol or petroleum – should be used in the manufacture of butadiene-styrene rubber.

After the outbreak of the war, a few academics turned their attention to solving some of these problems. At McGill University, for example, the head of organic chemistry, R.V. Nicholls, and his young graduate

student, Roger Hatch, worked on polymerizing butadiene and styrene
into a general-purpose synthetic rubber. The young Hatch would later
join the Canadian synthetic-rubber project and play a key role as an expediter of essential wartime materials. Outside the halls of academe,
private enterprise was also grappling with these problems. At Goodyear Tire and Rubber Company, for instance, another of Polymer's future faculty, Ralph Rowzee, was busy designing a pilot plant for the
production of synthetic rubber. But again it was only on a laboratory
scale. There was little impetus for large-scale synthetic-rubber production while the natural rubber plantations in the Far East were in
friendly hands. Thus, the art of synthetic-rubber production remained
underdeveloped.

Nevertheless, Nicholson was sure that the experimental dream
could become an industrial reality. And Howe had every faith in his
man. As a result, on 21 January 1942 Howe authorized the immediate
construction of a massive synthetic rubber complex at Sarnia, Ontario.

At the crossroads of the Great Lakes continental economy and as the
point of entry for the biggest, most reliable, and most secure flow of
crude oil into Canada from the United States, Sarnia was the ideal location for the new industry. There, on the banks of the broad St Clair
River, its first plant would have easy access to raw materials and markets. The river itself would be a natural source of the comparatively
low-temperature water needed for the plant's cooling system. The Imperial Oil refinery next door would supply the required petroleum-
cracked gases for the production of butadiene, as well as taking back
residual hydrocarbons. In addition, ethyl-benzene, from which came
styrene, could also easily be brought in by lake boat from the coke ov-
ens of the Steel Company of Canada at Hamilton and from Algoma
Steel at the Sault. In terms of markets, the rubber manufacturing industry was located almost entirely in southern Ontario, where a handful of large, multi-divisional American rubber companies had
established themselves early in the twentieth century in response to
the Canadian tariff.

To coordinate the massive and complicated task of constructing and
operating the first fully integrated rubber plant in the British Empire,
Howe decided to employ a familiar instrument: the public enterprise,
or Crown corporation. There had been a long tradition of public enterprise dating back to pre-Confederation days, as for example when
the state financed, built, and operated the canal system upon which
the commercial empire of the St Lawrence depended. Between 1850
and 1910 railways and the government were closely intertwined. In
1919 this notorious and lengthy intimacy was formally acknowledged

by the creation of the Canadian National Railway, a publicly owned and operated corporation. These early Crown interventions were prompted by various factors: Canada's heavy reliance on primary product exports, its chronic deficiency in capital and technology, the necessity to rationalize regional disparate markets, and the need to shore up the national interest in the face of American economic ambition.[24] According to Harold Adams Innis, the Crown corporation was an "effective weapon" by which the government was able to bring together "the retarded development and possession of vast natural resources, mature technique and a market favourable to the purchasing of raw materials."[25] Yet despite these early examples of publicly owned business ventures, it was not until the 1930s that the federal government displayed any marked inclination to experiment extensively with Crown corporations.

The economic depression of the 1930s, which put economics at the forefront of public policy, provided a new and immediate rationale for government intervention into the economy. Increasingly, Canadians of various political persuasions called on government to abandon, or at least modify, the laissez-faire principles of the previous generation and – as Canadian economist, humorist, and historian Stephen Leacock put it – "make things happen."[26] Some observers viewed the Crown corporation as the most effective method of intervention. "The problem of the twentieth century is to make economic government responsible to the public weal," political economist J.A. Corry declared. "[T]he solution is the fusion of government and business in the independent public corporation."[27] The statement resonated with a large segment of the population who were increasingly turning away from the "old orthodoxies" (e.g., a laissez-faire approach to economic matters). Among the "new orthodoxies" that were taking shape during this period was the belief in large-scale government intervention. The use of Crown corporations was consistent with this belief; they were viewed as an effective means of entering critical sectors of the economy. During the 1930s, the federal government created several Crown corporations in response to a number of structural problems. In 1932, the Conservative government of R.B. Bennett passed the Canadian Broadcast Act, creating a publicly owned Canadian Radio and Broadcasting Commission. The CRBC was given the mandate to provide programs and extend coverage to all settled parts of Canada, but it suffered from underfunding, an uncertain mandate, and unsuitable administrative arrangements.[28] As a result, when the Liberal government of Mackenzie King returned to power in 1936, it replaced the CRBC with a stronger agency, the Canadian Broadcasting Corporation. The CBC was a classic case of "defensive expansionism."[29] That is, in the face of American economic imperialism, the Canadian government expanded into an area of the economy that was vulnerable to takeover. In this case the choice was clear: it was the state or the United States. The trend continued throughout the 1930s. Between 1932 and 1938, central banking, wheat marketing, national harbours, and air transportation were all brought under partial or complete public ownership and control. The quest for monetary leverage and a national economy, as well as the challenge of new technologies, was prominent in these decisions.

C.D. Howe was the driving force behind many of these interventions. "I plead guilty to having been the moving spirit in forming a considerable number of crown corporations," Howe later recalled. "And I still believe them to be an efficient method of administration where government finds it necessary to enter upon business activities."[30] A free enterpriser at heart, Howe was willing to use the full force of government to accelerate development in niche areas of the economy. His use of Crown corporations was therefore pragmatic rather than ideological. Howe innately understood the structural limitations of the Canadian economy – its lack of technology, capital, and markets – and used public enterprise to overcome them. Usually, he did so at the request of business: his Crowns were established to create an environment within which private enterprise could function competitively. The instinct was deeply rooted in the Canadian economic experience. Howe was simply its latest interpreter. For Howe Crown corporations did not represent an attempt by the government to encroach on the field of private enterprise. On the contrary, they supplemented and tended to support the private sector of the economy by providing services, raw materials, and technology that would not otherwise be available.[31] War accentuated this tendency.

During the war, Howe established twenty-eight Crown corporations in order to overcome a number of structural barriers to national economic performance. Howe's tenure as minister of munitions and supply thus established "the corporate form as the instrument of choice for the execution of public policy."[32] Howe's Crown corporations served a number of production and administrative functions. For example, Research Enterprises Ltd was set up in July 1940 to hurry the development of radar and optical instruments – a field in which Canada previously had no technology or industrial expertise. Others were created to supervise the acquisition of critical raw materials. Others still were established to allocate scarce resources.

Not everyone, however, supported Howe's methods. For instance, the novice Conservative MP John Diefenbaker, who denounced big government in all its forms, was critical of Howe's interventionist bent, anticipating that his Crown companies would enjoy subsidies after the war that would enable them to compete unfairly with privately owned firms.[33] His use of the Crowns, charged Diefenbaker, was "the first move along the road to socialization."[34] Ironically, it was in the Red Tory urge to employ the state powers to collective economic ends that the Crowns were ideologically rooted. These roots, however, were ignored by Diefenbaker.

Conversely, observers on the left viewed Howe's Crown corporations as instruments designed to benefit the capitalist class. The fledgling Cooperative Commonwealth Federation (CCF), for example, charged that the Crowns were, in effect, the Trojan horses of capitalism. Having been established at enormous public expense and provided with invaluable plants, equipment, and technology, they would be sold off to private interests at war's end at a fraction of their intrinsic value, or so the CCF alleged.[35]

For his part, Howe thought these criticisms patently ideological and therefore misplaced. "This fetish in the minds of some people, that everything is wrong that is private industry, and in the minds of others, that everything is wrong that is public industry," he later stated, "is the most ridiculous situation."[36] Howe was a pragmatist, and in his reading of the Canadian marketplace he saw some situations that simply demanded state intervention, not as a panacea in its own right, but to hurry the development or protect the niche areas of the economy that either lacked capital and technology or needed the assistance of quasipublic management to establish themselves. Such was the rationale behind his establishment of Trans-Canada Airlines, Atomic Energy of Canada, Trans-Canada Pipelines, and the St Lawrence Seaway Authority.[37] Similarly, it was the rationale behind the establishment of Polymer Corporation.

On 13 February 1942, just two months after the fall of Penang, Howe created Polymer Corporation to coordinate the complex task of constructing and operating the largest synthetic-rubber plant in the British Empire. The order-in-council commissioning the project authorized Polymer "to forthwith proceed to acquire, construct, install and establish the necessary land, buildings, machinery, equipment and plant for the manufacture, production and storage of synthetic rubber."[38] The corporation would not have title to any assets (these were held in the name of the Crown) and would oversee the operation of the plant once it was constructed. Initially, therefore, Polymer's task was an administrative one – that of coordinating the diverse commercial and intellectual interests that would have to be brought together to make the vision of synthetic-rubber production a reality.

The technological know-how, staff, and management for the project
would have to come from private industry. The government had no
clue as to how synthetic rubber was manufactured, and private industry was almost as ignorant. To make matters worse, no single firm had
all the elements of synthetic-rubber production. Indeed, the tools of
the dark art were spread across several different industries. Polymer's
first task, therefore, was to bring these divergent industries together.

When the war broke out in Europe, only one North American company had full knowledge of the art of styrene production – one of the
three stages in the production of GR-S rubber. Dow Chemical had a
long and distinguished history in the field. The company was founded
in 1897 by Herbert Henry Dow to extract bromine and chlorine brine
around Midland, Michigan. To chlorine bleach, the company's first
product, Dow slowly added various other chemicals: chloroform in
1903, ethylene in 1915, and phenol in 1922. In 1937 Dow invented a
process for the commercial production of styrene, a product then used
mainly in the manufacture of plastics. At the time of the Japanese advance into Southeast Asia, Dow was the only commercial producer of
styrene in North America.[39] With that in mind, in the summer of 1942
J.R. Nicholson arranged for Dow, through its subsidiary, Dow Chemical
of Canada, to staff and operate the styrene plant at Sarnia.

The art of butadiene production, on the other hand, was the pur-
view of Imperial Oil, one of three large-scale, heavily integrated oil
companies operating in Canada. Like Dow, Imperial had a rich history.
It was established in 1880 by Joseph Englehart, an emigrant from
Cleveland, Ohio, the oil refining capital of the United States. In 1898
the company was acquired by J.D. Rockefeller's huge, vertically integrated business enterprise, Standard Oil. In 1907, as a result of the
U.S. government's antitrust action, Imperial Oil passed into the hands
of Standard Oil Company of New Jersey. Standard Oil was a pioneer in
the commercial production of butadiene and on the eve of the Second
World War was the world's largest producer of the product. It also held
patents in the field of butyl rubber production. In March 1941, four
years after the initial discovery of butyl rubber by its chemists William
Sparks and Robert Thomas, Standard Oil erected a ten-ton-per-day
plant at Baton Rouge, Louisiana. It was the only butyl rubber plant of
its kind. Nicholson thus concluded that the Canadian government
would also have to obtain the support of Imperial Oil. As a result, in
the winter of 1942 he negotiated an operating arrangement with the
company. When the construction phase of the project was finished,
Imperial established a subsidiary, St Clair Processing Corporation, to
oversee the butyl rubber and butadiene units at Sarnia.

Producing butadiene and styrene, however, constituted only two phases of the overall task of manufacturing GR-S rubber. To manufacture a finished product, these two monomers had to be copolymerized, that is, compounded into synthetic rubber. This third, rubber-compounding stage involved the intricate use of promoters, accelerators, vulcanizers, antioxidants, softeners, fillers, and other chemical agents that made the rubber suitable for manufacturing tires, tubes, and other fabricated products. On the eve of the Second World War, compounding was a highly developed and confidential trade secret confined to firms in the rubber industry. Neither the oil nor the chemical industry had knowledge of this highly technical art. Given this, Nicholson was driven to seek the help of Canadian Goodrich, Canadian Goodyear, Canadian Firestone, and Dominion Rubber, a subsidiary of U.S. Rubber. To Nicholson's credit, he managed to get these peacetime competitors to come together to manage the copolymerization and compounding process at Sarnia. On 26 March 1942 the four companies established the Canadian Synthetic Rubber Company (CSR) and selected Ralph Rowzee, a brilliant young engineer, to manage the operation.[40]

The structure and organization of the Polymer project thus paralleled other wartime efforts emanating from Ottawa. It was a two-pronged approach with industry contributing management know-how and personnel and with government, through Polymer, coordinating the overall production effort.[41] The government's involvement, which was criticized by many at the outset, was necessary in order to bring the divergent chemical, oil, and rubber interests together and set up synthetic rubber production in Canada. Time was of the essence. The problem was urgent; the country could not afford the luxury of waiting for private enterprise to mobilize. Government initiative was needed.

Three days after incorporating Polymer, Howe invited Colonel Arthur L. Bishop, the president of Consumers Gas Company, to accept the presidency of the new Crown corporation. Howe often turned to industry to oversee his enterprises. Indeed, much of the operational success of the Department of Munitions and Supply resulted from his decision to retain the services of what became known as the "dollar-a-year men": senior businesspeople who served the country in some executive capacity for the token retainer of a dollar a year. So many of these people came to Ottawa during the first few years of the war that the leader of the CCF, Major James Coldwell, declared that the Department of Munitions and Supply had become a "concentration point for the Canadian Manufacturers' Association and its friends." Bishop's appointment certainly did nothing to deflate the charge. He, like so

Buna-s (i.e. GR-S) co-polymerization process.

Buna-S Rubber polymer Unit

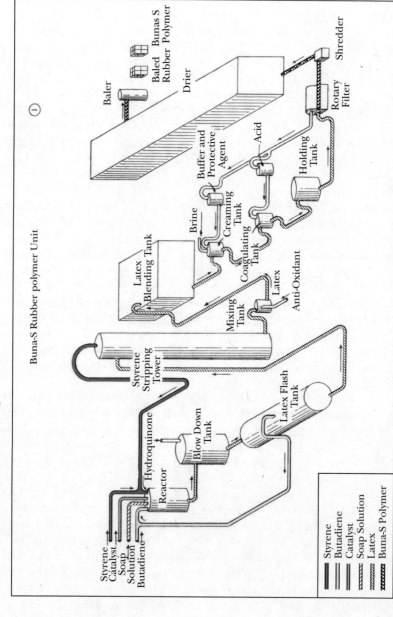

①

Source: St Clair Processing Corporation Ltd., *Synthetic Rubber: A Process Digest*, 26.

many of his fellow dollar-a-year men, was a captain of Canadian industry. In addition to being the head of Consumers Gas, he was a director of the Imperial Bank of Canada, Toronto Shipbuilding Company, and Consolidated Mining and Smelting Corporation. In the early part of 1942 Bishop had come to the attention of the Department of Munitions for his criticism of the government's handling of the war. A member of the Committee for Total War – a hawkish Toronto-centric, pro-Tory group – Bishop wanted the government to get on with the war more energetically. According to Bishop, there was only one way to wage total war: with total effort. No half measures, in his opinion, were consistent with national honour. In January he and his fellow committee members signed their names to a full-page advertisement in the *Globe and Mail* pointing out that there was a lot of talent around that needed to be put to effective use.[42] The advertisement came to the attention of R.C. Berkinshaw, who recognized Bishop's name. As chairman of the Wartime Industries Control Board, Berkinshaw had come into contact with him on several occasions. Berkinshaw thought Bishop a "sincere" and "conscientious" individual and admired his "forthright manner."[43] In Berkinshaw's opinion, he was well-suited to oversee the Polymer project, and he recommended him to Howe for the top position at Polymer.

For some at the department, however, Bishop was not the ideal choice. His educational experience was not in the chemical field, and – as he later confided to C.D. Howe – he knew "next to nothing about synthetic rubber or its manufacture."[44] But then again, who did? With the exception of Nicholson and a handful of chemists within academe, no one in Canada knew the secret of synthetic rubber production. Nevertheless, A.H. Williamson, R.A.C. Henry, and H.R. MacMillan thought Greville Smith, president of Canadian Industries Limited, a better man for the job. "We are all agreed that if we could get Mr. Greville Smith of Canadian Industries to undertake this responsibility, this would be one of the very best selections that could possibly be made."[45] Howe, however, had no time for wishful thinking. Wartime conditions demanded management-on-the-run. According to Howe, one simply had to grab the most qualified manager when one could find him and this time Bishop was that man. After three frenzied days spent winding up his affairs, Bishop assumed his responsibilities as president and chairman of the board of directors on 20 February and thereafter devoted most of his time to the activities of the company.

There was a slight delay in the appointment of the other directors to the board, since Howe did not consider it desirable to choose anybody from the rubber, petroleum, or chemical industries. Yet he wanted men accomplished in the ways of business, believing that knowledge derived from experience. "There is no substitute for having done the job before," he confided to J.R. Nicholson.[46] Thus, if the government was going to build a synthetic rubber plant, Howe thought it wise to put in charge individuals who had some first-hand experience with large-scale industrial construction. In late February 1942, Howe asked Nicholson and Berkinshaw to compile a list of such men from the financial and industrial sectors. With one exception, it was from this list that the rest of the directorate was appointed.[47]

Among the first to be selected were Wallace Campbell, president of Ford Motor Company of Canada, and Douglas Ambridge, assistant general manager of Ontario Paper Company. Campbell had been one of the first dollar–a-year men to come to Ottawa in 1939, serving as head of the War Supplies Board.[48] Ambridge, on the other hand, joined the Department of Munitions and Supply two years later, in October 1941, serving initially as the director of the shipbuilding branch. Howe's decision to appoint Ambridge and Campbell to Polymer's board of directors was by no means unusual, since he was frequently moving people between government departments and Crown corporations. Ambridge was an alumnus of McGill University, having graduated in 1923 with a BSc in chemical engineering. He had subsequently held several executive posts in the Canadian pulp and paper industry. What was also appealing about Ambridge was that in 1938 he had overseen the construction of a large-scale pulp and paper plant at Baie Comeau, Quebec. Howe needed such men. The construction of the synthetic rubber plant at Sarnia promised to be one of the most complex and expensive in Canadian history.

Albert C. Guthrie, the next of Howe's appointees, had also overseen the construction of a manufacturing plant and was a veteran of Canadian business. Guthrie had been involved in manufacturing since 1912, and at the time of his appointment was president and general manager of Simmons. Guthrie shared many characteristics with another of Howe's delegates, Gilbert C. LaBine, a hard-nosed mining promoter and president of Eldorado Mines. Both men had a deep determination to succeed and had demonstrated a willingness to dedicate themselves fully to the job at hand. Of the two, LaBine was the more adventurous. He had started business life as a prospector, searching for copper with his brother Charlie on the Canadian mining frontier. Instead of copper, however, the LaBine brothers found pitchblende at Great Bear Lake in the Northwest Territories. From pitchblende came radium and uranium. During the 1930s and early 1940s the brothers made, lost, and remade a fortune, first peddling radium – which during the 1930s fetched seventy-five thousand dollars per gram on the world market as a "wonder" cure for cancer – and then by selling uranium to the u.s. Army to make "uranium bombs."[49] In the summer of 1942, Howe, sensing the strategic need for uranium, nationalized the LaBine brothers' company. Eldorado Mines thus came into the fold of C.D. Howe's wartime Crown corporations.

The final director appointed was not on Nicholson's list, and for an obvious reason: A.J. Crawford was not a captain of Canadian industry but, rather, an agent of organized labour. When he was contacted by Howe six weeks after the other directors had been appointed, Crawford was working in Toronto as the Canadian general representative of the Sheet Metal Workers' International Association. For political and practical reasons, Howe decided that it would be desirable to have a representative of organized labour appointed to Polymer's board of directors.[50] Howe was particular as to the sort of individual that labour representative should be. He did not want anyone who might take a confrontational approach with the other directors. The Canadian synthetic rubber project was going to be challenging enough; there was no need to complicate things further, Howe thought, by appointing someone who might rock the boat. On the other hand, he wanted labour on the boat, paddling away in concert with business to reach a common wartime goal. He did not want labour strife in a key wartime industry. The reports circulating about the Department of Munitions and Supply suggested that Crawford was neither radical nor antagonistic and would accept Howe's appointment if asked.[51] "I have been given to understand that you would be a suitable person to serve as a director in this capacity," Howe wrote to Crawford on 24 April, "and that you would be willing to act if requested."[52] Crawford wrote back immediately accepting the appointment and assuring Howe that he would "co-operate with the president and directors at all times."[53] Crawford and the other directors – whom C.D. Howe celebrated as "the cream of Canadian industrial talent" and whom Stanley Knowles, a member of the ccf, condemned as the "usual who's who of big business"[54] – would guide the Canadian synthetic-rubber program through its crucial initial phase.

Between April and August 1942, the board of directors worked to pave the way for the beginning of construction, receiving tenders, establishing agreements, and signing contracts for goods and services, fine-tuning design plans, making housing arrangements for the construction workers (who numbered 5,579 at the peak of the project), working to have the machinery and equipment exempt from duties and taxes, and coordinating the numerous construction companies that were involved. As the end of the summer of 1942 approached, Canadians could take some comfort in knowing that their government had made the first steps towards resolving the rubber crisis. Nevertheless, most of the work lay ahead.

In the months leading up to production at Sarnia, the novel character of the synthetic rubber project again became apparent. This time it was in the debate over the appropriate raw material to be used in manufacturing butadiene, a debate that was rooted in scientific and technical uncertainty and political and economic interest. When in January 1942 Nicholson contacted his colleagues at the Rubber Reserve Company (RRC) in Washington with the Canadian plan to produce synthetic rubber, he was informed that crude petroleum was the best, that is, the cheapest and most readily available, of the raw materials.[55] On this information several critical decisions were made. Sarnia, as the point of entry for the largest flow of crude oil into Canada, was chosen as the site for the new Canadian synthetic-rubber plant. Imperial Oil was contracted to manage the butadiene-from-petroleum plant, and Standard Oil was hired to do much of the design and engineering work. During the ensuing months, however, a conjunction of technological, economic, and political developments gave pause to the initial decision to produce synthetic rubber solely from a petroleum feedstock.

At the time of Polymer's inception in February 1942, butadiene, which constituted approximately 75 percent of the rubber copolymer GR–S, could be manufactured in several different ways: from oil, natural gas, coal, or alcohol. The Canadian decision to use petroleum was based on advice from the RRC and the NRC that the cost of producing butadiene from oil, rather than from any other base, would be appreciably lower and would ensure production of synthetic rubber in commercial quantities at the earliest date.[56] As the summer of 1942 approached, however, there was a growing concern in Canada that the equipment and feedstocks necessary for the production of butadiene from petroleum would be difficult to obtain, due to developments taking place in the United States.[57] There, changes were being made to the system of priorities that had been set up in the summer of 1940 to control the flow of essential materials and equipment.

Nearly everything that went into the plant at Sarnia was on a priority list. Lists of priorities (i.e., general government instructions to producers and dealers requiring them to fill orders bearing a higher rating before they filled orders of a lower rating) were generated and administered by the War Production Board (WPB) in the United States, which had decided early on that in order to keep the war machine running, the use of certain vital items would have to be restricted. Those industries with a high priority rating, which had been assigned on the basis of military necessity, went directly to the head of the queue, no matter how many other consumers were there ahead of them. The more vital the item for the allied war effort, the greater the priority given to its manufacture and the higher the rating it received.[58] The first categories for priorities instituted by the WPB were simply A, B, and C, with each letter-section having ten subdivisions. But as the war production effort intensified, the As began to crowd each other in some factories, and a new system of lettering came into effect, using A-1-a, etc., and finally AAS and AAAS. Since over half the items to be used at Sarnia were to be imported from the United States, Polymer understood that it was imperative to obtain a high priority rating from the WPB if Polymer was to bring the construction of the plants to a speedy completion.

During the winter of 1942, Polymer had received assurances from a number of high-ranking U.S. officials that it would indeed be assigned a high priority rating. Nevertheless by the spring of 1942 it looked increasingly unlikely that Canada would get the petroleum and equipment it needed to manufacture synthetic rubber on time, not because of any discrimination on the Americans' part or because the American synthetic-rubber program was getting the vital material and equipment it needed while the Polymer project was not: the Americans, in particular the executives at the RRC, considered the Canadian project part of the larger American synthetic-rubber program.[59] Rather, the program was being delayed because of a broad continental scarcity of wartime resources.

This scarcity worried Ottawa. Specifically, it feared that the petroleum feedstock needed to manufacture butadiene would not be available once the Sarnia plant was erected.[60] Petroleum was, of course, in the highest demand during the war. As well as being an essential ingredient in synthetic rubber, it was used for lighting, heating, lubrication, and motor transportation. In mid-1942, it was becoming evident to the wartime authorities that there was not going to be enough crude petroleum to go around. Realizing this, the Army and Navy Munitions Board in the United States began pressuring Donald Nelson, the chairman of the WPB, to give its programs more of the existing supply of petroleum. Fearful that Nelson might acquiesce, the Canadian rubber authorities began to seriously consider using other feedstocks in the manufacture of synthetic rubber. Alcohol was foremost in their minds.

Earlier that year, C.D. Howe had received a letter from the consul general of Poland in New York, Victor Podoski, who was representing Waclaw Szukiewicz, a Polish engineer and coinventor of a catalyst for making butadiene from alcohol in a time-saving single step. Until that time, the use of alcohol in the production of butadiene had been both expensive and time-consuming. Alcohol first had to be converted to ethylene and then to butadiene. But Szukiewicz claimed to be able to convert alcohol to butadiene in one continuous operation. According to Podoski, Szukiewicz and his compatriot Boleslaw Przedpelski had perfected the method while living in Poland before the war. Following the fall of Warsaw in September 1939, Szukiewicz fled to Italy, where he was approached by the local authorities, who were eager to learn more about his scientific discovery. Fearful that his invention might fall into the wrong hands and increasingly concerned for his life, Szukiewicz again took flight, this time to the United States. In January 1942, he contacted Podoski, who, following Szukiewicz's wishes, in turn contacted the Canadian Trade Commissioner in New York, Douglas Cole, with the intention of making Szukiewicz's butadiene-from-alcohol method available to Ottawa.[61] Excited by the potential of Szukiewicz's breakthrough, Cole immediately forwarded Podoski's letter to C.D. Howe at the Department of Munitions and Supply in Ottawa.

As a man who had dedicated a good deal of his life to the applied sciences, Howe was excited by Szukiewicz's scientific formulations.[62] This was not out of character. Howe was often given to enthusiasms, especially for creative schemes with a hint of high technology like this one.[63] Nevertheless, Howe wanted the process fully reviewed by his technical experts before making any radical reconsideration regarding the raw materials to be used in the Polymer project. To that end, in February, Nicholson contacted C.J. Mackenzie, the president of the NRC and a former university student of Howe's, and asked him "to pursue the matter as expeditiously as possible."[64]

Mackenzie responded immediately, since the subject had of late been very much on his mind. Indeed, for the past two days he had been discussing the merits of the process with Boleslaw Przedpelski – the co-inventor, with Szukiewicz, of the Polish method. Mackenzie considered Przedpelski a "very reliable man" and thought his formulations scientifically sound.[65] On that basis, he was willing to endorse the butadiene-from-alcohol process. However, Mackenzie was quick to add that this issue could not be judged solely on scientific grounds. The question, he maintained, was "a broad one," which also involved economic and political considerations. "It appears to me," Mackenzie wrote to Nicholson in February 1942, "that the fundamental question is whether or not the economic and industrial conditions indicate a preference for alcohol over petroleum as the raw material."[66]

If the matter could have been settled solely on scientific grounds, perhaps the alcohol issue would have evaporated. But given that economic and industrial development discussions were involved, politics necessarily came into play. In the spring of 1942, the West began demanding that the federal government take "immediate steps" to establish factories in that part of the country for the production of alcohol from grain into synthetic rubber. In Saskatchewan the municipal councils of Moose Jaw, Duck Lake, Star City, Saskatoon, Regina, Weyburn, North Battleford, and Lloydminster all passed resolutions calling on their provincial and federal representatives "to insist day and night that surplus farm products shall be used in any industry where they can be economically used."[67] A similar resolution was subsequently adopted by the United Farmers of Alberta and the United Farm Women of Alberta.[68] Later the issue became a centrepiece of Tommy Douglas's CCF election campaign in Saskatchewan in 1944.

The issue resonated with the West's sense of alienation. During the First World War, the West had become frustrated by the government's unwillingness to decentralize Canadian industry and give it a greater role in national defence production.[69] The same sense of marginalization had given birth to Western political protest movements such as the Progressive Party, the CCF, and Bible Bill Aberhart's Social Credit – parties that haunted the federal Liberals. In the Western mind, the possibility of now producing butadiene from wheat alcohol offered an opportunity to right past wrongs. "[W]e must recognize the fact that a great deal of capital assistance has been given by the government to set up industry, chiefly in eastern Canada, for the manufacture of war munitions," stated James Ross, a Western farmer who was first elected as a federal Conservative MP in 1940. "Factories [for the manufacturing of wheat alcohol into butadiene] should be established in the prairie provinces," he continued, "to decentralize industry to some extent."[70]

The West had large amounts of surplus wheat stored in its grain elevators – many of the same grain elevators that C.D. Howe had helped build in the 1920s and 1930s while in private practice as a consulting engineer. The surplus wheat, Ross and others argued, could be used to manufacture alcohol, which could then be converted, using the Polish method, directly into butadiene. The possibility of butadiene from wheat therefore offered at one stroke development for an agricultural region and an alternative for an underused staple crop. In the minds of many Western leaders it offered the federal government a tremendous opportunity to solve two of the nation's most pressing problems simultaneously: the wheat problem and the rubber problem.[71]

The Department of Munitions and Supply had not ruled out using alternative raw materials in manufacturing synthetic rubber. In May 1942 the department's deputy minister, G.K. Sheils, wrote to Nicholson asking him if Polymer had made "a thorough investigation" of the possibility of securing butadiene from alcohol.[72] Given the difficulty of securing materials and equipment from the United States, Sheils felt that it offered "some hope" of obtaining butadiene and synthetic rubber at an earlier date than by the petroleum method. That same month, Howe appointed Dr Horace B. Speakman, a chemist and alcohol expert, to examine the butadiene-from-alcohol issue. Howe was skeptical about Polymer's board of directors possessing the technical expertise necessary to rule on the matter. They had been chosen for their managerial skill, not their scientific insights. "We have an enthusiastic Board of Directors in charge of the program," Howe confided to Speakman, "[but] I am afraid that the Board is weak on the technical side."[73] Howe was sanguine that Speakman would give him an expert and objective scientific evaluation.

Speakman certainly possessed all the required credentials to do so. He was a scientist by training, having graduated from the University of Manchester with an MSC in 1915. In addition to teaching basic science at the University of Toronto, he had held various high-ranking positions in both the British and Canadian governments. In 1928, the same year in which he received a doctorate in science, he was appointed director of research at the Ontario Research Foundation – a scientific think-tank that was established in 1927 to solve problems of production and processing for Canadian industries and natural resource developers.[74]

Speakman thus knew his stuff, and in May 1942 he travelled to Washington to discuss the issue with several other experts in the field. Of the greatest assistance to him was Sir Clive Baillieu, chair of the British section of the Raw Material Committee. Baillieu was widely considered an expert on the comparative advantages of producing butadiene from alcohol. Most opportunely, he was in Washington giving testimony before the Gillette Committee, a U.S. Senate subcommittee on the utilization of farm crops in the production of synthetic rubber – a subcommittee that took the name of its chair, the colourful Guy Gillette, a populist senator from the farm state of Iowa. In the United States, as in Canada, the decision to use petroleum in the manufacture of synthetic rubber was being passionately contested. Farmers, feeling cheated out of their own rubber industry, were pressuring their congressional representatives – who were facing a midterm election in November – to make a political issue out of the government's decision not to use grain alcohol in the production of synthetic rubber. Baillieu had done extensive research on the issue and had found that there were benefits to using an alcohol base, since the process was less complex[75] and involved fewer critical materials than the production of butadiene from petroleum. At a time when critical materials were increasingly hard to come by, Baillieu's findings delighted Speakman, and he immediately wrote Howe to report the "momentous news."[76]

When Speakman's letter arrived, Howe tucked it away in a file with several other documents he had recently received on the subject. Just one month earlier he had been sent a report prepared by W.H. Cook, a research scientist at the division of applied biology at the NRC. The report, which considered the merits of several alternative methods for manufacturing rubber from grain, contradicted many of Baillieu's findings. According to Cook, there were no "adequate facts" to support the claim that butadiene might be made from alcohol "more easily, rapidly and cheaply than from petroleum."[77] Instead, Cook concluded that a plant designed to produce butadiene from alcohol would be just as complex and exhaust just as many critical materials as would one designed to produce butadiene from petroleum. Furthermore, Cook maintained, it would cost almost twice as much to produce butadiene from alcohol as it would from petroleum. His conclusions, which were supported by those of Dr C.Y. Hopkins, another NRC chemist, directly challenged the conclusions of Boleslaw Przedpelski.[78]

By August 1942 Howe had had enough. He had never been one for drawn-out decision making. As a get-up-and-go engineering type, he detested indecision and inaction, and as far as he was concerned the alcohol versus petroleum debate, which was now into its seventh month, had gone on long enough. If it could not be conclusively shown that the butadiene from alcohol would guarantee synthetic rubber more easily, quickly, and cheaply than from petroleum, then he would not sanction it for use in the Polymer project. It was that simple: either it was scientifically proven to be cheaper or faster, or it would not be used. As a result, on 17 August 1942, one week after the first sod was turned at Sarnia, Howe quashed the butadiene-from-alcohol project. In a memorandum he advised the members of his department "that doubt has been cast on the process for manufacturing any butyl alcohol in existing distilleries to the extent that I have decided to drop the whole project of using butyl alcohol as a base for synthetic rubber."[79] Three days later, Howe advised Polymer of the same decision. "The point I wish to make is that the Polymer program is not to concern itself with the manufacture of alcohol into butylene or butadiene."[80] Instead, he continued, Polymer was to stick with the original plan to produce butadiene from petroleum.

His decision brought down the wrath of some. In a polemical pamphlet entitled *So That Man May Prosper*, Dyson Carter, a young Canadian research scientist who would later leave the laboratory and become internationally known for his literary writings, argued that Howe's decision was "an inexcusable and disastrous blunder."[81] Carter charged that Howe was in the pocket of the international oil trust, whose object was monopolistic control of Canadian rubber production. "Is it possible," Carter asked rhetorically, "that the Canadian authorities still cannot wipe the petroleum out of their eyes and see the truth?"[82] According to Carter, the Liberal government had deliberately turned away from a simple, fast wheat-to-rubber process, one that would have been Canadian controlled, for a method that was less efficient and benefited foreign interests.[83] But for Howe, who thought it was illusory to talk of Canadian industrial self-sufficiency, there was no turning back.[84] "Sooner or later a stage is reached when a decision must be made," he stated in the House of Commons, "and in this case that decision was made ... action was taken; and it is very difficult to turn back the clock at this stage."[85] Again, expediency ruled the day.

The year 1942 was filled with tension for those involved with the Polymer project. Overseas, the war had not yet turned in the Allies' favour. Closer to home, there was great difficulty acquiring materials and equipment for the construction of the synthetic rubber plant. The priority situation south of the border, which paradoxically was both cause and effect of the scarcity of resources, was slowing the pace of progress at Sarnia. This annoyed C.D. Howe, who was continually pressing for ground-breaking news. Howe felt that if a higher priority rating was not secured from the WPB, Canada would lose the "race against time."[86] Without the essential supplies from the United States, synthetic rubber production would remain a flight of fancy, with the very real consequence of gravely impeding the allied war machine.

Adding to the anxiety was the enormous cost of the project. The $50-million price tag represented the largest single government wartime expenditure. Although he later supposedly blurted out in the House of Commons, "What's a million?" this level of expenditure worried even Howe. "My difficulty," he informed Polymer's president, A.L. Bishop, in September 1942, "is that I am at present carrying the responsibility for the largest expenditure of public money involved in any single war project."[87] Perhaps this would not have troubled Howe so much if it had not been for the likelihood of disaster if things did not go according to plan. Bluntly put, Howe had committed $50 million of the people's money to an experimental idea. Thus far no synthetic rubber had ever been made in Canada outside the laboratory. But despite all this, despite all the obstacles and potential risk, Howe, whose incurable optimism was overshadowed only by a dogged determination to get things done, never once talked of throwing in the towel. This was a project that he was resolved to see succeed. His synthetic-rubber "boys" would simply have to dedicate more of their time and effort to the government's project. And if they could not, if they were unwilling or unable, Howe was confident that others could be found to take their place.

At Polymer, Colonel Bishop was having trouble meeting Howe's expectations. For several months, Bishop had been the butt of Howe's criticism. "Since you were appointed president of the company," Howe scolded Bishop in September 1942, "I think that you have been in my office only once and our correspondence has been almost nil."[88] Unlike the faith he placed in most of his "boys," Howe never fully trusted Bishop's business abilities and rarely relied on his economic judgment. Even on matters relating to the construction of the plant – supposedly Bishop's specialty and certainly an aspect of engineering with which Howe had some personal experience – Howe felt compelled at times to question his wisdom.[89] On one such occasion, Howe chided Bishop for an estimate he considered inordinately high. "I may say that I am rather shocked," Howe rebuked Bishop, "at your estimate for a pumping station ... I am sure that with proper appreciation of the type of construction needed ... this can be greatly reduced."[90] It was, in part, this lack of confidence that had caused Howe to go outside the corporation for advice on the butadiene-from-alcohol issue and, later, for an independent check on construction.[91] This was not the usual course of action for Howe. The confident Yankee from Port Arthur, Ontario, usually accepted, almost without question, the judgment and recommendations of those who worked for him. He rarely got involved in the day-to-day operational decisions, confining his energies instead to planning Canada's overall strategy for wartime production. The war and his management-on-the-run style demanded this. "I never give instructions," Howe once commented, "I just give responsibilities."[92]

Howe was a superb delegator of authority. He recruited men with proven records of achievement from business and bureaucratic circles. Each was then invested with sufficient authority to pursue the goals set for him and left alone. This approach was necessary in an expanding department such as Munitions and Supply, which at midwar had more than five thousand people employed by it directly and as many as twenty-five thousand others working for the Crown corporations that Howe had set up to handle war production. Above all else, Howe demanded results. If an executive in a wartime Crown corporation failed, Howe acted quickly to supplant him. Such was Bishop's fate.

On 24 September, Howe wrote to Bishop asking him to step down as president of the corporation.[93] With the Polymer project at a "critical stage," Howe wanted someone he could trust, someone who understood his managerial style, someone who would "get on with the job" and would keep him abreast of key developments. The following day, Bishop tendered his resignation, which Howe accepted without ado.[94]

To replace Bishop, Howe appointed Richard Berkinshaw, chair of the War Industries Control Board. Berkinshaw had been involved with the Canadian synthetic-rubber program from the beginning. Indeed, it was Berkinshaw who had first suggested naming the corporation Polymer and, somewhat ironically, who had recommended Bishop for Polymer's presidency.[95] A lawyer by training, Berkinshaw joined the Department of Munitions and Supply in 1941. Before coming to Ottawa, he had been general manager at Goodyear Tire and Rubber Company of Canada. Far from being the rubber industry's Trojan horse in Ottawa, ready to manipulate the levers of wartime government for the advantage of private industry, Berkinshaw pragmatically built up a new and more broadly applicable set of ground rules for the interaction of business and government. Howe was eager to have men like Berkinshaw working for him. He admired the business caste, its members' ability to clearly define objectives and to achieve their goals efficiently and effectively. He shared their values, spoke their language, and knew and appreciated how their minds worked. Thus, when Berkinshaw came to Ottawa in 1941, Howe immediately put him to work as director general of the Priorities Branch of the Department of Munitions and Supply. Although his stay was brief, the experience gave Berkinshaw an almost unrivalled knowledge of the priority system. This knowledge, C.D. Howe noted at the time of Berkinshaw's appointment as president of Polymer, "will play an important part in determining the date of completion of the [Polymer] project."[96]

On 5 December 1942, widespread frustration with the existing system of priorities led to a new program being launched in the United States. There, the directors of several programs, including the synthetic-rubber program, got together and persuaded Donald Nelson, chair of the WPB, to issue a list of fifty-six different vital wartime projects. To each Nelson assigned an "urgency number" based on their importance to the allied war effort. The numbers were officially declared to outrank any other priority symbol. The new system was initially viewed favourably by those at Polymer. "It should be of considerable assistance to us," R.C. Berkinshaw wrote to G.K. Sheils in mid-December.[97] But Berkinshaw and the others at Polymer quickly found out in the economic scrum of the war that the new system was not of very much assistance to the company at all.

When the new system of urgency numbers was devised, officials at Polymer were working under the impression that the Canadian plant

An early issue of *Poly-Progress*, the newspaper of the employees of Polymer (December 1942). On the front page is a picture of C.D. Howe and William Jeffers, the United States rubber chief, who is biting into a chunk of Canadian-made synthetic rubber. National Archives of Canada.

would receive the same rating as the American synthetic-rubber plants. But when the first list of urgency numbers was issued, the plant at Sarnia was not included. Concerned and somewhat agitated about this, Douglas Ambridge, a bombastic engineer who at times was given to pitbull-like pugnacity, travelled to Washington to obtain an explanation. There, at the office of the American rubber director, he met with the assistant deputy rubber director, Frank Creedon. Understanding and apologetic, Creedon informed Ambridge that the Army and Navy Board had yet again demanded that their program receive preferential

A view of the construction site at Polymer's plant, June 1943. When finished,
the state-of-the art plant would be one of the most fully integrated in the world.

treatment and that as a result the office of the rubber director had decided that in order "to get the thin end of the wedge into the door," it
was best to settle for urgency numbers for only the first 20 percent of
rubber plants then under construction.[98] As a result, Polymer was not
on the list. Still, Creedon assured Ambridge that the rubber director's
approach would ultimately compel the army and the navy to permit
the extension of "urgency numbers" to the remainder of the rubber
projects, including Polymer's.[99] While Ambridge was satisfied with
Creedon's explanation, he and the others at Polymer were unwilling to
sit idly by with the Polymer project hanging in the balance. Ambridge
felt that it was profoundly "unfair" that due to "administrative bicker-
ing" in the United States, Canada would have to wait months for essential parts before beginning operations. Ambridge was especially upset
because the Canadian government had extended top preference to its
synthetic-rubber program to such an extent as "seriously to disturb
other war programs."[100] Without reducing its efforts to secure an appropriate priority rating from the WPB, Polymer took it upon itself to
get the necessary supplies to finish construction on time.

In September of 1942, Roger Hatch was brought in to expedite materials, along with his fellow engineers Lee Dougan and Jack Sayre. Hatch was a natural for the job, having paid his way through university by selling Fuller brushes door-to-door on the East Coast. Peddling brushes had taught Hatch the basic hustling techniques needed to be successful in business, and when it came time to expedite materials, he put these techniques to effective use. He quickly made friends with the people at Crane Industries in Chicago and persuaded them to send some critical materials Polymer's way. During the winter of 1942–43, he and the others obtained additional equipment from all over Canada and the United States. Polymer had thus taken matters into its own hands and by so doing had kept the critical Sarnia project on schedule.

Despite all the trials and tribulations, by June 1943 Polymer's directors were able to report that the GR–S copolymer plant and the styrene plant were substantially completed. When the U.S. rubber director, William Jeffers, and his deputy, Colonel Dewey, visited the plant at Sarnia later that month, they were amazed by the pace of development. "The progress you and your associates are making in establishing the Number One synthetic rubber plant of the British Empire," Dewey commented to Berkinshaw, "is really fine."[101] The construction work proceeded with drill-sergeant regularity, and three months later, on 29 September 1943, thirteen months after the first sod had been turned at Sarnia, the first producing unit went into operation without a hitch. In February 1944, the final phase of the construction effort was completed when the butyl rubber plant was brought on stream.

The exigencies of war needs and timing dictated the compression into less than two years the accomplishment of a task that in more normal times might have taken more than five years. In the national press the event was celebrated as "little short of being a miracle, even in these days of war-bred industrial records."[102] The Sarnia *Canadian Observer* noted that the accomplishment was all the more remarkable given the incredible obstacles that had had to be overcome.[103] The scale and scope of the project was captured, for instance, in a series of photographs published by the *Moncton Transcript*.[104] One photograph was of Polymer's giant tower, which according to the *Transcript* had taken five days to move on three flat cars from Montreal. The image of the erect tower seemed to symbolize Canada's growing industrial prowess. Both the upward angle of the shot and the sharp contrast between the bright sky and caliginous steel gridwork emphasized Canada's newfound technological proficiency. The people associated with the Polymer project seemed to have mastered nature, taking control of elemental forces and siphoning them off for human use.

Polymer's strategy upon commencement of production was to produce as much rubber as possible. With its plant operating at near capacity, Polymer's corporate focus was thus initially production-
oriented. The emphasis was on quantity over quality. This was rubber
produced to meet urgent war needs and not to suit the more discerning demands of a consumer market. That objective would come later.
Between September 1943 and December 1945, Canadian rubber manufacturers received over eighty thousand tons of GR–S rubber and
close to fifteen thousand tons of butyl from the Polymer plant. This
was enough, Howe informed the House of Commons near the end of
the war, to avoid "a shortage, which would have crippled our production programme."[105] Under the stress of the national emergency, the
development of synthetic rubber reached an advanced stage in a remarkably short time. By June 1944 production was at such a high rate
that all restrictions on the use of this material were removed, and later
in the year exports to the United States commenced. By war's end, synthetic rubber had gained a spectacular record of production and development.

The Sarnia project was one in a series of challenges faced by C.D.
Howe that produced a government-business collaboration ideally tai-
lored to meet the demands of the wartime economy. The implementation of the plan for the project paralleled other wartime efforts, with
industry providing management, know-how, and staff and the government providing broad guidance, financing, and regulation. The monumental task of giving birth to a cutting-edge industry required the
utmost in cooperation between a multitude of competing private companies and the plethora of government agencies that were involved. By
bringing business and science together under the umbrella of his
Crown corporation, Polymer, C.D. Howe had hastened the development of a whole industry and overcome the country's almost total de-
pendence on foreign-grown natural rubber.

The project was the biggest wartime bet placed by Howe. When Ottawa undertook the project, no synthetic rubber had been made on the
continent outside of laboratories. "We were very much in the dark as to
costs," Howe later recalled, "and we were not at all sure that sufficient
engineering data was available to allow us to work out the process ... it
was ... a race against time with the possibility of disaster if the project did
not turn out well."[106] But the gamble paid off. In less than two years synthetic rubber had come to supply about 90 percent of total rubber requirements. Howe himself took some pride in the accomplishment.
"The best brains in science and business," Howe declared on the first an-

Symbolizing the extent to which rubber won the war, two Canadian brigadiers celebrate VE-day by taking a ride in a rubber raft. National Archives of Canada.

niversary of the opening of the plant, "have been used at Polymer to transform an experimental dream into an industrial reality ... Polymer," the minister continued, emphasizing every word, "has kept Canada in the war."[107] Like other Crown corporations before it, Polymer was thus the pragmatic product of public purpose in times of national duress.

As he had done in the past, Howe had used the full force of his public office to overcome a national emergency. In the process he pushed the country across the high-technology threshold. The exigencies of war compressed the enterprise's creation into a matter of months. Polymer's launching strategy – its initial crystallization in purpose and structure – was to produce as much rubber as possible. At first, Howe imposed the strategic vision for the fledgling company, which was then made operational by executives drawn from the ranks of his wartime managers. Ironically, Howe's ability to imperiously oversee Polymer (along with such other Crown corporations as Trans-Canada Airlines before it and Atomic Energy of Canada after it) was a function of the lax administrative framework that prevailed until the revision of Crown corporation legislation in 1951. Ultimately, however, it was not Howe but the dynamic men at Polymer Corporation who determined the success of the project. With its plant on the banks of the majestic St Clair River in Sarnia, Ontario, operating at near capacity, Polymer's corporate focus was production-oriented. Acting upon Howe's instructions, the wartime emphasis was on quantity over quality. This was rubber produced to meet urgent needs of a command economy. It was not suited to the more discerning demands of a consumer market. That would come later. For now, Polymer was serving a public purpose, manufacturing the rubber needed to win the war.

For the Country at War and the Country at Peace, 1945–1951

The plant at Sarnia is exclusively the property of the government of Canada; it will be operated by the government of Canada; its products will be at the disposal of the government of Canada, they will be owned by the government of Canada and will be sold in the interests of the government of Canada. So far as I know the situation will continue indefinitely. [I]t is the intention of this government to continue to operate the plant at Sarnia to make rubber for the country at war and the country at peace.

C.D. Howe (1943)[1]

The war proved to be an expensive time to build a synthetic-rubber plant. By most estimates, the $50-million price tag would likely have been half that during peacetime. Yet wartime expediency carried the day, and at war's end few questioned the government's decision to build when it did. Canadians of all political persuasions took pride in the pace and high calibre of the construction effort at Sarnia – a job that C.D. Howe heralded as the "most complex ... ever attempted in this country."[2] One trade journalist of the time commented that "the building of the plant is remarkable not only for its speed but also for its extent and complexities."[3] Another went further in his solemnization: "the story of Polymer's construction," he wrote, "is a Canadian classic."[4] In the House of Commons, a similar sentiment was expressed. In March 1944, Tommy Douglas, one of the CCF's ablest parliamentarians and generally a leading critic of C.D. Howe's handling of the rubber question, judged the plant at Sarnia to be a "splendid piece of engineering."[5] That same month, Douglas's political confrere, Stanley Knowles, added his congratulations to those already expressed to the engineers and technicians, who had designed what was in his words a "thoroughly integrated plant" through which "we have been able to make this very vital contribution to the war effort."[6] In the postwar boom, the Sarnia synthetic-rubber complex would become an icon of Canada's industrial prowess, eventually finding a place on the back of the ten-dollar bill.

As an instrument of public policy, Polymer had served its wartime purpose well. Between September 1943 and September 1945, Polymer had produced over eighty thousand tons of GR-S and fifteen thousand tons of butyl rubber, which was then manufactured into tires and other finished rubber goods by private enterprise. In so doing, Howe told the House of Commons, Polymer had acted as "the backbone of the rubber industry."[7] Like earlier Crown corporations, Polymer had been "facilitative" – to borrow a term from Marsha Chandler[8] – fostering the conditions necessary for the expansion of the private sector, in this case by supplying the rubber once furnished by the plantations of the Far East. Nevertheless, Stanley Knowles admitted to having "misgivings" about the future of the plant.[9] He was not alone.

In the immediate postwar period, a cloud of uncertainty hung over the Polymer project. Those who looked to the future anxiously noted that the plant at Sarnia had a capacity of fifty thousand tons per year, yet before the war Canadians were consuming less than half that amount of rubber.[10] There was no guarantee, skeptics argued, that consumption rates would increase after the war. Indeed, if history was any guide, the reverse would occur. After all, that is what had happened following the First World War – a war that had resulted in victory only to be followed by persistent unemployment, economic instability, and declining levels of domestic consumption. One of the great bugbears of the Depression had been industrial overcapacity. Canadians had recklessly overbuilt their leading industries, like pulp and paper, in the 1920s and had to carry much overcapacity and its attendant financial woes through the 1930s.[11] The anxiety regarding overcapacity resurfaced at war's end. Canadians, and especially industrialists, were haunted by the memory of the two prewar decades and, as a result, approached the prospect of peace with caution.

But even if history did not repeat itself this time around and even if there was no postwar economic slump, as there had been following the First World War, some calculated that the Canadian market could absorb only about one-third of Polymer's annual output.[12] By even the most charitable estimates, the maximum postwar domestic market for synthetic rubber would be only twenty thousand tons per year, and Polymer had to sell forty thousand tons annually merely to break even. The task would be made additionally difficult, predicted Douglas Ross, Conservative member for Toronto-St Paul's, by the fact that synthetic rubber would face competition from natural rubber once the Japanese had been driven out of the plantations of the Far East.[13] On this point, Ross was echoing the opinion of the majority.

A view of the sections of the 125-mile network of medium and heavy steam water and petroleum pipes on the 185-acre property of Polymer Corporation. The
largest steam plant in Canada, and one of the largest producers of process
steam in the world, the steam and power house at Polymer had a rated capacity
of 1,375,000 pounds of steam per hour at 450 pounds per square inch of pressure. National Archives of Canada.

Most industrial observers in Canada and elsewhere believed that natural rubber would dominate the postwar market, as it had the prewar
market, because of its cheaper price and superior qualities.[14] Long in-
ured to what seemed the immutable rhythms of staple-driven economic growth, Canadians tended towards the view that the market for
natural products always resonated itself. The more pessimistic of this
group even argued that the synthetic rubber industry would vanish as
quickly as it had emerged and that it would therefore be best for the
Canadian government to divest itself as soon as possible of this technological "white elephant."[15]

In the face of this cautious outlook, Polymer's weaknesses were all too
apparent. The Crown company, which had been set up to meet a wartime emergency, was without a postwar market for roughly two-thirds of

its operating capacity. In addition, the corporation's structure was designed to accommodate tightly regulated imperatives of wartime production rather than to compete aggressively in a free-market economy.
For instance, it was a structurally truncated enterprise that, unlike the
successful private prewar petrochemical enterprises, lacked a sales division and a department of research and development, crucial organizational elements in any free-market industrial success. Adding to its
troubles, many of the people who had guided the synthetic-rubber program to date and who had volunteered their services for the duration of
the war were now returning to their natural niches in private industry.
For example, Richard Berkinshaw, the soft-spoken Torontonian who
had so skilfully led the corporation since September of 1942, departed
from Polymer in 1945 to resume his full-time duties at Goodyear Tire
and Rubber Company. The corporation was thus losing some of its key
strategists at a time when it needed seasoned hands-on direction most.
In sum, at the end of the war Polymer was without a natural market for
much of its output, without a corporate strategy for postwar survival, and
without the necessary organizational structure for successful operation
in a consumer-oriented economy. The Crown company was without the
crucial ingredients that business historian Alfred Chandler identifies as
necessary for any industrial company's survival: a well-thought-out business strategy and a corporate structure to enable it to realize its objectives.[16] At war's end, therefore, the economic future of the Polymer
project was very much in question.

While Polymer had lost some of its principal personnel, the minister
responsible for bringing the company into existence remained in office. C.D. Howe was reelected by the people of Port Arthur in the general election of 1945 and thus retained the political authority to
determine Polymer's postwar fate. The majority of people in Sarnia –
or Lambton West, to be more exact – did not, however, vote Liberal in
the 1945 election. For various reasons, they supported the Progressive
Conservative candidate, Joseph Murphy. A lawyer and successful businessman, Murphy joined sixty-six other Conservatives in the House of
Commons. In the years that followed he pressured the government to
privatize Polymer, arguing that this would generate additional tax revenue for Sarnia in the form of municipal taxes – something that before
1951 Polymer, as a Crown corporation, did not pay.[17] "Crown Companies should make some contribution," Murphy stated indignantly in
1949, "by way of taxes to the municipalities in which they do business."[18] Statements such as these endeared him to the people of Lambton West, and he was reelected in 1949, 1953, 1957, and 1958.

Despite Murphy's personal success, the Liberals returned to power in 1945 with another majority government – 125 of 220 seats – on the promise that they had the competence and the blueprint for postwar reconstruction. Planning for postwar recovery had, however, begun well before Canadians went to the polls in June 1945. During the last eighteen months of the war, the Liberal government had taken the initial steps to ensure that there would be no postwar industrial slump, as there had been following the First World War. In order to prevent the sharp economic dislocations that accompanied much of the two prewar decades, Mackenzie King's Liberals developed a complex series of plans and programs to ensure the smooth transition from the economic conditions of war to those of peace. For example, in 1944 the Industrial Development Bank was established as a subsidiary of the Bank of Canada to ensure the availability of credit to small and medium-sized businesses.[19] In June of that same year, the Department of Veterans' Affairs was created to implement a wide range of benefits for returning soldiers, including subsidized mortgages, health-care benefits, job training, and education allowances. As well, in 1944 a monthly family allowance was introduced to put spending money in the pockets of Canadian consumers. The program was consciously Keynesian, designed to stimulate aggregate demand. All these measures were part of the Liberals' overall strategy for postwar socioeconomic reconstruction.

In setting postwar priorities the King government was formatively influenced by Keynesian prescriptions for economic stability, which assumed that the federal government would, in the words of political scientist Donald Smiley, "ensure appropriate levels of aggregated demand through generalized fiscal and monetary policies and through lowering barriers to international trade and investment."[20] The striking change in general equilibrium theory that John Maynard Keynes initiated in his classic 1936 treatise *The General Theory of Employment, Interest and Money* and that a generation of civil servants embraced shifted the attention of Canadian opinion makers to the implications of improperly managed economic policy. As a result, there was a conscious effort on Ottawa's part after the war to regulate the level of demand in the economy by fiscal adjustments. The "Ottawa men" (to use Granatstein's term) were also sanguine they could maintain a "high and stable level of employment" – a phrase enshrined in the Canadian lexicon by the 1945 *White Paper on Employment and Income* (discussed below) – through supplementary countercyclical policies.[21] The pursuit of higher levels of welfare – through the implementation of such programs as the family allowance – was seen not only as good in itself but also as a way of sustaining consumer demand. If people could be kept spending, the Keynesian logic went, then their demands would create the jobs and profits necessary to allow continued consumption. "Success," in the words of economic historians Ken Norrie and Doug Owram, would thus be "self-fulfilling."[22] In Canada, Keynes' ideas were embraced and disseminated by a dynamic group of public-policy economists who had been recruited into government service during the war. W.C. Clark, Louis Rasminsky, R.B. Bryce, J.J. Deutsch, A.W.F. Plumptre, and W.A. Mackintosh each played an active role in aiding in the diffusion of Keynesian doctrines throughout the upper echelons of the Ottawa bureaucracy.[23] As a result of their efforts, when the war ended, a strong central authority and a Keynesian mentality pervaded Ottawa thinking.

Among the attractions of Keynesianism was the preeminent role it envisioned for the national government in directing economic activity. Not since the end of the nineteenth century had Ottawa held such sway in the economic affairs of the nation. By the end of the war, Canadians had come not only to accept but also to appreciate the "visible hand" of government intervention. This was certainly the message of the 1945 election. With the exception of the extreme laissez-faire Tory fringe, Canadians wanted their national government to take a firmer hand in directing the economy. Unlike the feelings after World War I, there was little inclination for a return to normalcy. The political/ideological conundrum lay in just how much firmer the government grip should be. The June 1945 election seemed to reveal that a majority of Canadians did not favour the super-firm hand of the CCF – "Turn Left, Canada" – but rather the lighter grip of the Liberals – "Let the Liberals finish the job" – a grip that still allowed for a variable tenacity.

C.D. Howe, who in 1944 was appointed minister of reconstruction, was a Liberal who favoured the lightest grip. Unlike the CCF and left-leaning Keynesians within the Liberal Cabinet and the Ottawa mandarinate, Howe thought the market would settle most economic matters. He had confidence in the "judgment of business" to make the right microeconomic decisions.[24] "In Canada," Howe stated shortly after the end of the war, "the initiative to industrial expansion rests largely with private individuals and private companies."[25] This did not mean that the government resigned its role in the economy. On the contrary, public policymakers in Canada, as elsewhere, sought to counteract global forces and assert greater control over their economic destiny by extending the direct role of the state as investor and producer.[26] Howe's record as a public servant was full of examples of his using government to boost Canada's presence in certain strategic or frontier industries. Polymer was simply the latest example of his interventionist bent. Before the war he had used the full power of the state on several occasions to overcome private industry's inability or unwilllingness to provide critical goods and services. In 1936–37, for example, when Canada was in need of a national intercity air service, Howe wasted little time before creating Trans-Canada Air Lines as a government-owned and government-controlled company.[27] Because no private firms were capable of making the leap to national-carrier status, Howe created his own Crown company made up primarily of American aviation men who brought with them practical experience and technological know-how. As he did during the war when Canada needed a secure source of rubber, Howe used government to put the necessary industrial structure into place, not in order to compete with private industry but in order to provide it with goods and services it would otherwise be without. According to Howe, simply priming the market alone, as Keynesians recommended, would not be enough in a small, technology- and capital-deficient economy like Canada's to push the economy in a new direction.

In looking beyond the exigencies of wartime, C.D. Howe was generally more optimistic than most Keynesians about Canada's economic prospects. The economic dislocations of the Great Depression would not return, he believed; indeed, the basic problem of the postwar era would be ensuring sufficient supply, rather than stimulating demand.[28] Thus, he was less worried than most observers about Polymer's "excess capacity." At war's end, Canada was a "nation on the march."[29] The war had produced new economic opportunities, according to Howe, particularly in the areas of electronics, communications, and petrochemicals. It had provided a broadened industrial base and had modernized the technological core of the country. No longer was Canada composed merely of hewers of wood and drawers of water. "Today," Howe stated proudly shortly after the end of the war, "Canadians are both an industrious and an industrialized nation."[30]

He had a point. After all, in less than three decades (decades that paralleled Howe's own business and political career), the Canadian economy had changed its status from one mainly dependent for its livelihood on primary industries to one deriving its main wealth from processing primary products and manufacturing various capital and consumer goods. In 1919 agriculture was Canada's most important industry, contributing 44 percent of the total new value of commodity production, as against 33 percent for manufacturing. By 1939 this position was almost the reverse, with manufacturing contributing 41 percent, as against 23 percent for agriculture. When the war ended six years later, manufacturing had increased its lead to 52 percent. This change pleased Howe. In his mind, it was essential for the Canadian economy to be mixed, with manufacturing firms like Polymer playing a leading role.[31]

As minister of reconstruction, Howe considered it his task to help maintain the balance and buoyancy of the economy. The objective was fully outlined in his department's 1945 *White Paper on Employment and Income.* "The program of reconstruction," the white paper stated, "is a complicated task of combining the demobilization of the armed services and war industry with the rebuilding of an ampler and more stable Canadian economy."[32] For six years industry had relied upon a war market, with the government as chief purchaser. But now that the demands of war were no more, it was widely accepted that normal patterns of trade would have to be restored. For Howe and officials at the Department of Reconstruction, this goal meant first liquidating the industrial and military war effort, which at its peak absorbed about half of Canada's resources. Thereafter, they would have to encourage the expansion of business serving peacetime purposes to take the place of large-scale government buying of munitions and war equipment. With his task defined, Howe matter-of-factly got down to the business of dismantling the siege economy that he had built up over the previous five years.

When it came to the demobilization of the war-created industrial structure, Howe had to deal with the question of what to do with the twenty-eight Crown corporations he had established during the war. After all, they were designed for a wartime economy and theoretically had no purpose and therefore no place in a peacetime, consumer-oriented world. Howe's own industrial vision acknowledged this. It made sense, therefore, for him to put his wartime Crown corporations into private hands, especially now that the pressures of war were over. The Canadian economy was a free-enterprise system, and like Howe, the vast majority of Canadians were committed, at least in principle, to private ownership of industry. This was not the case, of course, in the United Kingdom and France, where industry was nationalized after the war in accordance with the socialist belief that the state should take over "the commanding heights of the economy."[33] In those countries there was an ideological commitment to state ownership in critical sectors of the economy.

Ideology played a far less important role in Canada. On the question of state ownership, Howe took a decidedly pragmatic approach. He considered the merits of retaining each Crown corporation on a discrete basis and kept only those with a strategic postwar purpose: those like Eldorado, Canada's uranium company, whose continued operation was viewed as necessary for reasons of national security after the detonation of the atomic bomb.[34] Similarly, the continued state operation of Wartime Housing – a company that ultimately merged with the National Housing Administration and the Central Mortgage Bank to become the CMHC – was seen as warranted by the acute postwar housing shortages, particularly for returning veterans.[35] For the rest, the auction block awaited. By June 1946 only three of the twenty-eight Crown corporations that Howe had established during the war were still active; the majority had been sold to private interests through the War Assets Corporation.[36] Polymer completed the triumvirate.

On the shores of the majestic St Clair River, the company's state-of-the-art plant continued to churn out synthetic rubber in peace, as it had done in war. In mid-1944, Polymer's executive cabal had gone to see Howe to ask that the Crown corporation be allowed to continue operations after the end of hostilities. Contrary to the skepticism of the majority, Polymer was bullish on its peacetime prospects. As early as 1943, J.R. Nicholson had voiced his belief that synthetic rubber had a place in the postwar world. "I agree ... it is unlikely that synthetic will ever wholly supplant crude rubber," he wrote A.H. Williamson in October 1943, "but both products have their uses and a well established synthetic rubber industry will keep this continent away from the mercy of other lands as to stocks and prices."[37] Douglas Ambridge, who ascended to the presidency in 1945, agreed. "The first thing that strikes me," he wrote to C.D. Howe and R.C. Berkinshaw in November of 1943, "is that we, as Canadians, can never abandon the synthetic rubber business, come what it may [sic] in the crude rubber market."[38] Whether or not Ambridge knew it, he was preaching to the choir. Berkinshaw was among the most bullish about the future of the synthetic-rubber industry. In his expert opinion, synthetic rubber would have "a prominent place in Canada's future."[39] He was sanguine that in the years to come the industry would be able to reduce its costs and improve its products to such an extent that it would become competitive with crude rubber. [40] "Synthetic rubber must earn its place in the postwar market," he stated in 1945, "but in the competitive field it will not be weaponless."[41] Of course Berkinshaw, as a senior executive with Goodyear Rubber and Tire, had a vested interest in seeing the project continue. With Polymer producing rubber, private industry would have an alternative and uninterrupted source of supply when the natural rubber cartel "unfairly" manipulated world prices. Likewise, Howe was confident that the Canadian synthetic-rubber industry would be well armed to compete in the postwar world. "What will happen when natural rubber competes with synthetic rubber, I cannot say," the minister declared in September 1944. "But I do know that synthetic rubber is here and here to stay."[42] Howe's "hard-hitting comments" – as the president of the RRC, Colonel Dewey, termed them[43] – were welcomed by those associated with the Polymer project.[44]

The question for Howe, therefore, was not whether manufacturing synthetic rubber was a viable postwar enterprise. He was sure that it was. Rather, the issue for him was in whose hands – the government's or private industry's – the Polymer project would be placed once the hostilities had ended. In August 1942 Howe gave the first clue of his intentions. "I think that operating costs will be low enough," he confided to a colleague, "to warrant [Polymer's] peacetime operation as a Government enterprise."[45] The following year, when he was asked by Conservative MP John Diefenbaker about his postwar plans for the Polymer project, Howe stated that it was his aim to continue to operate the plant at Sarnia as a government-owned and government-controlled enterprise "to make rubber for the country at war and the country at peace."[46] Howe felt that he had a valuable asset in Polymer.[47] Since beginning operations in September 1943, the plant at Sarnia had been running to capacity, supplying the needs of Canada in full with a fairly substantial margin for export. "In light of what has been achieved," Howe stated in September 1944, "Polymer need not fear the future."[48] Looking ahead, there seemed to be "every reason" for putting Polymer "on its own as a [government] corporation operating for profit."[49]

The task of determining exactly how profitability was to be accomplished the minister was willing to leave to Polymer's executive team. "It will be the job of Polymer to sell sufficient rubber to keep its operations at an economic level," he wrote Nicholson in November 1944, "and I am quite willing to leave the method to you and your Board of Governors."[50] Howe's decision to take a hands-off approach to Polymer ultimately guaranteed the long-term success of the firm. The purpose of Polymer was to generate a profit, and Howe was willing to give the firm tremendous autonomy to achieve its aim. In so doing, he established a pattern of ministerial behaviour that his successors would emulate. Howe was confident that as a postwar government-owned and government-operated commercial enterprise, Polymer would be able to sell enough high-value-added goods to turn a profit. Polymer was being asked to produce for profit and given a wide margin of managerial discretion to do so.

While Polymer's postwar commercial viability was the determining factor in Howe's decision to retain the corporation, there were additional – albeit incidental – reasons. In Polymer he saw the possibility of an industrial polymath. As an instrument of state-led development strategy, Polymer would play several roles. First, by being a profitable commercial enterprise Polymer would incidentally generate export earnings. The white paper had stressed the need for increased export markets if the federal government's demand-management policies were to work at home. Polymer would aid the government in this task.

The Crown company's synthetic rubber would be sold in world markets, thus taking its place alongside Canadian uranium, aluminum, iron ore, petroleum, and natural gas as the latest in a long line of products for export. Second, the Crown company would act as "pump primer" to a whole new petrochemical industry in Canada. Since being elected to office in 1935, Howe had endeavoured to modernize the Canadian economy. He was especially interested in developing science- and technology-based industry. In 1945, he expressed to J.R. Nicholson his desire for "making Sarnia a center of Canada's great organic chemical industry."[51] Howe believed that Western civilization was at "the dawn of a chemical age" and that the Polymer undertaking could become "the very hub of a group of complementary chemical and other industries."[52] By the end of the war, Polymer was producing surpluses of styrene, ethylene, and butylene, all of which would be the basis of substantial industries. Polymer would thus be the cornerstone of a whole new petrochemical industry, helping to propel Canada across the high-technology threshold.

By 1948 there were already signs that Howe's industrial strategy was working. In the fall of 1945 Dow Chemical had begun construction of a $10-million plant on land adjacent to Polymer to polymerize styrene into plastic.[53] At that time, an agreement was reached whereby Polymer would supply Dow with its principal raw material. This arrangement proved enormously successful, generating a stable income for Polymer while protecting it from fluctuations in the rubber market. About the same time Fiberglass (Canada) announced that it would soon begin construction of a $2.5-million plant in Sarnia.[54] Later, Standard Chemical Company and the General Aniline and Film Company made similar announcements. The war had increased Canada's appetite for chemicals. Between 1939 and 1945, chemical consumption had doubled.[55] After the war, the craving remained. Between 1945 and 1955, chemical consumption as a percentage of the gross national product averaged 4.5 percent.[56] By 1951 the chemical industry in Canada employed 45,644 people.[57] Of these, 2,055 were employed by Polymer. In more ways than one, therefore, Polymer had catalyzed the industrial development of the region.

Howe's decision to retain Polymer was in marked contrast to the decision taken by his counterparts in the United States. At the end of the war, Polymer's u.s. counterpart, the RRC, was wound up, and the factories under its control were either sold to private interests or shut down for use at a later date. Even before the ultimate ratification of the Rubber Producing Facilities Disposal Act of 1953, early steps had been taken in general accord with the belief in the United States that the government should get out of the rubber business. Between October

1946 and December 1948, eighteen of the fifty-one original synthetic rubber facilities in the United States were sold under authority of the Surplus Property Act. By the time Congress passed the Disposal Act in 1953, roughly half the government's rubber plants had been sold to private industry.[58] The remaining plants, those for which a private purchaser could not be found, were mothballed in case of another national emergency.

This course of action was never considered by Howe. If the Liberal government had chosen to close its plant, Canadian manufacturers would have again become reliant on foreign supplies of rubber. The dangers associated with this were etched in the national memory. During the war, Canada's dependency on foreign sources had exposed the vulnerability of the Canadian economy. After the war, there was no desire to return to a situation of dependency. When in December 1946 Howe was approached by Peter Campbell, a Liberal senator and prominent Toronto lawyer who was representing a group of investors interested in purchasing Polymer from the Crown, Howe stated that he was "inclined to think that the government should keep Polymer if only as a protection against our rubber supply in future years."[59] Furthermore, mothballing the plant would have been inconsistent with the government's commitment to "a high and stable level of employment and income." In 1946 Polymer was employing roughly two thousand workers directly and was indirectly creating employment for thousands of other men and women who worked for the companies that provided Polymer with the necessary brine, soap, benzol, sulphuric acid, petroleum gas, and other raw materials used in synthetic rubber production. In the context of the Liberal government's overall postwar strategy for reconstruction, writing off the plant and closing it was as unpalatable as privatization. Thus, the major argument in favour of Polymer's continued operation as a state-run enterprise was as much a reflection of the macroeconomic downside of all other alternatives as it was of its intrinsic desirability.

The government's decision gave Polymer the confidence to plan strategically. Not since the founding of the corporation had there been such a momentous juncture in its short history. But there was no time for self-congratulation. An arduous task lay ahead. The corporation would have to live up to its own high expectations and those of C.D. Howe. Polymer would have to quickly formulate a strategy for survival and adjust its corporate structure so as to function as a profitable commercial enterprise. Like other enterprising Canadian companies, such as Alcan, Algoma Steel, and Inco, which had emerged from the war with excess capacity, Polymer would have to locate and develop new markets.[60]

Polymer Corporation's synthetic-rubber plant at Sarnia, Ontario, 1946. National Archives of Canada.

Howe's public declaration that he was retaining Polymer came some months after his private directive to Polymer's board that the corporation would continue operating in pursuit of profit. During this interval, executives at Polymer began formulating a strategy for success in the postwar world. The imperatives of wartime expansion were gone, and if the company was to profit in the postwar economy, it would have to shift from a production-oriented to a diverse product-oriented enterprise.

The new corporate mission that emerged had three key elements. Given the plant's overcapacity in relation to Canada's domestic needs, the company needed to develop export markets for synthetic rubber. In addition, it would have to develop a greater variety of products to meet the needs of peacetime consumers and reduce the cost of producing existing ones. "To insure a long term future for synthetic [rubber]," an internally generated technical paper noted, "prices must definitely be lowered and quality improved until it is directly competitive with crude rubber ... Failing this, the demand will fall off to a negligible volume with a consequence of writing-off the huge Sarnia investment."[61] And finally, the company would have to increase its sales of the by-products of synthetic-rubber production so as to break the dangerous dependency on staple-oriented production.

Polymer Corporation Limited Organization Chart

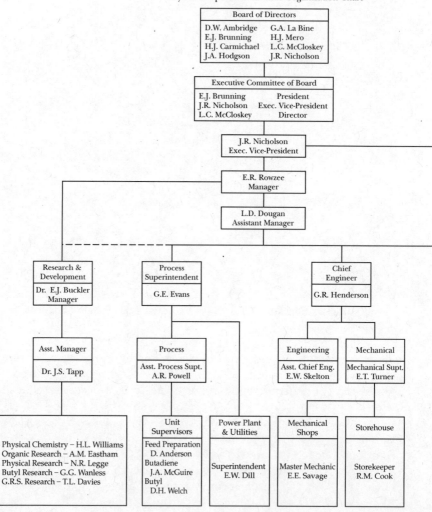

Board of Directors

D.W. Ambridge	G.A. La Bine
E.J. Brunning	H.J. Mero
H.J. Carmichael	L.C. McCloskey
J.A. Hodgson	J.R. Nicholson

Executive Committee of Board

E.J. Brunning	President
J.R. Nicholson	Exec. Vice-President
L.C. McCloskey	Director

J.R. Nicholson
Exec. Vice-President

E.R. Rowzee
Manager

L.D. Dougan
Assistant Manager

Research & Development
Dr. E.J. Buckler
Manager

Process Superintendent
G.E. Evans

Chief Engineer
G.R. Henderson

Asst. Manager
Dr. J.S. Tapp

Process
Asst. Process Supt.
A.R. Powell

Engineering
Asst. Chief Eng.
E.W. Skelton

Mechanical
Mechanical Supt.
E.T. Turner

Physical Chemistry – H.L. Williams
Organic Research – A.M. Eastham
Physical Research – N.R. Legge
Butyl Research – G.G. Wanless
G.R.S. Research – T.L. Davies

Unit Supervisors
Feed Preparation
D. Anderson
Butadiene
J.A. McGuire
Butyl
D.H. Welch

Power Plant & Utilities
Superintendent
E.W. Dill

Mechanical Shops
Master Mechanic
E.E. Savage

Storehouse
Storekeeper
R.M. Cook

Main Committees	Sub-Committees
Management	Budget
E.R. Rowzee	I.P. Cameron
Staff	Accounting
L.D. Dougan	G.C. Weir
Research & Development	Laboratory
Dr. E.J. Buckler	J.F. Gilbert
Operating	Safety
H.R. Emmerson	G.L. Underhay
Operators Co-ordination	Materials Standards
E.R. Rowzee	J.R. Millar
	Editorial Committee
	of "Polysphere"
	W.J. Dyke

Associated Operating Companies

Canadian Synthetic Rubber Limited		Dow Chemical of Canada Limited	
A.G. Partridge	President	N.R. Crawford	President
C.H. Madsen	Manager	L.D. Smithers	Works Manager
G. Bracewell	Secretary-Treas.	P.D. Scott	Asst. Works Mgr.
R. Dance	Prod. Manager	J. Hacking	Plant Supt.
Operating	Producing	Operating	Producing
G.R.S. Plant	G.R.S. Rubber	Styrene Plant	Styrene
	Buna-S Latex		Ethylbenzene
	G.R.S. Latex		

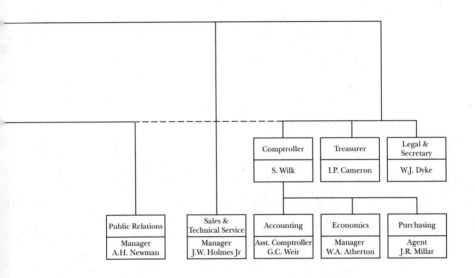

	Comptroller	Treasurer	Legal & Secretary
	S. Wilk	I.P. Cameron	W.J. Dyke

Public Relations	Sales & Technical Service	Accounting	Economics	Purchasing
Manager A.H. Newman	Manager J.W. Holmes Jr	Asst. Comptroller G.C. Weir	Manager W.A. Atherton	Agent J.R. Millar

Consultants	
Legal	Technical
General Counsel W.A.G. Kelley Canadian Patent Counsel E.G. Gowling	Standard Oil Development Co. H.G. Acres & Co. J.W. Livingston Dr. G.S. Whitby J.J. Moriarty

The implementation of the new strategy necessitated altering the organization's structure. This was a common progression in the growth of the successful industrial enterprises during the twentieth century. It was also a necessary development if the firm was to compete successfully and function effectively in its environment.[62] "A new strategy," the business historian Chandler writes, "required a new or at least refashioned structure if the enlarged enterprise was to be operated efficiently."[63] Structure, in Chandler's famous dictum, followed strategy. At Polymer after the war a similar chain of events occurred.

One of the first organizational changes to be made came in late 1944 when Polymer established a research department to develop and improve products scientifically. This objective was decidedly distinct from the one that led to the establishment of research and development departments at General Electric, America Telephone and Telegraph, and Kodak. All these firms had organized research laboratories to protect their technological leads from competition.[64] But Polymer's rationale was far more activist. From the outset the goal of the department was to produce with the greatest possible efficiency a synthetic rubber that could aggressively compete, in terms of both price and quality, with natural rubber once that product returned to the marketplace. Polymer was thus among the first Canadian firms to acknowledge that economic growth could be knowledge-based and science-driven.

The war had taught Polymer the power of science. The establishment of a research department would now put that power toward peacetime commercial ends. "A well directed research and development program," R.C. Berkinshaw wrote to the president of the NRC Dr C.J. Mackenzie, in May 1944, "can be expected to more than justify its cost by its contribution to cost reductions and product improvement and to contribute materially toward ensuring a successful future for Canada's huge synthetic rubber program."[65] The statement was consistent with the objectives of Howe's Department of Reconstruction, which in 1947 released a report on research and scientific activity in Canada.[66] The report reiterated the department's position, which had first been stated in the white paper, that the application of science to industry was "an essential of modern industrial development."[67] Howe had held such a view since his education at MIT. Not only was science transforming older industries but it was creating new ones associated with radio, electronics, combustion processes, and petrochemicals. Building on earlier initiatives, the 1947 report promised new funds to firms like Polymer engaged in R&D activity.

To head the new department Berkinshaw chose Ralph Rowzee, the general manager of Canadian Synthetic Rubber. Rowzee was a strong advocate of the need for an R&D program. "I feel that if Canada's synthetic plant is to compete in world markets after the war," he wrote to Berkinshaw in October 1944, "we will have need of the best research and development facilities that are available to assist in establishing this plant in a competitive position."[68] During the war, Rowzee had overseen the copolymerization process at Sarnia and was generally thought to have done an outstanding job. "The remarkable success which attended his work," Berkinshaw wrote to Howe of Rowzee in November 1944, "has greatly impressed those of us who have been closely associated with the enterprise."[69] When Berkinshaw proposed Rowzee's name to C.J. Mackenzie, Mackenzie responded that if the services of Rowzee could be obtained, he would be "an ideal man to head up the Polymer program."[70]

The comments were well justified. Rowzee had graduated with honours in chemical engineering from MIT in 1930 and had obtained his MSc degree from that institution in 1931. Later that year he was one of a group selected, on the recommendation of the faculty at MIT, to join Goodyear Tire and Rubber Company of Akron, Ohio. His first two years with the company were spent in the chemical engineering division, but in 1933 he was transferred to the research division to do some preliminary work on synthetic rubber. He was there in 1934 when the news broke of IG Farben's discovery of a new method of synthesizing rubber by polymerization of butadiene and other monomers. The news prompted Goodyear to resume its independent research in the field and Rowzee was assigned to the company's first scale-up program from laboratory work. He was actively engaged in the work of designing, engineering, and constructing the plant required and upon its completion was placed in charge of its operation.

In 1942, Goodyear loaned Rowzee to Canadian Synthetic Rubber for the duration of the war. Rowzee, however, chose not to return to Goodyear once the hostilities had ended. He was convinced that synthetic rubber was "here to stay" and that the Crown company on the banks of the St Clair was going to be a pioneer in the field. In a 1945 address to the Chemical Institute of Canada – an institute that he would later head – Rowzee outlined the reasons for his optimism. "Again and again," he stated, "time has shown that the synthetic product is capable of supplanting the natural product. It is my belief that history will again repeat itself and eventually Sarnia's products will supplant natural rubber."[71] The Second World War had revolutionized the chemical industry by greatly accelerating the rate and extent of the displacement of natural substances by synthetic polymers. Rowzee was sanguine that in the succeeding years natural rubber too would be "on the way to joining natural dyes, natural drugs and other products that have been replaced almost 100 percent by synthetic products."[72] His optimism was rooted in a faith in the Promethean power of science and its practitioners. "The future of the synthetic rubber program," he stated soon after his appointment as director of research, "is squarely in the hands of the rubber chemist ... I believe that he will successfully improve the present synthetics and concurrently discover new superior types of synthetics which can be produced economically."[73] Armed with this belief, in the fall of 1944 Rowzee began recruiting all the chemists that his relatively tiny R&D budget would allow. The department grew steadily after the war and by 1951 was employing over a hundred chemists and technicians. This level of growth was not unfamiliar to the industry in other industrialized countries; now Canada's synthetic rubber industry was falling into line with global corporate strategies and structures.[74]

Aided by the federal fiscal incentives that were available to all businesses (e.g., tax deductions for all expenditures and investments made in research facilities), between 1945 and 1951 Polymer's new research department worked to develop a synthetic rubber that would equal or surpass natural rubber in uniformity, special properties, and cost. The postwar petrochemical and polymer developments were monumental, and aggressive techno-economic competition with natural rubber was the order of the day. Under Rowzee's leadership and later under the direction of E.J. Buckler – a brilliant Cambridge-educated chemist, who replaced Rowzee as director of R&D when Rowzee was promoted to general manager in 1946 – the research department played a highly significant part in the translation of pure science to applied industrial use.[75] Of the six technological break-throughs during the period (i.e., cold-resistent butyl rubber, the black masterbatch technique, the improved butadiene catalyst, "cold" rubber, high-abrasion carbon blacks, and oil-extended buna-s), Polymer, remarkably, played a principal role in three.

One of Polymer's greatest successes came in 1947 when the research and development department solved the problem of cold-weather buckling. Postwar butyl rubber tended to grow brittle and crack at low temperatures. As a consequence, butyl-rubber inner tubes would rupture, causing travellers to get stranded – often in blizzards. The problem became so acute that the manufacturers of inner tubes announced that "the use of butyl rubber would become optional" – a polite way of saying that natural rubber would henceforth be used for inner tubes. The news was shocking. A large portion of Polymer's profits derived from butyl-rubber sales. Thus, if no solution could be found, there would be a devastating effect on Polymer's balance sheet.

Polymer's board of directors and executive cabal, 1946. In the back row, from left to right, are Stan Wilk, Lee Dougan, Roger Hatch, W.J. (Bill) Dyke, E.J. (Bill) Buckler, and Ian C. Rush. These men, along with Ralph Rowzee (seated centre right), would lead the corporation for the next quarter century, taking it to dizzying heights.

Polymer manufactured butyl as a licensee of Standard Oil of New Jersey and was bound by agreement to a mutual exchange of patents and technical information. The company was therefore obliged to turn first to Standard for assistance. But Standard was indifferent to the problem of cold buckling.[76] As a result, Polymer tackled it on its own. Having in mind Canada's cold winter climate, Polymer sent its engineers to Winnipeg to experience the problem firsthand. From the data gathered there, Polymer was able to evolve a new theory of the structure of butyl rubber, which E.J. Buckler presented to the industry in June 1948.[77] More importantly from a commercial point of view, the buckling problem was solved by making a high-molecular-weight version of butyl rubber and extending it with oil of a specific composition. The added oil made the rubber less brittle and thus far less likely to crack in cold weather. Since oil was much cheaper than the other inputs, the innovation not only improved the rubber's quality but lowered its cost as well. The net result was to render butyl preeminent as an inner-tube rubber under all weather conditions.

Despite these innovations, R&D meant little if markets could not be found. In 1945 the market for Polymer's output was overwhelmingly North American; less than 3 percent of total output was exported to countries outside the United States, while domestic consumption

totalled approximately thirty-five thousand tons.[78] Polymer's success at
home was largely a result of two factors: stronger-than-expected postwar demand for rubber products and the protection afforded by ongoing wartime controls. The board of directors anticipated that neither
of these phenomena would last for long.[79] They were right.

In the spring of 1947, C.D. Howe followed through on his promise to
deregulate the rubber industry, ending five years of government controls. After Pearl Harbor, the Canadian government had decided to
limit the amount of natural rubber used to manufacture tires and
other products. This decision guaranteed synthetic rubber a certain
portion of the marketplace and, in effect, protected the nascent industry. The protection was purely incidental, however, since the principal
purpose of the government's regulation was to ensure that existing
supplies of natural rubber were not depleted unnecessarily. At the end
of the war, with access to the rubber plantations of the Far East re-
gained, the rationale for such controls vanished, and talk began in Ottawa about bringing an end to the wartime regulations. Howe had
never intended to protect Polymer from postwar competition – a point
that he had made abundantly clear to the board of directors when they
had approached him with their recommendation to keep Polymer in
business after the war.[80] He made a similar declaration before parliament in May of 1946. "The fact that the government owns a synthetic
rubber plant," Howe asserted in the House of Commons, "will not be
used to deprive anyone from the privilege of purchasing natural rubber."[81] In Howe's opinion, nothing should interfere with the right of
Canadian industry or consumers to purchase either synthetic or natural rubber. He wanted nothing to do with the old "infant industry"
mentality that had coddled Canadian industry since the 1870s.
    At Polymer, however, the whole notion of decontrol sent shivers
down the collective spine of the corporation. The board feared that it
would "throttle the new industry before it ... has had a chance to develop continuing peacetime markets and before the public has had a
chance to evaluate its good qualities."[82] It further worried that if the
rubber regulations were summarily suspended, as was being suggested,
the domestic demand for their product would drop off precipitously.
Some of the more pessimistic estimates predicted that if decontrol
went through, synthetic rubber would lose over two-thirds of its domestic market share to natural rubber. In an effort to prevent such a ruin-
ous event, Polymer's board of directors – in addition to stepping up
their efforts to develop new markets abroad, while embarking on a
campaign at home to heighten public awareness about the qualities of

their products[83] – wrote to Howe asking that the wartime regulations be continued. In true Canadian form, they were asking Ottawa to consider them a needy infant industry.

The argument put forth by the board was well-rooted in Canadian economic thought, dating from John Rae's classic nineteenth-century *Statement of Some New Principles on the Subject of Political Economy*.[84] As an infant enterprise, the board argued, the synthetic-rubber industry should not, indeed could not, be expected to compete with a fully developed industry like that of natural rubber. "The baby should not be treated as a full grown man. We must not suddenly feed it the adult fare of full de-control if we expect it [i.e., the synthetic rubber industry] to reach maturity," the Polymer board told Howe in true protectionist spirit.[85] This argument had an honourable lineage in Canadian industrial history. Alexander Galt had used a similar argument as early as 1859 to justify "incidental protection" of Canada's nascent industrial economy. John A. Macdonald again used it in defence of the National Policy of 1879.[86] Yet C.D. Howe would have none of it. As he had previously instructed the board of directors, Polymer would either "profit or perish" as a competitive agent on the free market. "I feel that there is no excuse for controls after a commodity comes into adequate supply," Howe wrote to an interested observer at the time.[87] "I feel that the Sarnia plant must stand on its own feet, and that it is quite capable of doing so."[88] Howe's position on Polymer was consistent with his general approach to postwar industrial planning. He rejected the old cloistered protectionist outlook that had traditionally governed Canadian industrial development and opted instead for an approach that was largely free of dependency on tariffs, direct government succour, and foreign capital and research and development ideas.

In November of 1946 the board made a final appeal to Howe to extend controls on the purchase and use of natural rubber so as to leave the Canadian market open to them.[89] The implacable Howe responded that Polymer could expect no more than four additional months of regulation.[90] As it turned out, the company got five. In April 1947, Ottawa removed all wartime restrictions on the use of natural rubber and Canadian rubber-consuming manufacturers became free to use as much natural rubber as they chose in tires and other products. Remarkably, private industry did not abandon synthetic rubber altogether, despite the pent-up consumer demand for natural rubber products and the fact that natural rubber was usually cheaper to purchase than synthetic rubber. According to Arthur Plumptre, a Queen's University economist who had studied under Keynes at Cambridge before being recruited into government service during the war, this was because private industry understood that it was in its long-term interest to have an alternative source to that of natural rubber. Still, Howe's decision to remove government controls frustrated Plumptre. Commenting in *Saturday Night*, he put forth a rather complex argument for continued government regulation. Taking into account developments in the United States, consumer demand at home, and long-term levels of employment and income, Plumptre concluded that if one agreed that it was in the "public interest" to continue having a synthetic rubber industry in Canada, then it was up to government and not to industry to make sure this happened. "This is a matter on which the government should make its own decision," Plumptre stated, "rather than pushing it onto industry."[91] Despite the force of Plumptre's argument, Howe maintained his position. His intransigence was not without its consequences.

Natural rubber's return to the marketplace, brought on by decontrol, led to dramatic shifts in the pattern of domestic consumption. Of the approximately 42,000 tons of rubber consumed in Canada in 1945, 36,100 tons, or 85.9 percent, was in the form of synthetics. Two years later, synthetic rubber's share of the marketplace had fallen to almost half that. Of the 61,455 tons of rubber consumed in Canada in 1947, 32,270 tons, or 52.5 percent, was in the form of natural rubber.[92] In 1948 only 20,500 tons (or 33.1 percent) of all rubber consumed in Canada was from Polymer's 50,000-ton plant. This was dismaying news given that the Crown company had to sell forty thousand tons just to break even. This trend continued until 1952, when synthetic rubber once again pulled even with natural rubber, accounting for 50.1 percent of domestic rubber consumption.[93] By then the superior properties of synthetic rubber in certain applications were fully recognized. The return of natural rubber to the international marketplace therefore had an immediate and almost devastating effect on the Crown company. With the plantations of the Far East tapping prewar levels of natural rubber and synthetic rubber production remaining steady at wartime levels, a glut in the international marketplace occurred. The price of rubber – both natural and synthetic – flattened as a result. In 1947, the price of natural rubber fell to roughly 14¢ a pound – approximately the figure that prevailed in August 1939. In an effort to retain its market share in this "buyer's market," Polymer dropped its price to 15¢ a pound – a rate very close to the company's production cost. Price, which had been a secondary consideration during the war, was now a decisive factor in the fierce battle for rubber markets. Howe's determination to deregulate rubber consumption in Canada had given Polymer a bracing baptism in the postwar marketplace.

Market dynamics had changed dramatically since the end of the war. In 1946 there was still a world-wide shortage of crude rubber and the pent-up demand for rubber products enabled the company to dispose of its entire output at prices that included a reasonable margin of profit. This was reflected in the company's financial position. In March 1947 the company reported a net profit of $3.9 million on sales of $22.5 million.[94] But in the twelve months that followed, an increase in competition from crude rubber, which was readily available at low prices, weakened the company's financial position. Between 31 March 1947 and 31 March 1948, Polymer experienced what C.D. Howe termed its worst year on record.[95] With decreases in domestic sales not matched by increases in sales abroad, the Crown company posted a razor-thin net profit of $25,000 on sales of $17.3 million – a volume that was only about two-thirds of that recorded in 1945. Still, it was a profit – however slight – and as a result there was no talk of shutting the company down.

Fortunately, the company's strategy of selling the by-products of production – the second string in the company's bow, as Howe had termed it[96] – had its desired effect of safeguarding the company from uncontrollable fluctuations in the marketplace. During the year, large quantities of styrene, ethylene, butane, toluene, isobutylene, electric power, and steam were sold, and the gross realization from such sales amounted to $2,599,100.[97] Looking ahead, officials at Polymer were cautiously optimistic. "We feel confident," E.J. Brunning, who had recently replaced Douglas Ambridge as president, stated, "that a year of steady progress and sound development lies ahead."[98]

Part of the reason for Brunning's optimism was that since the end of the war the company had made notable strides developing export markets abroad. Energized by the threat of decontrol, in the autumn of 1945 J.R. Nicholson crossed the Atlantic and set up an overseas sales and technical organization to service Europe. Outside the United States, which Polymer continued to supply at a rate of between 9,000 and 25,000 tons per year during the period, the war-ravaged countries of Western Europe were the most logical place for Polymer to establish a commercial presence. Both Nicholson and Rowzee had travelled there in the closing days of the war and were struck by the scale and scope of the potential market for Polymer's products.[99]

The war had left Europeans rubber hungry and rubber starved. Ever since Columbus had returned from the New World with stories of the inhabitants playing games using balls prepared from the gum of a tree, Europeans had been fascinated by rubber's properties. This intellectual curiosity turned into a commercial appetite during the industrial revolution and continued to increase thereafter. The quest for rubber was a crucial pressure behind European expansion. By the time the world went to war for the second time in the twentieth century, Germany, France, Italy, and the United Kingdom were among the world's most voracious consumers of rubber. In 1939, these four countries together consumed more than 275,000 tons of raw rubber, nearly one-third of all the rubber consumed in the world that year. The war only heightened Europe's appetite for rubber, and according to executives at Polymer, it would soon reappear in the peace.

At the end of the war, world demand for rubber was far in excess of supply. Although the plantations of the Far East had been recovered, the Japanese had left them in such a devastated state that it took several years before they were producing natural rubber at prewar levels. On the synthetic-rubber front, only four countries had substantial production at the end of the Second World War – Germany, Russia, the United States, and Canada – and only Canada was in a position to supply European markets. Germany would play no immediate part in meeting postwar demand, because under the terms of the armistice it was not allowed to produce synthetic rubber until 1951. Russia, on the other hand, was engaged in its own rebuilding campaign and demonstrated no interest in exporting what little synthetic rubber it had to Western Europe. Indeed, as Nicholson later wrote to Howe, Russia looked as though it too would soon be a net importer of synthetic rubber, since it and its satellite countries were falling far short of their domestic requirements.[100] The United States would offer no immediate competition either, since a political decision was made not to export synthetic rubber to Europe – a decision reached primarily for the benefit of its wartime ally, Great Britain, which had a substantial politicoeconomic interest in seeing the plantations of the Far East return to their prewar prominence. As a result, at the war's end Canada was the only country in the world with the political will and industrial capacity to aggressively attack the foreign rubber market.[101] In light of Ottawa's determination to build postwar prosperity on exports, Polymer was ideally suited to align its corporate strategy with national macroeconomic goals.

Nevertheless, the going was initially tough. Nicholson, who proved to be as energetic at selling rubber in the industrial jungles of Europe as he had been in organizing the initial project in Canada, found two formidable obstacles facing him in Europe. The first was an ignorance about and, at times, an outright prejudice against, synthetic products. The very word "synthetic" had come to possess a negative meaning in many European countries after the war. People there associated it with the German word *ersatz*, which had been applied to many second- and third-rate substitutes during the war. Synthetics symbolized wartime sacrifices on the home front, and their continued presence was for many an unwanted reminder of all those items that had been denied them during the war. Much of the ignorance about synthetic rubber stemmed from the fact that during the war Europeans had not suffered the same shortages of natural rubber as North Americans and that as a result they had not been forced to use large quantities of the synthetic substitute. Unaware of the steady improvement in its qualities, many Europeans simply tarred synthetic rubber with the same brush as other synthetic products. Before Nicholson could make any progress in selling Polymer's products in Europe, a sales force had therefore to educate potential customers, virtually from scratch, about all aspects – scientific, technological, and economic – of the product.

During the war, IG Farben had made a point of providing technical advice to users, a fact that Rowzee became aware of on a technical mission to Germany in 1944. Rowzee was taken with the German approach and believed that, if combined with an appropriate level of personalized customer service, a consumer-oriented sales strategy could be important in gaining and keeping new markets. Technical assistance would ultimately come from Canadians like Roger Hatch and E.J. Buckler. But it would be communicated to the European manufacturers through the European agents that Polymer contracted to sell its products. Roger Hatch had already demonstrated energy, technical skill, and diplomacy as an expediter of material during the construction phase of the project. Having been born in German-speaking Alsace, Hatch had grown up in Paris and was therefore fluently trilingual. His knowledge of the English, German, and French languages and cultures played an important role in Polymer's "going global" after the war. Equally significant was the ability he shared with Buckler to explain in easy-to-understand terms the complex technical and scientific aspects of their products. Both men had backgrounds in the sciences. Hatch, who would later become vice-president in charge of marketing, had graduated from Mount Allison University in 1941 with an honours degree in chemical engineering. After graduation he had gone to McGill, where he helped Professor R.V. Nicholls produce synthetic rubber on a laboratory scale. Buckler, on the other hand, was a Cambridge University PHD who in the years to follow would become known world-wide for his practical contributions to polymer science. The early efforts of each were essential to establishing a market in Europe.

The second obstacle facing Nicholson was more difficult to overcome. After the war Europe suffered from a shortage of hard currency. While there was a strong emerging European demand for Polymer's products by 1948, thanks largely to the efforts of Nicholson and

Hatch, few customers had the ability to pay – an endemic problem in postwar Europe. The situation continued until the summer of 1948, when the American government implemented George C. Marshall's plan to offer comprehensive economic aid to all European countries. Under the plan, the Americans would provide European countries with the necessary hard currency to buy the goods and services to re-build their industry. Whether or not it "saved" Europe from a postwar economic collapse,[102] the plan benefited Canada.[103] As a North American nation, Canada was included in the program and designated as a source for what was being called Marshall Plan "off-shore purchasing." Canada's good luck under the plan was that it permitted American-dollar purchases in Canada. The results were astonishing. By June 1950 fully U.S.$1.155 billion had been spent in Canada for European consumption. Marshall Plan dollars, in the words of historians Robert Cuff and Jack Granatstein, "were a major catalyst in the 'revolution' in Canadian trade that Howe sought to maintain."[104]

One of the items Europeans were spending their Marshall Plan dollars on was synthetic rubber. The plan benefited Polymer specifically because synthetic rubber was considered essential enough to permit large allocations of U.S. dollars to the European rubber-manufacturing industries. Marshall Plan aid, combined with the company's creative sales approach and strategy of invariably setting the price of its GR-S rubber – which in 1947 was given the trade name Polysar-s – at 1.5¢ per pound less than the London and New York price for the top grade natural product – proved a successful mix. Whereas Polymer was shipping less than 3 percent of its total rubber production to Europe in 1945, by 1949 roughly one-quarter of its output was destined for the European marketplace.[105]

Polymer had gained a reputation for personalized customer education and service, with considerable attention being paid to the importance of the small, as well as the large, customer. By 1950 Polymer was supplying nearly all the larger manufacturers of rubber products in Western Europe. Among its principal customers were tire makers Pirelli of Italy (which had factories in England, Spain, Belgium, and South America), Michelin and Kleber of France, Continental of Germany, and Trelleborg of Sweden. Polymer's success abroad was thus the product of aggressive sales and technical service, matched by aggressive product pricing and a fillip from the early Cold War.

In March 1950 the company reported a net operating profit of $800,000 for the preceding twelve months of operation. While this was a healthy profit, it was still a good deal shy of the multimillion dollar profits the Crown corporation had recorded during its first three years of operation.[106] Polymer, which on 8 December 1948 was transferred from Howe's Department of Reconstruction and Supply to his new Department of Trade and Commerce, continued to face increased competition from natural rubber at home and abroad. That year, world consumption of natural rubber was 50 percent higher than that of synthetic rubber.[107] Although from then on the situation improved, the outlook for synthetic rubber did not change materially until war again provided another fillip to the young corporation and its products.

The outbreak of the Korean War in June 1950 provided an immediate stimulus to the Canadian economy and concomitantly to the Canadian synthetic-rubber industry as the war created a demand for Canadian products, especially for those with a military purpose, like rubber. The general increase in demand could not be met from natural-rubber production alone. This gave Polymer the chance to finally prove to Howe that he had done the right thing four years earlier by extending the Crown corporation's lease on industrial life.

The onset of the Korean War resulted in accelerated strategic stockpiling of natural rubber, as Western democracies looked apprehensively at communist insurgency in and around the rubber plantations of Malaya and Indonesia. At the heart of the Cold War's industrial campaign was the notion that strategic materials had to be hoarded in anticipation of any potential hostility. The Cold War also underlined the shrewdness of having secure sources of strategic material beyond the reach of ideological and national exigencies.

The accelerated stockpiling consequently increased the price of natural rubber. During these postwar years the supply of natural rubber was relatively inelastic and therefore its cost could surge in times of high demand or restrictions of supply. The supply of synthetic rubber was, on the other hand, more elastic (e.g., one could build factories), and therefore its price could fall if demand rose. Thus, any global crisis like the Korean War was likely to play into the hands of synthetic-rubber producers.

Understanding these market economies made Howe's decision to keep Polymer in business after the war a very prescient one. Given a growing postwar economy and the imperatives of the Cold War, synthetic rubber was bound to prosper, while natural rubber was bound to hit a ceiling. This is exactly what happened in 1950. In the early part of the year, natural rubber was priced slightly below its synthetic competitor, at approximately 18¢ per pound. By November 1950 the price of natural rubber had surged to above 85¢ per pound, roughly four times that of synthetic rubber.[108] The net result was a greatly increased demand for the man-made substitute. In July the *Financial Post* noted that Polymer's plant was "going full blast," producing at an annual rate of more than

50,000 tons.[109] Polymer's sales position changed markedly as a result. Sales for the year ending 31 March 1951 reached $35 million dollars, an increase of more than $9 million over the previous year. The increase was responsible for the company recording its largest net profit to date, $4.2 million. Howe could not have been more pleased. "I congratulate you and your fellow Directors," he wrote to his one-time coal controller and present Polymer president E.J. Brunning, "on the splendid results indicated by this Annual Report. Obviously, the improvements in operating procedures effected since the war days are producing results … Please convey to your Board the appreciation of myself and the Government for their services so freely and effectively given."[110]

The favourable seller's market was not without its problems, however. In light of a pre-Korean War forecast that the requirements of the Canadian industry for 1950 would be less than for 1949, the company had increased its efforts to develop new outlets in the United States, Europe, and South America, in order to offset the anticipated reduction in domestic sales.[111] The company consequently found itself in a difficult supply position when the requirements of the Canadian industry increased unexpectedly early in the year. As a "Canadian government company" operating a plant paid for with Canadian taxpayers' money and established with the very substantial technological aid of the major rubber manufacturing companies, Polymer was expected by some to satisfy domestic needs first.[112] Goodyear, Goodrich, and Dominion Rubber, and Asbestos Corporation, for instance, demanded that their feedstock requirements first be satisfied before any Canadian rubber was released for sale abroad. The request was certainly reasonable. Howe had rationalized Polymer's continued operation, in part, on public policy grounds, i.e., on the grounds that Polymer would guarantee private Canadian tire and rubber manufacturers a stable and affordable supply. These companies therefore felt justified in seeking government support for their position.

Polymer's board of directors had a different view, however. In its opinion, there were both moral and commercial reasons for Polymer to continue supplying the foreign market. After all, it was the foreign market that had secured Polymer's postwar survival. There would have been no continuing Canadian synthetic rubber industry at all, the board argued, if the corporation had relied entirely on domestic demand during the postwar years. To survive, it had had to acquire markets in Britain, France, Italy, Belgium, Germany, and the Scandinavian countries. As a consequence, all these nations were now heavily dependent on Polymer for rubber.[113] The board argued that the Crown company, therefore, had a moral obligation – one with long-term strategic commercial implications – to meet foreign requirements.

But in the opinion of the board there was an economic as well as a moral imperative for continuing to serve the company's foreign-customer base. The board had recently received a strategic report from Ralph Rowzee regarding the short- and long-term sales outlook for synthetic rubber in Europe.[114] The report predicted that foreign demand for synthetic rubber would reach unprecedented levels in the years ahead, as the postwar economic recovery took root in Germany.[115] Rowzee was of the opinion that Polymer was in a good position to exploit this demand, given the relationships the company had established in the previous years. However, he warned, any advantage would be lost if these markets were not supplied at this critical juncture. One of the men who had been instrumental in establishing Polymer's presence in Europe, Roger Hatch, agreed. "If you let them down now you'll never get back in," Hatch cautioned, employing the rhetoric of international business. "They'll never trust you again."[116] The flip side of Polymer's imposed dedication to a diversified global strategy was therefore the need to wean itself from inflexible reliance on the domestic market.

After a good deal of debate, Polymer's position prevailed in Ottawa – the company would allocate its product as it saw fit, according to its own commercial objectives and not according to the wishes of government or private enterprise. The development was significant for two reasons. First, it demonstrated the government's increasing willingness to grant the corporation independence to manoeuver. Second, and perhaps more importantly for students of public enterprise, it illustrated that in Polymer's case, when public policy and commercial goals were at variance, Ottawa would privilege profits over politics. In so doing, Ottawa had taken its steps along the road to state capitalism – when financial results became the principal criterion by which to evaluate performance of public enterprise. Polymer was thus unique, and its history challenges accepted paradigms and periodizations. According to Laux and Molot, it was not until the late 1970s that the state took on commercial roles usually assumed by private enterprise and adopted the "logic of business."[117] In the immediate postwar period, Crown corporations were used primarily as public policy instruments, salvaging jobs and providing infrastructure and services to private enterprise. But by retaining Polymer and privileging profits, the state expanded its role to become a producer in a competitive and profitable industry earlier than has traditionally been recognized. To be sure, Crown corporations are "twin-headed creatures" that are expected to perform both policy and commercial roles.[118] Remarkably, at Polymer the emphasis was on the latter function.

Polymer had managed to survive the transition to a peacetime, consumer-oriented economy. Upon the recommendation of its managerial cabal, the strategy of the firm was changed to emphasize *profitability* over public service. It was a bold, new direction.[119] Polymer was seeking to be government-owned but profit-oriented. Once it had been crystallized in the firm's strategy and structure, the objective moved the company beyond the parameters of its original mission. C.D. Howe proved to be remarkably willing to aid in the firm's evolution. Nevertheless, he was offering no protection. The company would have to sink or swim as a free agent on the open market. "You will profit or perish," he told the firm. It was a remarkable statement not only because it broke with a protectionist tradition that dated from the mid-1800s but also because it sanctioned a course of action that stretched the boundary of the state's presence in the marketplace.

Given virtual freedom of action, the company overcame its weakness of excess capacity and turned it into a strength. By devising a postwar strategy and creating a multidivisional organizational structure, Polymer aggressively attacked foreign markets while maintaining sales at home. Through sales savvy abroad, Polymer triumphed over the cultural bias towards its products and the stiff international competition from the natural-rubber cartel. Driven by global-market sensitivity rather than domestic-market imperatives, Polymer was one of the first Canadian companies to "go global."[120] This was no lazy, coddled Crown corporation. Like such successful private firms as Alcan, Massey Ferguson, MacMillan Bloedel, and Seagram, Polymer had discovered strategic planning, reorganizing its growth to depend on science and research and development. In so doing, it was among the first Canadian companies to emphasize the role to be played by science and knowledge in the growth of the firm. Through innovation it had developed profitable specialty markets and sold the by-products of its operation. It had reinvested its profits to expand its operation and had in part also channelled its profits to the Canadian treasury. Polymer was flexible, diversified, and technologically adept, an agile Crown corporation, backed but not insulated by Ottawa. In Polymer there was indeed a remarkable conjunction of state purpose and industrial initiative.

4

The Prosperous Years, 1951–1957: Chemistry, Consumers, and the Great God – Car

By most measures, the period 1951–57 was a prosperous time for Canadians. Total industrial output went up by half and productivity soared, thanks to technological innovation like the innovation taking place at Polymer Corporation. C.D. Howe's incentives to business, together with the hospitable monetary and fiscal environment created by his colleagues in the finance portfolio, led to unprecedented levels of investment. The fact that much of the investment capital was American in origin did not concern Howe as it did others at the time and since.[1] Howe firmly believed that profit-motivated behaviour was not affected by nationality, and he was convinced that foreign investment brought net benefits to Canada in the form of added economic growth. If statistics are any guide, he seems to have been correct. Except in 1954, when output actually declined, the rate of economic growth in Canada was consistently above 4.5 percent per annum and reached a dizzying postwar high of 9.5 percent in 1955. With the economies of Western Europe rebuilding using Marshall Plan dollars, Canada readily found export markets for its goods. The nation's standard of living was second highest in the world, after that of the United States. With the unemployment rate often below 4 percent, there were jobs for most Canadians looking for work. University graduates, an increasing proportion of whom were in chemistry and chemical engineering, easily found jobs in this sellers' market. The Liberal government's fiscal stabilization and demand-management policies continued to have their desired effect. People were working and people were spending. "The picture," Canadian economist David Slater stated in 1957, "is one of rich people becoming richer, of people with ... many items of household equipment, of a nation ... with many automobiles."[2] It was a kind of Keynesian prophecy come true – steady, high consumption levels supporting steady, high employment levels.

There were problems, to be sure. University graduates easily found jobs, but few Canadian men and women in the 1950s held a university degree. In many professions, this deficit was made up by inflows of highly qualified Europeans. While most people found work, women, Indians, Metis, and nonunionized workers were paid less than their unionized, white-male counterparts. And in Quebec and the Maritimes, some farmers, incapable of making a living, were forced to leave their land. Yet for the majority of Canadians, life was better in the 1950s than at any time since the Laurier boom.[3]

That was certainly the case for those who had come to Sarnia in the postwar period seeking employment in the flourishing petrochemical industry. From an economic perspective, times had never been better. Since the government had embarked on its synthetic-rubber project, Sarnia had experienced unprecedented growth and prosperity and as a result, by 1951 was, in the words of one observer, "busting out all over."[4] As C.D. Howe had intended, Polymer had stimulated the development of the region. Between 1945 and 1955, the regional population had doubled, industrial output had tripled, and the area of the city had quintupled. "It is not surprising," noted the *Canadian Geographic Journal* in 1957, "that even lifetime residents feel as if they are now living in some city other than the staid little Sarnia they knew in 1940."[5] The city had surely changed. In the south end, where there had once been an Indian reserve, a compound of petrochemical plants now stood. The site often evoked a sublime response: "My delegation and I are amazed by the enormity and complexity of your plants," noted the Malayan minister of commerce and industry, Tan Siew Sin, when he toured Sarnia in 1958. "It's all very wonderful."[6]As Howe had predicted, the petrochemical industry (i.e., the industry comprised of the manufacturers of synthetic commodities and fabricated materials from natural gas and petroleum feedstock) had taken off and was now booming.

The period 1950–73 was the industry's golden era. These years represented an apogee in the life cycle of the industry, as profit margins and sale volumes grew rapidly.[7] The growth in the demand for petrochemicals, along with the diffusion of technology, led to a proliferation of producers. In North America and Western Europe, chemical and oil companies entered the petrochemical field to add value to their products. The charter of Sun Oil, for example, was amended in 1952 to allow it to engage in the manufacture and sale of petrochemicals.[8] The following year Sun Oil built a plant at Sarnia. In the late 1940s and early 1950s Standard Oil (Indiana) gradually extended its involvement in petrochemicals, on the basis of research conducted at its Whiting, Indiana, refinery, culminating in the construction of a major complex at Chocolate, Bayou Texas, in 1968.[9] The availability of indigenous natural gas provided the boost Italy and France needed to enter the industry in the late 1950s. In West Germany, Bayer renewed its quest for supremacy in synthetic-polymer production – a quest that would ultimately bring the German petrochemical giant to Polymer's door.[10] The growth of the polymers market was the main reason behind the petrochemical industry growth as a whole. Polymer science was still relatively young, and there were plenty of opportunities for innovation and substitution. From 1949 to 1969 synthetic-polymers production grew by an astonishing factor of thirty. Synthetic rubber was one of the main applications for polymers, and its production grew at an equally astonishing rate, with each producer manufacturing several different types of rubbers.

These, consequently, were Polymer's prosperous years, a time when the prescient strategy of the preceding period set the stage for unparalleled corporate growth and development. The company's earlier decision to "go global," to diversify its product line and improve its research and development efforts, placed it in a position of advantage, so that when the economic boom of the 1950s materialized, it fully capitalized. So profitable were these years that Polymer's new president J.D. Barrington (a miner with the mouth and irrepressible optimism to prove it) felt that there was no need for any change in the corporation's strategy.

During the period 1951–57, sitting on a foundation of unprecedented consumer demand for such large-scale durable goods as automobiles, Polymer witnessed its sales volume increase by approximately 100 percent (see table A1). Output doubled, as productivity soared due to technological innovation. By the end of the decade, Polymer produced fully one-tenth of the world's synthetic rubber. Net profits concomitantly increased more than 150 percent during the period, averaging a remarkable 13.2 percent annual return on the government's investment.[11] "Our financial statements," J.D. Barrington proudly boasted in 1953, "give real proof that our industry is permanently established to play a major role in Canada's business."[12] Polymer thus offered an example of a technologically driven, wholly Canadian-owned industrial endeavour, a striking departure from the derivative industrialism of the prewar National Policy–framed economy. Indeed, there was a good deal of evidence of this after the Second World War as well, as the branch plant economy continued to grow in many economic sectors.

Both macro- and microeconomic factors led to this phenomenal growth. At the macroeconomic level, the period witnessed a worldwide economic boom. As a producer's commodity with a derived demand, rubber had its fortunes tied to ebbs and flows in the business cycle. When times were good and people were spending, particularly on cars, rubber did well. Needless to say, when rubber did well, Polymer did well. Polymer was also fortunate in that during these years it had to face little competition from other synthetic-rubber producers at home and elsewhere. All this created a climate for innovation that was probably the most creative in the company's history. At a time of great confidence in humankind's technocratic ability to govern its material destiny, Polymer's research chemists rearranged the basic elements of their product, which led to new and better chemically engineered consumer goods. Their success was celebrated in the press and reflected more generally by a new cultural awareness and acceptance of synthetic products.

It has often been said that business success is a function of circumstance and purposive action, or – as Michael Bliss has put it – "the interplay of enterprise and opportunity."[13] During the 1950s at Polymer these forces came together to produce unprecedented corporate growth and development. These were thus the prosperous years.

When Barrington assumed his position as president of Polymer in June 1951, he ushered in this period of unparalleled prosperity. Barrington was taking over for E.J. Brunning who, while remaining as chairman of the board, was stepping down as president, so as to dedicate more time to his principal function as president of the Consumers Glass Company of Montreal. Brunning would be missed, C.D. Howe stated upon his departure, but Howe felt confident that the corporation would continue to thrive under its new president.[14]

Howe, who was now doing double duty as the minister of defence production and minister of trade and commerce, had seen Barrington at work before. Shortly after the outbreak of the Second World War, Walter Segsworth, president of Moneta Porcupine Mines, had gone to see Howe to ask what his firm could do for the war effort. Howe in his usual blunt way told Segsworth that Canada needed magnesium and that if he and his firm really wanted to help they should go out and find mineral deposits containing the substance so crucially needed as an alloy and explosive component. Ultimately, the job fell to the company's manager J.D. Barrington. Ever productive, Barrington did not take long to discover that the cliffs of Niagara Falls and the surrounding area were composed of rocks that were about one-third magnesium. It just so happened that the technological process for extracting magnesium from this type of ore had recently been worked out by Dr Roy Pidgeon, a scientist at the University of Toronto. Barrington knew Pidgeon from his days at the university and persuaded him to help design and build a full-scale plant based on his laboratory model. Work started on the project a few months before Pearl Harbor, and by August 1942 Barrington was extracting magnesium from the region at a rate of five thousand tons per year. By helping solve Canada's magnesium problem, Barrington established himself in Howe's eyes not only as a man of science but as a practical man who could get things done. Thus, when E.J. Brunning resigned as Polymer's president in June 1951, Howe wasted little time seeking out Barrington and appointing him the first full-time president of the Polymer Corporation.[15]

Despite being a man of science, Barrington knew next to nothing about synthetic-rubber technology and production at the time of his appointment. This deficiency was not specific to Barrington alone, of course. With the exception of Douglas Ambridge, all the preceding presidents of the corporation had assumed their duties without knowing the basics of polymer science, synthetic-rubber technology, or the political economy of rubber. This situation had reflected Howe's penchant for placing executives' abilities before their specific knowledge. This approach had not hampered performance in the past and therefore did not dissuade C.D. Howe from looking outside the corporation once again when finding a replacement for E.J. Brunning. To Barrington's credit, he fully acknowledged his lack of understanding of synthetic-rubber production. But he was eager to learn and throughout his presidency reached out to senior staff and line management for guidance.[16]

While there were few, if any, outward signs, Barrington did, however, initially struggle with the idea of assuming the top job at the Crown corporation. He believed firmly in the merits of working one's way up the corporate ladder and of paying one's dues along the way. Before coming to Polymer, he had spent fifteen years at Moneta Porcupine Mines doing just that. But the temptation of being a part of a corporation on the cutting-edge of technology was too great, and when C.D. Howe offered him the presidency, Barrington accepted. "I look forward to being part of your high technology team," he wrote to Howe shortly before his appointment was made public.[17] Despite the enthusiasm for his new job, Barrington was determined not to rock the boat once he assumed his duties. He recognized that Polymer was on a productive trajectory. He understood that the existing corporate strategy had served the company well in the past and, by all indications and opinions, would serve it well in the future. He was therefore determined not to do anything that might jeopardize the company's performance going forward. In his inaugural address to a gathering of Polymer's working men and women, he stated that there would be no change in corporate strategy; the company would continue to develop and produce quality rubber to customer specification, expand markets at home and abroad, and diversify the produce line at both the upper and lower ends of the market.[18] The changes that he made were structural.

It is somewhat ironic that Barrington ultimately proved to be as conservative an executive as he did, given that he headed the corporation at a time of unprecedented corporate freedom and power. Unlike his predecessors, his strategic options were virtually unrestricted. Part of this freedom was the very result of the corporation's postwar performance. Success had silenced the critics. Gone was the chorus of criticism demanding that the government divest itself of the "technological white elephant." Polymer had proved itself a viable commercial enterprise, and by the end of 1952 even the omnipotent and omnipresent C.D. Howe was reluctant to intervene in the corporation's affairs. The shift in the external view of Polymer brought two structural changes that furthered the Crown corporation's autonomy.

The first occurred in the latter part of 1951, when the last of the contracts with Polymer's operating companies were terminated. For the first time the company became a free-standing, public industrial enterprise. For some time, C.D. Howe had wished to bring these contracts to an end. As early as 1944 he had suggested to J.R. Nicholson terminating the operating agreement with St Clair Processing – the company that managed Polymer's butadiene and butyl-rubber units.[19] Howe was not alone in wanting to see these agreements concluded. Many in parliament had long advocated ending outside involvement in the plant. In 1944, for instance, a bipartisan parliamentary committee – a committee that had been set up to examine wartime expenditures – recommended that "as soon as possible" after the war, Polymer readjust its relations with the companies administering the different plants "with a view to Polymer as a government-owned company operating and administering all of these plants itself."[20] Earlier, in the House of Commons the CCF had recommended a similar change, in order to remove suspect private interests from participation in a public enterprise.[21] Howe agreed with the CCF's recommendation, although not for the same reasons. He was not motivated by any suspicion of private interest or any ideological commitment to the position that private and public concerns are always at odds and therefore should be kept separate. Indeed, he had initially conceived of Trans-Canada Airlines as a mixed enterprise. Rather, Howe had come to the same conclusion as the CCF for more pragmatic reasons. As he noted, Canada now possessed the necessary people, science, and technology to go it alone. Canadian technicians had been trained to run and were capable of running the plant without outside assistance. In addition, the fundamental scientific knowledge for synthetic-rubber development – knowledge that had originated in Germany and the United States – was now in Canadian hands. The day had arrived, therefore, when Polymer could stand entirely on its own feet and control its own operations and destiny.[22]

The decision to go it alone made sense from an economic standpoint as well. It was economically inefficient, Howe maintained, to have "a crown company within a crown company."[23] The termination of the three operating contracts would eliminate the duplication of services and, ultimately, save Polymer money. From the beginning of operation to the time of Barrington's appointment as president, Polymer had paid out over $4.3 million in management fees.[24] According to Howe, it made little sense to continue to pay such large sums for services that could be, and to a certain extent already were, provided for by Polymer itself. The merger of the companies would thus allow definite economies of scale and improved efficiency. The position was echoed by the company's new president and its board of directors.[25]

In May 1946, the operating contract with St Clair Processing was terminated. Four years later Polymer assumed full responsibility for the operation of the three sections comprising the styrene unit. In 1951 Polymer took over the general-purpose rubber unit, which to that point had been managed by Canadian Synthetic Rubber. Thus, by the end of 1951 the last of the management contracts had been terminated, and Polymer was in full control of the facilities within its gates.

The second structural change occurred on the heels of the first. In March 1952 all the plant's assets, which until then had been in the possession of the Crown, were transferred to Polymer. Before the transfer Polymer, from a financial perspective, was a corporation in name only. It owned no assets and still depended on the government for working capital. This structure, while seen as necessary during the war, came to be viewed as incongruent with the corporation's actual postwar status as a "commercial plant operating in a commercial community."[26]

Howe did not like such inconsistency and determined that the time had come to put Polymer on a more normative financial footing. In March 1952, after a good deal of preliminary planning, he announced his intentions before parliament: "Now that Polymer Corporation has demonstrated a substantial earning power, which will enable it to pay annual dividends to the crown, it seems desirable to provide a capital structure for the company which will serve as a proper background for the considerations of owner-customer-labour relations ... and against which to assess and compare the operations of the company with similar operations."[27] Polymer was no longer a production-oriented company operating in a command economy to meet a wartime emergency; rather, it was a product-oriented firm competing in a consumer-oriented market economy for the purpose of earning a profit. Given the change in strategic purpose, Howe considered it desirable to create a capital structure that would permit comparability with other commercial enterprises and thereby promote increased productivity and sound management. Since his days at the department of transport, he had put a premium on efficiency and accountability. These attributes were essential, he believed, if government and its corporations were to act responsibly for the benefit of all Canadians. At the end of the war Howe had stated in a letter to J.R. Nicholson that he would like "to demonstrate through Polymer that the government can be efficient and progressive in a government-owned industry."[28] The financial restructuring of Polymer was the latest in a series of steps towards the ultimate realization of that goal.

In June 1951, Howe called Polymer's board of directors to his office in Ottawa and informed them that it was time the financial arrangements between the government and the company were put on a more "normal investment basis." To bring this about, he suggested transferring the plant's assets to the corporation in return for Ottawa getting cash and stock in the firm. For its part, the board felt that Howe's plan was "highly desirable."[29] The company had been given the mandate to prove itself as a commercial undertaking and since the end of the war had made strategic decisions based on business criteria and not necessarily designed to appease public-policy makers. To Polymer's way of thinking, the restructuring would acknowledge all that it had done to date and give it additional freedom to manoeuver. "The reorganization will give us a greater degree of autonomy," Barrington stated, echoing the position of the board, "and enhance our position in the eyes of customers, suppliers, distributors and the community."[30] The quest for autonomy was to have a long life in the history of the firm.

With the support of all involved, the restructuring received royal assent on 31 March 1952.[31] As a result, title to all the assets, valued at $53,793,946, passed from the Crown to Polymer. In return, the government received $3 million in cash and $8 million worth of a 4 percent debenture, maturing at a rate of $1 million per annum. The balance was covered by the issue of 1,999,996 no-par-value shares, of which the government received all but the few held, one a piece, by the directors of the Crown corporation during their term in office.[32] A value of $39,640,916 was placed on the issued shares for the purpose of the agreement. The dividends received from the ownership of these shares would pay richly in the years that followed. Nothing in the restructuring agreement was to contravene the Financial Administration

Act of 1951 – an act that rationalized the system of government agencies that had evolved over the previous thirty years.[33] Polymer would continue to pay income tax, as well as provincial imposts, including corporate taxation. Summing up the effects of reorganization in the House of Commons, Howe stated that the rearrangement of the financial structure made no change in the beneficial ownership of the enterprise.[34] It did, however, provide those in charge of the operation with "yardsticks by which the efficiency and success of the enterprise may be considered."[35]

When examined in conjunction with the Financial Administration Act, the restructuring of Polymer can be seen as an attempt by the Liberal government to define the terms of its public accountability. The financial reorganization had created an individual corporate structure that ensured managerial flexibility and freedom from the rigid framework of government financial and personnel controls. Nevertheless, Polymer, like all other Crown companies, was still an instrument of public policy. The firm had been given a job to do – to produce synthetic-rubber and, after 1945, to sell it at a profit.

The Liberal government wanted some way of making sure that this task, as well as the tasks assigned to its other Crown corporations, was being pursued efficiently and effectively. Before 1951, there was no common criterion or rationalized system – beyond some vague notion of serving the public good – to ensure that any of this was taking place. In Polymer's case, the Crown corporation had been responsible to one man: C.D. Howe. Fortunately, although not surprisingly, there was a sort of symbiosis between Howe and executives at the Crown company. For the most part, they all shared the same business values and were dedicated to the same strategic objectives. Thus, when measuring the effectiveness of the firm, they had all used the same standards, the standards of international business (e.g., operating costs, level of profit or loss, rate of return on investment). Howe's financial restructuring was an attempt to apply these standards more scientifically. Nevertheless, as before, the company was accountable first and foremost to the bottom line. The Liberal government had thus given expression to a kind of hybrid capitalism, accountable to the state but equipped to operate in the free market.

Before the ratification of the Financial Administration Act, there was nothing stated in law to ensure that subsequent ministers of the Crown would apply Howe's standards. This lacuna concerned Louis St Laurent's Liberals, who worried about the day when Howe was gone and they were no longer the governing party. They worried that a less "responsible" party in power would employ different standards of accountability, perhaps personal standards that, God forbid, might actually be as

arbitrary as Howe's own. For his part, Howe, too, was concerned about
the prospect of a less "business-oriented" party assuming the reins of
power. He had once stated that the only danger to public ownership
was that the CCF might actually get into a position of political responsibility someday and allow its prejudices to interfere with its "obligation"
to keep the management of the nation's Crown corporations in an "efficient state."[36] "That", declared Howe, "was the real menace to government ownership."[37]

The Financial Administration Act, which, among other things, established the minimum standards of financial behaviour for Crown corporations, was thus intended to institutionalize the Liberals' standards of
accountability. It would obtain when the Liberals were no longer there
themselves and ensure that Howe's corporations were kept in an "efficient state" once he was gone. Henceforth, Polymer – a class D, or proprietary, corporation under the terms of the act – would be legally
responsible to the bottom line.

With the ratification of the Financial Administration Act and the restructuring of Polymer complete, C.D. Howe could now stand back
and dedicate himself more fully to other megaprojects (e.g., the building of the Trans-Canada Pipeline and the St Lawrence Seaway) knowing that Polymer was in good hands. With its structure now in line with
its strategy, the company was primed to seize the opportunities of the
1950s. As the company would soon find out, there would be plenty of
them, for this was the age of mass consumerism and the "great god –
Car."

The 1950s were a time when Canadians earned more, spent more, and
owned more things, a time when people used their money to support
leisure activities, to gratify the five senses, and perhaps indulge in the
seven sins, to define a lifestyle, if not a persona itself. It was a time
when people spent freely on big-ticket consumer items such as cars. It
was a time of mass consumerism.[38]

To meet the unprecedented demand for consumer goods, giant
shopping malls with everything under one roof were erected in the
emerging suburbs of the nation. Another of Howe's dollar-a-year men,
E.P. Taylor, used his Argus Corporation in these same years to give Canada its first designed suburb – Don Mills. Billboards materialized at the
side of the nation's expanding highways inviting Canadians to spend
for their good and that of the nation.

One of the main themes of the 1945 *White Paper on Employment and
Income* had been the need to maintain aggregate demand at home. If
people and businesses kept spending, the Keynesian logic went, they
would create jobs and profits and consumption would itself continue.

Consumption was thus the key to economic growth and stability. Of course, as the white paper noted, in a small, open economy like Canada's any attempt to maintain aggregate demand at home would eventually fail if international markets were not found for Canada's products. Nevertheless, domestic consumption was viewed as critical to Canadian prosperity, and after the war the Liberal government, in conjunction with the various provincial governments, did everything in its power to put more money into people's pockets so that they would continue to consume.

While the Liberal government provided Canadians with a fiscal incentive to go out and spend, business schemed to give them the psychological incentive to do so. The 1950s witnessed aggressive advertising campaigns, as businesses tried to entice would-be consumers to buy their goods and services. "Ours is the first age," wrote Marshall McLuhan in his 1951 satirical examination of popular culture, "in which many thousands of the best-trained individual minds have made it a full-time business to get inside the collective public mind."[39] As advertisers, these "best-trained" minds urged the Canadian consumer to purchase everything from Leonard's "leisure line" appliances to Sunworthy prepasted wallpaper. "Nearly everybody wants a big, new Ford", one advertisement read.[40] "Come and get it!" read another.[41] The Admiral Television Company enticed shoppers to buy its products with promises of "whiter whites and deeper blacks, and the full range of in between shades." Mass advertising such as this extended the world of commerce and consumption ever more completely to all corners of society. It constituted an attempt by Canadian business to penetrate and open up the sphere of culture as a new territory for producing exchange value.

In 1953, Polymer embarked upon its own advertising campaign when it began running a series of advertisements in several Canadian editions of *Time*, the *Financial Post*, *Maclean's*, and the French Canadian magazine *Le Samedi*, all with the objective of creating "interest and confidence in the company and its products."[42] Barrington and the other executives at Polymer had become concerned by the lack of knowledge on the part of the general public as to the advantages and uses of synthetic rubber and even about the company itself. To bridge the knowledge gap, at a cost of just under seventy thousand dollars a year the company hired Harold F. Stanfield Limited to prepare an advertising program to "generate good will for the company and its products."[43] The first advertisements began to appear shortly after the new year and stressed the role the company had played in the postwar product revolution. "Today, Polymer's research and development technicians brush aside the imperfections of nature," proudly proclaimed one of the first advertisements, "and use chemical science to give a wide variety of consumer and industrial products new qualities with Polysar materials."[44] With the words "There's been a revolution in rubber" blazoned across the page, a series of subsequent advertisements informed readers and consumers that they were likely to be among the majority of Canadians who were "now riding on a comparatively new kind of tire – one built of chemical rubber."[45] How would someone know if s/he was in the majority, the advertisement asked. By the performance of the tire, no less. Tires made with Polysar rubber, the company claimed, were the "toughest in tire history,"[46] able to "defy wear for tens of thousands of miles."[47]

A tougher tire, however, was just one of the many innovations, the company assured Canadians, that had resulted from its scientific endeavours. It had also enabled manufacturers to produce rubber tiles, creating floors that did not scuff; comfortable foam rubber cushioning for car seats, mattresses, and upholstered furniture; and, for the army of do-it-yourselfers that emerged in Canada after the war, rubber-based paints that made just about anyone a professional painter.[48]

Advertisements such as these helped overcome the public's resistance to synthetic products. In Canada and the other industrialized nations where the company ran its ads, the wartime stigma of being *ersatz* was replaced by an image of synthetics as modern materials that could guarantee better living. No longer were synthetics taken as an unwelcome reminder of wartime sacrifices. Instead, during the 1950s people came to perceive synthetics as "high-tech" commodities with superior qualities capable of democratizing consumption. Such chemically engineered consumer goods as Tupperware, Vinylite, and Polymer's own Polysar butyl rubber were revered by manufacturers and many consumers for their versatility, convenience, sanitation, predictability, and low cost.[49]

At one level, the change in perceptions was a consequence of an aggressive advertising campaign by the chemical industry to promote its products as superior to what nature had to offer. "Nature doesn't make rubber that holds air like this," read one Polymer advertisement, proffering a picture of a fully inflated inner tube.[50] "Nature doesn't make the tough resilient rubber for today's flooring," proclaimed another.[51] The manufacturers of synthetic fibres, such as polyester, acrylic, and nylon, seduced consumers with promises of wash-and-wear apparel. "Taking a 'Terylene' dress on your holidays," assured one ad, "is the next best thing to taking a personal maid."[52] Other advertisements of this genre pitched a sort of "damp-cloth utopianism" – to borrow a phrase from the cultural historian Jeffrey Meikle – of laminated walls, plastic dinette tops, and upholstered furniture.[53]

Polymer advertisements of the 1950s. *Maclean's* magazine.

While advertisements that emphasized the extraordinary material superiority of chemically engineered goods helped overcome the public resistance to synthetics, they could not have done so if they had not appealed to some underlying cultural logic, or what the neo-Marxist sociologist Robert Goldman terms "deep social assumptions."[54] As historian David E. Nye points out, corporate advertisements such as Polymer's were not only shapers of values, moulders of roles, and effective promoters of needs but also mirrors of "otherwise unspoken assumptions about the social order."[55] Advertising leaders recognized the necessity of associating their selling messages with the values and attitudes already held by their audience.[56] They sought to strike only those notes that would evoke a positive resonance. In this way advertisements not only constituted but were constituted by the dominant social ethos. In Polymer's case the company's advertisements, perhaps intentionally, tapped into the postwar confidence in humankind's "determining" capacities.

For a majority of North Americans there seemed little that was beyond human control. Not only could humanity harness the nation's economy through the use of macroeconomic policy, but it could control the material environment through chemical science. Only such confidence in humanity's abilities could have led the Liberal government to commit itself in its 1945 white paper to "a high and stable level of employment and income." Only such confidence could have led Polymer's Ralph Rowzee to predict that chemistry would soon render obsolete one of the world's longest-lasting and most elastic commercial substances, natural rubber.[57] On a broader plane, only such confidence could have prompted the majority of philosophers in Canada, the United States, and Great Britain to reject as senseless the emphasis of traditional philosophy on such issues as metaphysics and theology and embrace the logical positivism of Ludwig Wittgenstein and the Vienna Circle. It was no coincidence that both Keynesianism and logical positivism were rooted in the same mathematical-empiricism that led to the rise of modern chemical science. Thus, when Polymer claimed in its ads that its chemists could manipulate chemical elements "at will" to produce better rubber than nature offered, there was a cultural bias working in favour of Polymer's message.[58] The claim had a social validity, or, if one prefers, it had truth.

During the 1950s, advertising campaigns such as Polymer's played a consequential part in getting Canadians to go out and satisfy their pent-up yearning (a yearning formed by years of depression and wartime deprivation) for the things that they longed for. The efforts of advertisers and those of the federal government resulted in unprecedented levels of real consumption expenditures in Canada.[59] Contributing to the spending frenzy was consumer credit, which became available in the 1950s when the 1954 Bank Act revision allowed banks to finance such purchases as cars through taking chattel mortgages. With the aid of this readily available consumer credit, Canadians were purchasing not only small items such as rubber-soled shoes, latex paints, nylon stockings, Terylene dresses, and plastic hula-hoops but large-scale durable goods such as refrigerators, household furniture, televisions, and cars. Of all these material goods, the automobile – with more than two hundred rubber parts – came to occupy a special place in Canadian society.

After the war, the dream of automobile ownership was probably second only to that of home ownership in the minds of Canadians. In an age that glorified technology, the automobile symbolized the good life: security, status, and freedom. To the lament of some, the car attained a god-like status. "For the god," historian Arthur Lower wrote in 1958, "no better name could be found than simply – CAR!"[60] During the decade, its places of worship – dealerships, drive-in theatres, and drive-through restaurants – came to dominate the Canadian landscape.

Increasingly, life was taking place in and around the car. As a result, sales of new automobiles mounted as Canadians bought sleek American Fords and Chevvies, traditional British Morrises and Austins, and after 1953, the more utilitarian German Volkswagen Beetle. The car-selling slogan of 1950, "You auto buy now," encouraged Canadians to purchase a record 324,900 new passenger cars that year.[61] The auto industry kept the public buying by promising glamour and status in bigger and splashier models with gleaming chrome, two-tone colors, tail fins, and white-wall rubber tires. "You'll be the leading man in any company in a beautiful new Chrysler," one 1954 advertisement proclaimed, appealing to the postwar cult of masculinity.[62] Between 1945 and 1952, car-ownership doubled in Canada.[63] By 1953, more than 50 percent of Canadian families owned a car. By 1960, two-thirds of households had a car, and 10 percent had two or more. Like the gods of yesteryear, the "great god – Car" was seemingly everywhere.

This, of course, was not solely a Canadian phenomenon. It was also taking place in the United States and Western Europe. South of the border, Americans were buying cars in record numbers. Between 1950 and 1960, 58 million new cars were sold. The number of automobile registrations increased by 21 million, and the total of motor-vehicle miles travelled rose by 75 percent. And critics complained of "auto-sclerosis" – the clogging of urban arteries. Cars sporting such names as Marauder and Barracuda came in colours ranging from "passion pink" to "lilac mist" – with rubber moldings to match – and they were powered by engines capable of reaching more than twice the existing speed limit.

During the fifties "bigger was better, and Americans, it seemed, wanted bigger cars every year."[64] Advertisements like the one for the 1952 Ford invited people to step inside the new "coach-craft bodies" and feel the relaxing comfort of the "deep, wide seats cushioned in soft foam rubber." Cars were also celebrated for their power – real and symbolic. The 1955 Ford, for instance, featured Trigger-Torque "Go" Power and that year's Pontiac boasted the Sensational Strato-Streak v-8. As McLuhan pointed out, car advertisements such as these made it plain that there was widespread acceptance of the car as a womb symbol and, paradoxically enough, as a phallic power symbol as well.[65] By 1960, 75 percent of all Americans owned at least one car. These were good years for the American auto industry, which had a strong corporate presence in Canada, and as a consequence, for the rubber industry as well.

In most Western European nations, car registrations almost trebled during the decade, and in some places they increased nearly tenfold. In Germany, for instance, the number of registrations jumped from 500,000 in 1950 to 4.5 million in 1960.[66] In 1953, close to 13 million cars were in use in Western Europe. A decade later that number had jumped to over 40 million.[67] Most of these cars were European in origin. Foreign aid helped car manufacturers in Germany and Italy to rebuild their factories after the war. In Germany, external aid came in the form of a British army officer, Major Ivan Hirst, whose managerial talents kept alive Hitler's dream of a small, cheap People's Car. Having spent months scouring the devastated German economy for steel, rubber, and other critical materials to keep the plant going, Hirst got Volkswagen back in business by 1946, when the company produced 12,000 cars. Ten years later, the company, which was once again under German management, was turning out ten times that number – or about 7 percent of the 2 million cars manufactured in Europe in 1973.[68] Within another twenty years, the Beetle would surpass the Model T Ford in sales, and Volkswagen would emerge as the fourth largest car manufacturer in the world.[69] For Polymer, the success of Volkswagen and of the automotive industry in general was very good news.

In the 1950s people were buying cars, car makers were buying tires, and tire manufacturers were buying rubber. Corresponding to the growth in the automotive industry, world consumption of rubber more than doubled in the ten years following the end of the Second World War, from 780,000 tons in 1946 to over 1.5 million long tons in 1956.[70] In Canada annual rubber consumption increased during the same period from 47,000 to over 100,000 tons. Polymer's accomplishment lay in changing the composition of consumption during the period, as synthetic rubber came to represent a larger percentage of rubber consumption. In 1951 synthetic rubber accounted for 37 percent of all domestic rubber consumption; by 1957 that amount had increased to 54 percent.[71] "Almost half of all new rubber used in Canada today," proudly declared a 1956 Polymer advertisement, "is Polysar."[72]

In part, the change had been brought about by the company's aggressive pricing strategy. During the decade, except for a brief recessionary period at the end of 1953 and early 1954, prices for Polymer's GR–S rubber were below prices for natural rubber. Increased productivity due to technological innovation had allowed the company to lower costs to the point where natural rubber found it hard to compete on a price basis. The only task that remained, therefore, for the confident young Crown company on the banks of the broad St Clair River was to stretch natural rubber to the breaking point, by improving the quality of its synthetic products. To do this, the company turned to the rubber chemist.

One of the three elements of the company's postwar strategy for survival had been to produce rubbers that would equal or surpass natural rubber in terms of quality. The strategy was continued under J.D. Barrington, who emphasized the need for initiative and innovation in research and development. "At Polymer," Barrington stated shortly after his appointment as president, "we realize that we must step up our research efforts if we are to hold our position in the industry."[73] Barrington was a firm believer in the idea that nothing was as perishable as an established product and that without a resourceful R&D department the company would not continue to prosper.

J.D. Barrington was a man of science. He appreciated the powerful effects it could have on industry. After graduating from the University of Toronto in 1926 with a bachelor's degree in science, he had gone to work in the mining industry as a field engineer. The industry was one of the first in Canada to recognize the role that science could play in achieving strategic objectives. At a time when most Canadian firms lagged behind the rest of the industrialized world in research and development, Canadian mining companies used science to achieve corporate goals. For example, such firms as Shawinigan Company, the Consolidated Mining and Smelting Company, and Barrington's own Moneta Porcupine Mines used magnetic anomaly detection to locate, excavate, and refine the earth's minerals. Barrington's years at the University of Toronto and at Moneta Porcupine Mines had taught him that research, as a method of bold endeavour and good aim, was one of the best assurances of industrial success. When he came to Polymer, he brought this proactive philosophy with him.

Barrington arrived at Polymer at a unique time in the industry's history. In 1951 there were twenty-nine commercial enterprises in North America engaged in synthetic-rubber research and development. Polymer continued to have the distinction of being the sole participant operating outside the United States. While many of the u.s. government's synthetic-rubber plants had been sold to private interests by this time, it continued to regulate the industry through its agency the Reconstruction Finance Corporation (RFC). Not only did the RFC set prices and restrict exports, but after 1948 it regulated and funded research and development as well. By mid-1949, the u.s. government had allocated just over $13.5 million to industrial companies for synthetic-rubber research.[74] In return for this funding, the recipients pledged to turn over all their discoveries and innovations to the government. The program thus removed the profit motive as a spur to technological innovation and, as a result, was a complete failure.[75]

Ever since John Rae made his *Statement of Some New Principles on the Subject of Political Economy* in 1834, economists have theorized about the connection between commercial self-interest, new knowledge, technological innovation, and productivity and economic growth. Today, such theorizing takes the form of the "new endogenous growth theory" of Robert E. Lucas, among others.[76] In 1954, the American economist, Robert Solo, studied the effect of profit as a motive for technological innovation in the synthetic-rubber industry. He concluded that there was little incentive for technological innovation without "commercial self-interest" and that for this reason the u.s. government's research program had been nearly a total disaster.[77] Not one of the six major technological breakthroughs of the period, Solo pointed out, had been accomplished by a participant in the government's program. Instead, they had come from those companies – four in total – that remained outside the program and, therefore, that were free to exploit for profit the fruits of their own research.

Since it was a Canadian firm, Polymer had of course never been offered RFC funds, and even if it had been, in all likelihood it would not have accepted them, given C.D. Howe's devotion to the profit system as a measure of efficiency. At liberty to profit from its own research and development, Polymer participated in three of the period's major innovations. The company would perhaps have accomplished even more if it had not had to deal with the disadvantages of being a medium-sized firm. Without the capital resources of a large industrial enterprise like Du Pont or Dow Chemical, Polymer had to choose its research and development projects carefully, evaluating each in terms of cost and potential profit before proceeding. The Crown corporation did not have the necessary resources to achieve a major advance in basic research, which was generally aimed at discovery of new knowledge. Polymer emphasized applied research, therefore, adapting basic knowledge to practical and profitable ends. During this period, the Crown company worked almost entirely in fields that had already been studied by investigators in Germany and the United States, bringing to the point of commercial production what had been previously discovered in the laboratory.

It was the pensive and imaginative E.J. Buckler who spearheaded the drive for flexibility and selectivity in research and development. As director of the research department, he viewed it as his task to pursue the profitable goals that were attainable given corporate resources.[78] It was his responsibility to ensure the overall success of the department. In fact, as he stated with characteristic modesty in 1953, this function was the "only excuse" for his existence as director of industrial research.[79] More specifically, Buckler took it upon himself to review all possible R&D problems at Polymer and select the ones that were most likely to succeed. In addition, it was his role to judge whether a project should be abandoned or accelerated and expanded.

Like many of his generation, Buckler believed in the positive powers of chemistry; he was confident that through science humankind could overcome economic scarcity and improve their material lot in life. In a speech given in Sarnia in October 1955, Buckler outlined the recent accomplishments of his profession. "We are all well aware of the effect that research has had on our daily lives," he confidently stated, "and can see very clearly the march of progress within living memory – radio, television, radar, nuclear fission, high-octane gasoline, nylon, dacron, synthetic rubber and so forth."[80] According to Buckler, the driving force behind most of these innovations was free enterprise and the profit motive. Industrial research, from which came technological innovation, he stated, grew out of the desire "to make more and compete effectively with other industries to the eventual benefit of the public."[81] In Buckler's opinion, there was no substitute for the discipline of the market. It fostered both efficiency and innovation, with the ultimate effect of improving the standard of living. Innovation in and of itself meant little if it was not done economically. Indeed, if innovation was undertaken without observing the "hard facts of economics," he cautioned in November 1953, "then the standard of living would actually go down."[82] As head of research and development at a medium-sized firm, Buckler was profoundly conscious of the need to economize. Only through the efficient allocation of resources could Polymer compete in the international marketplace with large, multidivisional firms. The application of science alone would not yield a more prosperous future; only in combination with economics would it do that.

"In their combination," Buckler stated, "lie the nature, problems and aims of research in industry."[83]

Buckler had come to St Clair Processing in 1942 with a background in chemistry and engineering. While his doctoral work at Cambridge University in England had no direct bearing on his work at Sarnia, it did help define his vision of a modern industrial research department. Since research was the most speculative of any industrial operation, Buckler believed that the organization of the department had to be "very flexible."[84] There was, for instance, really no hierarchical structure at Polymer, as there was at Du Pont. Buckler gave his research chemists free rein to pursue the problems of industry. Often his time was spent outside the department, conferring with people in marketing and sales to ensure that theoretical advances would find a practical commercial purpose. To foster flexibility and interaction, Buckler created an academic-like setting, although the values of academia did not apply. This was research undertaken for economic ends, not to make a contribution to abstract knowledge. At Polymer, the research chemists would freely and critically exchange ideas in the pursuit of technological innovation and profit. Buckler felt strongly that industrial research could not be conducted in isolation. "It is vital that thoughts and the results are shared with others, so that everyone can make his contribution to solving the problem."[85] This was necessary, Buckler believed, in any young industry like synthetic rubber.

In this new field there was still plenty to discover and many an opportunity for the eager and able rubber chemist. Yet despite these practical challenges, it was not always easy attracting new PHDs. Buckler had to persuade them to abandon their dreams of achieving academic immortality by the publication of original discoveries in a new field and instead concentrate on innovation, that is, on reducing fundamental research to the level of practice, sales, and profits. When Buckler succeeded, he did so in large part by assuring his chemists that the intellectual challenge was just as great as doing basic research and that the reward was, if not fame, at least continuing employment. By 1955 the department had grown to employ over 180 people, of whom 40 were university graduates. Among the graduates were 12 who had administrative and nontechnical training, 24 who had BSC and MSC degrees from Canadian and European universities, but only 4 who had PHD degrees and special training in research. [86] In comparison, Du Pont had roughly 1,600 employees with PHDs on its payroll.[87] On occasion Buckler's group undertook work of a basic nature, to close the gap between original discovery and reduction to practice,[88] but for the most part the department concentrated on innovation in pursuit of profit.

Following its recent success in solving the problem of cold-weather buckling of butyl inner tubes, Buckler's department turned its attention to improving the properties of GR-S rubber – the principal type of synthetic rubber used in automobile tires. Given the global demand for automobiles, this project was viewed as crucial to the success of the firm, indeed, to that of the whole industry. Rubber for use in tires still accounted for approximately 75 percent of rubber consumption. If the synthetic rubber industry was to continue to grow, it would have to supplant natural rubber as the input of choice for tire manufacturers. While the properties of GR-S rubber had been substantially enhanced since the product was first developed in the late 1920s by IG Farben scientists Walter Bock and Edward Tschunkur, it was still inferior to natural rubber in terms of wear resistance, processability, and strength. Thus, after the war there was a concerted effort on the part of all synthetic-rubber research groups to produce a stronger and more malleable general-purpose rubber for use in automobile tires.[89]

For their part, the fraternity of rubber chemists felt that they were more than up to the task. Among this group, there was a confidence, a certitude – indeed, a cockiness – that perhaps accompanies only those of a young age who are working with a new science. In so many ways, the rubber chemists of the 1950s resembled the computer scientists of the 1990s. They were bold and brash, seeing themselves as the keepers and practitioners of a whole new knowledge with seemingly limitless potential. In less than a decade, they had seen their science progress from its infancy into the full stature of young adulthood. "The results of synthetic rubber research, on this continent, have proved so amazing," Ralph Rowzee stated immediately following the war, "that even the sober scientist cannot hide his enthusiasm."[90] It seemed as though each week brought news of another discovery and some sort of fresh knowledge. These were heady days, indeed, a time when the rubber chemist was potentate. Buckler's crew, which after 1953 had the luxury of working in a new state-of-the-art research laboratory, nick-named the Buckler Hilton, were enthusiastic, energized, and ready for any challenge.[91]

In their task of developing a better form of GR-S rubber, the postwar rubber chemists were assisted by developments that had taken place in Germany during the war. There, in the laboratory, chemists had succeeded in producing a GR-S rubber with improved tensile strength by lowering the temperature at which polymerization occurred, that is, by lowering the temperature of the emulsion in which the butadiene and styrene molecules joined together to form the long polymer chains that eventually constituted the synthetic rubber. Previously, chemists

on both sides of the Atlantic had been unsuccessful in effecting polymerization at any temperature below fifty degrees Celsius. But the Germans had developed a polymerization recipe for a "cold rubber," using
sugar, organic peroxide, and iron as principal ingredients, which allowed the same mixing process to occur between zero and ten degrees
Celsius. Polymerization at this lower temperature was desirable because it suppressed secondary reactions between growing chains so as
to make each of them more linear. The more linear the chain, the
stronger the synthetic rubber, and the stronger the synthetic rubber,
the more wear-resistant the rubber tire. Not since Tschunkur and
Bock's innovation of the butadiene-styrene copolymer had there been
such a revolution in synthetic-rubber technology. For commercial petrochemical companies, like Polymer, seeking to make inroads into the
tire industry, the German discovery was a major breakthrough. "It gives
promise," Ralph Rowzee stated shortly after his return from Germany
in 1945, "of being better ... than any product available to us."[92]

The transfer of this fundamental research from Germany to North
America was a result of the Allied victory in Europe. The Second
World War, unlike any war in history, was a war of science.[93] The brains
and industrial techniques of Allied scientists and engineers were
matched against those of the Germans to produce the most advanced
and effective devices in pursuit of military supremacy. "The Second
World War gave new meaning to the concept of total war," notes the
Canadian historian Donald Avery in his recent study, *The Science of War,*
"both in the mobilization of national resources and in the utilization
of science."[94] The forces of science and industry were marshalled to invent and develop new devices, all of which were held under a tight
cloak of military security. Each warring nation spent hundreds of millions of dollars on fundamental and applied research that, while primarily intended for the purpose of war, presented a unique form of
war booty as the conflict came to a close. Project Paperclip, the American operation that brought Werner von Braun and the team of German rocket scientists to the United States after the war, was but one
aspect of a much more comprehensive and systematic "intellectual
reparations" program to exploit German scientific and technical
know-how. Germany's substantial advances in numerous industries –
especially rocketry, optics, pharmaceuticals, plastics, and synthetic rubber – were seen by the Allies as the industrial spoils of war and, given
the outcome of the conflict, rightfully theirs to exploit.[95]

In August 1944 the Allied combined chiefs of staff established the
broad umbrella agency to plan for and administer the orderly exploitation of enemy secrets. Called the Combined Intelligence Objectives

Sub-committee (CIOS), this new control centre was responsible for compiling lists of "target plants," allocating the technical experts to investigate them, and processing and distributing the resulting reports. Its scope and cooperative purpose was reflected in the number and nationality of the agencies it represented. Canada was among the first of the Allied nations to establish formal and functional links with CIOS. The prospect of obtaining German science and technology titillated the Canadian government and private industry in Canada. According to Gordon Henderson, Polymer's chief engineer, the acquisition of German industrial secrets was of "first-rate importance to Canadian industry."[96] As a result, between 1944 and June 1945, the Canadian government established two agencies – the Joint Committee on Enemy Science and Technology (JCEST), which was based in Ottawa, and the Canadian Advisory Targets Committee (CATC), which was based in London, England – to coordinate Canadian activities with CIOS and other related allied organizations. Early on, CIOS and its Canadian counterparts recognized that the success of its "technical missions" to Germany depended in large measure on the quality of the investigators.[97] Thus, they recruited only the best: scientists of broad interest, able to comprehend wisely and quickly; scientists of deep learning, capable of strong analysis and critical thinking; scientists with practical training, whom their German colleagues would respect for scientific attainment. In short, people like Polymer's Ralph Rowzee.

In the spring of 1945, Rowzee, who was at that time Polymer's director of research, was selected by Howe's department of reconstruction to be part of the CIOS team being sent to Germany to investigate the synthetic-rubber industry.[98] With his extensive knowledge of all aspects of synthetic-rubber production, Rowzee was considered the most qualified Canadian to make the sortie. As J.R. Donald, director-general of the chemical and explosives production branch, put it: Rowzee was without a doubt the "best qualified man in Canada to undertake this important technical mission."[99] In mid-March 1945, Rowzee travelled to London, England, by Liberator bomber to join up with other scientists from Great Britain and the United States. He was to be given an honorary commission in the Canadian Army and to wait until he received the confidential details of his mission.

By early March 1945 the Allied armies had reached the banks of the Rhine. On 6 March they took Cologne, and the next day, by remarkable luck, they seized the bridge at Remagen before the Germans could blow it up. Troops poured across the Rhine. From then on, the war and the Allied investigational work speeded up greatly. Accompanying each of three main armed divisions on the Western Front was a so-called T-force, whose responsibility was to go into the "target" industrial plant with or immediately after the combat units, in order to prevent looting, sabotage, removal of documents, and the escape of key personnel. Once the plant was brought under control and put under T-force guard, a message was sent to London informing CIOS that the plant was ready for investigation. Within a matter of hours, a group of investigators were dispatched to the target.

Rowzee's first trip to Germany came in the middle of April 1945. Along with six Americans, he was ordered to investigate the IG Farben synthetic-rubber complex at Hüls and Leverkusen near Cologne. There, he spent almost two weeks poring over scientific and technical data, questioning key technical personnel, and studying equipment and processes. He subsequently did the same at the Phoenix Rubber Company's plant at Hamburg and the Continental Rubber Company's plant at Nordhaven.[100] Rowzee was not, however, overly impressed with the German synthetic industry. Soon after his return to Canada in June 1945, he noted that Polymer's GR-S was "at least as good as the best German tire rubber and in one most important characteristic, processability, it was far superior."[101] Furthermore, Rowzee found "no indication" that the Germans had produced a rubber of the butyl type, leading him to conclude that "our GR-I [i.e., butyl rubber] was far superior to any rubber used for inner tubes in Germany."[102] Despite Rowzee's general belief that the Polymer project was better than its German counterpart, he was nonetheless forced to admit that there were a few areas in which the Germans did excel. For instance, he found that the infrastructure setup for R&D at Leverkusen was on "a scale far exceeding any rubber research laboratories on this continent."[103] He was also impressed with much of their equipment, which he later found was available through the "repatriation" initiative.

Based on Rowzee's investigation, Polymer's directors implemented "operation Leverkusen" to bring German equipment and technology back to Canada. Characteristically, it was Nicholson who spearheaded the drive.[104] As he had so often done in the past, Nicholson first turned to C.D. Howe for assistance. Long a forceful arbiter of business-government relations, Howe believed that it was the role of government to assist Canadian business to locate and acquire German industrial science and technology. To that end, in January 1946 he appointed Roy Geddes as economic advisor to the newly opened Canadian Military Mission in Berlin. Under the command of General Maurice Pope, the Canadian Military Mission functioned as an emissary between the Canadian government and the Inter-Allied Reparations Agency (IARA), a body created in December of 1945 to oversee the allocation of German assets. In September 1949, Howe also solicited the support of L.B. Pearson, secretary of state at the department of external affairs (and future prime minister), to help him bring German synthetic-rubber knowledge and technology to Canada.[105] The process was long and drawn out, given the number of competing nations interested in German technology. But in the end the effort paid off. In 1950 Polymer's chief engineer, Gordon Henderson, went to Germany under the auspices of the IARA and brought back several thousand tons of the German research equipment to Sarnia.[106]

But research equipment was only a small part of the Allies' war booty. CIOS and its spin-off agencies also took tons of scientific and technological documentation out of Germany at the end of the war, information on everything from German pharmaceuticals and optics to synthetic fuel and leather tanning.[107] It was from these technical missions that the Allies and, ultimately, the North American synthetic-rubber industry, acquired the fundamental theory and method for the production of "cold rubber."[108]

After the war, based on what CIOS had learned in Germany, a number of North American chemical concerns began manufacturing their own version of cold rubber. All used Polymer's polymerization recipe, which it had donated to the RFC free of royalties, in return for the assistance it had received during the war. Polymer's version was introduced in 1950 and marketed under the trade name Polysar Krylene. It, like all other cold rubbers at the time, was an improvement over regular GR-S rubber and three times as good as natural rubber in terms of wear resistance in car tires. Unfortunately, however, tire manufacturers complained that the new cold rubber – whichever brand name it was marketed under – was difficult to process and no cheaper to purchase than the old, "hot" buna-s rubber. If cold rubber was to be a successful commercial product, it would have to be made more attractive in terms of processability and price. The task that preoccupied Buckler and other rubber chemists, therefore, was to develop a longer-lasting, less expensive, and more processing-friendly form of cold rubber, a rubber that was cheaper than natural rubber but that, like natural rubber, was malleable enough to be fabricated directly into tires. In short, the goal was to retain the positive properties of cold rubber while making it more affordable and more plastic. Here, applied research took over from war-prize science.

By 1948 the task was already under way. At B.F. Goodrich, a young research scientist, Dr Emmet Pfau, theorized that the relative strength of cold rubber and its lack of malleability derived from the same source: the long, intermingled chains of the butadiene molecules. He theorized further that it might be possible to introduce oil directly into the polymerization process of an unmodified butadiene-styrene rubber, so as to produce a sufficiently plastic material without compromising the strength derivable from the longer linear chains of cold rubber. Replacing some of the costlier styrene and butadiene with cheap oil would have the additional benefit of reducing the overall cost of production.[109] In a strict sense, Pfau's idea was not new: by this time plasticizers like oil were common in rubber factories. What was novel about his approach was that he suggested pushing oil extension to an unprecedented level (37–45 parts of oil for every 100 parts of polymer) and carrying out the blending at the latex stage, rather than in a mixing factory.

Pfau had marked success testing his innovation at the laboratory level, but the research chiefs and upper management at B.F Goodrich were not interested in taking his work to the next step. Because they had joined the U.S. government's subsidized research program, there was no financial incentive for them to proceed any further with Pfau's ideas.[110] With no prospect of commercial benefit, B.F. Goodrich pulled the plug on his research. The decision proved to be extremely short-sighted.

Unable to interest B.F. Goodrich in his work, Emmet Pfau left the company in 1949 and joined the General Rubber and Tire Company. General Tire, along with Phillips Petroleum, Dow Chemical, and Polymer, was one of the four industrial companies engaged in synthetic-rubber research and development that had opted out of the U.S. government's subsidized program.[111] It therefore could benefit commercially from Pfau's research, whereas B.F. Goodrich could not. Thus, when Pfau approached the company with his idea for an oil-extended cold rubber, company executives at General Tire welcomed him aboard with open arms. Still, before General Tire could fully exploit the fruits of his research, one more legal obstacle had to be overcome. While General Tire was legally free to develop his ideas, its operating agreement with the RFC prohibited it from doing so in the facilities it operated for the U.S. government. In order to avoid any legal complication with the RFC, therefore, General Tire decided to develop Pfau's process outside the United States.[112] It needed a firm already producing "cold rubber" in commercial quantities, which narrowed the field considerably. At the time, there was in fact only one firm in the world that fit the bill: Canada's Polymer Corporation.

Between 1950 and 1951, the two companies worked closely together to bring Pfau's process to the point of commercial production. Indeed, the cooperation between the two companies was so great that one technical journal, *Chemical and Engineering News*, mistakenly reported that Polymer Corporation had joined General Tire to form a "jointly owned company."[113] While J.D. Barrington quickly set the record straight, the oversight was perhaps understandable given the close relationship between the companies. Not since the war had there been such a level of cooperation between Canada and the United States on synthetic-rubber science and technology. Polymer's contribution came in the form of an efficient polymerization recipe. Without it there would have been no way of controlling the molecular weight of the base polymer. Unlike the recipes developed in the United States (recipes that contained enough iron to severely limit the tolerance of polymer for oil in Pfau's oil-extended process), Polymer's recipe included only a minute trace of iron bound to a sequestering agent, which enabled the company to make and dry a very high-molecular-weight polymer, like the one Pfau was suggesting, all without degradation. The recipe was essential to bring Pfau's process to the point of commercial production.

The joint venture proved fruitful. In 1951, Polymer began the commercial production of a high-grade, oil-enriched, butadiene–styrene copolymer known as Polysar Krynol. As had been intended, the desirable properties of cold rubber were retained, but owing to the incorporation of a comparatively low-cost oil, the overall cost of the final product was reduced considerably. The new rubber also proved easier to mix, extrude, and handle in rubber-factory equipment than any other type of synthetic rubber produced. "The development," the *Financial Post* noted in April 1951, "marks a new era in synthetic rubber manufacture."[114]

In terms of research and development, the twelve years that followed the Second World War were thus the most productive in Polymer's history. The transfer of German science and technology gave an immediate stimulus to research on the North American continent. The ill-conceived policies of the American RFC had dramatically narrowed the number of companies positioned to reduce this research to commercial practice. As a result of Howe's postwar faith in Polymer, the Crown corporation had built sufficient R&D to compete and cooperate on a continental basis – a remarkable lesson for "little" Canada. By 1957, however, the RFC was no longer regulating the synthetic-rubber industry in the United States, and new technology was emerging that would lead to types of rubber never made before. Buckler and the others sensed that success in the future would be more difficult to achieve and efficiency in production much more important. But for now they could have pride in all that they had accomplished and watch as those in charge of sales did their job. Here too Polymer found its opportunities.

When J.D. Barrington arrived in Western Europe in the autumn of 1952 to meet with customers, he found a region flourishing with economic activity. In seven short years, with the benefit of Marshall Plan

aid Western Europe had managed to rise from the ashes of war, recon-
structing most of its major industries and establishing whole new ones.
The dispatch of Barrington to Europe symbolized the importance the
corporation attached to the region. After the war, when the decision
was made to "go global," it was to Europe that the company first
turned. The going had initially been tough, but due largely to the efforts of Polymer's executive vice-president, J.R. Nicholson, the company had managed to persevere. Polymer's good reputation in Europe
was primarily a product of Nicholson's way of doing things: the fact
that he never promised anything he could not deliver, the way he lived
up to the terms of his agreements, and the level of the personal service
he gave to his clients. The company had worked hard to generate
goodwill for itself and its products in Europe and by 1951 had established a reputation as a reliable international supplier of rubber.

But just as the company was poised to reap the benefits that accom-
pany such a reputation, the man largely responsible for establishing it
announced his resignation. In June 1951, after a decade with the firm,
J.R. Nicholson was stepping down as executive vice-president, to assume a senior position with Brazilian Traction, a Toronto-based opera-
tor of Brazilian utilities.[115] The Canadian synthetic-rubber program
had never been without Nicholson. Indeed, the whole project was
largely his idea. He was the first officer of the Department of Munitions and Supply to be delegated to study the synthetic-rubber situation, and he had almost single-handedly paved the way for the work of
the first board of directors. In addition, he had arranged for the transfer of technological know-how and scientific knowledge from the
United States – without which there would not have been a Canadian
synthetic-rubber industry. In the years that followed, he had overseen
nearly every legal aspect of the firm and had personally developed
Polymer's export markets in Europe. "It was largely Nicholson's efforts, continued over the years," Howe stated on the eve of Nicholson's
departure in 1951, "that has brought Polymer Corporation from an
idea to the large and successful corporation that it is today."[116] Nicholson had proved himself a new kind of Canadian business executive: an
aggressive international salesman with intellect, passion, and determination that was rarely matched. He was the quintessential "Howe boy."
Now he had moved on, with Howe's blessing, to work with another of
Howe's wartime acolytes, Henry Borden, who, as president of Brazilian
Traction, oversaw Canada's largest overseas investment. Nicholson
would be missed.

In an attempt to mitigate the damages resulting from Nicholson's
departure, Polymer immediately dispatched two of its most able personnel to Europe. Ralph Rowzee and Roger Hatch spent three months

overseas reassuring agents and customers that the company would continue to do things "Nicholson's way." Meetings held with the company's principal customers – Michelin and Kleber of France, Pirelli of Italy, Continental of Germany and Trelleborg of Sweden – went remarkably well. Rowzee and Hatch were successful in calming alarmed clients and in getting them to renew their existing contracts.[117]

Rowzee's trip to Europe served as the basis for a report that would establish the corporation's sales policy for almost a decade. Rowzee believed that from the standpoint of both financial return and long-term growth possibilities, Europe was Polymer's most attractive export market. He anticipated that in the decades to come the demand for rubber would outstrip supply and that therefore Polymer should step up its sales efforts in Europe.[118]

Given the attractiveness of the European market, Rowzee further recommended decreasing exposure in the United States. While the United States, with its unparalleled number of cars and consumers, appeared like the greenest of pastures, once there Polymer had found the grazing not so good. Due to the RFC's "no-profit–no-loss" pricing policy as well as its 10 percent duty on all synthetic-rubber imports, Polymer had found it difficult, and at times impossible, to make money. Nevertheless, Rowzee was not willing to go as far as to recommend withdrawing from the U.S. marketplace altogether. "Polymer must maintain its U.S. market for the next five to ten years," he stated, "if only as an insurance policy."[119] Given the strong level of demand for rubber south of the border, Rowzee believed that it would be possible for Polymer to get rid of its product at short notice if currency difficulties, slumps in rubber consumption, drops in the price of natural rubber, or increased competition should affect Polymer's sales elsewhere.[120]

Rowzee's report became corporate strategy, and as a result, the U.S. market became less important to the firm's success. In 1952, approximately twenty-four thousand tons were exported to the United States, or approximately 26 percent of total sales. In 1956, by contrast, less than ten thousand tons were sold south of the border, or less than 7 percent of total sales. France and Great Britain were now both larger consumers of Polymer's rubber than the United States. In contrast, exports to Europe more than doubled during the period, from just under thirty thousand tons in 1951 to just over seventy thousand tons in 1956.[121]

Polymer's success in Western Europe was largely a result of three factors. First, as in North America, the Western European economy was booming after 1950. In Germany, Italy, France, and Great Britain, reconstruction was achieved quickly and with remarkably little political dispute. In each of these nations, real incomes continued to rise. As a result, sales of durable goods such as cars increased. Second, Polymer faced little or no competition from other synthetic-rubber producers during the period. While prospective competition was a serious threat and caused Polymer's executives no end of concern,[122] the threat did not become an industrial reality until the end of the decade. It was only then that the United Kingdom, Germany, Italy, and France followed through on their earlier plans to build their own synthetic-rubber plants. Furthermore, it was only then that American synthetic-rubber producers began aggressively selling their product in Europe.[123] Thus, for most of the decade Polymer had an uncontested market for its product. The only real competition that the company faced was from the natural-rubber cartel, and even on this front Polymer was winning the war.

The third factor contributing to Polymer's success was innovation. In production the company had been able to increase output rapidly, to meet demand in Europe without new plant additions. Polymer had thus benefited from socioeconomic conditions. That said, it made the most of its opportunities.

While circumstances had benefited Polymer, after twenty-two years the times were no longer showing the same beneficent consideration to C.D. Howe and the Liberal government. By 1957, the political tide had turned against the "government party." The Conservatives' and the CCF's charges that the Liberals were arrogant, overbearing, undemocratic – indeed dictatorial – had of course, been made before; the difference was that now they were starting to resonate with the electorate. Howe himself was the target of much of the opposition's criticism. His invoking of closure during the Trans-Canada pipeline debate of 1956 caused the Conservatives to cry foul. Howe, they charged, was a "dictator" who had "contempt for parliament" and for democratic practices.[124] Increasingly in the House of Commons, Howe looked like an old bear under attack by a pack of tenacious hounds. Occasionally the opposition drew blood in the form of a politically unwise outburst by Howe – "What's a million?" "Who can stop us?" "Nuts!" Such infamous one-liners served to confirm the Conservatives' characterization of him and his party.

Looking old and tired, Howe was the visible symbol of the government's ossification. Ironically, the least bureaucratic of men had come to embody the Ottawa attitude that the electorate so decisively rejected during the election of 1957.[125] Suffering from internal decay and discredited by the pipeline debate, the Liberals were defeated in June at the polls by John Diefenbaker's Progressive Conservatives. That year, the Progressive Conservatives won more seats than any other party in Canadian history (208 of 265). Riding on Diefenbaker's coattails, the party finally managed to appeal to voters in the West and in Quebec without alienating their base in Ontario. As they had done in every election since 1945, the people of Sarnia voted for the Progressive Conservative candidate, reelecting Joseph Murphy. Ironically, Murphy had managed to get himself reelected, in part, by identifying himself with one of Howe's most successful economic ventures – Polymer Corporation. In the years leading up to the election of 1957, Murphy celebrated Polymer at nearly every turn. "Polymer is a very successful corporation," he declared in the House of Commons in January 1956, "which is operated pretty much the same as any private corporation."[126] Murphy was no longer in favour of privatization, defending the status quo whenever the issue came up.[127] Perhaps just as ironic was the fact that the man responsible for Polymer's formation, C.D Howe, was not reelected in 1957. His behind-the-scenes genius in plotting the strategies and structures of Canada's industrial success had largely been hidden from the electorate.

Like so many of the old Liberal guard – men like the minister of finance, Walter Harris, the minister of public works, Robert Winters, and the long-time Liberal power broker, Stuart Garson – Howe was unable or, more likely, unwilling to reinvent himself and was thus forcibly retired by the voters. After twenty-two years in office the Liberals had finally managed to offend more people than they had gratified.

Never one to remain idle, Howe moved to Montreal and was soon finding new business challenges to match his enormous talents. From time to time he spoke out on public policy issues, on one occasion defending the need for Crown corporations like Polymer.[128] He had always taken great pride in Polymer's accomplishments. For Howe, Polymer was a shining example of everything that was good about the government being in business. It remained to be seen if Diefenbaker's Conservatives thought likewise.

The period of Barrington's presidency, 1951–57, was by many indications the most prosperous in the company's history. The corporate strategy, which had been formulated shortly after the war, positioned the company to take advantage of the international economic boom of the 1950s. Barrington had done his part, in a sense, by changing nothing at all, by staying the course. Early on, he recognized the merits of continuing along the same path, of utilizing chemistry to create new and diverse products for both domestic and international consumers. Once the financial reorganization of the company had been completed and the company's structure brought into line with its strategy, it was set to seize the opportunities that accompanied an age of mass consumerism and the great god – Car. Polymer was very fortunate in the combination of economic and political factors that operated during the period. Once the nascent petrochemical industry had taken off after the war, Polymer's political godfather, C.D. Howe, was content to let Polymer's management run the show. To Polymer's credit it did not abuse the latitude given it by Howe. It made the most of the chances it was given and by so doing continued to reward the Crown.

5

Worldly Wise:
Growth and Multinationalization,
1958–1966

There are those who would like to convince us that further growth is inadvisable or impossible for Polymer. The arguments they use are that it is inappropriate for a Government-owned Company to grow to satisfy markets which private interests stand ready to serve; that the export market for synthetic rubber is finished; that those who do not have plants in the Common Market area are finished; and that it will be impossible for Polymer to establish an effective position in the solution polymer field. In answer to the arguments as to why Polymer should not grow, I submit that the export market is going to grow and that it may be in Polymer's best interest to establish manufacturing facilities in Europe. In regard to the solution polymer development, I believe that Polymer can and will establish a strong position in that field.

Ralph Rowzee (1960)[1]

The 1950s and 1960s witnessed the perfection of the "multinational enterprise" as expansion abroad became the strategy of growth for an increasing number of leading industrial organizations.[2] In many ways, the MNE became the epitome of postwar economic dynamism – flexible, efficient, and, as its critics would soon point out, imperialistic.[3] The MNE was not new, of course. Since the second industrial revolution in the late nineteenth century, many firms – with competitive advantages derived from economies of scale and scope – had established production facilities in foreign markets. Even Canadian capitalism, long a recipient of foreign economic attention, had participated in this global reach; as early as 1899 Toronto capitalists had carried Canadian expertise in urban transit and power generation technology to Latin America.[4] Geographical expansion into distant markets provided a way for the modern industrial enterprise to continue to exploit

its competitive advantage. After the Second World War, an increasing
number of businesses embraced this strategy of direct foreign investment as a means to growth. Firms from around the world became successful challengers to Alfred Chandler's "first movers" – those
Parsonian industrial organizations like Ford, RCA, Du Pont, and Dow –
which had established branch plants in distant lands early in the twentieth century.[5] Having relentlessly expanded the output of their standard production line (i.e., increased their scale) and continually
introduced new sorts of products (i.e., expanded their scope), postwar
industrial enterprises invested in new products and new geographical
markets in order to grow.[6] As the economist Charles Kindleberger suc-
cinctly put it, "in going abroad, they grow abroad."[7] The multinational
enterprise thus evolved naturally out of the successful industrial corporation.[8] Often by way of joint ventures, these corporations set up subsidiaries in places where both the markets and the proprietary
technologies of production offered the greatest potential for exploit-
ing the economies of scale and scope.[9] While this phenomenon was
quintessentially American – le défi américain, as one European economist termed it – other industrial nations were not immune to its allure.
These, then, became decades of "global reach."[10]

Between 1945 and 1970, Canadian corporations such as Inco, Brascan, Noranda, Cominco, Alcan, MacMillan Bloedel, and Massey-
Ferguson made substantial investments abroad.[11] Alcan continued on its
"global mission," investing in new fabricating facilities in Mexico and
South Africa and expanding those already in operation in Switzerland,
Norway, India, and France.[12] After 1964 MacMillan Bloedel, Canada's
largest lumber forest products company, made acquisitions abroad,
thereby expanding its "empire of wood."[13] Likewise, Massey-Ferguson
expanded its existing plants in the United Kingdom, Germany, France,
Australia, and South Africa and began manufacturing in promising
third world countries such as India, Brazil, and Turkey.[14] Having earlier
developed its export market, Massey-Ferguson took the next logical step
and established manufacturing facilities outside its domestic market.
In recent years, Massey-Ferguson's international expansion – master-
minded by business-school-trained executives like A.A. Thornborough –
has been held up as a classic Canadian case of multinational growth.[15]
By establishing facilities abroad, this elite group of Canadian companies
was able to reduce manufacturing costs through an increased scale of
operation. Implicit in this new global outlook was a rejection of the old
national-policy mentality of Canadian manufacturing – a small, protected national market was no longer enough.

Another Canadian corporation became multinational during this
period. Remarkably, however, it was not a private but rather a public

corporation. In an effort to hold and expand its market in the face of increasing competition, Polymer embarked upon a program of growth through mulitinationalization. In so doing, it pushed state capitalism to a new extreme. In stark contrast to Canada's traditional policy of "defensive expansionism," Polymer pursued a strategy that furthered its, and Canada's, external commercial expansion. At a time when many Canadians were inward-looking, some to the point of being chauvinistic, Polymer strived to be worldly wise.

It did so in large part because of developments taking place within the petrochemical industry. The golden era in petrochemicals had brought with it a rush of new entrants into the chemical field.[16] The high profit margins of the immediate postwar period had led many in business to consider the industry the "place to be."[17] For over a decade Polymer had faced little competition in Europe from other petro-chemical producers. But by the mid-1950s large American oil, gas, and chemical companies, which were eager to emulate Polymer's earlier success, expanded into Europe. One of the main characteristics of the period, therefore, was the exploitation of economies of scale, which led to the construction of huge plants and to the realization of the in-dustry's global nature. Adding to the competitive environment was the fact that by the late 1950s Germany, France, and some other European countries were well on the way to becoming petrochemical producers of some size, with strong assistance from the international oil compa-nies operating refineries in these countries. Polymer's established mar-kets were now under siege. If Polymer was to hold and expand these markets, it would have to join the small and elite collection of Cana-dian companies becoming multinational.

In January 1960, Ralph Rowzee put forward a new strategic vision for the Crown company. "Polymer must grow," he stated, "to maintain its position as a major producer of synthetic rubber."[18] To do otherwise, he believed, would lead to a loss of the company's "competitive posi-tion" and hence to its "decline."[19] In Rowzee's mind, the greatest dan-ger to the company's status as a leading manufacturer of synthetic rubber was not any external phenomenon, like the emergence of new synthetic-rubber producers in Europe, but rather internal decay and complacency. Rowzee had no doubt that competition at home and abroad could be met so long as the corporation remained attentive of mind and dynamic in action. That, after all, was how it had met its challenges in the past. During the fateful postwar years of 1945–51, when the corporation was faced with extinction if it did not find a mar-ket for two-thirds of its output, Polymer had devised and undertaken an aggressive new corporate strategy that emphasized exports, R&D,

and diversification. According to Rowzee, similar actions were now required if Polymer was to meet the challenges of the 1960s. "Fifteen years ago," Ralph Rowzee proudly reminded the board of directors, "we had the courage of our conviction and made bold moves that were contrary to so-called expert advice. In the same manner, bold moves are now required to insure the future of Polymer."[20] The corporation, he emphatically declared, had to grow, or it would wither away.

It was now or never as far as Rowzee was concerned. In 1957 the European postwar economic recovery was reaching maturity and the external environment was becoming more competitive. American firms like Firestone, Goodrich, Esso, and Du Pont were now in Europe.[21] In addition, European firms – including Royal Dutch Shell, ICI, Dunlop, and BASF – had synthetic-rubber plants in operation or under construction in England, Germany, France, Italy, and Holland.[22] As a result of this rapid building of synthetic-rubber plants outside North America, global synthetic-rubber production doubled between 1956 and 1961, and Polymer's share of the market fell from 10 percent to 7.5 percent. Nevertheless, Rowzee was optimistic regarding Polymer's prospects. "I am convinced," he told the board of directors, "that Polymer has a tremendous potential for growth and that the synthetic rubber industry is on the threshold of another leap forward."[23] As a result of fifteen years of intensive marketing, R&D, and technical service, Polymer was in a position to hold a substantial share of world markets. All that was needed, Rowzee stated, was implementation of his aggressive strategy for growth.[24]

What Rowzee had in mind was an enormous undertaking: a $45-million expenditure to increase world-wide production by one-third, from 150,000 to 200,000 tons per year.[25] But that was not all. In one of the most radical proposals to date, Rowzee recommended that the company abandon its reliance on exports and meet the competitive situation head-on by establishing actual production facilities in growth markets around the world. "There are real advantages from the standpoint of cost and of customer relations," Rowzee informed a parliamentary committee examining Polymer's operations, "to locating production facilities close to the principal consuming areas."[26] If endorsed by the board of directors, Rowzee's idea to better serve existing and potential markets by locating facilities closer to them would mark a momentous change in corporate strategy from export sales to direct sales in the markets concerned.

A man of critical thought, Rowzee was profoundly aware of the risk involved in building plants overseas, especially given the global excess capacity in the industry.[27] Nevertheless, when weighed against the need to locate within these markets to prevent erosion of market share, he considered the risk worth taking.[28] Exports were becoming a more costly method of operation, open to the vagaries of foreign exchange differentials.[29] And while there was no tariff at this time on synthetic rubber entering the European common market, the cost of transportation alone was enough to compromise Polymer's competitive position overseas. "Transportation is an important factor," Ralph Rowzee informed the standing committee on public accounts. At almost 10 percent of Polymer's net return on sales, transportation costs were stretching Polymer's ability to compete overseas to the limit.[30] In an environment in which aggressive competition and excess industrial capacity were putting downward pressure on prices, such costs were deemed improvident.[31] To compete effectively in the European market, Polymer needed to eliminate these costs and, according to Ralph Rowzee, that meant establishing production facilities overseas.

Wise to the workings of a modern public enterprise, Rowzee fully appreciated the politico-economic ramifications of what he was suggesting. The Crown corporation was initially conceived in a defensive mentality – i.e., it was intended to hold the home front – but Rowzee's strategy revealed a new aggressive mindset. If endorsed by the board of directors and government, his program would see Polymer, a Crown company, operating on foreign soil: no longer only selling but also manufacturing its product overseas.

Never had a Canadian Crown corporation produced its product outside the national boundary. True, some Crown corporations performed on the international stage. For example, Teleglobe Canada, which was established by Louis St Laurent's government in 1949 to fulfill the terms of the Commonwealth Telegraph Agreement of the preceding year, functioned outside Canada's borders. Nevertheless, it did so to fulfil a public-policy purpose, that is, to coordinate Canada's external telecommunications services with the telecommunication services of other nations. While Teleglobe operated abroad, it did not manufacture overseas. No Crown corporation did, and for good reason. Before Polymer, the goal of public enterprise was to facilitate domestic industry. In so doing, it served a public-policy purpose. But to manufacture abroad, as Rowzee was suggesting, served no traditional public-policy purpose whatsoever. It would not create jobs for Canadians; it would not further Canada's political or cultural cohesion; it would not help stabilize domestic prices or incomes; it would not secure the supply of critical materials; nor would it help develop an underdeveloped sector of the Canadian economy. No, as Rowzee readily admitted before the Standing Committee on Public Accounts in May 1961, the move could be justified only on commercial grounds. Polymer needed to manufacture abroad to maintain "an efficient and profitable operation."[32]

Given the rationale, Rowzee wondered whether the Diefenbaker government would have the political courage to endorse such a unique endeavour.[33] He also worried about the attitude of foreign governments to having a Canadian government-owned company establishing operations within their borders.[34]But these were just two of the obstacles associated with continued government ownership that Rowzee identified as standing in the way of Polymer's future growth and prosperity.

There was also the problem of financing a major expansion program. If Polymer had been privately owned, it could have gone out and borrowed through the usual channels or sold additional shares. But as a Crown corporation it could not do so. Any expansion would have to be financed out of retained earnings. With a cash flow (after allowing for maintenance and improvement expenditures) of \$4–\$5 million per year, Polymer would have roughly \$20–\$25 million available over the next five years for new capital additions. But Rowzee's growth program called for an expenditure that was about twice that amount. It would therefore be necessary, Rowzee anticipated, to take on partners at certain junctures to obtain capital and market access.[35] But such linkages raised further questions. Would the government be willing to let one of its corporations go into partnership with what might well be a foreign, privately owned company?[36] Conversely, would private industry be willing to take on a partner that was government-owned? Rowzee was uncharacteristically skeptical. "If, as seems possible, we build a plant in Europe and desire a partner, there are not too many companies who would consider partnership with a government-owned company."[37]

These were serious problems of corporate status as far as Rowzee was concerned. Polymer needed to grow in order to continue to be prosperous, and in order to grow it needed venture capital and a manufacturing presence overseas. Rowzee did not rule out the possibility of successful expansion as a Crown corporation, but in his view the task would be much more difficult than if the corporation was privately owned. "Under conditions which continue to provide freedom of decision to the Board of Directors, a successful program of growth might be carried out," stated Rowzee cautiously, "but against considerably heavier odds than if the Company was privately owned."[38] Rowzee's preference for private ownership stemmed from his belief that under government ownership it was difficult to extend full authority to the board of directors and that it was almost impossible to prevent political considerations from coming into play – particularly in the event of conflict with private interests.[39] While C.D. Howe was in office, this problem was not as much of a consideration. For most of his tenure, there were no commercial synthetic-rubber producers competing with Polymer in Europe, and Howe was content to let Polymer do whatever it determined necessary to be prosperous. But Rowzee worried about the approach of future governments, especially given the rapidly changing macroeconomic environment. He questioned the capacity of future federal administrations to remain quiescent when political pressure from private industry and foreign governments came to bear. Unable to reconcile his strategy for growth with continued government ownership, Rowzee opted for growth and the privatization of the firm. "On balance and with the full support of the management group at Sarnia," Rowzee stated in January of 1960, "I wish to go on record as believing that Polymer stands the best chance of future success as a private company."[40]

Unlike at the end of the Second World War, talk of privatization was not academic. A number of private firms were now interested in purchasing Polymer, and here, Polymer executives sensed, was a means to their new-found global ends. No longer was the corporation viewed by business as a technological white elephant. In the financial press, Polymer was heralded as a "technological wonder,"[41] a "world leader in rubber developments,"[42] "one of Canada's most successful corporations,"[43] and "a shining gem in the diadem of Canadian industry."[44]

The financial press had reason to eulogize. Over the last fifteen years of operation, Polymer had developed a world-wide reputation for leadership in rubber research and development. And if past success was any indication, Buckler's R&D department would keep the company on the cutting-edge of technology. Whereas once Polymer had produced three distinct types of elastomers, now it produced ten.[45] It also produced fifty types of specialty products, whereas once it had manufactured only eleven. These products, as J.D. Barrington noted before his departure from the corporation in 1957, "were well-known and fully accepted, both in Canada and abroad."[46] Since 1946, when Polymer had begun organized R&D activities in response to the need for diversification and development, R&D expenses had been close to the level of 2.5 percent of cost of sales.[47] In 1960 the R&D department had an operating budget of roughly $2 million, a figure representing about 20 percent of net income. The Gordon Royal Commission Report of 1957 had argued that one of the systemic problems of Canadian manufacturing was its chronic lack of R&D – resulting from too high a level of foreign ownership.[48] But Polymer provided a counter-case – a Canadian corporation that had prospered because it controlled its own R&D.

On the marketing side of the operation, by 1960 Polymer had a network of sales representatives that literally circled the globe. The company had agents in over seventy countries, from Argentina to Singapore, Iceland to New Zealand.[49] Attempting to capitalize on this development, Polymer's advertisements that year read simply, "Polysar ... everywhere." Roger Hatch, who was determined to see each one of the company's agents become a millionaire from their commissions, continued to have nationals in the different countries do the selling.[50] This practice allowed the Crown company to overcome the cultural and protectionist barriers that stood in its way. While nationals did the selling, Polymer coordinated the sales efforts and provided technical service. Polymer also continued its earlier practice of sending its top executives on sales missions. On the basis of this world-wide sales organization, Polymer enjoyed a tremendous amount of goodwill within the industry. While Polymer was not the biggest synthetic-rubber producer, it was one of the world's most adroit.

Polymer's research, production, and marketing success was reflected in the company's financial performance (see table A1). Between 1944 and 1961, net sales increased nine-fold from roughly $10 million to over $88 million. As for net profits, on the other hand, the company moved from a loss of $400,000 in 1944 to a net gain, in 1961, of just over $10 million. In cumulative terms, between 1944 and 1961, Polymer had collected almost $90 million in profits on net sales of over $850 million. The number of employees increased from 1,810 in 1944 to 2,711 in 1961. At the expense of a total payroll increase of approximately 40 percent and an approximate doubling in the book value of facilities, the output of the plant had quadrupled.[51]

Since Polymer was a Crown corporation, the Canadian government reaped most of the financial benefits of all of this. By the end of 1961, it had received $46.3 million in dividends and $1 million in debenture interest. In addition, Polymer had repaid $10.4 million of the total government advance ($48.4 million) and retired $8 million of debentures. The *Financial Post* could properly state in 1960 that Polymer, with total assets of $85 million and profits representing 17.1 percent of the government's investment, was "the most successful and profitable of all the crown corporations."[52] Not even Eldorado, Canada's national uranium producer, recorded such lucrative financial results.[53]

The success and profitability of Polymer was not lost on the new Diefenbaker government, which in June of 1957 had won a narrow victory at the polls, thus breaking twenty-two years of Grit dominance. Ten months later the Conservatives fortified their position by winning the most spectacular landslide yet seen in Canadian politics. In May 1958, after six weeks of indecision, Diefenbaker appointed Raymond

The first service dinner, held in Kenwick Terrace in 1962. Seated at the head table, from left to right, Roger Hatch, Lee Dougan, Ralph Rowzee, and Stan Wilk. National Archives of Canada.

O'Hurley as the minister of defence production and therefore the minister with oversight for Polymer. For the next five years, Polymer's future would be in his – and Diefenbaker's – hands.

A full-blooded Irishman, O'Hurley was no stranger to business, although he was to federal politics. In 1956, at the age of forty-seven, he was enlisted by the Quebec premier, Maurice Duplessis, to run for the Conservatives in Lotbinière, Quebec. As a good soldier, he saluted smartly, ran, and was elected. In Ottawa, however, he was often out of his depth. His inexperience made him tentative and nervous. David Golden, who served as deputy minister of defence production between 1954 and 1962, later recalled that this behaviour added to the chaos of the Diefenbaker years.[54] Before entering politics for the first time in 1957, O'Hurley had worked for twenty-two years as a timber grader on the Ross Seigneury in Quebec. He was thus rooted in Canada's old, staple-oriented economy. This was a more bucolic business experience than the one that had taken place at Polymer. Nevertheless, even O'Hurley knew a successful modern enterprise when he saw one. In September he wrote to the prime minister praising Polymer's past performance.[55] "The actions of management," he reported, "have been in the public interest and in keeping with sound business practice ... The operation has been a success."[56] It was a message he later reiterated in the House of Commons.[57]

To some, O'Hurley's statement must have come as a shock, not because it was factually incorrect – it was not – but because, while in opposition, the Conservatives had been critical of the government trespassing
into the realm of private enterprise.[58] The party was committed, at least
in principle, to the idea that government should not tread where private
industry could ably proceed. Given its preference for private ownership
of industry, it was widely anticipated that the Conservative government
would dispose of Polymer soon after coming to power.[59]

During his years in office, C.D. Howe had been approached only
twice by individuals interested in buying the Crown corporation: once,
in 1946, by the Liberal senator Peter Campbell, who was representing
a less than fully committed group of anonymous investors, and more
recently, in 1957, by J.D. Barrington. Perhaps private industry thought
that raising the matter with Howe would be a waste of time given the
minister's avowed attachment to the Crown corporation. Publicly,
Howe had not given any indication that he was prepared to hand over
"his" enterprise to private industry. That is not to say that he was averse
to the idea. According to J.D. Barrington, his offer to purchase Polymer was received favourably by the minister, but nothing had come of
it because Howe did not want any disruptions in public policy before
the 1957 election.[60] It is quite likely that had the Liberals won that
election, Polymer would have been sold – perhaps not to Barrington
and perhaps not until after 1960, when Rowzee had made his pragmatic appeal for growth and denationalization, but in all likelihood it
would have been sold. Polymer had become profitable and capable of
fending for itself as an instrument of national economic sovereignty,
and Howe had a tradition of picking good puppies, of raising them,
and then letting them out of the pound. But the Liberals lost the 1957
election, and history took a different course.

Believing the Conservatives were ideologically committed to selling
the firm, a number of private companies initiated behind-the-scenes approaches to the Diefenbaker government in an effort to obtain an interest in Polymer. The companies that coveted the Crown corporation
were diverse in their backgrounds. Canadian Industries Limited, Canada's largest chemical manufacturer, was "extremely interested."[61] And
quite understandably. Polymer had consistently outperformed CIL.[62]
Shawinigan Chemical and the Dominion Tar and Chemical Company
were also enticed by Polymer's strong financial performance.[63] Several
American companies, including Allied Chemical Corporation of New
York, Goodrich Rubber and Tire, Courtaulds of North America Limited, and Dow Chemical, added their names to the list of companies in
pursuit of the Crown's industrial jewel.[64] In 1961 the Bay Street investment firm Wisener, Mackellar and Company went into partnership with

the Montreal engineering company Mannis for the purpose of acquiring Polymer. Two years later they were still pursuing their objective.[65] Likewise, J.D. Barrington was proving resilient. Having had nothing come of his initial bid, Barrington, in his capacity as president of Ventures, a subsidiary of the mining giant McIntyre-Porcupine, approached the Diefenbaker government in 1959 with a $75-million offer to purchase Polymer.[66] The offer was discussed in Cabinet but at that time it was decided that the enterprise was "too successful" to be disposed of.[67] As a consequence, the Cabinet determined that there "should be no discussion now at all with Mr Barrington."[68] Accordingly, when Barrington wrote to the prime minister asking for an appointment to discuss a deal, he never received a reply.[69] Not to be discouraged, Barrington continued to lobby the government until the Conservatives' electoral defeat by the Pearson Liberals in 1963.[70]

Many industry observers, including Polymer's former president R.C. Berkinshaw, considered Barrington's offer reasonable.[71] While Polymer had assets of approximately $125 million, critics noted that the plant was getting older and in the near future would need some expensive renovations. The depreciated value of the plant was already down to $32 million. In addition, the company's raw materials position was not fully secure. In 1960 Polymer was supplementing its own production of butadiene with purchases from Imperial Oil across the road and with imports from the United States. This practice would continue to be seen as a problem and would ultimately lead to a risky backward integration into feedstocks. Finally, it was generally anticipated that the buyer would have to invest another $45 million over and above the cost of the existing plant to hold a competitive position in world markets. A corporation in the ethos of profitable private enterprise needed constant injections of capital to stay flexible, competitive, and efficient. Howe seemed to realize this and thus was prepared by the mid-1950s to let the government-succoured infant industry go private. Given the anticipated capital expenditures, most of the offers to purchase Polymer were in the $75–$80 million range.[72] The one exception came from a group of investors represented by Julian H. Ferguson, a Progressive Conservative MP who was first elected to the House of Commons in 1945; they offered the government almost $100 million for Polymer.[73]

But the government was not selling, at any price. "The Government," the minister of finance, Donald Fleming wrote to Julian Ferguson in April 1959, "has at no time indicated any interest in the sale of the Polymer undertaking."[74] In what was fast becoming a pattern of ministerial behaviour, Fleming was reluctant to do anything that might undermine the success of the firm. There is no indication that Fleming realized the ongoing implications of this stance – i.e., that Polymer would have to be fed capital. When asked in the House of Commons about the government's plans for Polymer, Raymond O'Hurley stated that he had "no views" about the future of Polymer but then went on to note that he saw no reason to dispose of Polymer so long as the "best interest" of Canada's only producer of synthetic rubber was being well served by the status quo.[75] In all likelihood that would have been the end of the matter if it had not been for developments that were taking place at Polymer itself.

Ralph Rowzee had always had a tremendous amount of influence on decisions by the board of directors, and this instance proved no different. In June 1960 his suggestion that Polymer be transferred to private industry was endorsed by all but one member of the board of directors. The lone dissident was John Bruce, labour's representative on the board. Bruce, a union organizer who had been appointed to the board in 1947 by C.D. Howe, thought that the company could meet competition and carry out its growth program satisfactorily as a Crown corporation.[76]

It was no coincidence that this position was also taken by the local unions. "There is no justification, in our opinion," stated Anne Blair, chairperson of the legislative committee of Local 535 of the United Electrical, Radio and Machine Workers of America, "in turning this valuable property over to those who reap large profits. Rather we suggest the government use the profit to expand this industry and other crown corporations."[77] The Oil, Chemical and Atomic Workers' Union, Polymer's largest union, also went on record as "opposing the surrendering of the Polymer Corporation into private hands."[78] This sentiment had already been expressed by the Canadian Labour Congress: "The Polymer corporation, which was created by the investment of public funds at a time of national emergency and made such an outstanding contribution to our successful war effort, should be retained by its owners, the people of Canada, and not sold for the private advantage of a small group within our nation."[79] But unfortunately for labour, this position was not endorsed by the majority of Polymer's board of directors and as a result Rowzee was granted his wish.

On 16 June 1960 Rowzee was authorized to advise minister O'Hurley that each of the directors, with the exception of John Bruce, was "strongly of the opinion that the Company can best meet competitive conditions and take full advantage of opportunities for growth, in Canada and abroad, as a private enterprise."[80] Raymond O'Hurley had once tentatively stated that if any new circumstances made the government's ownership a liability, the government would sell Polymer.[81] Now Polymer's high command was telling him exactly that.

Unfortunately for those advocating privatization, the matter was not solely O'Hurley's to judge. A decision of this magnitude would first need the support of Cabinet. To that end, in the spring of 1960 the Diefenbaker government formed a special Cabinet committee to examine Polymer's status. Specifically, the committee was given the task of considering two issues: Rowzee's three-pronged program for growth and the merits of private ownership. The committee was composed of some of the most powerful men in Diefenbaker's government. In addition to O'Hurley, who was appointed chairman of the committee, there was the minister of finance, Donald Fleming. The epitome of the right-wing Tory, Fleming often disagreed with Diefenbaker on matters of public policy. Yet he remained ferociously loyal to him while the party was in power. Gordon Churchill, a one-time school principal and wartime army officer, was House leader and minister of trade and commerce. Churchill, like David Walker, the final committee member, was part of Diefenbaker's inner circle. Walker, who occupied the public-works portfolio, had been one of the first to support Diefenbaker's leadership bid and for that reason had the prime minister's ear on most issues. Together it was the responsibility of these men to determine the government's best course of action with regard to Polymer Corporation.

In May and June, Ralph Rowzee; Stanley Wilk, Polymer's vice-president of finance; and Lee Dougan, Polymer's vice-president of operations, travelled to Ottawa to meet with the government's special Cabinet committee. There, Rowzee reiterated the need for establishing plants overseas and the problems associated with government ownership. The bottom line, he said, was that Polymer needed to expand to remain competitive and that the best way this could be accomplished was for Polymer to be removed from the hands of government.[82] The committee was sympathetic to Rowzee's position. His arguments for privatization resonated well with those members, particularly Donald Fleming, who were opposed to government ownership of industry. Nevertheless, the committee expressed concern about the possibility of Polymer falling into foreign hands.[83]

While the Diefenbaker government was not radically opposed to foreign ownership of Canadian industry, it was politically sensitive to the fact that the issue was important to a growing segment of society. Walter Gordon, the chairman of the 1955–57 royal commission on Canada's economic prospects, which had put the issue of foreign investment on the public agenda, was gaining power within and outside the Liberal Party. Gordon had warned that foreign direct investment had a "snowballing" effect in any national economy. During the election campaign of 1957, Diefenbaker had echoed some of the views of

Gordon's royal commission about the effects of too much American capital investment in Canada. It had been óne of Diefenbaker's election promises to increase the proportion of domestic ownership of Canadian industry. Between 1958 and 1960 his government made various reforms to the state's regulatory power in order to protect Canadian ownership (e.g., it placed limits on foreign direct investment, CALURA (Corporation and Labour Union Return Act) obligations on foreign corporations to report their activities, and set up the Public Commission on Energy). In 1960 the prime minister and Alvin Hamilton, the minister of northern affairs and national resources, considered establishing a national development corporation to encourage Canadians to invest in, and ultimately, retain control of, Canadian industry.[84] Due to the firm opposition of Donald Fleming, however, the government dropped this idea.[85] Ironically, the proposal was later resurrected by Walter Gordon in the form of the Canada Development Corporation.[86]The Conservatives were all too aware of the fact that Gordon, a staunch economic nationalist, was determined to see their demise, and they were therefore unwilling to provide grist for his mill by letting Polymer slip into foreign hands.[87]

The committee further feared that if Polymer became foreign-owned, Canadian jobs would be lost. It had been another of Diefenbaker's election promises to end the agony of unemployment. Yet after three years in power, the Conservatives had been unable to turn their political rhetoric into an economic reality. In 1960, the unemployment rate was 7.5 percent, the same as it had been in 1957 when the Conservatives took office and more than double its 1956 level. While much of this unemployment was due to structural weaknesses in the economy, the Conservatives did not help matters by being indecisive and at times inconsistent when formulating and implementing economic policy. At the Department of Finance, Donald Fleming appeared not to have heard the government's commitment to the unemployed. Abandoning Keynesian countercyclical fiscal stabilization principles, Fleming waged war on the budgetary deficit, attempting in vain to balance the books. To the further horror of Keynesians within and outside the government, the governor of the Bank of Canada, a maverick by the name of James Coyne, refused to tackle the problem of unemployment directly.[88] Contrary to the government's position, Coyne insisted that the principal economic problem afflicting society was not unemployment but inflation.[89] Despite the relatively high rate of unemployment, inflationary pressures had persisted after 1957, as the inflow of external – primarily American – long-term capital continued to strengthen. Under these conditions, Coyne insisted that unemployment could not be vanquished without first obtaining domestic price stability, and he thus refused to increase the stock of money by any utilitarian extent.[90] Coyne's heretical stance caused the government untold political embarrassment.[91]

Fortunately, it had more control over public works, and in 1959 it instituted a winter works program, under which Ottawa paid half the labour costs of approved municipal work projects to combat the seasonal rise in unemployment. In addition, the Conservatives oversaw the construction of a small number of roads and facilities as part of their grand "Northern vision" – a largely oratorical scheme to open up the (alleged) vast economic potential of the Canadian North. While the Northern vision did not live up to its billing, it did at least create some jobs, which was more than could be said about the government's handling of the Avro Arrow development program.

When the government cancelled funding of the CF-105 in February 1959, after two years of indecision, A.V. Roe, the Malton, Ontario, company that was slated to manufacture the supersonic jet, immediately let go all its fifteen thousand employees. While it later recalled some twenty-five hundred workers, the majority did not return. Thousands of Canada's best-trained scientific and technical personnel were thus lost to the United States forever – just the reverse of the effect that Polymer had had in drawing talent and ideas into Canada.[92] Whether or not the decision was correct from a military standpoint, it cost the government a good deal of political capital in the industrial heartland of Ontario.[93] Thus, when it became time to rule on Polymer's future, the government was not about to further alienate Ontario voters by doing anything that might cost jobs. Nor was it about to frustrate the national body politic by letting another of Canada's technological possessions come under u.s. control. These considerations (i.e., the delicate problems of returning a corporation to the private sector in peacetime) provided a contrast to the act of creation in an atmosphere of wartime expediency.

In August 1960, on the heels of the Avro affair and with the economy showing further signs of weakening, the special Cabinet committee considering Polymer's future tabled its final report.[94] Having weighed all the evidence, it came to the unanimous conclusion that the "corporation ought to be sold."[95] Unwilling, however, to allow this technological asset to pass into the hands of u.s. interests, it made its recommendation subject to the condition that "satisfactory assurances" be given by the purchaser that "the company would be under Canadian control on a continuing basis."[96] To prevent the further loss of technology-driven jobs in Ontario, the committee demanded that Polymer continue to be operated as an integrated unit, that the research and development program be maintained, and that Rowzee's strategy for growth be implemented by the purchaser.[97] Having committed itself to the privatization of Polymer, the committee wanted to do everything in its power to mitigate the possible negative effects arising from the sale of the firm.

Despite the safeguards stipulated in the committee's final report, some members of Cabinet were opposed to the recommendation that Polymer be sold. Several worried that no matter what safeguards were attempted, continued Canadian control could not be guaranteed and that if Polymer did fall into foreign hands the government would be roundly criticized.[98] Privatization, from their political perspective, was a risky business. Others in Cabinet agreed with the conclusion but for different reasons. "It would be a serious political mistake, to sell one of the very few public enterprises that had paid regular dividends," it was argued. The general public was unaware of the intrinsic problems of government ownership, and given Polymer's profitable status, its disposal might be seen as the government selling out to its friends.[99] Faced with these concerns, the Cabinet was reluctant at this stage to endorse the committee's findings and authorize Polymer's disposal. Instead it was decided to postpone any concrete decision until a later date.[100]

On 7 September 1960, when the Cabinet next met to consider Polymer's future, Raymond O'Hurley and the other Cabinet committee members were determined to get approval for Rowzee's growth program. While a decision on privatization could wait, the judgment on growth could not. Early on, the committee had gone on record as stating that the approval for the plan for growth "should not depend upon, nor await a decision as to, the future status of the company."[101] For some months, work at Polymer had been under way, and the company was now at the point where it had to either go ahead or turn back. A decision, O'Hurley informed the Cabinet, was "required urgently."[102]

Despite O'Hurley's appeal, the Cabinet chose to settle the matter of ownership first. Again the discussion flowed endlessly and repetitively. The pros and cons of private ownership were discussed without resolution. To further complicate matters, a new proposal was tabled recommending that Polymer be sold on the basis that 50 percent of the equity be acquired by domestic industry, 25 percent by the Canadian public and 25 percent by the Crown. It was argued that such a structure would allow the government to partially privatize the corporation without losing the ability "to exercise considerable influence over the policies of the company."[103]

It was a remarkable notion given the hands-off approach successive governments had taken toward Polymer. There was a precedent, however, for such an arrangement. In 1954, the Social Credit government in Alberta had established the Alberta Gas Trunk Line (AGTL) as a "defensive," or "province-building," response to C.D. Howe's plans to build the Trans-Canada pipeline. AGTL was a hybrid corporation, or "half-way house," as political economists John Richards and Larry Pratt put it, created to carry all the natural gas produced within the province for export.[104] Alberta's premier, Ernest Manning, was opposed to public ownership both in principle and practice, but he needed a corporate vehicle to protect and promote Alberta's interests in the field. AGTL was the structural solution. It was owned by the province's gas producers, gas exporters, and gas utilities, and by government. Despite this precedent, however, there was opposition to the proposal in the Diefenbaker Cabinet. The opponents argued that while they could conceive of no technical problems with such a structure, there would be "real" political problems associated with it. The government, critics argued, would be forced to "make decisions which other shareholders might not like or, to acquiesce on decisions which might not be in the best interest of the country."[105] The Cabinet was again at an impasse.

Perpetually preoccupied with the political ramifications of its decisions, the Cabinet was unable to reach a decision regarding the sale of Polymer. The neophyte minister O'Hurley, who was often out of his depth in Ottawa, was neither powerful nor persuasive enough to force a resolution. Instead, the Cabinet decided to first "test" the public's reaction to a possible sale by making public the recommendations of Polymer's directors and management.[106] Incessantly calculating and recalculating the possible impact of its political decisions, the Cabinet could not bring itself to put to rest, once and for all, the matter of privatization. It was still under review two years later when the Glassco Royal Commission on Government Organization concluded that public ownership of Polymer was "unwarranted."[107] "The corporation," the commission determined, "cannot be regarded as an instrument of public policy. Its ownership by the Crown is in no sense essential, on security or other grounds, to any of the programs of the federal government."[108] The commission did recognize, however, that the transfer of Polymer to private ownership "presents certain practical problems which so far, have proved very obstinate."[109] While the commission's recommendation renewed private industry's quest for Polymer, it did little to prompt action on the part of the government. As was so often the case (for example, when considering whether to accept American nuclear warheads for Bomarc missiles) the government's indecision ultimately resulted in paralysis. Remarkably, the government's inaction did not hurt Polymer. The company was innovative enough to prosper in spite of continued government ownership.

While the Diefenbaker government was unable to settle the issue of privatization, it did have the foresight to authorize Rowzee's plan for growth. In its report, the special Cabinet committee considering Polymer's future warned of "far-reaching consequences" if the government did not support the growth program.[110] In September the Cabinet took notice and "approved the growth program recommended by the Board of Directors of Polymer and endorsed in principle by the special cabinet committee."[111] Soon thereafter, Raymond O'Hurley explained the government's decision to industry: "Polymer cannot stand still. Change and growth are for it, as for all organizations, the inescapable conditions of life ... A growth program now seems to be essential if Polymer's position in international markets is to be maintained and enhanced."[112] "We are going ahead with the expansion now," O'Hurley stated elsewhere, "without thought as to whether the government will sell Polymer or not."[113]

For the second time in its history, Polymer's intellectual cabal had determined government policy on an issue of national importance. The first time had come at the end of the war, when the board of directors – on the merits of Rowzee's argument – had won approval for the plant's continued operation under government ownership. That decision had proved remarkably provident. It remained to be seen if the government's latest decision would prove similarly sagacious.

It had always been Rowzee's contention that Polymer's growth as a Crown corporation was possible, albeit more difficult than if the corporation was privately owned.[114] There were obstacles to growth as a Crown corporation that would not have existed had Diefenbaker privatized the firm. But he had not done so, and now these obstacles would have to be overcome. First and foremost was the problem of financing the expansion. Rowzee's plan called for an expenditure of approximately $45 million, but positive cash flow would provide only half that amount.[115] If the program was to succeed, therefore, Polymer would have to be very creative in developing the financial and organizational structure to implement its corporate strategy for growth.

In late 1960 the company aggressively moved into the European market, establishing Polymer Corporation SAF to build and operate a specialty-rubber plant in France. Since the end of the war, the French had been Polymer's best single customer among the European nations. As Rowzee informed the standing committee on public accounts in 1961, Polymer was "well and favourably known in the Rubber industry in France which is very large and well organized."[116] Roger Hatch had developed close relationships with all Polymer's customers in France, but he was particularly close to the Michelin family – Polymer's largest customer in Europe. Due in large measure to Hatch's efforts,

Polymer Corporation's (SAF) plant in Fribourg, France. National Archives of Canada.

the French market in 1957 represented 15 percent of Polymer's total sales volume.[117] But sales dropped off thereafter, as a result of import restrictions that favoured American firms. To circumvent these restrictions, Polymer decided to construct a $12-million plant at Strasbourg to produce roughly ten thousand tons of specialty rubber per year. To help finance the project, Polymer SAF took on the Banque de Paris et des Pays Bas as a minority shareholder. While the French bank's stake was only 5 percent, it provided valuable assistance in arranging the financing, in obtaining the necessary government approvals, and in counseling Polymer about business practices in France.

Rowzee's growth plan also called for expanding production of butyl rubber – thus continuing Polymer's move away from general-purpose rubbers, for which the technological know-how was now readily available. After a period of relative decline – due to the introduction of the tubeless tire in 1954 – demand for butyl rubber was again on the rise. As a result of new applications (e.g., automobile weather stripping and seals, pharmaceutical stoppers, emulsion paint and roof coating) and the successful marketing of a butyl passenger tire, consumption of butyl rubber bounced back after 1957. Over the next five years, annual consumption increased at a rate of approximately 10 percent.[118] When Rowzee took over the presidency from Barrington in 1957, Polymer was supplying approximately 29 percent of the world demand for butyl. But by 1961, the company's share of the market had dropped to just over 15 percent. Polymer's principal competitor, Esso, a subsidiary of Standard Oil of New Jersey, was acting aggressively in the field, developing new uses for butyl rubber and expanding into foreign markets. Due to Esso's initiatives, Polymer's share of the market had been reduced considerably, and executives at Polymer worried that if the company did not increase its output soon, its market share would shrink even further.[119]

Polymer desperately wanted to retain the butyl market, from which a good deal of its net income was derived. Polymer was one of only two companies in the world – the other being Esso – that possessed the technology for its manufacture. At a time when burgeoning world production and increasing competition were gradually knocking down world prices and profit margins on general-purpose rubber, the price of butyl rubber remained relatively high. As early as 1951, Rowzee had anticipated these developments. But at that time, due to the shifting requirements of Canadian industry, he had argued against increasing production of butyl rubber.[120] By 1962, however, circumstances had changed, and Rowzee's pragmatic mind had changed along with them. Now he and the rest of Polymer's brain trust believed that with general-purpose type rubber, it was better to sell know-how to new foreign manufacturers or take a small participating interest, rather than to engage in production directly.[121] As a result, during the mid-1960s Polymer took a "know how" participation in styrene-butadiene rubber (SBR, formerly designated GR-S) plants in Mexico and South Africa. While the 1960s witnessed the proliferation of SBR producers around the world, the duopoly in butyl rubber remained.[122] The complex manufacturing process created a barrier to entry that could not be overcome even by the most innovative and industrious firms.

Once Polymer had committed itself to expanding butyl production, the question that remained was where to locate the new facility. Three locations were initially considered by the board of directors: Sarnia, the United Kingdom, and Belgium. Sarnia was quickly ruled out, however. At a time when Polymer was exporting roughly 90 percent of its butyl rubber to Europe, expanding the facilities in Sarnia simply did not make business sense.[123] It was estimated that if the Sarnia facilities were expanded the company could hold a 15 percent share of the market. But if a plant was built in Belgium or the United Kingdom, Polymer's share could be increased to 20 to 25 percent, due to its proximity to the major consuming areas. The United Kingdom was considered desirable because it represented a large domestic market with a business climate and methods very similar to Polymer's own.[124] Belgium, on the other hand, had a relatively small domestic market

Butyl rubber manufacturing process.

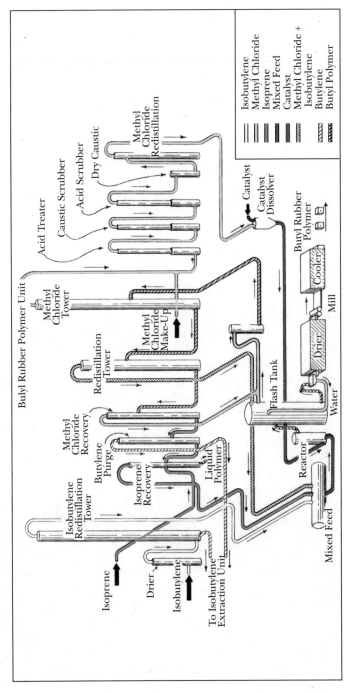

To this day, the production of butyl rubber is one of the most complicated commercial processes in the world. By reaction with itself (polymerization) and a small amount of isoprene, isobutylene forms a butyl rubber. This polymer forms instantly when the reactants, diluted in an inert solvent and at the extreme cold of − 140°F, meet a catalyst. The isobutylene and isoprene are mixed with methyl chloride in exact proportions in the mixed-feed tank. As shown in the diagram, this mixed feed enters the reactor, where it meets a solution of aluminium chloride in methyl chloride. On contact with this catalyst, solid white particles of butyl rubber polymer are formed. The methyl chloride carries the suspended polymer particles into the flash tank where hot water evaporates the gaseous methyl chloride, leaving the polymer suspended in the water. The butyl rubber polymer is separated on a vibrating screen, passed through a drier, and formed into a continuous sheet. The sheet is cut into slabs for shipment to the rubber factories.

and a somewhat different way of doing business. However, the patent situation in the United Kingdom was precarious. Esso claimed to have the sole right to license butyl production, and it was not willing to extend the right to Polymer. The patent situation in Belgium was less problematic, since Esso held no Belgian patents in the field. In the end, what decided the matter was the fact that it would be easier to finance a plant in Belgium than in the United Kingdom.

During the early 1960s, the Belgian government, eager to attract industry, was offering incentives in the form of construction loans to multinational companies like Polymer. Up to 60 percent of the capital requirements could be borrowed at a guaranteed rate of 2.5 percent for twenty years. The incentives appealed to the Crown company, which was looking for ways to finance its expansion program, since, unlike in France, Polymer could build without having any equity held by outside interests. At the board of directors meeting held in July 1961, it was unanimously agreed that the company should proceed with building the plant in Belgium.[125]

The aggressive international competition that drove Polymer into manufacturing operations in Europe was also the decisive force behind the establishment of an international marketing centre in Fribourg, Switzerland. Marketing efforts overseas had always received major emphasis in the corporate setting, but the new competitive environment demanded stronger ties with distributors and customers. It was believed that by establishing a separate division responsible for sales outside North America, Polymer could better coordinate production and marketing and that this, in turn, would achieve cost savings, as well as improvements in the efficiency of product distribution. Thus, in 1962 Polymer set up Polysar International SA (PISA) in Switzerland to market all its products outside North America and provide technical services in all export marketing areas. To head the new international marketing organization the board appointed Roger Hatch, who was the obvious choice, since Polymer's success in Europe had been largely a result of his sales and marketing efforts over the past fifteen years.

The decision to locate in Fribourg, Switzerland, was again primarily a financial one. Always working the numbers, Polymer's vice-president of finance, Stan Wilk, had determined that by establishing an international marketing centre in Switzerland, the company could avoid excessive taxation on repatriation of earnings from overseas operations. To do this, Wilk suggested a complex series of arrangements that would see Polymer's majority stake in Polymer SAF transferred to PISA, whose equity, in turn, would be transferred to a holding company in Holland. The holding company, Polysar Nederland N.V., would thus serve as a vehicle by which profits from Polymer's European subsidiaries could be transmitted to Sarnia under the favourable tax conventions between Switzerland and the Netherlands and the Netherlands and Canada.

Wilk was a master of such savvy schemes. Indeed, it was his creative thinking on financial matters that had brought him to the attention of executives at Polymer in the first place. During the war, Wilk, an American-born chemical engineer by training, had been a key member of the economic division of the U.S. Office of the Petroleum Administration for War (PAW). While at PAW, Wilk had helped Polymer negotiate a number of contracts with American petroleum companies. At the end of the war, Nicholson and Rowzee persuaded him to come and manage Polymer's petroleum economics in Sarnia. When Rowzee became president, Wilk was promoted to the position of vice-president of finance, and when the Dutch company was formed, he was given the top post.[126]

While Wilk's creative proposal was viewed favourably by the board of directors, some critics in Diefenbaker's Cabinet argued that Wilk's proposal was tantamount to tax evasion, an action unbecoming to a Canadian corporation, especially one that was government-owned.[127] But others in Cabinet took a more sympathetic stance. Having studied the implications of Wilk's proposal, O'Hurley, Fleming, and the secretary to the Cabinet, R.B. Bryce, concluded that the arrangement was "in line with normal business practice."[128] Polymer would simply be doing what other commercial firms seeking to maximize their profits were already doing in Europe. They therefore recommended that Polymer be authorized to go ahead with Wilk's proposal. The majority in Cabinet agreed, and in mid-1962 Polysar Nederland N.V. went into operation with Wilk as its head. By structuring its operations as Wilk had suggested, Polymer managed to save roughly $4 million dollars a year in taxes. In the years that followed, the increased cash flow was used to finance the growth effort.[129] Through creative schemes like this, Polymer moved closer to realizing Rowzee's objective of "serving the world."[130]

In the meantime revolutionary technological developments were taking place. In 1952 the director of the Max Plank Institut für Kohlenforschung in Mülheim in Germany, Dr Karl Ziegler, a German chemist with a strong eye for practical applications, announced a new class of catalysts that could bring about polymerization of ethylene, propylene, and other olefins at low pressures. For some time, scientists had appreciated the importance of the catalyst in the production of straight-chained polymers. During the 1930s and 1940s, the subject had engaged many leading polymer chemists – Herman Mark, Maurice Huggins, Paul Flory, and Calvin Schildknecht. But it was the work of

Ziegler that demonstrated to the world just how fundamental catalyst technology was to achieving the requisite high degree of control and regularity in synthetic structures.[131] Ziegler, who was later awarded a Nobel prize in chemistry for his discovery, found that mixing aluminum alkyl in a hydrocarbon solution formed a black precipitate that initiated the polymerization of ethylene at low pressure. The important feature of Ziegler's catalyst was that it allowed the polymer chemist to control the spatial arrangements of the monomer molecules during polymerization. Ziegler's discovery excited the engineering community. "Using these [organo-metallic] catalysts," Ralph Rowzee stated in 1959, "the polymer chemist can [now] come closer to preparing a polymer having a specific molecular configuration than ever before."[132] "I feel justified in suggesting to you," he continued, "that polymer chemistry and the synthetic rubber industry have entered a new phase in their development."[133] Ziegler's discovery of a new way of putting the building blocks of polymers together promised a whole new class of polymeric materials. Sensing this, during the 1950s American petrochemical companies flocked to Ziegler's laboratory in Mülheim, Germany, to procure the necessary licences to use his catalyst technology.

It did not come cheaply, however. The American chemical giant Hercules, for example, paid $350,000 for a nonexclusive one-year option on Ziegler's know-how with respect to ethylene polymers, copolymers, and other olefin polymers.[134] Du Pont, on the other hand, paid $50,000 in advance just to get a look at Ziegler's laboratory notes.[135] Goodrich-Gulf, a joint company established in 1954 to commercialize petroleum-based plastics, also paid Ziegler $50,000, in this case for a one-month option to examine samples of Ziegler's polyethylene and reach a decision about a permanent licence.[136]

In 1954 Polymer joined those making the pilgrimage to Mülheim. That year Buckler visited Dr Ziegler to explore the possibility of using these new catalysts. He found Ziegler to be most hospitable and engaging. The two men discovered they had a good deal in common: each held a PHD in chemistry, Buckler from Cambridge, Ziegler from Marburg University. Each had become too interested in practical applications of science to remain in the world of academe or take up a position elsewhere as a "pure" scientist. Each, instead, had entered industry and had created R&D departments that encouraged communication, cooperation, and creative thinking. Each was passionate and philosophical about his work and enjoyed early success.[137]

While appreciative of the long-term implications of Ziegler's work, Buckler decided that at this stage Ziegler's discoveries were not of direct interest to Polymer's synthetic-rubber operation. In the following year, Buckler and Dougan made a second visit to Mülheim to follow up on further advances. They learned that Goodrich-Gulf and Phillips Petroleum had taken out restricted licences to investigate the use of these catalysts to polymerize butadiene and isoprene. In December 1955 Goodrich-Gulf announced that a catalyst composition had been found that would convert isoprene to a polymer (i.e., cis 1,4 polyisoprene) having substantially the same structure as natural rubber. Nearly a century after the Englishman Greville Williams had succeeded in doing exactly the reverse, Goodrich-Gulf had achieved an almost exact synthesis of natural rubber from isoprene. Goodrich-Gulf quickly made the news public. "American scientists have finally succeeded in reproducing the molecule of crude, or tree-grown rubber," stated the president of Goodrich-Gulf. "It is a major scientific achievement," he continued, "a goal of world scientists for generations."[138] Moreover, Phillips Petroleum had announced another variation of this type of catalysts that converted butadiene, that was much less expensive than isoprene, into polybutadiene – a substance that showed promise as a tire rubber. These announcements were stimulating widespread research in the field, and Polymer decided that rather than taking out a licence at that point, it would be better to become knowledgeable in the field and await clarification of the overall patent position.

Polymer had learned that introducing a new tire rubber was a very risky business. Tire failures could lead to fatalities that could put a tire manufacturer in jeopardy. Expensive, large-scale testing was thus felt necessary before adopting any major change in raw rubber, both in making the tires and in evaluating tire performance. Furthermore, no tire company wished to rely on a single source of tire rubber unless they made it themselves. Hence, the correct strategy for Polymer to follow was to wait until the tire companies had decided what they wanted and then to use its commercial, geographic, and technical position to negotiate licences.

In the late 1950s the general opinion in the industry was that polybutadiene was the preferred material. Small-scale testing had shown that it had phenomenal wear resistance and resilience, far exceeding the properties of natural rubber or synthetic polyisoprene.[139] Polymer was urged therefore to undertake manufacture in Canada of polybutadiene in order to provide the tire companies with raw material for truck tires. Based on its own studies and pilot-plant developments, Polymer decided finally to take a licence from Goodrich-Gulf for its catalyst to make polybutadiene, rather than know-how from Phillips Petroleum. Shortly before the Polymer polybutadiene plant came into operation, however, information came to light, first from a company in the United Kingdom and then confirmed in the United States, that polybutadiene was extremely "nervy" and difficult to mix and extrude in the factory. Even worse, the treads of truck tires made from polybutadiene developed severe "chipping" and "chunking" and fell to pieces after only a few weeks of heavy service. Studies by several groups, and particularly by Polymer, suggested that the phenomenon was due to progressive cross-linking of the polybutadiene chains arising from free radicals generated by chain scission during deformation.[140] The problem did not arise in treads made from natural rubber, because the free radicals produced from polyisoprene are much less reactive and are destroyed without causing damage.

No means could be found for preventing the chipping and chunking in treads made wholly or mainly of this type of polybutadiene. However, it was found that the effect was suppressed when the polybutadiene was blended with about equal parts of ordinary styrene-butadiene rubber. These blends were not sufficiently resilient for truck tires, but the superior wear resistance of polybutadiene carried through and produced a superior tread stock for passenger tires. (The blend is to this day the standard composition for all passenger tires). It was also found by Polymer that a few percentages of this type of polybutadiene markedly reduced the brittleness of polystyrene plastic; the polybutadiene made with the Goodrich-Gulf catalyst was preferred over other types because it was almost colourless.

Despite these innovative efforts, narrowing profit margins within the industry led some company members to question whether Polymer could survive in the future solely as a synthetic-rubber producer.[141] As early as 1962, Buckler had predicted a stormy future for independent manufacturers of general-purpose rubber (i.e., SBR).[142] "The SBR plants under the greatest challenge will be the independent producers, particularly those depending to any degree on export business."[143] Only those heavily integrated companies with captive or protected markets, he predicted, would survive in the field. Buckler was sanguine, however, that Polymer would continue to prosper as producer of specialty rubbers so long as the research and development program was expanding.[144]

In 1966 Buckler pondered the future for Polymer Corporation as a manufacturer of synthetic polymeric materials. "To survive," he stated, "it must supply the long-established materials in quality, price and quantity with such efficiency that the fabricators do not seek to manufacture their own materials." In addition, Buckler maintained, the company must use its resources "to launch new materials and nurse them through their early uneconomic stages."[145] Others, however, were less optimistic and argued that the company should diversify into unrelated areas of production. Lower net income in 1966 and 1967 served to further fuel the pessimism.

Dr E.J. Buckler addressing industry executives in Fribourg, Switzerland on recent innovations in the synthetic rubber field, 1964. National Archives of Canada.

The company had followed through on Rowzee's strategy for growth, and from a technical point of view it had done everything right. It had formulated a bold strategy and implemented an innovative structure that saw production double between 1960 and 1966. It had created an international marketing company to better serve its customers. It had invested in state-of-the-art technology and R&D, which had caused productivity to soar.[146]And finally, it had expanded geographically to gain a manufacturing presence in its most important markets. In the process, Polymer had helped redefine state capitalism in Canada. Polymer's external commercial expansion was in stark contrast to the "defensive expansionism" that had traditionally defined Canadian economic policy.

Unfortunately, however, net income did not increase as had been anticipated. In 1960, Rowzee had confidently stated that "a successful growth program would mean … a possible doubling of the profit over the next ten years."[147] But this increase did not happen, for various reasons. Although sales were increasing, selling prices were not, as the price-cost squeeze throughout the industry continued, especially with respect to salaries and wages and feedstock prices. Rising costs, combined with surplus world capacity, offset the productivity increases of more efficient plants. This was – as one observer noted – a "strange boom, indeed."[148] Investment in inventories also grew as the company sought to balance economies of scale and market demand. Another important factor was the increased cost of the debt financing. The capital expenditure programs required large amounts of long-term debt. The rising cost of doing business reduced Polymer's 1967 net income to its lowest level in many years – $5.8 million (see table A1).

Nevertheless, from a long-term perspective, Rowzee's growth program was a success. During the period 1960–66 – a time of aggressive competition and narrowing profit margins – net income as a percentage of net sales and other income remained at roughly the same levels it had been during the period 1953–59. Polymer thus continued to profit the Crown.

The challenge that Polymer faced during the period 1958–66 was to maintain its previous level of prosperity in the face of increasing global competition. The global petrochemical industry had always been highly competitive, but after 1960 the competition became cutthroat. Faced with losing market share, Polymer embraced a strategy of multi-nationalization. Again Polymer's managerial cabal called on the government to widen the parameters of its mission. Polymer maintained that by building manufacturing plants overseas, it would be better able to meet the demands of its foreign customers. Going global was risky business and quite different from serving a staid domestic market. To survive in the global economy, a corporation needed to be agile, strategic of vision, and ready to feed its hunches with capital and R&D. During the period under review, Polymer had done this and in the process had broken the historical pattern of Canadian manufacturing. By creatively structuring its expansion and developing its organizational capabilities, Polymer had managed to maintain a favourable position throughout the world, despite U.S. competition and despite the fact that every industrialized nation was showing a determined intention to produce and market its own synthetic rubber. The Crown company abandoned the old branch-plant mentality, which was satisfied with hand-me-down technology, and began stressing R&D and demonstrating a constant vigilance for new technology. This was a new world for Canadian manufacturing. Polymer had managed to overcome the obstacles to growth and, despite continued government ownership, had continued to prosper in the international marketplace.

6

Decade of Discord:
Diversification and Denationalization,
1967–1977

If Polymer were to continue on its old course the best we could expect would
be a levelling-off and ultimate decline of profitability despite substantial new
capital. Our answer to this is to follow an aggressive program of expansion and
diversification to convert Polymer into a broader based aggressive business
force.

Ralph Rowzee (1969)[1]

The late 1960s and the 1970s witnessed the rapid adoption of diversification as a strategy for corporate growth.[2] Mature firms around the industrialized world strategically expanded into both related and
unrelated industries in an attempt to sustain their growth and development.[3] This became the age of the protean multinational corporation,
an enterprise dedicated to internationalization and the pursuit of synergies – a seemingly magical mixture of business activities that were
stronger and more profitable together than they were apart. As Alfred
Chandler has noted, in the 1960s and 1970s the drive for growth
through diversification "had almost become a mania."[4] In 1972, even
the Liberal government in Ottawa got caught up in the exuberance
when it created the Canada Development Corporation (CDC), a publicly sponsored, diversified conglomerate with portfolio investments in
mining, oil and gas, petrochemicals, life sciences, and information
processing. Without entirely abandoning old product lines, mature
companies embarked upon the production of new and intermediate
products, expanding their "basic areas" of manufacturing in the process. Increasingly, the "single business" or "specialized firm" became a
rarity. In 1969, for example, over 90 percent of the *Fortune* 500 companies were diversified to some extent.[5] The drive towards diversification

was facilitated by the stock market, which – at least in the 1960s and early 1970s – rewarded high-growth companies with high stock prices. As a result, many companies that had once made a handful of products began making hundreds, if not thousands, and many companies that were once involved in one or a few businesses expanded into many.

Beyond the rewards of a higher stock price, there were several more fundamental reasons why industrialized firms chose to diversify. As a strategy for corporate growth and development, diversification allowed a mature firm – at least in theory – to utilize its management skills more fully, spread its risk across several business cycles, and, concomitantly, seize opportunities for synergy. As early as 1955 business theorists like Peter Drucker began arguing that good managers needed to master certain general principles of management that were applicable in any business setting.[6] Drucker's *Practice of Management* became standard reading for a whole generation of corporate executives and led to a widespread belief in "general management skills." Given the currency of Drucker's ideas, it was not a great leap for many in the business community to conclude that "professional managers" – armed, as they were, with the latest portfolio techniques developed in consulting firms – might be able to use their skills in a variety of different business settings.[7] At one extreme, conglomerates like Canadian Pacific and E.P. Taylor's Argus Corporation sought growth by entering a wide range of different businesses. Similarly, in the 1970s Bell Canada, under the leadership of a savvy young lawyer named Jean de Grandpré, abandoned its conservative approach to business and joined what the editors of *Fortune* magazine termed the "conglomerate commotion."[8] The top managers of these conglomerates believed that they possessed distinctive general-management techniques and that by applying them to a large number of different businesses, they could grow profitably.

But diversification was not limited to firms seeking to utilize corporate competencies more fully. During the 1960s and 1970s, many other industrial companies diversified to spread their risk across a variety of different business cycles. When a company's core business was maturing, as Polymer's was by the late 1960s, corporate managers looked for growth opportunities in new areas of production. In part this approach was a response to the rapidly changing macroeconomic environment. After the Second World War, many traditional industries and markets experienced slower rates of growth as demographic shifts and technological innovations affected product markets. At the same time, intensified R&D and rising consumer incomes generated new goods and services. Given the shifting socioeconomic environment, many "old" industries faced with lagging demand chose to diversify into unrelated areas of production – those areas having nothing in common with the firm's other activities or resources – rather than limiting themselves to the destinies of their existing markets. In so doing, they situated themselves in several business cycles, thereby spreading their risk across a variety of ventures and reducing the volatility of their performance. A large firm with many products in many markets and producing in many different places was in theory less dependent on individual markets or technologies and therefore was less vulnerable to any single set of unfavourable circumstances. Such a strategy also opened up the possibility of cross-subsidization from mature to developing enterprises. In effect, these large diversifying firms rejected the classical doctrine of comparative advantage and embraced their own form of mercantilism. In place of specialization for higher returns, they substituted diversification in hopes of greater security.

By the 1980s, however, many diversified, multibusiness companies were encountering performance problems, and widespread skepticism about the ability of companies to manage and add value to multibusiness portfolios gained ground. Diversification was thus no panacea but required careful balancing and synergy. Du Pont's diversification program, which invested about $100 million in various generally unprofitable ventures, including a $50-million building materials debacle, was a strategic and financial failure.[9] The chemical giant was one of a number of companies that had embraced diversification only to find that the synergies it had anticipated simply were not there. Du Pont's Canadian subsidiary did not fare any better in "digging for profits" by diversifying into mining.[10] And Canadian Industries Limited's diversification into real estate did nothing to return the company to the profit level it had attained during the mid-1960s. The poor performance of firms like Du Pont, CIL, and CP Enterprises prompted a rethinking of both the role of the corporate centre and the sagacity of diversification.[11] Moreover, consultants and academics such as Tom Peters, Robert Hayes, and Michael Porter were increasingly hostile towards diversification, with several of their studies showing that diversification had generally performed poorly.[12] As a consequence, they and others advocated a renewed focus on selected "core" businesses. During the 1980s corporate restructuring in Canada and the United States began to reverse the trend of the previous two decades, and the percentage of diversified firms declined among the *Fortune* 500.[13] The period became one of "de-conglomeration" and "de-diversification," as corporations "shed assets" and got "back to basics." The trend was continued into the "lean and mean" 1990s. During the 1960s and 1970s, however, the tendency in business was towards diversification.

Polymer was not immune to the lure of diversification, further symbolizing that it was not a typical Crown corporation perpetually cloistered in a discrete sector of the economy. Indeed, its experience was remarkably similar to that of other multinational companies, particularly those in the petrochemical industry. Like Du Pont, CIL, Hercules, and Monsanto, Polymer's "core" business was maturing. In all its essential characteristics, synthetic rubber was now fully developed. The rapid technological innovations that had characterized the industry's infancy had thus tapered off. Polymer's product markets were established, and there were seemingly few new frontiers. As is often the case in a mature industry, competition for existing markets became the order of the day. In 1967, there were twenty-one nations producing synthetic rubber, more than double the number that there had been a decade earlier. World capacity, as a result, was in excess of demand. And while the gap between supply and demand for synthetic rubber was narrowing in North America, it was widening disproportionately in the rest of the world. This global overcapacity, in turn, caused a sharp decline in prices. Early in the life of synthetic rubber, when there were few competitors, profit levels were high. But these high profits, along with technological changes in the form of major and minor process innovations, attracted additional competitors into the field. As the number of producers increased, price cuts caused profit levels to decline.[14]

Since ascending to the presidency in 1957, Ralph Rowzee had witnessed the price of SBR, the principal product of the synthetic-rubber industry, decline by almost 23 percent in North America and somewhat more in Europe. The price of polybutadiene showed a similar trend, declining 33 percent since first being commercially produced in 1960. Although butyl rubber continued to retain its value on world markets, the overall pattern in the rubber market was disturbing as far as Rowzee was concerned, and it led him to question whether there was a place in the future for an independent, undiversified synthetic-rubber producer like Polymer.[15] Adding further to Rowzee's anxiety was the fact that inflationary pressures were increasing the cost of materials and services. Salaries and wages, particularly in Canada, were rising faster than corresponding gains in productivity, leading to higher labour costs. Rising costs and declining prices reduced net income in 1967 to the lowest level since 1959, the year of the ninety-day strike.[16]

Polymer's management was no less concerned about the 1967 results – which carried over, to some extent, into 1968 – than would private sector entrepreneurs have been in similar circumstances. Even the perennially upbeat Rowzee, who in 1967 was entering his tenth year as president of the corporation, was forced to concede that the company's financial performance was "disappointing."[17] He had not anticipated the "profit squeeze" seven years earlier when he put forward his strategy for growth and multinationalization.[18] No one at Polymer had. But in 1967, for the second year in a row, there was a marked rise in the cost of doing business and a corresponding decline in profitability.

To be sure, Rowzee had experienced the cyclical nature of the rubber trade before. As a young research chemist working at Goodyear Tire and Rubber Company during the Depression, he had seen the bottom drop out of the rubber market. And after coming to Polymer in 1942, he had witnessed several cyclical downturns, the most severe of which came during the period 1957–59, when net income fell in each succeeding year. But the downturn in 1967 was far more unsettling to Rowzee and others at the corporation, in that, unlike before, it occurred at a time of increasing sales. Indeed, Polymer had never sold as much as it did in 1967 – $128.9 million worth of products and services. That was over $1.3 million more than the preceding year, and yet net income was just over half of its 1966 level.[19] This new and disconcerting phenomenon led some industry analysts to conclude that Polymer was in a "declining business" from which it needed to escape.[20]

The "profit squeeze" and Polymer's declining fortunes precipitated a crisis in managerial confidence. In 1967, for the first time in its history, Polymer's management began to doubt its own entrepreneurial competence.[21] Some senior managers, like Roger Hatch, felt that Polymer had stayed too long with a technology that had a disappearing premium and that the company had failed to anticipate changing conditions with timely action.[22] Further down the corporate ladder, others began to question whether Polymer's executives were capable of realizing the full potential of the rubber business.[23] Occasionally, fingers were pointed. The marketing department, for example, accused the department of research and development of being out of touch with the needs of consumers. The company's renowned esprit de corps, which had been the hallmark of earlier years, seemed to vanish during what one observer termed "the traumatic experience of 1967–1968."[24] The unity and harmony of the postwar years was increasingly hard to muster in this age of declining prices and increasing competition.

The tendency toward condemnatory introspection was reflected in the virtual suspension of executive action. For more than a year between 1967 and 1968, Polymer's solution to the profit squeeze was to cut costs and take a more critical approach to existing methods of operation. In 1967 Rowzee was still sanguine that an increase in productivity would generate the profits necessary for the next leap forward in synthetic-rubber development. Only such an advance, he informed the International Institute of Synthetic Rubber Producers in Montreal in

April 1967, would save synthetic rubber from becoming "a commodity article, with price alone being the basis for competition."[25]

But by 1969, Rowzee and other top executives at Polymer had decided that a more radical response was needed. Polymer would have to expand into new areas of production in order to survive and prosper in the future. "It is imperative that the Company diversify," Roger Hatch stated, "so that it is less dependent on the vagaries of the rubber business."[26] Rowzee agreed. In December 1969 he wrote to the minister of supply and services in Ottawa, James Richardson, stating that he was now convinced that "the risks of continuing as a one purpose company are far too great to be accepted."[27] "In the future," he continued, "we intend to be a broad-based business force."[28] As in the past, Ottawa's response was that the Crown corporation knew best.[29]

The strategic groundwork for Polymer's diversification program was laid down in a lengthy 1969 report written by William F. Ackerman, a business consultant from New York. At a time when Rowzee was looking for an outsider to help him determine the future course of Polymer's activities, Ackerman came highly recommended by Russell Baker, one of Polymer's long-time advisers on international corporate structure. Ackerman's final *Report* set the company's strategic course for the next decade. According to Ackerman, in order to survive, Polymer would have to diversify into related and unrelated areas of production.[30] The world, he maintained, was becoming a more complex and competitive place. The trend in business was toward integration, diversification, and conglomeration. Within the petrochemical industry, integrating pressures on both feedstock suppliers (the oil companies) and their customers (the rubber fabricators) were great and growing. Polymer, as a relatively small and specialized firm, was out of step with these international business developments and, as a result, was vulnerable to a takeover bid by a larger firm. Ackerman warned that if Polymer was to survive as an independent entity, it would have to think anew and head in a different strategic direction.

Ackerman suggested a "drastic break" with the past.[31] To date, Polymer's strategy had been to develop and produce a variety of synthetic rubbers and to sell them aggressively in emerging markets around the globe. This strategy had been foreshadowed in 1944 when Polymer established its research and development department. In the early 1960s, an international marketing centre and manufacturing facilities were established overseas to augment the corporate structure in pursuit of Polymer's business strategy. But Ackerman wanted Polymer "to think [about] synthetic rubber less."[32] If it did not, he warned, the old "one-purpose company" mentality would eventually lead to the extinction of the firm.

Ackerman was skeptical that Buckler's R&D department, which was relatively small and underfunded, could sustain its high level of innovation. This was not a criticism of Buckler per se or of the members of his department. It was simply that in Ackerman's mind, research could not do much to force the overall trend of technology now that the synthetic-rubber industry had reached its maturity.[33] Without the dramatic technological breakthroughs of the past, Ackerman predicted that on its current course Polymer's return on equity would approximate just 6.75 percent per annum within eight years.[34] That kind of return, he maintained, would not be enough to guarantee Polymer's survival. "Another year like 1967, in which several harmful developments coincided, would produce heavy losses," Ackerman cautioned, "and would weaken Polymer irretrievably."[35] At that point, he continued, Polymer would be absorbed at a distress price by a larger foreign company.[36]

The possibility of the company being taken over by a larger, integrating company sent shivers down the corporate spine. Rowzee, Hatch, Buckler, and Rush shared an unassailable feeling that Polymer was *their* corporation. "It was our baby," Roger Hatch later recalled, "and we were determined to see it continue to grow under our direction."[37] The feeling stemmed from a common history, a history that in 1969 stretched back over a quarter of a century and consisted of a number of defining moments. At the end of the war, for example, when most observers had consigned Polymer to oblivion, the board of directors, on the advice of Rowzee and upper management, had decided to carry on, and they ultimately proved to Canadian nay-sayers that synthetic rubber was a commercially viable industry. In the years that followed, a number of American firms had in fact emulated Polymer's move. The result, ironically, was stiff international competition and again the critics were quick to write off Polymer. But once more Polymer confounded its critics, this time by becoming a multinational operation with manufacturing plants and a marketing centre overseas. "The white elephant," noted the *Financial Times* in 1964, "has [again] made good."[38]

From its birth, the company had been immune to the protectionist mentality that had held sway in Canada since the 1870s. Despite being government-owned and government-controlled, Polymer had prospered without subsidies or protective tariffs. Such prosperity had consequently given Polymer's informal executive cabal a strong attachment to the firm. Rowzee and the others did not want to see control pass from their hands. Diversification appealed as a natural antidote to such a possibility. Polymer was at "a critical point," Ackerman stated in his report, and as at the end of the war, upper management and the board of directors had a difficult strategic decision to make. In his opinion, Polymer could either conservatively continue down the same path or, as before, boldly plot a new course to convert Polymer from "a take-over prospect to an increasing threat to take over a large fabricator, a large oil company, or both."[39] Ackerman was convinced of the wisdom of the more daring course and claimed to have the road map necessary for heading in a new strategic direction.

In addition to continuing to cut costs to achieve maximum efficiency and developing effective systems in order to upgrade end products, Ackerman had argued that Polymer needed to diversify and expand into related and unrelated areas of production. "Diversification," he stated, "is essential to Polymer's long-term future."[40] In terms of related, or what Ackerman termed "congeneric" diversification, he felt that it would be necessary for Polymer to expand into areas of manufacturing that would further utilize the firm's existing organizational capabilities.[41]

This course of action had proved successful for Du Pont in the second decade of the twentieth century, to Hercules in the 1920s, and to Union Carbide in the 1930s.[42] It had allowed these multidivisional chemical companies to exploit the economies of scope existing in their major functional units – production, distribution, and research. The top and middle managers at these firms were able to draw on their experiences and skills in order to make the strategic decisions necessary to achieve and maintain first-mover advantages for their new products.[43] For Polymer, however, expansion into related areas of production alone would not be enough, according to Ackerman, to generate the rate of growth necessary for survival, presumably because these related diversifications, by definition, would still be in the petrochemical field, a field that Ackerman felt was in relative economic decline. Thus, he maintained, diversification into unrelated fields would also be necessary. According to Ackerman, Polymer would have to "seek out and acquire basic positions in newer, faster-growing, and preferably technically oriented industries ... that combine a high growth rate and acceptable profits."[44] In these cases the investment projects would have nothing in common with Polymer's other activities. They would be unrelated to existing facilities and capabilities.

Ackerman's recommendations were received enthusiastically by Rowzee. Feeling that Ackerman's report provided the focus, framework, and direction that was urgently required, Rowzee sent a memorandum on 6 May 1969 to the company's senior personnel. "I am happy to be able to present to you a plan for our future," it stated. "It is one in which I have great confidence."[45] Echoing Ackerman, Rowzee maintained that if Polymer was to continue on its "old" course, the

Ian C. Rush at his desk shortly after being appointed executive vice-president of operations in 1969.

best that could be expected was a "levelling-off and ultimately a decline of profitability." The answer to this, he stated, was to follow an aggressive program of expansion and diversification that would "convert Polymer into a broader-based aggressive business force."[46] Ackerman confidently predicted that by following this new strategy for growth, Polymer would see a tripling of sales within the next eight years and a return on equity of 13.72 percent by 1977.[47] It was anticipated that by that time, about half of Polymer profits would be derived from new businesses. "The goal," Ralph Rowzee informed the *Chemical and Engineering News* in 1970, "is to reach a 50–50 mix of rubber-nonrubber sales within the next 10 years."[48] The day after Rowzee's memorandum, the *Financial Post* reported "a strong new note of optimism at the top-management level at Polymer Corporation."[49]

To implement the new strategy, management was split into two main divisions. One would seek to maximize profits in the old rubber and latex operations. The other would look for new investments in related and unrelated fields of production. To oversee Polymer's existing businesses, Rowzee appointed Ian Rush as executive vice-president. Rush was a no-nonsense chemical engineer who, after receiving an MSC from the University of British Columbia in 1943, joined Canadian Synthetic Rubber. When CSR was absorbed by Polymer in 1950, he was appointed Polymer's assistant technical superintendent. Early on, Rush demonstrated his mettle at making difficult business decisions, and in 1962 he was appointed director of corporate planning. Tough, competitive, contemplative, and calculating, Rush did not suffer fools gladly and expected perfection both from himself and from those around him. To many, Rush was aloof and stand-offish. Indeed, more than one former colleague described him as a "cool fish."[50]

The man that Rowzee chose to oversee the development of new business activities, on the other hand, was in many ways the very antithesis of Rush. Outspoken, restless, and gregarious, Roger Hatch was first and foremost a salesman. He was always on the go, always marketing, always looking to the next big adventure. During the 1950s Hatch had pioneered sales to China, believing that if he could put just one pair of rubber-soled shoes on each "Chinaman," he and Polymer would be set for life. Hatch was a ship in full sail. Thus, when he was offered the position of executive vice-president responsible for new enterprise development, he enthusiastically accepted. He was among the first to advocate diversification and was eager to see the rapid development of new businesses.

Time, according to Hatch, was of the essence. The feedback Hatch was receiving from his many friends within the industry was that Polymer's competitors had already begun to diversify. So committed to diversification was Monsanto, for instance, that in 1964 it dropped the word "chemical" from its name. Three years later, it created a new enterprise department to search out new business ideas inside and outside the company. The new fields in which it invested included electronics, graphic systems, educational toys, engineering composite systems, and protein foods.[51] In hopes of boosting its "inherent growth rate," Hercules had also established a new enterprise department in the late 1960s and diversified into such unrelated areas as information systems, health care, and prefabricated modular housing.[52] Du Pont's adventures in unrelated diversification bore remarkable parallels to those of Hercules. In the 1950s, Du Pont executives determined that they too needed to diversify by acquiring "small, highly technical companies" outside the petrochemical field. Thus, when Polymer embarked upon its diversification program at the end of the 1960s, it found itself a relative latecomer to a movement that had already been underway for almost a decade.

This did not discourage Hatch, however. It simply meant that Polymer would now have to be "fast on its feet."[53] In a letter dated 22 September 1969, he warned Ralph Rowzee to expect a good deal of competition when acquiring new businesses.[54] "A really good business opportunity," he stated, "usually involves several potential buyers."[55] To be competitive in such a situation, he continued, would require that his new department be given "the authority and financial backing" necessary for making a quick acquisition. In many instances, he predicted, time would not permit the "depth of study" that was normal during an expansion phase. Instead, the decision making would have to be "more intuitive and entrepreneurial or the business opportunity would likely be lost."[56]

In a memorandum prepared for the board of directors entitled "A Strategy for Growth," Hatch identified business opportunities in five broad areas – plastics systems, housing systems, computers, environmental controls, and pharmaceuticals – in which he felt Polymer should concentrate its development efforts.[57] Each he considered to be a "high-growth area," with good or high profit potential and with high technological content.[58] In the past almost all Polymer's efforts began with discovering new materials that might be useful in some way. What Hatch wanted to do was to turn this process on its head by starting with a market need and then looking for technologies to fill it.

Roger Hatch was most bullish about what he termed the "profitability potential" of housing systems. He predicted that the need for housing would accelerate in the near future and that new industrialized systems for housing would capture a large share of the market. At Expo 67, Hatch and other Polymer executives had been awestruck by Moshe Safdie's revolutionary Habitat.[59] The modular-housing complex, which was only a short distance from Polymer's own pavilion, was seemingly a graphic demonstration that industrializing the building process would create better and cheaper ways to house people. "It is almost axiomatic," Hatch wrote to Ralph Rowzee in September 1969, "that the traditional methods of home building will give way to an industrialized or factory approach whereby the efficiencies of mass production can be achieved in a similar manner to … the automobile industry."[60] Just as Henry Ford recognized the importance of "bringing the work to the workers," Hatch calculated that the centralization of materials and workers would result in tremendous savings and thus allow Polymer to provide affordable housing to the maturing baby-boom generation. When he looked out at the highly decentralized nature of the housing industry in Canada, he saw thousands of disorganized, unsophisticated builders needlessly duplicating their efforts. Hatch predicted the industrialization of the housing process would revolutionize the industry, leading to a few omnipotent nation-wide builders, of which Polymer, with its experience in cutting-edge technologies, would be one.[61]

In the late 1960s several American firms were developing the technology for industrialized home building. Hatch singled out Stressed

The coincidence of Polymer's twenty-fifth anniversary and the country's one hundredth anniversary led to an exciting centennial project – the Polymer Pavilion at Expo 67 in Montreal. Called Curiosity: A Way of Looking at Things, the white concrete pavilion was ingeniously constructed to represent a giant molecule. Its theme focused on the importance of human curiosity and how it had changed and enriched life for humankind. Polymer's pavilion was a short distance from Moshe Safdie's revolutionary Habitat. National Archives of Canada.

Structures Inc. (ssi) of Denver, Colorado, as the front runner in the field.[62] ssi had developed a patented technology named the "uniment system" for volume production of lightweight, completely serviced, reinforced concrete housing modules. The technology used a special concrete that expanded as it dried, elongating the reinforced steel in the three-dimensional structure and simultaneously placing the concrete under compression. This new technology allowed for very thin (2.5 inches thick), prestressed, load-bearing walls that made the finished prefabricated units remarkably light and therefore portable. The bulk of work could thus be done within a factory, rather than on site, bringing about economies of scale. In a statement prepared for the financial press, Polymer stated that it was unable to find any existing system that combined the architectural versatility, the high degree of industrialization, and the economic advantages of the uniment sys-

Roger Hatch, left, and George Bracewell examine the company's newest product line from Polymer's building systems division. National Archives of Canada.

tem.[63] "We believe that the technology for the building of chemically prestressed housing," Polymer's vice-president of corporate finance, George Bracewell stated, "is the best in the field and will prove itself superior to other modular systems."[64] In late September 1969, Polymer's board of directors endorsed Hatch's planned expenditure of $3.25 million to acquire a 13 percent stake in Stressed Structures Inc. and to license its technology for exclusive use in Canada and in Europe.[65] The board's approval was welcome news to Hatch, who had been pressing hard for an expansion into housing.[66]

From the start, however, the housing program was plagued by problems. Late delivery of key equipment delayed the start-up of Polymer's plant at Milton, Ontario. And after the plant finally came into operation in the latter part of 1972, factory operating problems were encountered, interrupting construction progress at key development sites. Such interruptions did not help Polymer's bid to industrialize the home-building industry. It was proving difficult enough to get real estate developers interested in the new technology and the delays at the

Milton plant were simply making matters worse. The principal reason
for the lack of enthusiasm on the part of developers was that the new
technology was turning out to be – to the shock and horror of Polymer's management – fundamentally flawed.[67] The concept of stressing
by using concrete that expanded during setting was demonstrated to
have worked well on small blocks in the laboratory. But remarkably,
Polymer, in its haste to diversify away from rubber, had not demanded
scale-up pilot-plant trials before purchasing the technology from SSI.
When building-sized sheets of concrete were fabricated, the relative
movement between the ends of the expanding concrete and the ends
of the reinforcing elements was so large that slippage occurred. The
concrete lost its grip on the embedded reinforcing steel and thus pre-
stressing could not be achieved. As a result, the modules had to be of
normal thickness and could not be stacked several stories high as had
been anticipated.

In an effort to overcome some of these problems, H.W. Suters,
former managing director of the Ontario Housing Corporation (OHC),
was brought in to oversee the building construction department. It was
hoped that Suters could use his contacts within the industry, particularly
those at OHC, to stimulate demand for Polymer's prefabricated, modular housing. He could not. After only a year of operations, the department had incurred "substantial" losses. In an effort to reverse the trend,
a new strategic plan was formulated for the division. Initially, the objective had been to build the prefabricated units and sell them to public
and private contractors who would use them for the construction of
condominiums, hospitals, and hotels. But the new plan widened the department's scope from builder to builder-developer. The division's new
objective was outlined in the company's 1973 annual report: "We seek a
position as a major builder-developer furnishing high quality housing
based on the modular concept at a cost competitive with that of the conventional business."[68]

The new plan required not only changes in design and production
methods but also investment in land. The move proved to be disastrous. Polymer had no experience in the field of land speculation. Almost immediately, it found that it was unable to compete with
traditional builder/developers who, ironically, were "faster on their
feet" and more adaptable to the changing demands of the housing industry. To make matters worse, in 1974 the extended boom of the preceding ten years came to an end. That year, real GDP growth in Canada
fell to 4.4 percent from 7.7 percent a year earlier. Despite the slowing
of the economy, consumer prices did not fall, and the annual inflation
rate jumped to over 10 percent. The cost of consumer borrowing rose

as a result, killing the Canadian consumer's appetite for housing. This, in turn, was a factor in the depressed state of the home-building market. In 1974, the number of housing starts in Canada dropped to 169,437 from 211,543 in the previous year.[69]

Unlike traditional builder/developers, who had little fixed overhead and therefore could easily downsize in the face of declining demand, Polymer's cost were fixed. The plant at Milton was of fixed scale and scope, which froze Polymer's investment even when there was a slump in building. In practice, therefore, conventional construction technology was, relatively, very flexible and cost effective and could be adapted to many different building styles in many locations. Polymer's modular housing technology could not.

With losses mounting, the decision was made to withdraw from the housing business. Four years of experience in the industry had convinced Polymer that modular housing was a dead end. The revolution in housing construction, which Hatch had bet on, had not occurred. Polymer had gambled and lost big. All the division's assets were subsequently written down to net realizable value and placed on the market. In total, the diversification into housing systems had cost Polymer over $20 million. This was hardly the start to diversification that the company had wanted or anticipated.

Polymer's diversification into the information-processing field was only slightly more successful.[70] In his 1969 report, Hatch predicted that in the years ahead the use of computers would extend to an ever increasing spectrum of business activities. "The use of computers in business," he presciently wrote to Rowzee in September 1969, "is only now scratching the surface."[71] Hatch was particularly interested in computer timesharing and therefore in Com-Share, one of the industry's leading companies. Incorporated in 1968, Com-Share entered the Canadian market with a business strategy based on the use of hardware developed in the United States. It emphasized software and application packages in step with computer hardware improvements. According to Hatch, Com-Share had "excellent technology and marketing capabilities" that would enable it "to meet the needs and demands of a wide range of organizations."[72] As a high-technology firm, Com-Share was considered a complement to Polymer's own emphasis on knowledge-based growth. In December 1969, the board of directors authorized another expenditure of $3.25 million, this time to acquire a 50 percent interest in Com-Share (Canada) and to expand its operations into Europe.[73] Under the terms of the sale agreement, Polymer would have six seats on Com-Share's eleven-person board of directors. In April 1970 Hatch, Bracewell, Dyke, Willoughby, Lewis, and Hibberd were elected.

Hatch felt that by acquiring an established business, Polymer could avoid some of the out-of-pocket costs for equipment and facilities, as well as overcome some of the managerial and technical difficulties that often bedeviled a firm entering a new area of production. He also believed that diversification through acquisition was the quickest way of gaining access to new business areas. Hatch intrinsically understood that there were basically two methods of expansion open to the firm: it could build new plants and create new markets for itself – what Hatch termed "grassroots expansion" – or it could acquire the plants and markets of already existing firms.[74] For the expeditious Hatch, expansion through acquisition was the preferable method. "Grassroots entries," he wrote to Rowzee in 1969, "will take considerably more time, greater pre-investment in staff and research resources and greater risk."[75] In Hatch's mind, therefore, the acquisition of Com-Share was the best and quickest way for Polymer to become "a major vendor offering on-line computer services."[76]

Unfortunately, in its haste to gain access to the computer field, Polymer overestimated Canadian demand for Com-Share's services. It had been blithely assumed that the Canadian market was similar to the U.S. market. But what executives failed to recognize was that many Canadian plants were subsidiaries of U.S. companies whose information processing was done in the United States. Thus, there was not the demand for Com-Share's services that had been anticipated. This poor assessment of the characteristics of the Canadian marketplace resulted in a loss of over $700,000 in 1970.

In the following year Com-Share did not fare any better. Technology and monitoring problems resulted in an operating loss of over $1.2 million. In September 1972 Hatch wrote to the board of directors that the investment in computer systems had fallen short of expectations. "In summary," he stated, "our investment in Com-Share Limited has to date failed to achieve the projected results."[77] In two and a half years of operation, Com-Share's Canadian and United Kingdom operations had lost over $3.3 million. It was not until 1977 that Com-Share finally generated a profit.[78]

By nearly every measure, the diversification into information systems and modular housing was a failure. Impelled by new incentives, Polymer's managers had moved away from the proven principles of earlier achievement toward a more frenetic and ultimately self-defeating search for profits. The synergies that Polymer had expected did not materialize, primarily because top managers had little specific knowledge of the technical processes and markets of the divisions and subsidiaries they had acquired. Without the product-specific experience needed to evaluate proposals and to monitor the performance of their operating

managers, Polymer's senior management often found itself wandering
in the dark. It had been assumed by nearly all advocates of diversification that because Polymer was a high-technology firm, it was somehow
innately capable of successfully acquiring and operating other "cutting-
edge" businesses. The assumption was presumptuous and misguided.
Perhaps even worse from a long-term perspective, the diversification
effort jeopardized Polymer's core competency in synthetic-rubber science and technology.

During the first twenty-five years of operation, synthetic-rubber science
and technology at Polymer was the driving force behind the growth of
the firm. R&D was encouraged, emphasized, and, indeed, enshrined.
But during the decade 1967–77, with the company experiencing economic stress, turmoil, and change, R&D was de-emphasized. The research and development department underwent reorganization and
retrenchment, and, apart from one important exception (i.e., the development of bromobutyl rubber, a revolutionary innovation that
ensured a permanent place for Polymer in the synthetic rubber industry), concentrated on the progressive improvement of existing products and processes.

Given the widespread belief at Polymer, especially among its corporate planners, that the synthetic-rubber business was in decline, it was
decided to postpone the commercial development of a number of innovations and instead to "concentrate efforts in the fields to which the
corporation is now committed."[79] For instance, in 1968 work was suspended on the development of ethylene-propylene rubber – a stereo-
specific rubber used in the production of wire and cable insulation. It
was not until twelve years later, after the decision was made to get "back
to basics," that the project was reinitiated. But by that time markets had
been lost and Polymer found itself at a comparative disadvantage. Likewise, work had been halted on the development of thermoplastic block
elastomers. These compositions could be molded like plastics when hot
and behaved like rubbers at room temperature.

Used primarily in manufacturing toys, insulation, and mechanical
goods, the main purpose of thermoplastics was to avoid the expensive
curing step needed for conventional rubber. Polymer had enjoyed
some early success in this burgeoning field (during the 1980s thermoplastic rubbers were the fastest-growing segment of the specialty-rubber
market).[80] Nevertheless, the marketing division came to the conclusion
in 1970 that the world demand for thermoplastic rubber of the block
type would be large enough to support only one producer, namely
Shell. Thus, the program was shut down, along with associated work on
living polymerization, lithium, and block polymers. "The decision,"

Dr E.J. Buckler, in 1977, delivering a speech to the
French Rubber Association.

Buckler later recalled, "broke my heart."[81] Buckler had always known a
revolutionary product when he saw one. Thermoplastic rubber definitely fit the mold. But during the drive to diversification, the product
was dropped.

At the same time, the ABS resin program came under pressure and
was also terminated. The operation in Canada was not large enough to
support the research, development, and technical service necessary to
compete with the large U.S. producers who had established branch
plants in Canada. Thus, it too was shut down. Polymer was heading in a
new and, unbeknown to it, dangerous direction.

The progressive reduction of the research and development activities in Polymer's basic businesses created a surplus of technical and scientific personnel. In response, Ian Rush decided to lay off three
hundred research scientists. Rush had taken over the presidency from

Rowzee in 1971, much to the consternation of Roger Hatch. Hatch had always believed that he was Rowzee's natural heir. He had, after all, done more than anyone else, with perhaps the exception of J.R. Nicholson, to promote Polymer products abroad, and his tenure with the company predated that of Rush. Nevertheless, the board of directors selected Rush to succeed Rowzee, who agreed to stay on with the company as chairman of the board. The reason for the board's preference is unclear. Perhaps it was Hatch's opposition to the Sarnia Olefins Aromatics Project (SOAP) – a mammoth program that would see Polymer and its partners invest three-quarters of a billion dollars in a plant to manufacture feedstocks for the regional petrochemical industry. Perhaps it was the disappointing start to the diversification effort over which Hatch had presided. Perhaps it was that in this age of corporate planning, the board wanted a corporate planner like Rush at Polymer's helm. Or perhaps the board sensed that it was Rush who would be more effective at implementing the tough cost-cutting measures that lay on the horizon. Whatever the reason, Rush was appointed Polymer's seventh president in 1971, and he immediately got to work reorganizing and downsizing the existing operations, so as to generate the money necessary for further diversification.

In 1971 the corporation was decentralized along divisional lines to promote efficiency and cost-consciousness. The functional structure of the corporation was disbanded, and each line of business was made into an autonomous centre responsible for its own financial performance. Polymer was among the first Crown corporations to be reorganized along these lines. Several years later, when the profit-seeking Roger A. Bandeen took over as president of Canadian National Railways, Canada's oldest and largest federal Crown corporation, he followed Polymer's move, reorganizing the company into "profit centres." Bandeen argued that this would give CN's management a more accurate yardstick for measuring the success of the firm.[82] The move was momentous, because it reflected a fundamental change in CN's strategic focus. The Crown company was aiming to be more like Polymer: that is, profitable and market-oriented. Emphasizing profitability, market demand, and strategic business-unit appraisals, the new mission was a radical departure for CN, which since 1919 had primarily served a public-policy purpose. The route to commercialization was not without its obstacles, however. It proved very difficult, for instance, to jettison its public-service corporate culture. It was a similar story at Air Canada.[83] It, too, experienced turbulence on the route to commercialization.[84] This was not the case, however, at Polymer. Its public-policy phase, 1942–45, had not been long enough to instill non-profit-oriented behaviour. Polymer had been functioning like a private enterprise for so long that it had become accustomed to periodic structural reorganization. Thus, the move to restructure along divisional lines went relatively smoothly.

Within the new corporate structure, each line of business had direct control over its research and development activities and authorized each one to select the development programs and personnel it favoured. The supporting R&D activities, such as pilot plants and analytical and compounding laboratories, were centralized into one department to provide services to all product lines. Scientific and technical personnel from the research and marketing divisions were formed into a new group, the technical-development division, and a small research group was established to explore the remaining interesting ideas not included in the divisional programs. While the reorganization had the desired effect of reducing overall costs, it weakened communication links and compromised Polymer's core competency.

Despite Rush's cost-cutting measures, in 1971–72 Polymer was still having trouble generating the funds necessary for further diversification. In his report, Ackerman had maintained that Polymer would have to generate roughly $8 million in equity each year to finance the diversification program.[85] But in 1971 the Crown corporation recorded an after-tax profit of just $500,000 on sales of $174.7 million (see table A1), the lowest level of net earnings since the financial reorganization in 1952 and well short of the amount that was required to feed further diversification.[86] With the profit squeeze affecting the petrochemical industry getting tighter, management struggled with ways to come up with additional capital. The solution that it formulated was to tap the international capital market by transforming the Crown company into a publicly traded enterprise.[87] But the federal government had different plans for the firm: Polymer would be sold to the Canada Development Corporation (CDC).

In January 1971, after almost a decade of political deliberation and procrastination, the Liberal government, in response to a rising nationalist tide, introduced legislation to create the CDC. A government-sponsored venture capital and holding company, the CDC was conceived to prevent Canadian companies like Polymer from falling into foreign hands. The fear of losing control of Canadian companies to larger foreign – particularly American – firms was very much a part of the Canadian consciousness during the 1960s and 1970s. The takeover of such venerable Canadian businesses as Ryerson Press, a leading Canadian publisher, by large American enterprises did much to invigorate nationalist sentiment. Associations such as Walter Gordon's Committee for an Independent Canada and Mel Watkin's Waffle Group gained unprecedented public support for their nationalist stance on economic issues. "The major threat to Canadian survival today is American control of the Canadian economy," the Waffle Group warned. "The major issue of our times is not national unity but national survival, and the fundamental threat is external, not internal."[88] In the late 1960s Gordon established a task force, under Watkins, to examine the problem of foreign control of domestic industry and to recommend ways to increase Canadian control.[89] The task force's subsequent conclusions reflected the growing anxiety in Canada about the foreign presence in the economy.

The rising concern over foreign takeovers of Canadian firms was also reflected in the literature of the period. A number of books, such as Richard Rohmer's best-selling, albeit un-Canadianly dramatic, novel *Ultimatum* and Al Purdy's *New Romans*, warned Canadians of the inherent dangers of American economic imperialism.[90] In his novel *Takeover*, the esteemed Canadian historian Donald Creighton told the story of the annexation of an established Canadian distillery by an American syndication.[91] Within the world of academe, a number of social scientists, particularly from the disciplines of sociology and political science – but certainly not limited to them – fashioned a new type of economic literature that supposedly embodied Canadian values.[92] Their goal was to undermine the hegemonic neoclassical paradigm that in their view rationalized what Ontario economist Ian Macdonald termed a "derivative economy" and justified "a neo-colonial situation."[93]

The passive concern over foreign direct investment witnessed at the time of Walter Gordon's 1957 royal commission on Canada's economic prospects was transmogrified over the ensuing decade into the more activist approach outlined in the Gray *Report*.[94] The Gray *Report* of 1972 set out a number of options for controlling direct foreign investment inflows, one of which was government intervention in the investment process. The *Report* reflected the growing economic nationalism. A 1972 Gallup Poll showed that 67 percent of Canadians thought that Canada had enough capital from the United States.[95] It was the large, often dominant role played by foreign – and mainly American – capital that was widely perceived as both a prime cause and a chief consequence of Canada's alleged chronic inability to marshal adequate domestic savings to fund its economic and technological development.[96]

For their part, Polymer's senior executives were not swept along by the rising nationalist tide. They profoundly understood that Polymer had benefited from open access to foreign markets and from the free flow of capital and ideas across the national boundary. They instinctively sensed the cosmopolitan roots of their industry and their own careers in it. Canada's liberal immigration laws had brought many of them to Sarnia in the first place. Rowzee and Stanley Wilk, who were both American by birth, had come to Canada during the war to lend their expertise in synthetic-rubber production. Buckler and Ian Rush had emigrated from Great Britain, and Roger Hatch had come from France. These men, all of whom later became naturalized Canadians, were present at the dawn of the Canadian synthetic-rubber program and were acutely aware that it was German *cum* American technology and scientific know-how that had given the program its start.[97] After the war, Polymer's ability to think, and ultimately perform, in a global context determined the firm's success. Facing the limitations of a small domestic marketplace, the young, pioneering Crown corporation had "gone global" in search of emerging markets. "To have become insular," Rowzee later recalled, "would have been fatal."[98] From that time on, Polymer's global vision had remained strong.

.For his part, Rowzee felt that vision needed to be shared by more Canadians. "Our experience," he told the *Globe and Mail* in June 1971, "leads me to conclude that more Canadians need to look outward and not inward to achieve a perspective that will ensure policies which encourage and support dynamic enterprise."[99] Later, in an address to the Canadian Manufacturers' Association entitled "In Pursuit of Global Markets," he stated that Canadians had to avoid the obsession with national ownership of industry if Canada was to attract the productive capital necessary to flourish in a challenging global economy.[100] "Canadian ownership itself," he stated, "is not a panacea in the business world we face."[101] Rather, securing a healthy and growing industry for Canada would, in Rowzee's opinion, depend on whether the Canadian economy was competitive in a world sense. Only then would Canada attract capital for productive use.

But the majority of the population did not share Rowzee's neoclassical views. Neither did the federal government. On the heels of the Gray *Report*, legislation was introduced in the House of Commons establishing the Foreign Investment Review Agency. In April 1974, FIRA began screening foreign acquisitions of Canadian businesses. The agency was just one of the ways the Liberal government of Pierre Elliot Trudeau attempted to discourage foreign direct investment and promote Canadian control of domestic industry. Another effort was made in 1975 when the federal government created Petro-Canada. A Crown corporation with broad powers, Petro-Canada was created to take back control of the domestic petroleum industry. Along with the National Energy Program, Petro-Canada was attempting to promote total energy self-sufficiency in Canada.[102]

The logic behind the CDC also had a decidedly nationalist bent: to develop and maintain strong Canadian-controlled and Canadian-managed companies in the private sector. By channelling funds into

Canadian industrial development, the CDC would close the gap in Canadian capital markets that inhibited equity holding by Canadians and facilitated it by foreigners. In one sense, the CDC would act like any other large diversified holding company, picking businesses that were thought to be the "winners" in their respective fields, in order to generate a profit for its shareholders. In another sense, however, it would be very different from other conglomerates, because its shares would be owned only by Canadians and "the national interest was supposed to be very much a part of its objectives and operating policies."[103] The CDC would thus have both a commercial and public-policy purpose.

It was widely anticipated that once the CDC became an institutional reality, Polymer and two other "profit-oriented" Crown corporations, Eldorado and Northern Transportation Company, would come under its control.[104] With net assets of roughly $230 million, Polymer would be the largest of the CDC's holdings. In terms of net assets, Polymer had more than tripled in size since 1960. Polymer would thus give the CDC the scale, cash flow, and respectability that it would need to achieve its commercial and public-policy objectives.

The CDC had first been proposed by Walter Gordon during the election campaign of 1962–63 as an instrument to curb foreign takeovers of Canadian industries and to encourage Canadians to invest more in domestic enterprises. Gordon's plan, however, ran into heavy criticism, both from political opponents and from representatives of the financial and business communities. Those on the right, like the former Tory finance minister Donald Fleming and his friends on Bay Street and in the financial press, viewed the CDC as a "socialistic monster."[105] Neil McKinnon, the chairman of the CIBC, for instance, argued that the CDC was incompatible with the principles of the free-enterprise system and marketplace economics.[106] Ironically, it was another of the CIBC's senior personnel, Marshall Crowe, who became the first president of the CDC when it was finally established in mid-1971.

In an address delivered to the Canadian Club of Toronto on 17 January 1966, McKinnon took issue with Gordon's position that foreign investment in Canada was detrimental to the nation. Gordon had long maintained that there was a debilitating gap in Canadian capital markets and that this gap, in turn, was compromising Canadian economic sovereignty. The CDC was conceived by Gordon as a partial remedy to this "worrisome situation"; it would provide equity finance to Canadian ventures that might otherwise be compelled to turn to foreign sources for funds. McKinnon agreed with Gordon that there was a shortage of investment funds in Canada but argued that this shortage was not a distinctly Canadian phenomenon. Therefore, it did not warrant Gordon's radical remedy.[107] Gordon, of course, disagreed.

While those on Bay Street and on the political right opposed Gordon's CDC because they felt it would lead to too much government intervention in the economy, those on the political left objected to it because it would not extend the principle of government intervention far enough. United behind the basic tenet of functional socialism – that a greatly increased level of government intervention was the most appropriate response to the problems created by and in a capitalist society – the NDP and others on the left played an active and aggressive role in the debate over the CDC. They opposed Gordon's suggestion that the government should retain only 10 percent ownership of the CDC's shares, arguing instead for total government ownership and control. If economic power had to be concentrated, the left argued, then the best place for that to occur was in the hands of government. This would assure that the collective national need transcended that of the individual investor.[108] In the end, they almost got their wish. Faced with investor apathy, skepticism, and conservatism, the Canadian government was forced to retain a 47 percent ownership in the CDC well into the 1970s. The CDC was thus not the privately owned development corporation that Gordon had envisioned but a mixed enterprise – a firm owned jointly by the government and private investors.[109]

The left's objections to Gordon's plan did not end there, however. Soon after his appointment as finance minister in 1963, Gordon began hinting that Polymer would be among the CDC's first acquisitions.[110] Gordon was a great admirer of Polymer. He viewed the corporation as a symbol of Canada's managerial and technological competence.[111] In an address to the Canadian Club in Sarnia in October 1965, he celebrated the achievements of the firm. "The Corporation's success amidst highly competitive business conditions," he stated, "has been the result of efficient businesslike operations free from interference from the outside."[112] Gordon was profoundly aware of the earlier efforts to take over the Crown corporation and had strenuously objected to the Diefenbaker government's plans to privatize the firm. But at that time he was unable to conceive of a solution that would free Polymer from government ownership without control passing into foreign hands. It was only later that he came up with the idea of selling Polymer to the CDC. The benefits of doing so, he told his Sarnia audience, would be multiple. Polymer would get not only the access to capital and markets it needed but also the freedom it deserved. In return, the CDC would get "a large and immediate income and some diversification."[113] Without such a start, Gordon maintained, the commercial future of the CDC would be subject to a number of uncertainties, thus making the sale of its shares to the public more difficult.

But perhaps most importantly, as far as Gordon was concerned, by selling Polymer to the CDC, Canada would retain ownership and control of one of its most innovative companies, thereby ensuring the health and stability of the Canadian petrochemical industry.[114]

Nevertheless, many on the left considered Gordon's plans for Polymer a "regressive step." As things stood, all Canadians shared in the profits of Polymer, noted the editors of *Canadian Dimension* – a left-leaning, neonationalist periodical. But if Gordon's legislation was enacted and Polymer was sold to the CDC, the major portion of the profits would go to only a handful of citizens – i.e., the shareholders of the CDC.[115] That would be unacceptable, declared Stanley Knowles, the NDP's elder statesman.[116] To take Polymer, a government-owned corporation being run by "the people" for the benefit of "the people," and turn it over to a few capitalists, was in his opinion a bankrupt idea. Knowles maintained that despite Gordon's statements to the contrary, there was no way to guarantee the nationality of the shareholders of the CDC and therefore no way to guarantee that Polymer would continue to be operated by Canadians for the benefit of Canadians.

As the pace of globalization accelerated, Knowles and others on the left came to view the nation's Crown corporations as the last bastions of Canadian capitalism. In 1974 Herschel Hardin, echoing the sentiments expressed some time earlier by the historian Frank Underhill,[117] argued that public enterprise was central to Canadian economic culture and hence the national identity. In his treatise *A Nation Unaware*, he singled out Polymer for special praise: "Created by public enterprise, Polymer also endured and excelled in public enterprise. Over and above that it manifested, in its operations, a recognizably Canadian public enterprise style … The best single adjective for it is 'civilized' – a civilized style that in Polymer's case, stemmed from the ambiguous character of Canadian nationalism itself."[118]

In this time of increasing global reach, Hardin and others on the left implied that the nation needed more Crown corporations, not fewer. Indeed, Mel Watkins and his disciples within the Waffle Group of the NDP argued for the nationalization of all industry as a defence against American "corporate imperialism."[119] For the Waffle Group, the nationalist left wing of the NDP, the major threat to Canadian survival was "American control of the Canadian economy." The group's solution was to replace capitalism with socialism, including "national planning of investment" and "public ownership of the means of production."[120] While not everyone on the left supported Watkin's socialism, most agreed that the denationalization of Polymer was a strange way to go about repatriating the Canadian economy. Thus, they strenuously

objected to the idea of selling Polymer to the CDC.[121] "Polymer corporation is 100 percent Canadian owned and controlled," stated Ran-
dolph Harding of the NDP in the House of Commons. "Let us keep it
that way."[122]

When news of Gordon's plans reached Polymer, the reaction was
mixed. On the one hand, a sale to the CDC would, as Gordon maintained, remove Polymer from the hands of the government, and so it
was viewed in a positive light. Since 1960 Polymer's brain trust had been
advocating the denationalization of the firm, and while a sale to the
CDC would not eliminate the government's involvement altogether, it
was seen as a step in the right direction.[123] It had long been felt at Polymer that with government ownership there was always the possibility of
political interference in its affairs. To be sure, to date Polymer had operated virtually free of political intervention. Nevertheless, management
and the board of directors continually worried that this situation would
not last. "It is a fact that in the past the Canadian government has accepted [our] 'decisions of change' when they were required," Ralph
Rowzee stated in 1969. "However, changes in Governments and Government policies bring with them the likelihood of changed attitudes
toward a Crown Corporation and what it should be doing."[124] Rowzee
was convinced that as a commercial enterprise with no directive from
Ottawa other than to turn a profit, Polymer needed the freedom of
choice and action that was enjoyed by other profit-oriented firms. "Con-
tinuance of our long-established principles of operation and continued
independence of decision," he stated shortly after meeting with Walter
Gordon in February of 1965, "are, in my opinion, essential to the future
well-being of the Company."[125] The position was later voiced to other
ministers of the Crown. If incorporation in the CDC could guarantee
Polymer's independence, Rowzee maintained, then the proposal would
have the full support of management and the board of directors.[126] The
problem was that Gordon's proposal was so vague in terms of the details
that no one at Polymer seemed to be sure whether incorporation into
the CDC would give the firm more or less independence.

This was a common problem with Gordon's economic proposals and
policies. Concerned with broad politicoeconomic issues, Gordon seldom thought through the finer points of his proposals.[127] This was certainly the case in regard to the plan to sell Polymer to the CDC.
Although he addressed the topic in October 1965, many of the details
of his proposal remained unspecified.[128] Was the purpose of the CDC to
"buy back" Canadian industry or to maximize profits for its shareholders? If the former, would Polymer be mixed in with what Rowzee termed
"a nondescript group of companies which were not money makers?"[129]
Would Polymer be "milked" – as was suggested by the Canadian Trade

Committee, the blue-ribbon industrial lobby group[130] – to shore up the less-prosperous companies owned by the CDC?[131] Would Polymer's operations still be based on sound business principles and the profit motive? Would Polymer continue to develop and expand within the CDC or would incorporation in the CDC retard Polymer's growth? Would the CDC take a hands-off approach to Polymer or demand a say in the way the firm was run? To these questions Gordon had no satisfactory answers, and as a result, those at Polymer withheld their support from Gordon's proposal. "Until we know what form [the] CDC will take and how it will operate," Rowzee wrote to the board of directors, "we cannot properly evaluate this facet of a change of ownership ... For this reason, I believe we should withhold our support."[132]

But by 1972 Rowzee had changed his mind. In need of capital to finance the ailing diversification effort, Rowzee threw his full support behind a sale to the CDC. Despite strong political opposition and the declining political fortunes of Walter Gordon, the idea of creating a corporation to promote Canadian ownership and control of domestic industry had not gone away, and in June 1971 the Trudeau government had brought the CDC into being. In addition to its primary task of counteracting the multinational challenge, the CDC, somewhat paradoxically, became the instrument through which the government denationalized a number of its "profit-seeking" Crown corporations.

The Trudeau government could see no logic in retaining a Crown corporation that served no public-policy purpose other than to generate a profit.[133] Successive federal governments had been uneasy about the socialist implications of public ownership of institutions like Polymer, which functioned by every practical test as a member of the private sector. Yet they had struggled with how to go about denationalizing these firms without compromising Canadian ownership and control. A sale to the CDC offered a practical way out of the philosophical mire. But Ottawa was reluctant to act without Polymer's approval. That came in March 1972: "Given a free choice," Rowzee wrote to the federal cabinet minister, James Richardson, "I would like to see [the] CDC acquire Polymer."[134] That position was also shared by Polymer's board of directors.[135]

Two things had prompted Polymer to shift its position. The first came in the form of assurances from the government and CDC officials that there would be strong and on-going support for Polymer's diversification program and that there would be little interference in the affairs of the firm. The second was that Polymer's market value had dropped to a level where it was questionable if the sale of its shares to the public would generate the capital necessary for further diversification and expansion.

With all sides agreeing to the decision, Polymer was sold to the CDC for $62 million in July 1972. "A new era is ahead," predicted Anthony Hampson, chairman of the CDC.[136] According to Hampson, who became part of Polymer's executive committee in August 1972, the sale would make Polymer "more aggressive, more private enterprise-oriented and more entrepreneurial."[137] The multimillion-dollar sale included an additional payment of up to $10 million, depending on Polymer's earnings over the next two years.[138] The payment was in the form of 6,142,000 common CDC shares with a book value of roughly $10 a share. At first glance, a $72-million selling price might have seemed low for a company with total assets exceeding $180 million and shareholders' equity of $123.5 million at the time of the sale. On the CDC's balance sheet there was $51.6 million of negative goodwill by which the net assets purchased exceeded the price paid. However, the three independent estimates obtained by the government before the sale, two by separate government departments and one by a leading investment dealer, all clustered around the $62–$72-million range of the CDC's purchase price.[139]

In the years following the sale, Polymer took advantage of the CDC's financial backing, both in terms of share issues and loans advanced, to provide the corporation with lower-cost equity financing. In February 1977, for instance, the CDC advanced $50 million to the company on an interest-free basis. In addition, Polymer used the CDC's backing to diversify backwards into feedstocks.

In his report, William Ackerman had suggested the need to integrate/diversify backwards to remain competitive in the synthetic-rubber field. He predicted that by the end of the decade only a handful of heavily integrated companies would be producing synthetic rubber. "Polymer's management," he declared, "should act as though one-profit integration into oil-rubber-fabrication will be a reality by 1980 ... [and seek] to take over a large fabricator, a large oil company, or both."[140] Increasingly after 1970, the high cost of feedstocks for petrochemical derivative manufacturing plants was a problem to the entire Canadian petrochemical industry. Small-scale, widely scattered and, in some cases, technologically antiquated production facilities, combined with the high cost of feedstocks, therefore placed the Canadian petrochemical industry at a competitive disadvantage. During the 1970s, foreign producers with modern, large-scale plants began penetrating the Canadian marketplace. As a result, Canada's trade deficit in chemicals and plastics grew at an alarming rate. Without revitalization of the industry in Canada, the future of domestic producers of petrochemicals looked bleak.

In Polymer's case, Sarnia-produced butadiene was becoming too high-priced vis-à-vis the butadiene available to its U.S. competitors. It was believed that the vagaries and uncertainties of the operating environment, including government policy, required a means of ensuring reliability of raw materials at reasonable costs. Polymer felt that if the declining profitability of the synthetic-rubber operation was to be reversed, it had to secure cheaper feedstocks.[141] At the time, there were seemingly two alternatives: Polymer could either purchase by-product butadiene from European or Japanese sources or expand its operations so as to once again become self-sufficient in butadiene production. The purchase of offshore butadiene would provide some temporary relief from cost pressures, but it could hardly offer a permanent long-term solution. This left the second alternative to be pursued further.

In the early 1970s a proposal called the Sarnia Olefins Aromatics Project (SOAP) began being developed at Polymer. In its final report, the committee set up to study the feedstocks problem had advised that a world-scale complex, utilizing the most modern technology and crude oil from Western Canada, be built at Sarnia. Not everyone saw the wisdom in integrating backwards into feedstocks, however. Some, like Roger Hatch, argued that SOAP would commit Polymer even more deeply to the "declining rubber industry" and thereby reduce its capital-raising capacity and limit its diversification prospects. What was the point, Hatch asked, in spending millions of dollars to produce the feedstocks for a product that was becoming increasingly unprofitable to manufacture? But Hatch's was a dissenting opinion, and after 1972 he was no longer with the company to make his objections heard. Disappointed at having been passed over for the presidency and unable to work under Ian Rush, a man whom he disliked, Hatch left Polymer to pursue other ventures.[142] He was not the only member of Polymer's informal executive cabal to do so. Stanley Wilk and Lee Dougan also decided to leave the firm. Polymer was certainly becoming a different company – strategically, structurally, and organizationally – and in March 1973, less than a year after its sale to the CDC, the company changed its name to Polysar Ltd to reflect the transformation.[143]

The SOAP project would dwarf all others of the decade. Once constructed, the plant would process approximately 170,000 barrels of Western Canadian crude oil a day into 1 billion pounds of ethylene and 2 billion pounds of other primary petrochemicals such as benzene, propylene, isobutylene, and butadiene. It would thus be the largest single consumer of Canada's oil production. Initially it was estimated that the complex would cost $170 million to construct; in the end, however, the cost was roughly four times that amount. Given its enormous scale, the project needed broad-based private and public financial support. In 1974, Petrosar Limited was established as a partnership between Du Pont Canada, Union Carbide Canada, Koch Canada, and Polymer to manage the SOAP project. That same year the project was fully endorsed by the CDC. Polymer originally held 51 percent ownership of Petrosar, thus giving it majority control, and Rush was named Petrosar president. Rush was the driving force behind the project. Under his leadership it became bigger and more expensive than anyone had anticipated. Once operations at Petrosar began, Polymer's contribution included $20.1 million in equity and $74 million in subordinated debentures. Polymer, along with the project's other participants, promised to provide the necessary funds to complete the project and to meet Petrosar's bank loans and customer payments.

Mirroring most other developments of the decade, the Petrosar project got off to a shaky start, hampered by delays due to strikes and the lack of skilled tradespeople. It was not until 1978 that the plant finally came on stream. The delays, combined with the cost overruns and the high cost of financing, made Petrosar a costly investment. By the end of 1977, Polymer had invested over $165 million in the Petrosar project, and the plant was yet to produce a single petrochemical feedstock. To make matters worse, when the plant finally did come on line, it did so in an unfavourable operating environment. In 1978, Petrosar's operations resulted in a loss to Polysar of $10.2 million, followed by a loss in 1979 of $6.2 million. In the years that followed, Polymer's investment in Petrosar continued to mount. So did the losses. Petrosar was thus a treble drain on Polymer.

Polymer put the best face on things, stating that the project was a success since it strengthened its "long-term international merchant market position" by ensuring a continued source of feedstock.[144] This came at a heavy cost, however, a cost that, in the years that followed, would become even greater due to the effects of the National Energy Program and world market conditions.

If there was any doubt that this decade was shaping up to be the worst on record, that doubt was laid to rest in 1976 when news broke in the national press that Polymer's European marketing subsidiary, PISA, had been engaged in kickbacks and other "questionable" business practices. The dubious behaviour, which extended back to 1970, involved millions of dollars of fraudulent transactions between PISA and a number of its largest European customers. The PISA affair – or "Polygate," as it was termed – shook the corporate world and set shock waves reverberating across society. In its wake, a number of sticky questions were raised about the proper role of enterprise. Ultimately, it would cause the federal government to rethink its relationship with business.

The issue of what standards of propriety should apply to corporations active abroad was not limited to Canada. American executives and politicians tackled the same issue throughout the 1970s. Late in that decade, the U.S. Congress attempted to establish standards for ethical corporate behaviour overseas by passing the Foreign Corrupt Practices Act. Such attempts at imposing social responsibility on American corporations prompted a backlash among many observers of American enterprise. The business of business, Chicago economist Milton Friedman insisted, was profits and nothing but profits. One practical outcome of this controversy was the proliferation of audit committees on boards of directors, as an attempt to bring independent outside evaluation to corporate accounts. While a step in the right direction, these audit committees did not bring an end to bad corporate behaviour.

Although the public was made aware of Polygate only in 1976, a handful of Polymer's executives had long known about PISA's questionable dealings. Remarkably, they had done nothing to stop them. In February 1973, Polymer's audit committee, which included Ian Rush, Tony Hampson, and two outside directors, Ronald Todgham and William McGregor, met in Toronto to discuss Polymer's 1972 financial results. They were joined there by Maxwell Henderson, the auditor-general of Canada and Gordon Cowperthwaite, a senior accountant with Peat. Never one for beating around the bush, Henderson immediately broke the news that he had discovered that PISA was helping its customers minimize taxes and avoid foreign exchange regulations by diverting certain "under-the-table rebates or kickbacks" either to another country or into a numbered Swiss bank account.[145] A principled and uncompromising man, Henderson told the audit committee that he had "reservations" about the way PISA was conducting its business and demanded the "questionable practices" be stopped or, at least, disclosed to the company's shareholders. Todgham and McGregor were utterly stunned. They had no idea PISA's transactions were being handled like that on the books. "It was clear," Henderson later recalled of Todgham's and McGregor's reaction, "they had no knowledge of what was going on."[146] The implication that Rush and Hampson did know was thus profoundly clear. Todgham immediately turned to Rush and asked for an explanation. "These are customary marketing practices," he responded, "in the highly competitive European market."[147] While the explanation satisfied Todgham and McGregor, it did not impress the auditor-general. Henderson did not share Rush's moral relativism, and he thus refused to endorse Polymer's financial statement. He also felt it was his duty to inform Prime Minister Trudeau about PISA's dealings in Europe. When Hampson heard this he erupted, questioning Henderson's findings and his proposed handling of the matter.

Nevertheless, Henderson was resolute, and on 22 March 1973 he wrote to Prime Minister Trudeau of the "existence of a serious contingent liability of indeterminable proportions arising out of certain transactions of [Polymer's] Swiss subsidiary, Polysar International S.A."[148] As Henderson later noted, he thought the situation raised "the very serious contingency that the government of one or more of the customers involved might simply decide to sue the multinational corporation owned by the government of Canada."[149] This would be a humiliation of international proportions. Henderson's revelations concerned the prime minister, who thought the matter required "immediate attention."[150] In a letter to C.M. Drury, president of the treasury board, Trudeau wrote that "while the government may not have complete control or direct responsibility because of the status of Polymer and the CDC, there are obvious possibilities for embarrassment."[151] The government was still the CDC's largest shareholder, having a 68 percent interest, and if it was shown that one of the CDC's subsidiaries was involved in illegal or immoral practices, it would reflect badly on the Canadian government. Trudeau therefore suggested that Drury find a quick solution to the problem and recommended he seek the advice of Finance Minister John Turner, Supply and Services Minister Jean Pierre Goyer, and Secretary of State for External Affairs Mitchell Sharp. Not knowing of Henderson's previous efforts, Trudeau also proposed bringing the issue to the attention of Polymer's executive, in the hope that it would give "serious consideration" to modifying its practices.[152] Drury, however, did little about the matter except to make a telephone call or two before dropping it altogether.[153]

Four years passed, during which it was business as usual at PISA. The company continued to artificially inflate prices and deposit the so-called "rebates" into numbered Swiss accounts for a small number of its clients.[154] Henderson had retired in March 1973, and his successor, James Macdonell, was denied access to Polymer's records on the grounds that the company had ceased being a Crown corporation in July 1972, when it was purchased by the CDC. The matter, as a result, remained hidden from the shareholders and the public until November 1976. That month, Macdonell presented a report to parliament that contained startling disclosures about bribes paid by another Crown corporation, Atomic Energy of Canada, in South America and elsewhere to secure purchases of its CANDU reactors. A member of the press called Henderson to ask his views on this matter and to inquire whether it was true that he had written the prime minister in 1973 about similar "bribes" made by Polymer. Henderson later recalled that he was "astounded by the question" and felt he had no choice "except to confirm" that he had written to Trudeau.[155] The reporter immediately asked Henderson for a copy of the letter, which he received and subsequently made public.

On the morning of Saturday, 27 November 1976, employees at Polymer woke to the news that their company had been involved in "questionable business practices" for more than five years. A large headline on the front page of the *Globe and Mail* read, "Polysar says paybacks normal, still makes them."[156] Bill Dimma, a cerebral business executive who joined Polymer's board of directors in 1974, remembered being "blindsided by the news."[157] He was not alone. Nevertheless, there were some people who had an intimate knowledge of the affair, but they were denying any wrongdoing. Having solicited legal opinion, Rush and Hampson were still maintaining that the practices did not violate Swiss law and therefore were not wrong. For this reason the transactions had not been stopped or disclosed to the shareholders.[158] When the story broke in the press, Rush dismissed it as a tempest in a teacup.[159] "The controversy which has arisen over Polysar International in Europe, following the common commercial practice of allowing rebates, and the unpleasant and inapplicable language used to describe it [by the press], are a great disappointment to me as a Canadian," he stated. "The customers were fully entitled to the rebates, which were therefore their property, and Polysar International was obligated to act in accordance with the customer's instruction on the handling of those rebates."[160] Rush's comments, however, did little to reassure investors and parliamentarians. Indeed, they seemed only to fan the flames of the controversy.

In the House of Commons there was an uproar. The NDP called on the Liberal government to put an end to these "transactions of a nefarious nature."[161] The leader of the NDP, Ed Broadbent, asked if the government of Canada thought that "we as a country should be setting the lowest possible standards for international trade?"[162] Broadbent demanded a public inquiry into the matter. He got what he wanted.

At the public hearing that followed, members of parliament heard from Polymer's own executives about how PISA had assisted its customers in concealing $15 million of sales.[163] David Stanley, a member of Polymer's board of directors who had been assigned to undertake an internal investigation of the PISA affair, along with Justice J.B. Aylesworth, told how PISA had invoiced its customers at artificially inflated prices and then had "kickbacked" the money to its customers through their foreign affiliates. The practice helped the customers shift profits from one tax jurisdiction to another. What seemed not to have concerned PISA was the fact that the practice often defrauded shareholders or host governments.[164]

When the parliamentary committee reported to the House on 5 July 1977, it criticized all the principal actors: PISA for engaging in improper business practices; Drury for not adequately investigating the practices and not reporting back to the prime minister when requested to do so; and the auditors, Henderson and Cowperthwaite, for not immediately bringing the practices to the attention of parliament.[165] In response to the overwhelming criticism, Polymer put a stop to the questionable transactions at PISA. That put an end to the matter at Polymer, which returned to the business of profits.

But the federal government was less willing to let the issue pass without further action. Ottawa felt it was losing control of its companies, owing to nonexistent audit or performance review criteria. Indeed, as late as 1982 the federal government still did not know how many companies it owned. To many observers the 1951 Financial Administration Act was woefully out of step with the times. As a result, a number of major Crown corporations had escaped political control, particularly those companies in pursuit of commercial objectives – firms like Air Canada, CNR, Atomic Energy of Canada, and Petro-Canada. Successive auditors-general criticized the actions of these Crown corporations. Both AECL and CNR were accused of paying "rebates" to secure contracts.[166] Air Canada, on the other hand, was charged with creating an unauthorized subsidy. Petro-Canada, critics maintained, had rapidly expanded beyond the parameters of its original mission. All these indictments had merit. Later events at the CDC would lend further support to the position that the Crowns were out of control. In 1981, for example, the Trudeau government attempted to persuade the CDC to bail out one of Canada's leading multinational corporations, Massey Ferguson.[167] The CDC refused, as it had done earlier when the government had "leaned on" the company to move its headquarters from Toronto to Vancouver. In an effort to gain more political control over the CDC, the Liberal government attempted to have two party supporters appointed to its board of directors – Petro-Canada's vice-president Joel Ball and investment consultant David Betty.[168] But the CDC rejected that attempt also. In the wake of Polygate, the federal government felt that something had to be done to rein in these maverick corporations.

In late 1976, the Privy Council Office (PCO) was instructed to examine the relationship between the government and its firms. One of the key questions that it was to consider was whether the government should be in business for profit. "[W]e have to make up our minds," Trudeau told Canadians in November of that year, "whether we want

Crown corporations to exist which have corporate and commercial enterprise as their object."[169] The answer, according to the PCO, was that we did not.[170] "[T]he pursuit of commercial goals was never intended to override the broad social, cultural or economic goals that Crown corporations were established to pursue, especially since many of those goals could never be justified on purely commercial grounds."[171] For those Crown corporations that were already pursuing commercial objectives, the PCO recommended that they be allowed to stay the course. The ultimate goal in this commercialization trend would be privatization of the Crown corporations. The PCO's 1977 report therefore set the stage for the final chapter in Polymer's history – the government disposal of its shares in the CDC and the purchase and subsequent flip by Nova Corporation.

From a strategic and financial point of view, the diversification program of the 1970s was a failure. It did not move the company in a new direction and did not generate an adequate return. It was Rowzee's hope to reach a fifty-fifty mix of rubber-nonrubber sales by 1979.[172] This did not happen. By the end of the decade, Polymer had withdrawn from both housing systems and information processing. Lacking the requisite technical expertise, Polymer was unable to pick the winners in unrelated areas of production. Thus, Polymer did not become the diversified industrial giant that Rowzee and others had envisioned. Nor did it become a darling of the financial community. In 1969 Ackerman had confidently predicted that by following his strategy of diversification, Polymer would make a return on investment to its shareholders of 13.72 percent per annum by 1977.[173] In fact, the company returned less than half that amount – 6.2 percent – that year, and this was one of the company's better years of operation during the decade.[174] In 1972 the company's rate of return on equity was 5.7 percent; in 1976, it was 3.7 percent. And in both 1971 and 1975, it was less than 1 percent. To even the most conservative investor, this return could hardly have been satisfying.[175]

The company had, however, become bigger. During the period 1969–77, sales had more than tripled, as Rowzee had hoped, from $160 million to $577 million (see table A2). The number of employees had also grown to over six thousand world-wide. Nevertheless, the profitability of the company had not increased. In 1969, Polymer recorded a net income of $12.6 million. Eight years later, after investing roughly $300 million in various diversification projects, Polymer's net income was not much more, at $14.4 million.[176] The CDC's acquisition of Polymer did not improve the firm's profitability. Perhaps even worse, from a long-term perspective the diversification program had reduced Polymer's ability to seize a number of opportunities that might have contributed to its core competency if diversification had not consumed its cash reserves and increased its long-term debt. For instance, the diversification effort cost Polymer an opportunity to gain a larger share of the profitable butyl rubber market. While butyl contributed only 35 percent to Polymer's sales revenues in 1971, it provided 90 percent of the operating profit of the rubber division.[177] At a time when Polymer's executives were "thinking synthetic rubber less," Cities Services – one of three producers of butyl rubber – became available for purchase, but Polymer made no effort to acquire the company. There was also talk that Esso was interested in getting out of the butyl rubber business. But again Polymer's priorities lay elsewhere. Top managers were unable to conceive of the diversification program as anything other than an expansion into new "faster-growing" businesses. There was no discussion of how the new businesses would contribute to Polymer's "core competence" – something that C.K. Prahalad and Gary Hamel, in their prize-winning 1990 article in the *Harvard Business Review*, claim is critical to a successful corporate strategy.[178] Nor was there any discussion of how Polymer would achieve synergy through these acquisitions. As a result, there was little sharing of activities or skills that might have enabled Com-Share and SSI to perform better than they did. The corporate restructuring of 1971 only added to the problem. For over a quarter of a century Polymer had been a pioneer in knowledge-based growth. And despite the obstacles associated with innovation in the Canadian climate, they had made a number of important contributions to synthetic-rubber technology.[179] But the diversification effort compromised the source of its growth and profitability. It jeopardized Polymer's core products – i.e., its polymeric materials – and its core competency, the technological know-how and scientific knowledge to make those products. Realizing this problem in the years that followed, Polymer got "back to basics."

7
Back to Basics, 1978–1990

Are we, their inheritors, capable of such efforts should the need arise again?
Robert Dudley, president of Polymer, 1981–88[1]

After the diversification mania of the 1960s and 1970s came a wave of divesting in the late 1970s and 1980s, as firms got "back to basics." Polymer was among these firms. During the diversification drive, many companies had diversified beyond what was optimal for them. Some firms, like Polymer, expanded into unrelated areas of production without the requisite capital and organizational capabilities, and as a result, their profitability and market value suffered. Worse still, from a long-term perspective these firms lost sight of what they did best. In Polymer's case, the company moved away from developing new and improved polymeric materials. In its zeal to diversify, it siphoned off money from its R&D and in so doing, compromised its core competency. Diversification was much more difficult to realize in practice than in theory. "It is not an activity," wrote business theorist Ralph Biggadike in 1979, "for the impatient or for the faint-hearted."[2] When successful, diversification took substantial resources and continual commitment. Polymer seemingly lacked both.

In light of its negative impact on profits and stock prices, diversification as a strategy for growth began to be questioned in the late 1970s by business theorists and corporate managers alike. In 1980, Robert Hayes and William Abernathy wrote a scathing article in the *Harvard Business Review* entitled "Managing Our Way to Economic Decline," which criticized the myopic management principles that had led to diversification and corporate America's competitive inertia. "Responsibility for this competitive listlessness," they wrote, "belongs not just to a set of external conditions but also to the attitudes, preoccupations, and practices of American managers."[3] In their opinion management had focused too much on short-term profits at the expense of developing the facilities and skills needed for long-term growth and competitiveness. The indictment was reminiscent of Adam Smith's scorn for the feudal lords who traded their leadership in return for a pair of silver buckles.

Among corporate managers the realization set in that they could not manage anything and everything. Peter Drucker was wrong. Instead, they needed to return to what they did best. The message was received loud and clear at Canadian Pacific Enterprises, for example, where management refocused on the company's basic business, shedding its steel and airline units.[4] Canadian Pacific was not the only conglomerate to "unbundle" itself so as to concentrate on its core concerns. As many as half the *Fortune* 500 firms de-diversified during the period 1981–87.[5] In most industrialized countries the average size of firms became smaller, not bigger, as divisions were spun off and out-sourcing was initiated. Perhaps the most obvious example occurred at International Telephone and Telegraph. In 1980, ITT was the world's largest conglomerate, with revenues of $23.8 billion per year. Under the direction of Rand V. Araskog, a no-nonsense West Pointer who was appointed president in 1979, the company sold off over forty of its subsidiaries. The selling was so heavy that in 1982 *Fortune* magazine declared that "the most famous conglomerate around has plainly made a U-turn."[6] Whereas the dictum of big business in the 1960s and 1970s had been "diversify, diversify, diversify," in the 1980s it was – in Peters and Waterman's famous phrase – "stick to the knitting."[7]

The de-diversifying was made more pressing by the emergence of takeover artists who – armed with junk bonds – threatened to acquire or break up any company with a depressed stock price. During the 1980s, buying and selling corporations became a business in its own right, abetted by the huge blocks of shares that pension funds and collective investors could trade. Corporate raiders such as Carl Icahn, T. Boone Pickens, and the "radical sheik" of the Canadian oil patch, Bob Blair, demonstrated that they could acquire even the largest companies, break them up, and realize huge profits. At the end of the 1980s, Polymer's parent company, the CDC, would itself become a target of takeover artists. The threat of a hostile takeover prompted companies to refocus on their core products and competencies and return to a more optimal level of diversification.

The de-diversification movement was heralded in the business and academic press as a managerial revolution that was producing more efficient companies for creating and distributing shareholder wealth. "Through refocusing," Constantinos Markides noted in 1991, "many firms have been able to streamline their operations and improve their competitiveness so that they are now more efficient global competitors."[8] Likewise, historian Michael Bliss, whose 1987 book *Northern Enterprise* upheld the discipline of the market and disparaged the state, argued that "the best business practice in response to the tough going of the 1980s was to return to fundamental values: market sensitivity, entrepreneurship, emphasis on leanness, motivation and the maximum use of human resources."9 *Fortune* magazine's "companies to watch" were no longer the large multifaceted businesses it had singled out in the 1960s and 1970s. Its eye was now on smaller companies that were focused, lean, and had a well-defined market niche; companies like Easton Aluminum, a manufacturer of aluminum sporting equipment, and Tyco Toys, a maker of "tried-and-true" playthings.10 The trend in the 1980s, as the *Economist* noted in 1989, was towards firms "drawing in their horns, not pushing them out."11 The 1980s and 1990s, therefore, were decades of de-diversification, a time when firms went "back to basics." This was certainly the case at Polymer Corporation.

Polymer had always been sensitive to trends in the business environment, and this time was no different. Sometimes it had to anticipate these trends – as was the case at the end of the Second World War when it decided to "go global" – and sometimes it had lagged behind. When Polymer joined the diversification drive in 1969, for example, the movement had already been under way for more than a decade. To make up for the lost time, it streamlined the decision-making process and rushed into areas of production that in hindsight it should have avoided. Until that time, however, Polymer had been a model of success. "Its record to date," noted one keen observer of public enterprise in 1969, "clearly demonstrates that it has been an outstanding example of entrepreneurial success on the part of the Canadian government and establishes it as a model against which other proprietary crown corporations might wish to measure their performance."12 Only during the "traumatic experience" of 1967 did Polymer fail to return a higher profit than the government could have realized by transferring its investment in the company into government bonds or, more logically, by reducing its own borrowing requirements by an equivalent amount.

To be sure, the Crown corporation had habitually benefited from good timing. It had entered the synthetic-rubber field at the dawn of the chemical age, when polymer science was in its infancy and there was therefore plenty to discover and plenty to improve upon. In the years that followed, few other synthetic-rubber companies had the position or know-how to compete, and Polymer prospered accordingly. That said, Polymer had made the most of its opportunities. After the war, the future of the nascent synthetic-rubber industry was far from certain. Natural rubber was superior in terms of quality and price, and its cartel had a well-established international network of marketers and distributors. In the United States these obstacles were considered too great to overcome, and most of the synthetic-rubber plants that had been established during the war were shut down. Polymer faced its own additional problems and thus was perhaps an unlikely candidate for industrial success. At the end of the Second World War, its capacity was twice that of domestic demand, and it was a long way from the rubber-hungry markets of Europe. In addition, as we have seen, C.D. Howe, Canada's postwar economic czar and the man who had overseen the birth of the enterprise, showed little interest in perpetuating a Canadian tradition by extending government protection to the infant industry. If Polymer was to survive, Howe maintained, it would have to do so as a free enterprise without the benefit of protective tariffs and direct government succour.

Despite all these obstacles, Polymer endured and prospered. By pioneering synthetic-rubber sales in Europe, it demonstrated to the world that the synthetic-rubber industry was commercially viable. In the process it had developed certain revolutionary sales techniques that were subsequently adopted by others in the industry. As a result of being the first North American synthetic-rubber producer in Europe, Polymer captured a substantial share of the market.[13] Thereafter, it restlessly expanded the output of its standard product line through technological innovation. Between 1945 and 1972, productivity increased more than fourfold. By applying science, it continually brought new sorts of products into commercial use. During the 1960s its growth entailed strategic investment in manufacturing facilities and organizational talent abroad.[14] As a consequence, Polymer became one of Canada's first multinational manufacturing corporations, taking its place alongside Alcan, Seagram Ltd, MacMillan Bloedel and Massey-Ferguson. For the first twenty-five years of its evolution, Polymer was a model of corporate growth and development, and, remarkably, it outperformed many of the private companies operating in the field.[15] Hardin was right: Polymer had "endured and excelled in public enterprise."[16] It had, as another observer noted in 1971, "confounded its critics for 29 years."[17]

During the next decade, however, its performance had not been so spectacular. Like most other petrochemical firms, Polymer was negatively affected by lower growth rates for most of its existing products, higher energy and feedstock costs, and a slowdown in the introduction of new technology. As early as 1960 there were signs that the industry was suffering from overcapacity and cost-cutting. Yet numerous manufacturers continued to bring new capacity on stream well ahead of anticipated demand. During the 1970s companies joined in the petrochemical gold rush, only to find many others working the same veins. Faced with declining profit margins, Polymer embarked upon a program of diversification. Unfortunately, the company lacked the requisite technical expertise to be able to pick and manage the winners in fields that were unrelated to its basic areas of production. As a result, its financial performance continued to suffer. Years later, Ian Rush, who had the distinction of presiding over these turbulent years, still maintained that diversification was the correct course of action given the discontinuities and uncertainties of the 1970s.[18] Others were not so sure.[19] Either way, at the end of the decade the decision was made to get back to basics.

The new corporate mission was outlined in the company's 1979 annual report. The firm, it stated, aimed to be "a profitable international company of significant standing in the petrochemical industry, through the development of influential positions in selected geographic and product segments."[20] The world petrochemical industry was quickly becoming restructured. Ackerman had been wrong about a good number of things, but he was not mistaken about the changing nature of the industry. By 1980 most of the oil giants had integrated their processes downstream, as he had anticipated ten years earlier, and had become major competitors in the petrochemical field. These giants invested heavily in new facilities and new products, forcing others in the industry to rationalize their operations.[21] In addition, new producers from oil- and gas-rich regions of the world entered the field, further adding to the competition. In the mid-1970s such oil-rich countries as Iran, Saudi Arabia, and Libya plunged headlong into petrochemical projects when the world oil crisis appeared to give them a springboard. In these countries there was a great deal of resentment over the past "imperialistic" policies of the Western petrochemical producers. While some countries, such as Kuwait, had managed to establish their own refining industries, most had left the processing of crude oil largely in the hands of the multinational oil companies. But after the first oil shock of 1973 and OPEC's subsequent success in wresting control of the world's crude oil supply from the major oil companies, Middle Eastern countries used their new wealth and leverage to build locally owned and controlled refineries and petrochemical plants.[22]

A similar sort of resentment had led the Alberta government to support and promote the development of a petrochemical industry in the province. Since the First World War, Alberta had felt left out of Canada's industrialization. The province's attempts during the Second World War to get Ottawa's economic overlord, C.D. Howe, to establish factories in the West for the production of alcohol from grain into synthetic rubber had, for instance, been unsuccessful. This, along with Howe's attempt to take control of the province's natural gas exports after the war, infuriated Albertans and seemed to confirm that the federal government was not interested the province's economic development. In response, the Alberta government became increasingly proactive on economic matters.[23]

The idea of establishing petrochemical facilities in Alberta as part of a provincial strategy of encouraging oil- and gas-based industrialization dated from 1949.[24] But it was not until the mid-1970s – after the energy crisis gave the province the leverage and opportunity to realize its ambition – that the idea came to fruition. In 1977 the Lougheed government announced its intention to sponsor and promote a major program to build plants for the production of ammonia, methanol, and various ethylene derivatives. This would be done through the use of Alberta's recently established Heritage Fund, into which the provincial government paid much of the windfall profits received as a result of the frantic escalation of crude oil prices. The friendly and stable political environment, combined with the perceptions of a raw-material cost advantage, brought corporations rushing into the province. New petrochemical plants were constructed. The fact that Central Canada already had ample petrochemical capacity did not faze the Albertans, who were known for their independent thinking and action. In fact, as a result of Alberta's relatively tough bargaining stance with Ottawa, as well as with foreign firms, their oil men soon became known as the "blue-eyed sheiks" of the North.[25]

Polymer believed that to be a major player in this new environment, it needed to reinforce its strengths, while reducing the drain caused by less productive activities. With that goal in mind, a new class of senior managers – made up of men like Firm Bentley, Dr Mark Abbott, Pierre Choquette, Bill Pursell, and Charles Ambridge – sent out directives to the various divisions emphasizing the need for growth in high value-added areas that offered attractive profit margins. During the 1970s Ralph Rowzee, Bill Buckler, Stanley Wilk, and Roger Hatch all left the firm. For thirty years these men had provided the company's intellectual leadership. Their direction in the areas of research and development, marketing, distribution, and finance had established Polymer as a world-class producer of synthetic rubber. Through their actions the Crown corporation had established its core competencies. Perhaps the greatest compliment that could be paid to these men was that in 1979 their successors decided to get back to basics, refocusing on the fields that they had so ably cultivated.

By 1983 Polymer's rubber operations were again the largest in the free world, with major production facilities in six different countries. That year rubber sales accounted for more than 60 percent of total revenues. Under the direction of Robert Dudley, who replaced Ian

Rush as president in 1981, renewed attention was given to technical and customer service – a hallmark of the early years. Where growth was deemed not to be the primary means of obtaining market leadership, increased importance was placed on productivity improvements and rationalization of existing operations to increase capacity utilization.

The new strategy brought a re-alignment of corporate responsibilities. The new organizational structure comprised three divisions: basic petrochemicals, rubber, and diversified products. Later, in 1986, a fourth division – the Asia-Pacific Group – was added. Its formation was the first concrete step in the corporate objective of establishing a physical presence in the Asia-Pacific region. Polymer viewed this region as "the fastest growing [market] in the world."[26] In 1986, after it had been engaged in business there for more than thirty years, only 5 percent of Polymer's sales revenue came from the region. Management wanted this percentage increased. As a consequence, the corporation broadened its sales base by adding manufacturing and warehousing facilities there. In addition, Polymer became the first Canadian manufacturing company to form a joint venture in the People's Republic of China. Located in Shanghai, Shanghai Gao Qiao-Polysar Company oversaw the production of three thousand tons of latex rubber per year. These key elements gave Polymer the competitive advantage it needed to increase its market share and to grow as an industry leader. The corporation's new strategic mission was to go back to what it did best, and that meant developing new and improved polymeric substances through innovation and R&D.

One area that had particularly suffered during the diversification drive of the 1960s and 1970s was research and development – the cornerstone of technological innovation. Companies fell into the habit of thinking that they could acquire others' technology rather than generating their own. By 1979 Canadian investment in R&D had declined to 0.9 percent of GNP from a high of 1.4 percent in 1967. What was even more disturbing to some business observers was the fact that most R&D in Canada was not being undertaken by industry but by government laboratories and universities.[27] Unlike in most other industrial countries, where about two-thirds of R&D was carried out by private enterprise, in Canada in 1979 industry undertook only 40 percent of research and development. Critics complained that due to the low priority it had placed on R&D, Canadian business had fallen behind its major competitors, particularly the Japanese, whose investment in R&D had continued unabated since the end of the Second World War. This situation would continue, warned the economist Charles McMillan, who would serve for a time as an adviser to Brian Mulroney, if

Productivity Growth, 1945–72.

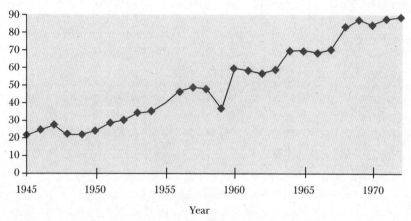

Year

As the graph demonstrates, the amount of rubber produced per employee (productivity) increased more than fourfold during the period 1945–72, from 21 to 88 long tons.

Canadian firms did not learn from the Japanese and invest more in the development of technologies. Only this investment would improve production processes and enable firms to shift product lines more rapidly in response to changing market conditions.[28] The business press agreed. "It's high noon for high technology," read a *Financial Post* supplement on innovation in 1980.[29] Canadian firms needed to invest more in applied research and rely less on borrowed technology if they were to remain competitive in an increasingly global environment. The dismal state of Canadian industrial research precipitated calls for government action.[30] But while there was a theoretical and intellectual awareness in Ottawa of the need to stimulate innovation, the federal government hesitated to offer any substantial fiscal incentive.

For the first twenty-five years of Polymer existence, R&D had played a leading role in the firm's success. Although it had never been undertaken solely for its own sake, research was the program that gave Polymer its competitive edge. Without the resources necessary to make a major breakthrough in basic science, Polymer focused on applying science to bring needed products into regular and profitable use. Often this strategy involved scouring the world for customers' needs and for technology from universities and research institutes in other industries. These two ends of the innovation chain were brought together in the R&D division. Under Buckler's guidance, the firm proved remarkably adroit at harnessing science to bring new consumer goods into everyday use.[31]

But during the period 1967–77, R&D was de-emphasized and the division entered its "dark ages." With profit margins eroding rapidly because of increasing competition and rising energy and raw material costs, Polymer had little incentive to undertake what were often high-risk, capital-intensive ventures. Under these circumstances, Polymer felt that it had no choice but to cut back on its R&D expenditures. While not given to confrontation, E.J. Buckler subtly questioned the long-term wisdom of this move.[32] That said, he fully understood the short-term pressures of running a business. "Innovation, like gambling and prospecting," he wrote in 1984, "initially costs money: money is rarely made until the innovative phase is over. The total orchestra of activities, including capital investment," he continued, "can only be practiced when profits are being made and must, regrettably, be curtailed when business is poor."[33] By 1970 the synthetic rubber industry had reached maturity, and the pace of innovation slowed. At the best of times, investment in R&D took years before it returned some sort of financial reward. During the diversification drive, Polymer lost its faith in the ability of R&D to produce a profitable and timely return. It wanted a higher and more immediate yield from its investment, and to get this, it thought it best to siphon off money from R&D and invest it in new, "faster-growing" areas of unrelated production.

With the decision to return to basics came a renewed emphasis on R&D. Robert Dudley was an ideas man who was committed to research and development. He understood the relationship between R&D and technological innovation. "You can not have one without the other," Dudley later stated. "They go hand in glove."[34] Born in Shanghai, China, Dudley obtained a masters degree in engineering from the University of British Columbia in 1951 and shortly thereafter joined Polymer as a process engineer. An ambitious young man, he slowly but steadily worked his way up Polymer's corporate ladder and dedicated himself to learning every facet of the rubber business. But polymer chemistry was his first love. Before becoming president in 1981, he had played a critical role in bringing bromobutyl – a brominated derivative of butyl rubber – into commercial production.

A revolutionary product, bromobutyl rubber used bromine as the principal element in its chemical construction. Bromine was a heavy, volatile, corrosive liquid element that could be mixed with the traditional components of butyl rubber. The end product had all the classic qualities of butyl rubber (i.e., resistance to tearing, flexing, and ageing, and impermeability to air, gas, and water), as well as the appeal of adhesion when cured in contact with other rubber stocks. Thus bromobutyl could be blended with other rubbers like SBR and natural rubber to obtain all the positive properties of each. Subsequent developments in the

marketplace made bromobutyl the product of choice among tire manufacturers, in particular after 1970, when the industrialized world gradually switched to radial tires. The transition occurred first in Europe but
shortly thereafter took place in North America. In 1981, fully
99 percent of all original-equipment tires were radials.[35] On the road,
the radial tire underwent a good deal of "flexing" in the sidewall region. As a consequence, manufacturers needed a tire with strong adhesion between the inner liner and the carcass. Bromobutyl rubber
allowed them to produce such a tire. Further, steel cord was becoming
preferred as the premium cord for radial tires, and it required an inner
liner giving the best-possible protection against air and moisture.
Again, bromobutyl rubber provided the industry with the means to
reach its desired end. As a result, bromobutyl quickly became the premier inner liner material. Polymer profited accordingly. "The commercial production of bromobutyl," Bill Buckler later recalled, "played an
important and perhaps crucial role in the survival of the Company."[36]

Dudley's role in bringing bromobutyl into commercial production reflected his belief in the productive power of R&D. As president he was
able to support his ideological conviction by substantial budgetary increases. While other areas experienced decreased spending and downsizing, R&D expenditures increased year after year, by more than
23 percent in 1980 and by more than 17 percent in both 1981 and 1982
– despite flat earnings and an actual loss in 1982. By 1986 spending had
increased to $48 million, ranking Polymer among the top twenty firms in
Canada in terms of R&D expenditures. More than half the R&D was undertaken in Sarnia and represented significant added value. The 1980s
were thus a radically different time for those associated with research and
development. Gone were the dark days of the 1970s. The faith in science
and innovation had returned to the banks of the St Clair River.

To further foster the spirit and the climate necessary for innovation,
an innovation fund was created. Dudley thought that corporate success
depended on encouraging people to come forward with their individual ideas.[37] A defining characteristic of Polymer's early years was the
tight internal communications loops that fostered idea sharing and, ultimately, innovation. But during the 1970s, as the corporation became
bigger, many channels of communication were lost. The innovation
fund was designed to restore them by reducing bureaucratic barriers so
that creative idea generation and problem solving could take place. In
many ways the fund was a reincarnation of the "coin-your-ideas" program that Polymer initiated after the war. Employees were rewarded for
coming up with new and more efficient ways of doing things. These
measures helped Polymer regain its reputation as one of the most innovative companies in the synthetic-rubber industry.

Sales Revenue by Market Area, 1986.

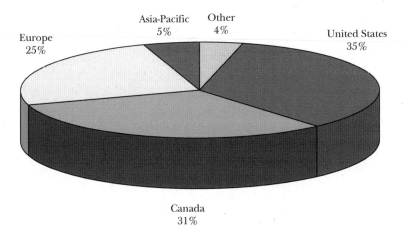

Initially these measures brought the desired results, as the decade commenced with stronger sales. But by 1981 the economy had entered a recession, dampening market demand and weakening prices. As the recession continued, so did high inflation, high interest rates, and high raw material prices. In 1982 Polymer experienced the worst results in its history, registering a $30.5 million loss on sales of $1.33 billion.[38] Polymer's Canadian operations were most deeply affected. While the corporation sought to maintain its momentum in terms of meeting its strategic goals, it was faced with plant shutdowns and lowered production. As it had done in the past when faced with declining revenues, Polymer curtailed its expenditures and focused on careful cash management. Unlike during the 1970s, however, this time it maintained its commitment to R&D. The commitment paid off in 1987, with the introduction of Tornac rubber – a heat and oil resistant rubber that would maintain its properties at 150°C for more than 1,000 hours. The development won the company the Canadian Award for Business Excellence – inventions category.

Instead of cutting R&D, the company put the completion of large projects, such as the new, state-of-the-art butyl rubber plant at Sarnia, on hold and initiated downsizing of existing operations. In this hostile climate, efforts to improve internal communications and innovation met with weakened morale, especially among employees caught in the uncertainty of the economic situation. The loss in 1982, a change from positive earnings of $22 million in the previous year, did not, however, divert the corporation from its strategic mission. As the global economic situation changed in 1983 and 1984, Polymer's own situation improved. The efforts at cost reduction and rationalization of services brought positive results in 1983 with a net income of $8.7 million, followed by a substantial increase to $36 million in 1984. By the end of 1983, Polymer had completed its major capital projects, including the Butyl II project, at a final cost of $360 million. Incorporating the latest technology, the Butyl II plant represented the largest single investment Polymer had ever made.

Polymer had thus returned to being an aggressive and agile corporate player. During the 1980s it moved into high technology and specialty products and into new geographic and product markets. The focus on R&D and technological innovation, which had been lost during the diversification mania of the 1970s, had reemerged. By the mid-1980s the strategy of getting back to basics was having its desired financial effect.

The return to profitability would have come sooner if the Petrosar situation had not impacted so negatively upon Polymer's performance. The giant feedstock operation was a money pit. At the beginning of 1980, Polymer held a 40.2 percent stake in Petrosar, while its parent company, the CDC, held an additional 19.8 percent interest. From a financial standpoint, Petrosar was a complete failure. At the close of 1984, it had losses totalling $159 million. No dividends had been received from the investment, while Polymer was committed to furnishing 48 percent of the additional funds necessary to meet Petrosar's debt obligations.[39]

When the project was undertaken, it was justified by the prospect that Petrosar would provide Polymer with competitively priced feedstock. For petrochemical producers, feedstock constituted between 60 percent and 70 percent of manufacturing costs. Thus, any reduction in feedstock expenses would enhance Polymer's competitive position relative to that of petrochemical producers elsewhere. During the world energy crisis of the 1970s the project seemed to make some sense. It appealed especially to those with a penchant for megaprojects. Nevertheless, even then plenty of thoughtful people questioned the logic of Petrosar. "I still find Petrosar a mind-boggling proposition," stated Michael Graham in his 1976 report on corporate concentration. "There would surely be very real problems if the Canadian oil price was to get excessively out of line with the U.S. oil price in particular."[40] Graham could not have imagined the prescience of his statement. Subsequent developments demonstrated the folly of the Petrosar project.

When the project began, naphtha – a product similar to the gasoline component of crude oil – was chosen as the feedstock for the Petrosar plant, for two reasons. First, it came closest to producing the range of primary petrochemicals required by Polymer and its partner companies. Second, it was the most economic feedstock for the chemical industry. However, when it became evident that naphtha could not be processed locally in a volume sufficient to sustain capacity operations, the decision was made to base the operation on Western Canadian crude oil. Consequently, an additional processing step was required to separate the naphtha from the crude oil, and in turn, the Petrosar project had to be expanded into something much larger and costlier than initially imagined.

The financial success of the project depended in part upon Western Canadian oil prices never getting excessively out of line with prices elsewhere, and particularly in the United States. While that was the case during the 1970s, it was not so during the early 1980s. As a result of the National Energy Program, by 1981 oil prices in Canada were higher than prices in the United States. The NEP, which was implemented by the Trudeau government in 1980 in order to achieve a greater degree of energy self-sufficiency, had created a pricing regime for domestic oil and gas that involved incremental rate increases every six months. The architects of the NEP believed that this regime would protect Canadian consumers from further shocks to the international energy market. Although the schedule of price increases anticipated a substantial rise in the price of oil to Canadian consumers, the architects of the NEP were confident that international prices would rise further and more suddenly than oil prices under their regime. They were wrong.

Almost as soon as the pricing mechanism was put into place, the price of oil on international markets began to fall. This decline gave petrochemical companies operating in more market-responsive systems, such as the one that prevailed in the United States, a tremendous competitive advantage. Unlike its major competitors, Petrosar was committed to purchasing higher-priced Western Canadian crude oil. This disadvantage was compounded by Petrosar's inability to use natural gas as well as crude oil. Petrosar's sourcing flexibility was being compromised; the company was unable to take advantage of price and market conditions. Because of the government's strategic decision to encourage a shift away from oil to natural gas in patterns of energy consumption, the NEP's schedule of price increases involved a more gradual rise in the price of gas than was involved in the corresponding program for oil. An incidental effect of this policy was to further improve the economics of the gas-based petrochemical industry in Alberta, since the regulated domestic price for natural gas was the principal variable determining the price of ethane feedstock.[41] It was not surprising, therefore, that many of Alberta's petrochemical firms, such as Bob Blair's Nova Corporation, were, on balance, supporters of the NEP.[42]

Before any additional strategic steps could be taken at Polymer, Robert Dudley felt that Petrosar had to be turned around. In Petrosar he felt Polymer had a "hideous monster."[43] The petrochemical animal would have to be brought under control if Polymer was to prosper in the future. Like Roger Hatch before him, Dudley had questioned the wisdom of the Petrosar project at the time of its conception, although as a young man striving to make his way up the corporate ladder, he was very careful with whom he expressed his doubts. He certainly did not share them with his mentor Ian Rush.[44] Rush did not tolerate dissent and Dudley knew it. Thus, like a good soldier, he fell into line and kept his mouth shut. In one sense, the approach paid off: Rush nominated Dudley as his successor when he stepped down as president in 1981. But with that change, the Petrosar problem became Dudley's problem.

Dudley was determined to make the best of a bad situation. Although he had never been a staunch supporter of the project, he was sanguine that if domestic oil prices were brought into line with world prices, a turnabout in Petrosar's fortunes would be possible. Existing profit margins within Petrosar were low, but changes in the price of raw materials would increase the profitability and viability of the operation. The first thing that had to go, therefore, was the NEP. In 1984, Polymer joined with others in the Canadian petrochemical industry calling on the government "to obtain market related prices for feedstocks."[45] The industry found the newly elected Mulroney government receptive to their position, and in 1985 the NEP was terminated and oil prices were deregulated.

In April of that year, Polymer took over complete ownership of Petrosar. Dudley felt that if Petrosar was to be turned around and made profitable, Polymer would have to have absolute control. One of his earlier objections to the Petrosar project was that there were too many competing interests involved. Now he was going to rectify the situation. In 1985 Polymer approached Union Carbide and Du Pont of Canada with an offer to assume their 40 percent stake. Union Carbide and Du Pont could not have been more receptive to the proposal. The Petrosar project had undermined their financial performance for far too long, and they were tired of throwing good money after bad. Thus, when Dudley proposed a restructuring of the corporation to allow them a graceful exit, they declared their unequivocal support.

The complex restructuring of Petrosar included the issue of nonvoting, nontrading redeemable preferred shares ($188 million) to Union Carbide and Du Pont and the purchase of the CDC's interest for a nominal consideration. The preferred shares would become the subject of much dispute two years later during the takeover battle with

Nova Corporation. Under the terms of the restructuring, Union Carbide and Du Pont also promised to buy $100 million in ethylene from Petrosar annually, as well to subscribe to shares in the CDC. The proceeds from the deal would provide Polymer with funds necessary to reduce Petrosar's debt, and to begin to convert some of its operations to utilize cheaper-priced natural gas.

The integration of Petrosar brought an improvement in Polymer's debt-to-equity ratio, lowering it from roughly 2:1 to 1.5:1. But it impinged upon Polymer's corporate results, since Petrosar's operating losses were now fully consolidated. In 1985 Polymer recorded a net loss of $520,000 on sales of $1.86 billion.[46] The loss would have been a $15 million profit if not for Petrosar's on-going financial troubles. Admittedly, thereafter the situation moderately improved. Nevertheless, Polymer would have been much better off if it had never embarked upon the Petrosar project. Between the beginning of operations in 1978 and the restructuring in 1985, Polymer's average after-tax rate of return on investment in Petrosar was a loss of 8.5 percent per annum. In only one year, 1980, did Polymer's share in Petrosar contribute positively – albeit ever so modestly – to Polymer's financial results. The losses had become particularly heavy in recent years: between 1983 and 1985 Polymer's share in the losses at Petrosar had totalled over $65 million.[47] Michael Graham was correct: Petrosar was a "mind-boggling proposition." It *had* resulted in "very real problems" and negatively affected Polymer's financial performance. Perhaps Dudley and others should have piped up when they had the chance. But Roger Hatch was the only one to do so. As a result, the megaproject had gone ahead, and Polymer had suffered accordingly.

The troubles at Petrosar were only a small part of the CDC's financial woes. An unwieldy collection of incompatible assets, the CDC had long been an economic underachiever. From the start, it had suffered from lackadaisical direction, an insurmountable debt load, and contradictory corporate objectives. Tony Hampson, who had been at the helm of the CDC since its inception, was not an inspired day-to-day manager. Under his watch the CDC became bloated, with very little in the way of strategic direction. Nevertheless, the board of directors was unwilling to demand Hampson's resignation until it was too late. In 1982 every division of the CDC except for tiny Life Sciences Inc. was showing an operating loss, and millions of dollars in bad investments had to be written off.[48]

The commercial performance of Polymer's parent company was poor by virtually any standard. The return on shareholders' equity in the CDC, for example, averaged just 5.1 percent during the period

1977–82. During the same period, the TSE 300 management companies' composite averaged 10.5 percent.[49] The CDC recorded a 3:1 price to earnings ratio in 1980 and a 2:1 ratio in 1981, compared with 7.6:1 and 6.0:1, respectively, for the TSE 300 management companies composite. In 1984 and 1985 several academic studies concluded that the CDC was being inefficiently run.[50] Summing up these studies, economist D.F. McFetridge stated that the "judgments regarding the contribution of the CDC to Canadian growth and development are as close to unanimity as occurs in the social sciences – namely, it has not made a contribution."[51] The failure of the CDC led McFetridge to conclude in his comparison of government, mixed, and private enterprise that the mixed enterprise "is more likely to constitute the worst than the best of all possible worlds."[52]

In May 1987, the tall, aristocratic Tony Hampson was finally forced to step down as chairman of the board. He was invited to remain as the CDC's deputy chairman – a corporate title that was the equivalent of the kiss of a mafia don. But Hampson refused. When asked why he was not remaining on the board, he stated that he was not the kind of person to hang around and fade away. "I'm not the shrinking violet type," he boldly declared. "I am too strong willed and too energetic."[53] And with that he took his leave of the company he had overseen since its formation in 1972. French-born Bernard Isautier, the one-time president of Aquitaine Company of Canada – an energy producer that was absorbed by the CDC in 1981 – replaced Hampson. Dubbed by the *Financial Post* "the most bankable senior executive in Canada," Isautier rapidly pared the CDC down to its "core business units."[54]

Isautier was an early convert to the new business orthodoxy of "sticking to the knitting." Companies, he maintained, should do what they do best, nothing more and nothing less. Given that, he disposed of the CDC's assorted investments in office and industrial equipment, venture capital, fishery products, pharmaceuticals, and mining. Polymer was among the few operations he left untouched. According to Isautier, being big was not necessarily better, and thus he set about streamlining the CDC's operations. The ultimate goal was to improve competitiveness and increase shareholder value. The payroll was consequently shrunk to seven thousand from seventeen thousand. The downsizing helped reduce the CDC's debt from $4.6 billion to about $2 billion.

Under Isautier, the CDC was becoming a different company. Like its subsidiary Polymer, the CDC was getting back to basics, attempting to focus on what it did best and scrapping the rest. By 1987, the corporation had a definite strategic focus and core competency. It was aiming to be a multinational oil and gas producer and maker of petrochemicals. To reflect the renewed emphasis on its core businesses, the CDC changed its name in 1987 to Polysar Energy & Chemical Corporation. Polysar Energy consisted of two main parts: Polymer Ltd, which remained the world's biggest synthetic-rubber maker and North America's third-largest polystyrene producer, and Canterra Energy Ltd, its oil and gas subsidiary.[55]

By the end of 1987, the new strategy and structure was already producing positive results. That year, Polysar Energy reported a net income of $227.5 million, up from a loss of $296.8 million the previous year.[56] Most of the gain was from the rubber and plastic operations, which generated $176.5 million in operating income.[57] The earnings were so good that the board of directors took the opportunity to thank its workforce. "To each of our employees, we say thank you for your efforts in a challenging environment and know that we can depend upon you – our greatest asset – in the months and years ahead."[58] Ironically, it was the last annual address the board of directors would give to the men and women of Polysar. Later that year the Mulroney government followed through on its early promise to sell its remaining share in the firm. While no one anticipated it at the time, the sale would trigger a battle for Polysar/CDC that would become one of the most vicious in Canadian business history.

The Mulroney government had come to power in 1984 on the promise of removing the state from the boardrooms of the nation. During the election the Tories were able to capitalize on the declining fervour for government-induced megaprojects (e.g., the Alberta tar sands and the National Energy Program) and the penchant of the government for "picking winners." Not all Crown corporations had performed as profitably as Polymer. During the 1970s the government had made a number of "investments in failure."[59] Canadair, a producer of advanced aircraft, was a prominent example. In 1976 the Liberal government had bought Canadair from General Dynamics for $38 million, with the aim of preserving jobs and stimulating high-technology manufacturing. Faced with declining demand for military aircraft and the firm's flagging water-bomber sales, Canadair decided to make a major entry into the commercial aviation market by producing a new executive jet, the Challenger. Ottawa and Quebec City provided most of the start-up capital for the project. The money was not well spent, however. In 1982, the corporation announced a loss of $1.4 billion, the largest corporate loss in Canadian history.[60] More than $1 billion of the loss was the result of the Challenger program. The taxpayers' money was never fully recovered. As *Maclean's* magazine noted in 1983, "for the Canadian taxpayers, the Challenger has proven to be a very, very expensive way to fly."[61]

For some the Canadair debacle was only the latest example of the shortcomings of state-owned enterprise. In 1976 the auditor general issued a scathing report on the federal government's mismanagement of its corporations that maintained that the federal government had lost control over its companies. "Polygate" certainly provided grist for the auditor general's mill. The federal government had no idea that one of its companies was engaged in improper business practices until the story broke in the national press, demonstrating that the government had become ignorant about its businesses. While in opposition the Conservatives had criticized the slipshod financial management practices at PISA, as well as at Atomic Energy of Canada[62] The fact that Petro-Canada had taken it upon itself to expand in nearly every direction – more than tripling in size between 1979 and 1984 – was further evidence that the Crowns were out of control. In Tory minds, the CDC, Petro-Canada, and AECL symbolized a "lack of accountability" that was intrinsic to all state-owned enterprise.[63]

The lack of accountability or profitability among many of the federal government's corporations seemed to confirm the Tories' presumption that the state had no place in the boardrooms of the nation. Like other neoconservative governments around the world, particularly Margaret Thatcher's in the United Kingdom and Ronald Reagan's south of the border, the Mulroney government viewed public enterprise as symptomatic of an intrusive state and accepted as axiomatic the benefits to be derived from privatization. Only the iron discipline of the market, the Conservatives maintained, could ensure a firm's efficiency.[64] The Tories often pointed to the CDC as evidence of the folly of state intervention. During the 1984 election campaign, Mulroney promised Canadians he would downsize government and the national debt by strengthening the market at the expense of the state. He committed himself to reducing the level of direct government ownership, then exceeding $53 billion in assets, by privatizing, eliminating, or otherwise restraining the Crown corporations. Gone was the Red Tory urge. Mulroney was, in belief if not always in action, a neoconservative.[65] He believed that free markets were the most efficient systems for allocating resources and distributing income. Correlated with this was the tropism of minimizing the role of the state in economic activity.

Mulroney's neoconservative rhetoric resonated with a population eager for change. As a result, the Tories took 211 of 282 seats in the House of Commons – a majority greater even than Diefenbaker's in 1958. After the Tory victory, the trend in public policy was away from state planning and nationalization and toward decentralization and privatization.[66] Between 1985 and 1990, the federal government moved in a "deliberate" manner to downsize the state by selling a number of Crown companies.[67] It divested its holding in five mixed-ownership corporations, privatized thirteen parent Crown corporations, and divested at least seven subsidiaries of parent corporations. Another eight Crown corporations were wound up. Among the Crown corporations that were privatized were Air Canada, De Havilland, Aircraft Canada, Canadair, Teleglobe, Northern Transportation Company, Canadian Arsenals, and Polymer's parent company the CDC.[68]

The federal government had been slowly selling off its shares in the CDC since 1982. That year the government offered 23 million shares for sale, to be distributed in two installments. The sale, which netted the state $241 million, reduced the government's stake in the corporation from 46.8 percent to just over 10 percent. Under the existing legislation the government could go no further, since the Canada Development Corporation Act of 1972 prohibited it from reducing its ownership in the CDC to less than 10 percent. But in 1985 the Tories introduced legislation in the House of Commons that did away with this provision and paved the way for the CDC's complete privatization.

The Tories could not conceive of any rationale for continued ownership in the company. Its primary objective no longer served a public-policy purpose. Instead, the CDC was in business for profit, although from the state of its balance sheet this goal was often hard to detect. In May 1985 the Progressive Conservative finance minister, Michael Wilson, stated that "any crown corporation that did not fulfill a policy purpose would be sold."[69] The CDC fit the profile. As a result, work began on its final privatization.

As president and CEO of the CDC, Tony Hampson was invited to appear before the legislative committee considering the sale of the government's remaining shares. In general, Hampson supported the idea of moving the Crown's holdings in the CDC fully into the private sector.[70] He and Ottawa had rarely seen eye-to-eye, and a sale would remove the government once and for all from the CDC's operations. In Hampson's mind, the primary purpose of the CDC was to generate a financial return for its shareholders. Ottawa, however, had historically been more inclined to see the CDC as an instrument of public policy. As late as 1982 the Liberal government had attempted to pressure the CDC into bailing out Dome Petroleum.

Started in 1950 by a thirty-four-year-old geologist nicknamed Smiling Jack Gallagher, Dome Petroleum was a Canadian energy giant with head offices in Calgary. During the 1970s and early 1980s Dome grew by making acquisitions in the energy industry. The most famous purchase came in 1981 when it acquired a 52.9 percent stake in Hudson's Bay Oil and Gas Company. For a while it seemed that Dome was heading for international greatness, but then the economy weakened. With almost $7 billion in debts from past takeovers, Dome teetered on the brink of bankruptcy. Never one to let his pride stand in the way of profits, Gallagher called on the government for help. He was a long-time Liberal party supporter and a personal friend of the deputy minister of Energy, Mines and Resources, Tom Shoyama. Indeed, in the late 1970s the two men sat on the CDC's board of directors together. Gallagher used his personal connections in an effort to get the government to bail out his debt-ridden firm. In mid-1982 the government began to "lean on" the CDC to intervene, but the CDC refused to help out, for commercial reasons.[71] Dome, the CDC correctly concluded, was a corporate basket case.[72] This, however, was not the end of government's efforts to direct the affairs of the firm.

In May 1982 Ottawa pressured the CDC's board of directors to have businessman and Liberal party stalwart Maurice Strong replace Wick Sellers as chairman of the CDC's board.[73] Again the CDC refused. Hampson hoped that the final privatization would forever remove Ottawa's very visible hand from the CDC's boardroom. Once that had occurred, Hampson informed the legislative committee in October 1985, the CDC would focus on creating an entrepreneurial, Canadian-based, and internationally competitive enterprise for its shareholders: "Our philosophy after full privatization will continue to be not to intervene in the day-to-day affairs of our companies but to put strong operating management in those enterprises."[74] He pointed to Polymer as an example of how things were done at the CDC.[75] But Hampson was being somewhat disingenuous, since Polymer had survived and prospered in spite of the CDC's ownership. ·

While Hampson strongly supported privatization, he had certain reservations about Bill C-66, An Act respecting the Reorganization of the Canada Development Corporation. Before the legislative committee considering the CDC's privatization, Hampson recommended a number of revisions "to deal with potential problem areas that could in certain circumstances allow an investor or an associate group of investors, either Canadian or foreign, to evade its intent."[76] The percentage stipulated in Bill C-66 for investors who were associated with each other gave Hampson the greatest concern. Under the draft legislation, one corporation was assumed to be associated with another if it owned more than 50 percent of its voting shares. In reality, Hampson maintained, many companies were effectively controlled with far less than a 50 percent stake. He had a point. In the mid-1980s Power Corporation had taken effective control of Consolidated Paper with 37 percent ownership of its shares. Likewise, Brascan had effectively controlled Noranda and Royal Trust with less than a 50 percent stake. In addition, Conrad Black's group controlled NorSand with less than 36 percent ownership. Thus, Hampson recommended amending Bill c-66 to a reduced percentage from 50 percent to 20 percent for investors deemed to be associated with one another. Without such a change, he warned, the 25 percent limit on any single Canadian shareholder proposed in the bill would be an "empty delusion." Hampson was thus attempting to protect the CDC from a potential hostile takeover.

The Tories ignored all Hampson's recommendations, however, and wasted little time passing Bill c-66 into law. As of 25 November 1985 the government was free to reduce its stake in the CDC to zero.[77] Within two years, Prime Minister Brian Mulroney's privatization minister, Barbara McDougall, announced the sale of the federal government's last 7,486,344 shares in the CDC. "Crown ownership in the CDC," McDougall stated at the time of the final sale, "is no longer needed to meet government policy objectives."[78] The sale netted the Canadian taxpayer an additional $120 million. In total, therefore, the government had sold its 48.2 percent stake in the CDC for $361 million. There was no vast giveaway here. In keeping with their principles for privatization, the Tories had not sold the government stake at a distressed price merely to transfer it to the private sector.[79]

Nevertheless, for some observers the CDC's privatization was a solemn moment. "The final CDC sale," lamented the journalist Don McGillvary, "marks the death of an old dream."[80] In the House of Commons economic nationalists within the NDP expressed a similar sentiment. Stephen Langdon, a disciple of Walter Gordon and MP for Essex-Windsor, declared that the CDC was a valuable asset that would have made a "tremendous contribution" to Canadian economic development if it had been allowed to continue.[81] Langdon, like others on the political left, grieved the passing of the statist impulse that had accompanied the CDC's creation. Gone was the economic nationalism of the early 1970s. The tendency was now away from state intervention and Canadianization. The CDC's final sale made that abundantly clear.

Why all the concern, Hampson was asked when he proposed changing Bill c-66 to protect the CDC from the potential of a hostile takeover. "Is there someone at the back door, or is there someone around the corner, who is waiting to go down that particular road?"[82] "No," replied Hampson. "If there is somebody skulking, he is in the bushes at the moment and has not declared himself."[83]

Bob Blair certainly had not declared himself. The maverick corporate wrangler who ran Calgary's Nova Corporation had made an art of lurking in the shadows until the time was right to strike. Only in 1987 did the industry become aware of Blair's intentions to acquire a big slice of the Polysar pie. When the government sold its final shares in the CDC, Blair's voracious Nova Corporation acquired the vast majority. The purchase began one of the most hotly contested corporate raids in Canadian history.

Nova Corporation was the successor of Alberta Gas Trunk Line (AGTL), which had been established by the Alberta government in 1954 to prevent Ottawa (i.e., C.D. Howe) from exercising legislative and regulatory control over the production, marketing and pricing of Alberta gas.[84] During the 1950s and 1960s AGTL had restricted its activities to the operation of a natural gas pipeline grid within Alberta.[85] But when Bob Blair took over as president of the corporation in 1970, AGTL spread its wings far and wide. Blair, who was later described by Peter C. Newman as "the thinking man's energy Baron,"[86] pursued two parallel strategies, revitalizing AGTL's transmission function and diversifying into other corporate areas. Blair's method of diversification was in at least one way similar to Polymer's in that he expanded into diverse fields through the acquisition of on-going concerns. Blair, however, proved much more savvy in making his acquisitions than Hatch and the diversification team at Polymer had been. In 1978 he brilliantly outmaneuvered both Petro-Canada and Dr Armand Hammer's Occidental Petroleum Corporation in a battle for the control of Husky Oil – a multinational oil producer and refiner.[87] Earlier, he had proved similarly artful in acquiring a controlling interest in the Alaska Highway Pipeline.[88] As a result of Blair's acquisitions, by 1980 AGTL was a major player in the Western petrochemical scene.

To reflect its growth and increasing diversity, in 1980 AGTL changed its name to Nova, An Alberta Corporation. Under Blair's direction, Nova continued to expand during the 1980s.[89] An ardent nationalist, Blair dreamed of creating a Canadian-based world leader in petrochemicals. "If you act on a purely financial basis and make your decisions entirely on dollar criteria – as though the world was without boundaries and Canada has no national spirit – in the long run, you lose track of reality because the existence of national attributes is just as much a fact of life as the existence of fiscal criteria."[90] In keeping with this philosophy, in 1987 Nova purchased the Moore Township polyethylene plant from American-based Union Carbide. About 40 percent of the plant's total ethylene feedstock – a natural gas derivative used in the manufacture of textiles and plastics – was provided by Polysar's plant at Sarnia. With supplies tight and prices skyrocketing, Blair felt Nova had to do something with respect to its long-term supply of ethylene. He also felt that by acquiring a venerable Canadian corporation like Polysar, he would move one step closer to realizing his dream of forming a Canadian petrochemical leviathan. Thus, he began purchasing large amounts of Polysar stock with the ultimate goal of taking over the corporation.

The fight for Polysar began in October 1987, when Nova acquired its first 9.7 percent stake in the firm. Three months later, Nova tried to raise its holding in Polysar Energy, Polymer's parent company, to 30.9 percent through a $14-per-share offering. Polysar's board of directors viewed the bid with hostility. The board was made up of such leading business luminaries as Bernard Lamarre, Bill Dimma, Kendal Cork, Pat Keenan, John Burk, Pierre Côté, Don Campbell, Don Lougheed, Bud McCuaig, and Bill Mongo. Also on the board was Bill Wilder, a veteran corporate director who had tangled with Bob Blair once before when trying to build a pipeline down the Mackenzie River Valley. Blair's aggressive tactics distressed these pillars of the Canadian establishment. Polysar's president, Bernard Isautier, who himself owned 40,000 shares plus stock options, charged that Blair was "nickel and diming" Polysar. Isautier thought the company would be valued somewhere around $25 a share if its $5.4 billion of assets were sold off. The two sides were thus miles apart.

Nova's hostile bid sent Polysar's boardroom into a state of panic. "It was as if we were mobilizing for total war," remembered Bill Dimma.[91] Time was of the essence: Polysar had to do something quickly if it was to defend itself. In January 1988 plans were formulated to ward off the Western corporate raider. Polysar realized that in order to survive, it needed to keep its investors loyal during the takeover struggle. As a result, the following month a complex restructuring of the corporation was proposed, in an effort to free up $900 million in cash and extra securities. Polysar's board of directors promised to distribute the funds to existing shareholders over a five-year period. The enormous sop was a defensive tactic. Re-capitalization had been employed successfully in the United States to discourage similarly hostile takeover bids. Nova Corporation issued a strongly worded response to Polysar's proposed restructuring: "It appears the implementation of the plan would not be in the best interest of Polysar Energy's shareholders and creditors," stated William Wilson, Nova's executive vice-president and chief financial officer.[92] The restructuring program, he warned, would neutralize the impressive financial gains made by Polysar over the previous year and hamper its ability to maintain capital spending at an optimum level. But Nova's attempt at moral suasion did not work, and Polysar's poison pill had its desired effect. It boosted the price of Polysar's common shares to $15.13 and thereby effectively killed Nova's opening bid of $14 a share.

Polysar was keenly aware, however, that the battle had just begun and that in order to survive in the long run it would need allies. Thus, it began soliciting support from other petrochemical producers to help fight off Nova's unwelcome offer. Polysar found a friend in Union

Carbide. On 22 February 1988, the two companies announced conversion of Carbide's 1985 nonvoting, nontrading preferred shares into 7 percent of Polysar's voting stock. If approved by the shareholders, the conversion would dilute the common equity and thus weaken Nova's hand. Realizing this, Nova attempted to block the private placement to Carbide. In early March, Nova filed a complaint with the Toronto Stock Exchange maintaining that the conversion was "an unfair defensive tactic" in Polysar's fight against Nova's takeover bid.[93] After a vicious court battle, the TSE ruled that the Union Carbide conversion had to be put to a shareholder vote. With the vote scheduled for 15 April 1988, both sides began mobilizing their forces. Nova enlisted the support of Noranda Inc., which threw its 10.5 percent share in Polysar behind Nova's initiative. With Noranda in its corner, Nova was able to block the placement. Nova's victory brought a swift and emotional response from Polysar's management: "Nova's tactics are absolute crap," stated Patrick Howe, Polysar's vice-president of corporate relations.[94] Robert Dudley later echoed Howe's sentiment, stating that Nova was guilty of debauched behaviour.[95] The unusually emotional tenor of what Peter C. Newman termed "the bitter Nova-Polysar slugfest" spilled over into the street, with observers and financial analysts taking sides.[96] The battle for control of Polysar was tearing apart the tightly knit Canadian chemical industry, as well as the usually detached financial community.

On 29 March 1988, Blair made another bid to acquire a controlling interest in Polysar. He was a tenacious suitor, and despite repeated professions of fading interest, he was not willing to walk away from his target. This time Nova was offering $17 a share. The figure was getting close to Isautier's desired price of $25 per share. As a consequence, Polysar's board of directors demanded some additional time to consider the offer. The ploy was reminiscent of another board of directors' delay on a takeover bid. After receiving a $456-million offer from Gulf Canada Resources, Asamera Inc. had delayed its response until the board and its financial advisors analyzed the offer. In the end, Asamera had rejected the offer and advised its shareholders to do the same. It was a similar story at Polysar. From Polysar's perspective, Nova's offer, while the best to date, was still not good enough. As a result, it too was rejected. "Our objective," Isautier stated, "is to maximize the value of our shares, and Nova has always been too cheap in its offers."[97] Isautier had no emotional attachment to Polysar. He was a cosmopolitan businessman who had made a name for himself by quickly turning around troubled companies. Usually this meant stripping them down to their basic assets by selling off incompatible business units. The proceeds would then be used to reduce corporate debt. Isautier believed that his responsibility was to the shareholder. His ultimate goal therefore was to raise Polysar's price per share.

In early June, officials from Polysar Energy & Chemical and Nova again attempted to reach an agreement on a deal, but negotiations broke off on 11 June 1988 amid renewed recriminations. With Isautier threatening to sell off more of Polysar's assets, including the all-important Sarnia plant, a deal was finally reached four days later. During the final stage of the negotiations, which took place in the stylish offices of Gordon Capital Corporation, atop Bay Street's Toronto-Dominion Bank Tower, Blair and Isautier stayed in separate rooms. The powerful but publicity-shy James Conacher, chairman of Gordon Capital, who had set up their meeting, shuttled between them with offers and counteroffers. Blair, whose principal objective was to gain control of the prized Sarnia plant, finally agreed to raise his offer to $20.31 a share. Isautier accepted; he had shown his mettle. Despite considerable pressure to do otherwise, he had turned down four Nova offers, in the process adding $1.4 billion to the value of Polysar's shares between January, when the bidding began, and June, when the deal was reached.

Despite the emphasis placed on money during the eight-month struggle, there was more to the deal than short-term financial gain. Polysar's major asset was its petrochemical plant at Sarnia. Queen's Park officials had already expressed their displeasure at Calgary-based Nova gaining a major share of one of Ontario's most valued industries. The sale also gave Nova control of over 80 percent of Canadian production of ethylene. This was one of the drawbacks of privatization. With Polysar in Nova's hands, the industry was further concentrated. In a telegram to the Bureau of Competition Policy, the federal agency that policed corporate concentration in Canada, Ontario premier David Peterson expressed reservations about the transaction. "Future plants to produce ethylene derivatives," he wrote, "will not be built in Ontario, despite clear commercial advantage." He was right. They were not.

Blair was in fact never committed to Polysar's rubber operation. He never viewed it as providing a strategic fit with Nova's other divisions. The technical focus of Nova was engineering – drilling gas wells, building and installing pipelines and compressor stations, and separating ethane and propane by distillation and cracking to make ethylene. The commercial side of Nova's business was all domestic, or at most North American. Customer service was minimal, except for polyethylene, and that was a fairly simple process. The technical basis for Polymer, on the other hand, was advanced chemistry at the polymerization level and at the compounding level. Unlike Nova, Polymer was involved with a complex patent structure. It required feedstock (e.g., butadiene, acrylonite, isobutylene, and isoprene) that was not related to Nova's line of business. In addition, Polymer's business, unlike Nova's, involved intense technical service with rubber users in many industries: manufacturers of tires, hose, mechanical goods, flooring, and soling. Finally, Polymer exported all over the world, whereas Nova did not. Polymer had overseas plants. It required staff with many capabilities, in chemistry, languages, and marketing, as well as unusual branches of engineering. About the only characteristic that Nova and Polymer shared was that their basic businesses were both based on hydrocarbons. For Blair, that was not enough. Soon after the acquisition of Polysar, Blair moved the rubber group's (i.e., Polymer's) headquarters from Sarnia to Toronto and began considering selling the division.

The takeover of Polysar had left Nova strapped for cash. Before the acquisition, Nova had had $700 million in nonutility debt. But as a result of the hostile takeover that figure had jumped to $2.9 billion. Adding to the strain on cash flow was the fact that almost immediately after the Polysar purchase, world prices of nearly every commodity produced by Nova fell. Polyethylene, methanol, and styrene all dropped at least 40 percent in value. As a consequence, Nova's cash flow collapsed. During the second half of 1989, the corporation had earnings close to zero, which prompted the Dominion Bond Rating Service to downgrade Nova's debentures from A to BBB, and analysts and financial observers expressed serious doubts about whether Nova's surviving cash flow would cover the carrying costs of its accumulated debt, let alone dividends.[98]

These adverse conditions, combined with the increasing pressure from investors to clean up Nova's balance sheet, caused Blair to rethink his corporate strategy. In late 1989 Nova too joined the companies getting back to basics by spinning off some of its noncore subsidiaries and thereby reducing its debt load. Blair's dream of creating a leading multinational petrochemical conglomerate was thus put on hold. "We concluded that we were doing too many big things at the same time," recalled Blair.[99] Other petroleum executives were undertaking similar wrenching corporate redefinitions. The recently appointed Petro-Canada president, James Stanford, for example, had put more than $300 million in assets up for sale as the Crown corporation attempted to slim down in anticipation of privatization in 1990. "The goal now is to do the things we do well," stated Stanford, "and not to continue carrying properties in which we hold only small interest."[100] Bob Blair had reluctantly come to share this philosophy. By selling off those assets that were not directly related to its core competency, Nova aimed at getting its long-term debt on its nonpipeline assets down to 30 percent again. (It had been up to 40 percent in 1989 because of the Polysar purchase).The sale of Polysar's rubber operation would help Nova achieve its goal. "We have a lot of business responsibilities and a lot of business opportunities, and they both take a lot of capital," stated Blair in 1990. "We decided to take the step [to sell Polymer], reluctantly, for the strengthening of the future of the whole corporation."[101] Blair thus had financial and strategic reasons for selling off Polysar's rubber division.

He had little problem finding a purchaser. There were several interested suitors with both the capital and technical capabilities to take over the business. The giant German chemicals and health care company Bayer AG had been eyeing Polymer for years. Best known as the manufacturer of Aspirin, Bayer was an industrial Goliath. In 1990, it had sales of $30.5 billion and employed 170,000 people worldwide. Its rubber operations dated from the turn of the century. After three years of research into solid synthetic rubber, the world's first patent for synthetic rubber was issued to Bayer in 1909. By 1915, the company had begun producing methyl rubber, the first commercially produced synthetic rubber, at Leverkusen, Germany. In the 1920s Bayer's continued synthetic-rubber research resulted in a number of developments that became the foundation of the synthetic-rubber industry and established Bayer as a technical leader in rubber and rubber chemicals. Bayer, therefore, was an expert in synthetic rubber and was profoundly aware of Polymer's history of innovative endeavours. Nevertheless, it had not jumped in to make a bid when Polymer was a rumoured sale candidate during the hostile Nova-Polysar fight, because it had a strict rule against getting in the middle of anyone else's hostilities. Bayer's major competition, Italy's Enimont and the Dutch firm DSM, however, did make several offers. When the rubber division came back on the market in the spring of 1990, these two companies again made bids. But their offers did not compare well to Bayer's $1.48 billion offer, which included $1.25 million for the cherished rubber division and Bayer's assumption of $230 million in debt and other liabilities.

Reaction to the sale was swift and harsh. Bernard Isautier, who was now the Paris-based chairman and CEO of multinational electronics giant Thomas International, said that the quick resale proved that Bob Blair had made a mistake. "The deal was worked out badly from the financial point of view and the national interest." Isautier claimed that

Blair had failed to create the Canadian-based petrochemical giant he had promised. And by selling the Sarnia plant to Bayer, Blair had relinquished a national asset. According to Isautier he need not have done so: "If Blair had settled for a merger with Polysar rather than a takeover, he could have achieved that goal."[102] These were remarkable statements for a man of international business. In the House of Commons similar charges were laid. This time, however, the nationalist rhetoric came from far more genuine sources. Federal and Ontario politicians, as well as union leaders at Polymer, also said that they doubted that the sale was in Canada's interest. Howard McCurdy, a former professor of biology and member of the NDP, called on the federal government to stop the sale. "Will this company, once cited as one of Canada's 10 greatest engineering achievements of the century and whose picture once appeared on the $10 bill, appear on the Deutschmark instead?"[103] The minister of state, Tom Hockin, responded that the transaction would be examined by Investment Canada. It was, but the sale went through as scheduled in September 1990.

The purchase of Polysar's rubber division was the largest acquisition in Bayer's 129-year history and made the company the world's leading manufacturer of synthetic rubber and synthetic latex, with an annual capacity of around one million metric tons. Together with its rubber chemicals, Bayer now offered the widest range of products for the rubber sector of any company in the world. The acquisition also extended Bayer's portfolio to include three important classes of rubber: emulsion styrene-butadiene, ethylene-propylene, and butyl. Polymer had truly become a global company.

It was fitting that Polymer should have ended up in Bayer's hands. After all, it was German technology, imported from the United States by C.D. Howe's department of munitions and supply during the war, that had given Polymer its start. Indeed, Bayer had been responsible for a number of prewar innovations. Having been engaged in the production of synthetic rubber since 1909, Bayer understood the polymer game. Like Polymer, it had been built on a powerful research and development tradition. But unlike Polymer, it was big and foresighted enough to have expanded into new polymers, as well as other chemicals. It thus had a broad technological base, and its various fields of expertise interacted with and reinforced each other in a way that Polymer in 1990 could not hope to match. Perhaps history would have been different if Polymer had not diversified in the 1970s. But it had, and as a result it was time for a final strategic move if Polymer was to survive. Otherwise, its products and processes would gradually become obsolete. Somewhat ironically, the main benefit of Petrosar proved to be that when it was bundled with Polymer, it formed a package that appealed to a Canadian purchaser, Nova. Polymer alone would have been impossible to sell to a Canadian company, because no one had the expertise, market position, and business connections to make a success of it, and for political reasons it could not be sold to a foreign owner. As soon as the combined package was sold, the Polymer component was offered for sale again, but now it could be offered to an international corporation.

During the 1980s Polymer had gotten back to basics, refocusing its efforts on producing new and improved polymeric materials. Polymer's performance in the innovation, manufacture, and sale of synthetic rubber was so outstanding that it attracted a world-class company like Bayer. Polymer was extraordinarily lucky in that events beyond its control led Nova first to buy and then to decide to sell and in that Bayer was the company finally able to buy.

More than a decade after the fact, the synthetic-rubber plant at Sarnia is still producing rubber, although there is some question as to how long this will continue.[104] During the 1990s the plant lost a good deal of money. In the early 1990s a major recession hit the rubber industry, resulting in substantial shakeouts and downsizing. Small and medium-sized firms found it increasingly hard to compete. Only those organizations with deep pockets and integrated business structures survived. Bayer was blessed with both of these qualities. A world-class company, Bayer had a long and venerable history. It had seen downturns in the business cycle before and had usually remained focused on long-term growth and competitiveness. As a medium-sized rubber company, Polymer would likely not have endured the economic downturn: in the global environment of the 1990s, only the big survived. That is not to say that Bayer was immune to the recession. In the early 1990s Bayer Rubber cut its workforce by roughly 30 percent. (The Sarnia plant had fourteen hundred unionized production workers at the time of the sale).[105] It was not the only petrochemical operation in Sarnia to do so: Nova, Dow, and Imperial Oil also laid off workers.

By the mid 1990s, the petrochemical industry had bounced back. In 1995, Bayer Canada had combined sales of $1.2 billion. Most of the 200,000 tons of rubber produced annually was destined south of the border for products ranging from car tires to chewing gum. The North American Free Trade Agreement benefited Bayer's Canadian rubber operations. Employment at the Sarnia plant returned to the thousand-person range – the same level that it had been at in 1987.

Throughout this period, the tradition of innovation continued. Under Bayer's direction the Sarnia operation developed new and improved polymeric materials. At the time of the sale, Bayer promised to

centre its entire North American rubber business in Canada, to increase R&D, and to invest $120 million in the Canadian operations
over the next three years. Bayer followed through on its promise. As
home of one of Bayer's two rubber R&D centres worldwide, the Sarnia
operation spent about $50 million in R&D annually, more than twice
the amount spent in 1987 – the final year of Polymer's operations under the CDC.[106] The effectiveness of Bayer's strategy was evidenced in
the number of patent applications filed each year. At the end of the
1990s, Bayer's synthetic rubber was used in more than forty thousand
applications worldwide. To be sure, the heady days of the 1950s and
1960s were gone. The pace of innovation had slowed. There was less to
discover and less to improve upon. Synthetic rubber was now a fully developed product, and as a result, its production had become a commodity business. The innovation period was over, and the competitive
edge once possessed by Polymer was now no longer available. Nevertheless, Bayer continued to pour money into R&D in the hopes of defending its market position.

To the extent that the synthetic rubber plant at Sarnia suffered during the 1990s, therefore, macroeconomic developments were the
cause, rather than the nature of its ownership. The business world had
been passing through a trough in activity and profitability, for several
reasons. When business revived in the mid-1990s, the synthetic-rubber
industry responded; it was a link in many different technologies.

Despite the turbulent times of the past decade, Bayer has been the
best custodian of the Polymer rubber business. A group less experienced and with lesser resources might well have given up, sold the butyl plant to Esso and the rest as scrap iron to Imperial. Of course, this
may happen eventually: much depends on how much overbuilding has
taken place in other countries. But butyl rubber will continue to retain
a unique position and will prosper, whoever owns the plant. The purchase by Bayer made the best of a bad situation, a better deal than
many other companies could have made.

Conclusion: Poor by Nature, Rich by Policy – State Intervention and Polymer Corporation

Twenty years ago, as the neoconservative revolution began to make its hesitant appearance in Canada, in an article entitled " 'Rich by Nature, Poor by Policy': The State and Economic Life in Canada," business historian Michael Bliss contentiously argued that government action had made Canadians poorer than nature had originally intended.[1] Through the application of protective tariffs, direct financial succour, and the creation of Crown corporations, the state had retarded the development of an otherwise well-endowed nation. State activism, Bliss vigorously maintained, had thus compromised, not bettered,Canada's productivity, efficiency, and standard of living. If Canada could just give up its "addiction to the positivist state" – an addiction that Dr Bliss equated to the dangerous effects of smoking – it would be healthier for it.

There is enticing historical evidence that lends anecdotal support to Bliss's thesis. For example, the National Policy tariff of 1879 probably did weaken Canadian industry in the long run and unnecessarily reduced the per capita income of Canadians.[2] Likewise, there is evidence to support the position that Canada's first transcontinental railroad, the Canadian Pacific Railway, was built prematurely and at excessive cost.[3] Similarly, the CPR's eventual competitor, Canadian National Railways, which was the first major Crown corporation to be established by the federal government, found it hard to stay out of the taxpayers' pockets. As Garth Stevenson observes, the government-owned and government-operated railway has experienced heavy financial losses since its creation in 1919. Between 1958 and 1968, CN was voted more than $432 million in payments to cover its annual deficits.[4] During the same period, it incurred a total interest expense in servicing its debt of almost $624 million. The deficits continued into the 1970s. In 1975, the Crown corporation recorded an unprecedented loss of $178.7 million.[5] Other Crown enterprises encountered persistent fiscal turbulence. Ontario Hydro became an irresponsible monopoly of questionable competence. Free from the discipline of the marketplace, this provincially owned Crown corporation had by 1999 amassed $38 billion of debt since beginning its operations as the Hydro-Electric Power Commission in 1906. "In the name of the people," H.V. Nelles writes of Ontario Hydro at the height of its expansion in 1919, "the Hydro-Electric Power Commission was literally running away with the provincial treasury, and no one had the courage to ask for what purpose."[6] The government's investments in such postwar enterprises as Bricklin, Canadair, Churchill Forest Industries, Deuterium, and Consolidated Computer were failures in the eyes of two prominent and opinionated observers of Canadian public policy.[7] These five government corporations cost the Canadian taxpayer billions of dollars. It was a familiar tale at Sysco, Nova Scotia's government-owned steel plant, as well as at Skeena Cellulose, a pulp mill on Canada's opposite coast, which in its five years of government operation lost the British Columbia taxpayers $350 million.[8] From a commercial point of view, the Farm Credit Corporation, which was set up in 1959 to provide low-cost loans to farmers, has had a dubious history.[9] During the first decade of operations, the corporation amassed serious deficits. Only in its inaugural year did it operate at a profit. And finally, the Canada Development Corporation, Polymer's parent company between 1972 and 1987, was a commercial underperformer. For neoconservatives, the financial performance of these government corporations – all of which were mandated to act in a "business-like" manner – suggested that they were a lethargic, inefficient, and ineffectual form of business enterprise. Here was the fodder on which would-be Canadian neoconservatives fed in the 1980s and 1990s.

But there is at least one persuasive example that contradicts the neoconservative position. From its wartime creation in 1942, Polymer Corporation, Canada's sole synthetic-rubber producer, played a critical and profitable role in the national and global economy. Initially, Polymer was an effective instrument of public policy. Through it the state "forced the pace" of the development of a new cutting-edge industry and, in so doing , helped the nation overcome its innate deficiency in natural rubber. By 1944, Polymer's gigantic synthetic-rubber plant on the banks of the St Clair River in Sarnia was producing *all* the rubber necessary to meet domestic wartime requirements. This remarkable Crown corporation undeniably helped Canada "win the war."

In the postwar environment, Polymer served a decidedly different purpose. As an instrument of state capitalism, Polymer operated primarily for the purpose of generating a profit. One cannot overstate the uniqueness of Polymer's postwar mission. For the first time in Canadian history, a Crown corporation had been assigned the *principal* task of producing a profit for the state. Polymer was thus the earliest example of truly market-driven state capitalism in Canada. Through Polymer, the state took on the dynamic role of investor and producer in a competitive and profitable sector of the economy. For most Crown corporations it was "business as usual" after the war.[10] The vast majority of Crown corporations continued to function as public policy instruments, usually providing the infrastructure necessary for private industry to function, but at the same time never testing the waters of the free market. They served in many ways as loss-leader enterprises for the nation, the loss being borne by the taxpayer. To be sure, Polymer *incidentally* fulfilled that role: as an instrument of state-led development strategy, Polymer generated much-needed export earnings and acted as "pump primer" to a whole new petrochemical industry in Canada. Largely as a result of Polymer's actions, by 1972 Sarnia had become Canada's "chemical valley," with more PHDs per capita than anywhere else in Canada. Polymer was thus responsible for a type of reverse brain drain attracting new industry and ideas to Canada. In addition, this industrial polymath continued to provide Canadian industry with an indispensable raw material. Nevertheless, making money was Polymer's overriding raison d'être.

And make money it did. This was no lazy Crown corporation. Between 1945 and 1988, when Polymer was purchased by Bob Blair's avaricious Nova Corporation, Polymer accumulated over half a billion dollars in profits. At no time during the period 1942–72 – a period during which the company was fully government-owned and government-controlled – did Polymer report an operating loss. During the same period, Polymer consistently outperformed such privately owned and operated chemical companies as Canadian Industries and Du Pont of Canada. Sometimes it did so by a very wide margin. For example, in 1960 Polymer's rate of return on investment was 15.2 percent, while privately held Canadian Industries' return was 5.1 percent and Du Pont's was 5.4 percent.[11] With the exception of 1970–71, Polymer's rate of return on investment was consistently above the average yield on the federal government's bonds (see table A3).

The government had thus made a wise financial investment; there was no "investment in failure" here. Having begun wartime operations with assets totalling approximately $50 million, by 1972 Polymer had total assets of roughly $230 million. By 1986 that figure had jumped to over $2.3 billion. And like any successful corporation, it paid dividends to its shareholders. Between 1952 and 1972, Ottawa received over $72 million in dividend payments from the firm. Having provided the initial start-up capital – seed money that was fully repaid by 1962 – Ottawa never advanced another penny to this self-sufficient Crown

corporation. All the firm's capital projects were financed either from
internal or external private sources. Over the course of its history,
1942–88, Polymer had sales of over $17 billion. So financially success-
ful was this unique Crown corporation that it eventually found its image on the back of the ten-dollar bill, thereby installing itself in the
iconography of Canadian national self-esteem. In the postwar industrial boom, the Crown company on the banks of St Clair River became
a symbol of Canada's industrial prowess.

Polymer's experience thus contradicts the neoconservative position
that Crown corporations are indolent and impecunious economic
animals. To be sure Crown corporations are " complex, twin-headed
creatures, performing both a policy and commercial role. "[12] What was
different about Polymer was that after 1945 the emphasis was always
on the latter function. Polymer made a practice of profiting the
Crown.

So what had caused Polymer to get it right? What factors had led this
government-owned and government-controlled firm to prosper and,
in the process, fulfill its public policy function? What lessons can be
drawn from Polymer's history? How had Polymer managed to succeed
where many other Crown corporations had failed?

Several seminal factors contributed to Polymer's success. Some, of
course, reflected plain good luck. It was good fortune, for instance,
that Polymer began operations at the dawn of the age of synthetic
chemical engineering, at a time when the polymerization field was ripe
for new discoveries. Polymer would simply not have prospered to the
extent that it did had it entered the field a decade later. In addition, after the war the United States had decided not to export synthetic rubber, thereby leaving an open field for export. Thus, until the late
1950s Polymer was fortunate to have world markets largely to itself.
Adding to Polymer's good luck was the coincidence that shortly after
the end of the war, oil was discovered in Alberta. Imperial Oil, which
had provided Polymer with the scientific knowledge, technological
know-how, and managerial expertise to operate the butyl-rubber unit,
became fixated on the potential profits lying under the earth in Alberta, to the exclusion of other postwar opportunities. Thus, when
C.D. Howe hinted that he might be willing to sell Polymer at the end
of the Second World War, Imperial Oil showed no interest. Its priorities lay elsewhere. As a result, Polymer was able to share a monopoly
with Imperial Oil in butyl-rubber production, the synthetic-rubber industry's most profitable field. Polymer was also lucky in that the postwar period also brought immense and unbroken economic prosperity.
People were spending, not only on small items but on large items like
cars. All these cars, of course, needed lots of rubberized parts, for ev-

erything from ash trays to windshield wipers. Polymer, which was all
too willing and able to supply the necessary material, benefited from
the roaring car culture and the booming consumer culture more generally.

The Crown corporation was also fortunate not to receive mixed messages from Ottawa. Its unwavering postwar mandate was to act like a
commercial enterprise for the purpose of generating a profit. You will
"profit or perish," C.D. Howe told the board of directors at the end of
the war. If that could be done, Polymer's political godfather C.D.
Howe maintained, all the other public policy objectives would take
care of themselves. Howe was tremendously insistent on this point.
Like other commercial enterprises, Polymer would have to "toe the
bottom line." This unambiguous directive provided tremendous motivation to the young men and women working at the plant. As Dr E.J.
"Bill" Buckler, a thirty-five-year veteran of Polymer's executive suite,
later recalled, Howe's edict "certainly put the staff's feet to the fire."[13]
It also fostered in them a proprietary interest in their firm, a concern
for Polymer's survival, and an esprit de corps. From the day the "profit
or perish" directive was promulgated, the logic and values of business
dominated Polymer's corporate culture.

The fact that Polymer had been given such a clear objective so soon
after beginning operations prevented a nonprofit-oriented mentality
from developing at the firm. This was not generally the case at Air Canada, the CBC, Atomic Energy of Canada, and Canadian National Railways. Trans-Canada Airlines, for instance, was obliged to buy airliners
that fit Ottawa's desire to create a national aeronautics industry but
did not suit the airliners' actual passenger-carrying needs. As a result
these firms found it much more difficult to make the transition to what
Barry Boothman terms "competitive commercialization."[14] Conversely,
at Polymer there was no such institutionalization of nonmarket-
oriented behaviour, and consequently, the transition to commercialization went far more smoothly. With remarkable ease, Polymer made the
shift from being a public-service-oriented corporation producing the
rubber needed to win the war to a commercially oriented firm operating for profit in a competitive environment.

The transition was further aided by the fact that C.D. Howe was unwilling to insulate the activities of his corporate managers from the discipline of the market. A free enterpriser at heart, Howe decided not to
extend old-styled protection to the nascent synthetic-rubber industry
at the end of the war. He refused to have anything to do with the old
"infant-industry" mentality that had coddled Canadian industry since
the 1870s. "The fact that the government owns a synthetic rubber
plant," Howe asserted in the House of Commons in 1946, "will not be

used to deprive anyone from the privilege of purchasing natural rubber."[15] To be sure, Polymer's executives were not thrilled by the news. Like other Canadian entrepreneurs they sensed the ongoing anxiety of dangling from the strings held by Adam Smith's invisible hand. Indeed, they lobbied Howe to maintain the regime of wartime regulations and state protection into the peace, but he refused. Polymer would thus either sink or swim as a free agent in a competitive marketplace. In the postwar environment, the firm was encouraged to seek out joint ventures and to coinvest, even with foreign firms, to enhance its research and development capability and thereby achieve flexible specialization – a characteristic that the political scientists Laux and Molot argue is essential to the successful operation of a state-run enterprise. The decision not to extend protection to the nascent synthetic-rubber industry benefited Polymer. It forced the company to be fast on its feet, think strategically, and operate efficiently. This was not generally the case at the majority of other Crown corporations, which had also been instructed to act in a "business-like" fashion. Crown corporations such as Petro-Canada, Air Canada, and CN obtained a strong and competitive position thanks to a long period of protection. "Governments have generally phased in direct competition, or lowered preferential status of the public firms, incrementally," observes Boothman, "a practice which allowed the executives time to make changes in internal administration and to adjust their firms to economic rivalry."[16] But this was not the case at Polymer, which was given a bracing baptism in the hurly-burly of life as a competitive agent in an open market. In the postwar period, Polymer thus became an agile industrial heavyweight because it was forced to survive in a competitive environment.

Polymer also benefited from the actions (or perhaps inaction is a more appropriate designation) of Ottawa's mandarins and politicians. For most of Polymer's history, Ottawa demonstrated a willingness to maintain an arm's length relationship with the firm. There were no political hacks appointed to Polymer's board of directors, and the minister with oversight for the corporation never got involved in the day-to-day operations of the firm. Again, this was not the case at most other Crown corporations. In the early 1980s the government had pressured Polymer's parent company, the CDC, for example, to undertake measures that served political, rather than economic, ends. Likewise, Petro-Canada was incessantly "leaned on" to pursue strategies that furthered Ottawa's short-term political objectives.[17] At Air Canada, the government kept a tight grip on the actions of the firm, dictating the policies it should adopt.[18] For example, in 1963 Ottawa applied political pressure to Air Canada over its decision to purchase the Douglas DC-9 aircraft in preference to the Sud Aviation Caravelle.[19] At Ontario

Hydro, the tradition of ministerial interference and patronage appointments dated from the 1920s. In the mid-1930s, the flamboyant leader of the provincial Liberal party, Mitch Hepburn, had come to power promising a "hydro clean up," meaning a purge of the politically appointed commissioners and their technical hirelings. Ironically, it was Hepburn who would subsequently perfect the technique of using Hydro – by then Ontario's largest construction company – for patronage appointments and sweetheart deals for suppliers.[20] Hydro's spending and debt charges soared, but the bills came due after Hepburn's premiership ended in shambles. The pattern continued under successive governments, resulting in a $38-billion debt load. The story was similar at Sysco. Having been taken over by the Nova Scotia government in 1967, the Sydney steelworks was subject to constant ministerial interference.[21] The Gagliano affair of 2002, in which a federal minister was alleged to have pressured Crown corporation officials at the Business Development Bank into commercially dubious decisions, suggested that political meddling in daily affairs of Crown corporations was not consigned to the past. Thus, both federal and provincial governments have generally found it disturbingly difficult to maintain an arm's length relationship with their firms.

At Polymer, however, Ottawa was willing to stand back and let the Crown corporation get the job done. "It will be the job of Polymer to sell sufficient rubber to keep its operations at an economic level," Howe wrote to J.R. Nicholson at the end of the war, "and I am quite willing to leave the method to you and your Board of Governors."[22] As long as the corporation was making money, Howe conceived of no reason to intervene in the affairs of the firm. After Howe was voted out of office in 1957, his successors took a similar approach. There was a sense in Ottawa that Howe had developed a winning formula, and public-policy makers were therefore loath to do anything that might take the shine off what one contemporary observer dubbed "the gem in the diadem of Canadian industry."[23] Polymer was therefore given the freedom necessary to efficiently achieve its commercial objectives.

Thus, Polymer had benefited greatly from good luck, fortunate timing, and a number of policy developments that were beyond its control. That said, Polymer had made the most of its opportunities, and thus its success was as much due to its own purposive action as to favourable exogenous circumstances. As Bliss himself writes, business history is "the interplay of enterprise and opportunity."[24] This was as true at Polymer as at any successful privately owned and operated corporation. Polymer's managers were not like those depicted by neoconservatives: they were decisive and intelligent, dedicated to making Polymer one of the world's leading synthetic-rubber producers. As

Howe once noted, they were part of "the cream of Canadian industrial talent. "[25] Some of them, like Ralph Rowzee, who served as Polymer president from 1957 to 1971, had left positions at leading North American corporations to be part of Howe's "high technology team." It was dynamic and prescient men like Rowzee who directed the affairs of the Crown corporation. These men were not the myopic and incompetent managers depicted in neoconservative discourse.

As a result, Polymer was innovative at the level of corporate strategy. Immediately after the war, it had embarked upon an aggressive strategy of exporting its products around the world. It built its own global reach in an era when most Canadian corporations rested content within the national market. In doing so, it became what the eminent Harvard University business historian Alfred Chandler has termed a "first mover" – i.e., a pioneering business force capable of cultivating and securing new markets. By 1950 exports accounted for roughly two-thirds of Polymer's sales. In the early 1960s, Polymer established manufacturing plants overseas to meet the surging foreign demand for its product. That year, the Polymer plant was supplying 10 percent of all the world's rubber needs. Not only did this pump money into the government's coffers, but it also improved Canada's balance of payments. Thus, again, Polymer was demonstrating itself to be a powerful instrument of public policy and an aggressive economic force.

In going global, Polymer joined an exclusive club of Canadian companies that were multinational in operation. In many ways, Polymer was the epitome of postwar economic dynamism – flexible, efficient and imperialistic. In going abroad – to borrow a phrase from the economist Charles Kindleberger – Polymer grew abroad. The only time that Polymer was derivative in its corporate strategy came in 1969, when the company decided to embark on a diversification program. The unfocused decision to diversify cost the company financially and strategically. Nevertheless, for most of its history Polymer was an innovator in its corporate strategy.

Polymer was also successful because it had pioneered unique sales techniques, including sending senior personnel overseas to spearhead sales missions. The practice was later adopted by all the large synthetic-rubber producers. In addition, Polymer pioneered the practice of providing technical service to its customers. By helping its clients use its revolutionary products, Polymer created a tremendous amount of goodwill, thereby doing more than any other synthetic-rubber producer to dethrone natural rubber as the reigning product of choice among manufacturers of rubber products. The world-wide rise of the synthetic-rubber industry was thus, in no small part, due to the actions of Canada's Polymer Corporation.

Finally, and most importantly, Polymer prospered and grew because it was habitually innovative in synthetic-rubber development. At a time when science-based growth was an enigma to most Canadian industry, Polymer embraced research and development as part of its corporate strategy. The growth of the firm was based on technologies that emerged in one way or another from discoveries and developments that were particularly susceptible to perfection through a scientific approach to problem solving. Scientific investigation and the systematic application of scientific knowledge to the process of production thus became a routine part of Polymer's operations. Through their ability to harness scientific and technical expertise, Polymer's technology-conscious managers created a corporate culture that recognized the umbilical relation of science and corporate prosperity. This group of scientist-managers dedicated themselves to transforming Polymer into a powerful and autonomous institution capable of shaping its competitive environment and pursuing independent strategies for growth. They were entrepreneurs in the classic Schumpeterian sense, that is, not as the riskers of capital, since the capital was not theirs to risk (it belonged to the people of Canada), but as the formulators of corporate strategy and the innovators of new industrial structures and technologies.[26] The best of them were visionaries, men like Polymer executives Ralph Rowzee, Bill Buckler, Roger Hatch, Stan Wilk, Lee Dougan, and Ian Rush, who could see a future for their industry when the majority of those around them could not. By applying science, Polymer persistently expanded the output of its standard product line and continually induced new sorts of products. In short, to use Alfred Chandler's terminology, Polymer relentlessly expanded its "scale and scope."

This strategy was not always easy, however, due to the peculiar nature of the Canadian marketplace. The limited size of the domestic market, the general lack of managerial skills and technology, the shortage of investment capital, and the branch plant nature of the Canadian economy all combined to make technological innovation more difficult in Canada than in the United States. In addition, Polymer faced the disadvantages of being a medium-sized (in global terms) government-owned firm operating in the same arena as deep-pocketed, privately owned petrochemical giants. Despite these obstacles, Polymer profited and grew by diligently bringing new products into commercial use.

Polymer stood at the forefront of technological innovation partly because of the intrinsically competitive nature of the petrochemical industry but also because of the company's middling rank among petrochemical producers. During the twentieth century the chemical industry was unusually dynamic: change was rapid, constant, and expensive.[27] The chemical industry was more technology-dependent, capital-intensive, and international in scope than any other industry in the development of corporate strategies and structures. Every successful competitor in the world chemical industry had to be agile and adroit. Polymer, a medium-sized Canadian competitor, had to be especially nimble. Unlike such larger companies as Esso, Dunlop, Du Pont, ICI, Bayer, BASF, and Hoechst, Polymer rarely enjoyed a commanding position in any particular major product market. As a result, it was obliged to choose its opportunities and weigh investments with unusual care and to reorient itself quickly in response to changing market conditions. While Polymer was a pioneer in science-based growth in Canada, in the international field of polymer research and development the company was generally a fast follower, adapting and improving upon the inventions and discoveries of others. Polymer was a process innovator rather than a pioneer in the field of basic research. In production, Polymer tended to avoid integration (backwards and, especially, forwards) because its operations lacked sufficient scale and financial resources. Instead, it purchased feedstock on the market. And in marketing, the company would attempt to focus on filling particular niches and on providing its customers with a high level of technical support and service. The strategy worked remarkably well. Polymer never overextended itself, and yet it made a number of significant contributions in the field of synthetic-rubber research and development.

These are the reasons for Polymer's success, and they indicate that under certain conditions public enterprise can be both an effective instrument of public policy and an efficient form of commercial enterprise. In many ways, it is a very un-Canadian tale. When a Crown corporation is given a single, clearly defined purpose that is without contradiction and the freedom to pursue that objective without political pressure or protection, it can further the wealth and welfare of the nation. This was Polymer's story. In Polymer there was indeed a remarkable conjunction of state purpose and industrial initiative. In this remarkable case, therefore, government action in fact made Canadians richer than nature had originally intended. With this in mind, Canadians might do well to see Polymer not just as a unique bit of our national history but also as a template for the future relationship of state and marketplace.

APPENDICES

APPENDIX ONE

Financial Statistics for Polymer Corporation

Table A1
Financial Performance, 1945–1986

Year	Rubber Produced (tons)	Number of Employees	Sales ($000s)	Dividends ($000s)	Profits ($000s)	Rate of Return on Investment (percentages)
1945	44,464	1,835	29,500	n.a.	1,600	3.2
1946	50,624	1,806	21,300	n.a.	2,600	6.1
1947	57,904	1,852	22,500	n.a.	3,900	8.4
1948	44,464	1,767	17,300	n.a.	25	0.1
1949	47,712	1,919	21,600	n.a.	700	1.5
1950	53,312	1,969	26,000	n.a.	800	1.7
1951	66,192	2,055	35,300	n.a.	4,500	9.4
1952	80,528	2,384	45,753	2,500	4,050	7.8
1953	90,048	2,343	50,614	3,000	5,097	10.9
1954	95,995	2,458	53,467	3,000	4,924	10.7
1955	115,472	2,556	61,836	5,000	7,531	15.6
1956	133,952	2,592	71,567	6,000	9,450	18.2
1957	146,496	2,723	74,615	4,000	6,823	12.5
1958	147,952	2,777	75,539	4,000	6,377	11.2
1959	109,984	2,669	60,253	3,000	3,690	6.4
1960	175,504	2,663	85,915	3,000	9,851	15.2
1961	180,544	2,711	88,514	3,000	10,220	13.9
1962	185,024	2,972	87,457	3,000	10,284	11.3
1963	217,952	3,310	97,806	3,250	9,138	8.8
1964	265,440	3,433	114,291	4,000	9,450	8.1
1965	277,536	3,605	117,503	4,500	10,303	8.5
1966	296,464	3,911	127,538	4,500	11,221	8.6

Table A1
Financial Performance, 1945–1986 (*Continued*)

Year	Rubber Produced (tons)	Number of Employees	Sales ($000s)	Dividends ($000s)	Profits ($000s)	Rate of Return on Investment (percentages)
1967	308,448	3,976	128,900	3,300	5,810	3.8
1968	342,496	3,722	143,900	3,000	7,050	4.5
1969	366,016	3,779	159,900	6,000	13,823	8.2
1970	400,512	4,273	156,700	3,000	7,060	4.3
1971	427,996	4,414	174,600	500	493	0.2
1972	479,024	4,856	205,000	750	7,058	4.0
1973	506,700	6,187	261,400	1,200	11,100	4.4
1974	461,600	6,034	392,400	2,500	22,820	7.8
1975	383,500	5,973	392,100	4,246	1,600	0.5
1976	464,700	6,189	457,600	8,804	7,500	2.0
1977	491,000	6,405	577,000	9,683	14,400	3.0
1978	540,000	6,264	747,800	11,900	18,500	3.0
1979	560,000	5,437	1,066,099	53,208	74,000	11.5
1980	561,000	6,144	1,180,600	10,334	73,400	15.1
1981	550,000	7,081	1,347,400	11,188	22,000	3.3
1982	n.a.	6,561	1,328,700	12,716	(30,500)	(2.7)
1983	n.a.	5,985	1,336,900	13,686	8,700	0.7
1984	n.a.	5,947	1,416,200	13,686	35,900	3.0
1985	n.a.	6,652	1,865,400	32,805	(520)	(0.1)
1986	n.a.	6,462	2,049,500	27,066	27,800	1.5

Source: Polymer Corporation, Annual *Reports* (1945–1986).

Table A2
Polymer Corporation, Net Worth of Assets, Net Profits, Rate of Return on Assets, Net Sales and Rate of Return on Sales, 1945–1987

Year	Net Worth of Assets ($000s)	Net Profit ($000s)	Rate of Return on Assets (percentages)	Net Sale ($000s)	Rate of Return on Sales (percentages)
1945	48,821	1,600	3.2	29,500	5.4
1946	49,610	2,600	5.2	21,300	12.2
1947	49,734	3,900	7.8	22,500	17.3
1948	49,004	25	0.5	17,300	0.1
1949	49,633	700	1.4	21,600	3.2
1950	50,793	800	1.5	26,000	3.0
1951	53,793	4,500	8.3	35,300	12.7

Table A2

Polymer Corporation, Net Worth of Assets, Net Profits, Rate of Return on Assets, Net Sales and Rate of Return on Sales, 1945–1987 (*Continued*)

Year	Net Worth of Assets ($000s)	Net Profit ($000s)	Rate of Return on Assets (percentages)	Net Sale ($000s)	Rate of Return on Sales (percentages)
1952	54,465	4,050	7.4	45,753	8.9
1953	53,275	5,097	9.5	50,614	10.0
1954	54,550	4,924	9.0	53,467	9.2
1955	56,155	7,531	13.4	61,836	12.2
1956	60,463	9,450	15.6	71,567	13.2
1957	63,058	6,823	10.8	74,615	9.1
1958	66,405	6,377	9.6	75,539	8.4
1959	65,164	3,690	5.6	60,253	6.1
1960	78,225	9,851	12.6	85,915	11.5
1961	84,199	10,220	12.1	88,514	11.6
1962	106,665	10,284	9.7	87,457	11.8
1963	131,278	9,138	6.9	97,806	9.3
1964	137,751	9,450	6.8	114,291	8.2
1965	141,351	10,303	7.2	117,503	8.8
1966	163,671	11,221	6.8	127,538	8.8
1967	179,510	5,810	3.2	128,900	4.5
1968	187,123	7,050	3.7	143,900	4.9
1969	207,374	13,823	6.7	159,900	8.6
1970	223,714	7,060	3.2	156,700	4.5
1971	233,088	493	0.2	174,600	0.3
1972	237,064	7,058	2.9	205,000	3.4
1973	341,451	11,100	3.3	261,400	4.2
1974	397,950	22,820	5.7	392,400	5.8
1975	415,515	1,600	0.4	392,100	0.4
1976	530,519	7,500	1.4	457,600	1.6
1977	646,385	14,400	2.2	577,000	2.4
1978	766,109	18,500	2.4	747,800	2.5
1979	909,932	74,000	8.1	1,066,099	6.9
1980	1,044,136	73,400	7.0	1,180,600	6.2
1981	1,402,488	22,000	1.5	1,347,400	1.6
1982	1,438,348	(30,500)	(2.1)	1,328,700	(2.3)
1983	1,452,985	8,700	0.6	1,336,900	0.6
1984	1,468,652	35,900	2.4	1,416,200	2.5
1985	2,431,203	(520)	(0.1)	1,865,400	0.0
1986	2,386,288	27,800	1.2	2,049,500	1.3

Source: Polymer Corporation, Annual *Reports* (1945–1986).

Table A3
Comparison of Polymer's Rate of Return on Investment with the Average Federal
Government Bond Yield, 1945–1971, Percentages

Year	Polymer's Rate of Return on Investment (1)	Average Federal Government Bond Yield 10 years and Over (2)	Difference (1) – (2)
1945	3.2	2.93	0.27
1946	6.1	2.61	3.49
1947	8.4	2.57	5.83
1948	0.1	2.93	−2.83
1949	1.5	2.83	−1.33
1950	1.7	2.78	−1.08
1951	9.4	3.24	6.16
1952	7.8	3.59	4.62
1953	10.9	3.68	7.52
1954	10.7	3.55	7.15
1955	15.6	3.36	13.04
1956	18.2	4.10	15.40
1957	12.5	4.14	9.06
1958	11.2	4.48	7.22
1959	6.4	5.07	1.33
1960	15.2	5.18	10.02
1961	13.9	5.04	8.66
1962	11.3	5.11	6.19
1963	8.8	5.08	3.72
1964	8.1	5.18	2.92
1965	8.5	5.22	3.28
1966	8.6	5.44	3.16
1967	3.8	5.94	−2.14
1968	4.5	6.73	−2.23
1969	8.2	8.30	−0.10
1970	4.3	6.99	−2.69
1971	0.2	7.15	−7.08

Source: Polymer Corporation, Annual Reports (1945–71), and Bank of Canada, Statistical Summary (1945–71).

APPENDIX TWO

Polymer's Senior Personnel

PRESIDENTS OF POLYMER, 1942–87

Arthur L. Bishop	March-September 1942
Richard C. Berkinshaw	1942–45
Douglas W. Ambridge	1945–47
Ernest J. Brunning	1947–51
John D. Barrington	1952–57
Ralph Rowzee	1957–71
Ian C.M. Rush	1971–81
Robert S. Dudley	1981–87

DIRECTORS OF POLYMER, 1942–87

A.L. Bishop	1942–43
D.W. Ambridge	1942–50
W.R. Campbell	1942–46
G.A. Lebine	1942–63
A.C. Guthrie	1942–47
A.J. Crawford	1942–47
R.C. Berkinshaw	1942–45
J.R. Nicholson	1943–51
J.A. Hodgson	1945–70
H.J. Mero	1946–52
L.C. McCloskey	1946–50
H.J. Carmichael	1946–50
E.J. Brunning	1947–65
J.W. Bruce	1947–61
C.A. Massey	1949–70
E.R. Rowzee	1950–78
F.A. Sherman	1951–63
J.D. Barrington	1952–59

E.C. Row	1952–56
R.W. Todgham	1956–75
J. Connolly	1961–66
E. Laflamme	1962–71
W.H. Rea	1963–73
F.H. Sherman	1963–73
F.W. Bruce	1965–71
W. Ladyman	1966–79
P. Lorange	1966–73
W.S. McGregor	1970–75
F.C. Wilkinson	1970–86
P.R. Gendron	1971–84
I.C. Rush	1971–87
H.A. Hampson	1972–85
F.E. Cleyn	1973–74
M.A. Crowe	1973–74
D.C. Stanley	1973–87
W.A. Dimma	1974–87
A.J. Ellis	1974–84
D.C. Jones	1975–85
F.W. Sellers	1975–84
D.C. Morrison	1975–76
P.K. Powell	1977–79
J.B. Hague	1979–87
H.S. Ladd	1981–87
R. Dudley	1981–87
G. Kraijenhoff	1983–87
P. Côté	1984–87
R.H. Marchessault	1984–87
D.P. Owen	1984–87
B.F. Isautier	1985–87
J.W. Johnstone Jr	1985–87
E.K. Cork	1986–87

POLYMER'S CHIEF EXECUTIVES, ADMINISTRATIVE OFFICERS AND
SENIOR MANAGEMENT, 1942–87

M. Abbott
General Manger, Latex, 1978–80
Vice-president, Technology, 1981–85

C. Ambridge
Vice-president, Rubber, Europe and Rest of the World, 1978–80
Vice-president, Europe and Rest of the World, 1981–82
Vice-president, 1983–85
Group Vice-president, Rubber, 1985–86
Group Vice-president, Corporate Development, 1986–87

D.W. Ambridge
Vice-president, 1942–45
President, 1945–47
Chairman of the Board, 1946–47

J.D. Barrington
President and Managing Director, 1952–57

J. Beaton
General Manager, Latex, 1981–82
Vice-president, Latex and Synthetics, 1983–84
Vice-president, Diversified Products, 1984–85

F. Bentley
Vice-president, Rubber, Europe and Rest of the World, 1974–80
Group Vice-president, Rubber and Plastics, 1981–85
Group Vice-president, Basic Petrochemicals, 1985–87

R.C. Berkinshaw
President, 1942–45

A.L. Bishop
President, March-September 1942
Chairman of the Board, 1942–43

G. Bracewell
Vice-president, 1969–71
Vice-president, Corporate Planning, 1971–72
Vice-president, Finance and Planning, 1972–76
Vice-president, Planning and Development, 1972–77
Vice-president, Corporate Projects, 1977–78

E.J. Brunning
President, 1947–51
Chairman of the Board, 1947–65

E.J. Buckler
Manager, Research and Development, 1947–58
Vice-president, Research and Development, 1958–62
Vice-president, 1963–70
Vice-president, Research and Development, 1971–79

P.S. Byrne
General Manager, Latex Division, 1985–86
Vice-president and General Manager, Latex, 1986–87

P. Choquette
Vice-president, Diversified Projects, 1981–83
Vice-president, Rubber, North and South America, 1983–86
Group Vice-president, Rubber, 1986–87

A.T. Cousins
Treasurer, 1981–84
Vice-president, Finance and Administration, 1984–86
Senior Vice-president, Finance and Administration, 1986–87

W. Critchley
Vice-president, Finance, 1976–77
Group Vice-president, Finance and Administration, 1977–83

W.A. Dimma
Chairman of the Board, 1978–87

Lee Dougan
Assistant Manager, 1946–51
Plant Manager, 1951–57
Vice-president Operations, 1957–63
Vice-president, Antwerp and Strasbourg Operations, 1963–68

R.S. Dudley
Vice-president, 1969–71
Group Vice-president, Rubber and Latex, 1971–78
Executive Vice-president, Operations, 1978–81
President and Chief Operating Officer, 1981–87

W.J. Dyke
Secretary-Treasurer, 1952–53
Secretary and Chief Legal Officer, 1953–82

M.E. Erlindson
Treasurer, 1972–80

R.C. Flakes
Vice-president, Plastics, 1975–77
Group Vice-president, Chemicals and Plastics, 1977–80

H.A. Graham
Vice-president, Corporate Personnel, 1976–82

R.B. Grogan
Controller, 1978–83
Treasurer, 1984–85
Vice-president, 1986–87

S.J. Goldenberg
Vice-president, Personnel, 1983–87

R.E. Hatch
General Sales Manager, 1954–57
Vice-president, Marketing, 1957–63
Vice-president, 1963–69
Executive Vice-president, Development, 1969–71
Group Vice-president, 1971–72

D.A. Henderson
Vice-president, Rubber and Plastics, Europe and Rest of the World, 1983–85
Group Vice-president, Diversified Products, 1986–87

G.M. Hicks
General Manager, Latex, North and South America, 1983–84
General Manager, Asia-Pacific, 1985–87

G.A. LaBine
Vice-president, 1945–46

J.R. Nicholson
Manager, March-July 1942
General Manager, 1942–43
Managing Director, 1943–46
Vice-president and General Manager, 1946–47
Executive Vice-president, 1947–51

J.H. Langstaff
Vice-president, North and South America, 1974–77

R.J. Lhonneux
Vice-president, 1971–72

C.A. McKenzie
Vice-president, North and South America, 1969–73
Vice-president, Europe and the Rest of the World, 1973–74
Vice-president, Chemicals, 1974–77
Vice-president, Project Development, 1977–78

J.R. Provo
Vice-president, 1969–75

E. Rhodes
Vice-president, Technology, 1986–87

E.R. Rowzee
Director Research and Development, 1944–46
Director of Sales and Manager, 1946–51
Vice-president and Manager, 1951–57
President and Managing Director, 1957–71
Chairman and Chief Executive Officer, 1971–72
Chairman of the Board of Directors, 1972–78

I.C. Rush
Manager Special Projects, 1960–62
Director of Corporate Planning, 1962–64
Vice-president, 1964–69
Executive Vice-president, Operations, 1969–71
President and Chief Executive Officer, 1971–81
Chairman of the Board of Directors, 1981–83

H.W. Suters
Vice-president, 1970–73

M.L. Wasik
Chief Legal Officer, 1981–83

S. Wilk
Comptroller, 1952–53
Treasurer, 1953–57
Vice-president, Finance, 1957–64
Vice-president, 1964–71
Vice-president, Corporate Finance, 1971–72

G.C. Wier
Assistant Treasurer, Controller and Assistant Comptroller, 1942–53

D.E. Wood
Divisional Manager, Chemicals, 1978–80
General Manager, Diversification, 1981–82
General Manager, Corporate Development, 1983–85

Glossary of Technical Terms

acetylene   A colourless, highly flammable or explosive gas, C_2H_2, with a characteristic sweet odour. It is the simplest member of the alkyne series of unsaturated hydrocarbons and can be manufactured by heating methane to $1500°C$ in the presence of a catalyst. Often also called "ethyne," it can be polymerized easily at high temperatures to give a range of products.

acrylonitrile   A colourless, liquid organic compound, $H_2C:CHCN$, used to manufacture acrylic rubber and fibres.

aluminum alkyl   A highly reactive compound containing an aluminum and alkyl radical, e.g., triethyl-aluminum; used as an initiator for the catalysts in polymerization.

butadiene   A colourless, highly flammable gaseous hydrocarbon, C_4H_6, obtained from petroleum and used to manufacture synthetic rubber.

butyl rubber   A synthetic rubber produced by copolymerization of butylene (98 percent) and isoprene (2 percent). Outstanding in gaseous impermeability, it is used in tiers and insulation.

co-polymerization   A chemical reaction in which two different monomers are joined together to form a molecular chain.

elastomer   A synthetic rubber or rubberoid material that has the ability to undergo deformation under the influence of a force and regain its original shape once the force has been removed.

GR-S rubber   A general-purpose rubber manufactured by copolymerizing styrene and butadiene. Also known as buna-s and SBR.

isoprene   A colourless and volatile substance produced by pyrolysis.

neoprene   A synthetic rubber produced by polymerization of chloroprene and used in waterproof products, adhesives, paints, and rocket fuels.

olefin   An unsaturated, open-chain hydrocarbon containing at least one double bond (e.g., ethylene or propylene).

petrochemical   Any chemical product derived from petroleum (e.g., ethylene, propylene, and hydrocarbon resins).

polymer High molecular-weight material existing naturally or obtained by joining together many simple molecules (monomers) linked end to end or cross-linked.

polymerizing The formation of very large molecules from small molecules, normally by using a catalyst. The resulting material is a polymer.

polymethyl methacrylate A clear synthetic material used exclusively as a substitute for plate glass.

polystyrene A polymeric form of styrene used either as a hard, rigid plastic for molded articles or as a white, light, expanded foam for packing and thermal insulation.

polyvinyl chloride (PVC) A thermoplastic resin used in a wide variety of manufactured items including raincoats, garden hoses, phonograph records, and floor tiles.

pyrolysis The chemical decomposition of a substance by heat.

scale-up An increase in the size of an operation, such as going from a laboratory to a pilot plant or from a pilot plant to an industrial or a commercial-sized plant.

styrene A colourless oily liquid, C_8H_8, with an earthy smell. It is used extensively in the rubber industry and in the manufacture of drugs and dyes.

synthetic A term describing a substance that has been made artificially, i.e., one that does not come from a natural source.

thermoplastic polymer A polymer that can be repeatedly softened by heating.

vulcanization The process discovered by Charles Goodyear (1839) of mixing rubber with sulphur and applying heat to make the rubber resistant to temperature changes.

Notes

INTRODUCTION

1 Underhill, "O Canada," 227–9.
2 Ibid., 228.
3 Wilbur, *The Bennett New Deal*, 81.
4 Corry, "The Fusion of Government and Business," 303.
5 Peers, *The Politics of Canadian Broadcasting*, chap. 4.
6 Smith, *It Seems like Only Yesterday*, chap. 4.
7 See Bothwell, *Nucleus*; Bothwell, *Eldorado*; Bothwell and Kilbourn, *C.D. Howe*; Borins, "World War II Crown Corporations," 437–75.
8 Clarke, *The IDB*; chap. 2.
9 Fossum, *Oil, the State and Federalism*; Dimma, *The Canada Development Corporation*.
10 Ibid.
11 Aitken, "Defensive Expansionism," 184.
12 See, for example, Creighton, *The Commercial Empire*; Neill, *The End of National Policy*, chaps. 10–12.
13 Aitken, *The Welland Canal Company*.
14 Stewart, *Uneasy Lies the Head*, 165.
15 *National Post*, 7 September 2001, 1.
16 Penrose, *Growth of the Firm*.
17 Lazonick, *Business Organization*; Klein, *A Social Scientist in Industry;* Warmington, Lupton, and Gribbin, *Organization Behaviour and Performance*.
18 Chandler, *Scale and Scope*, 36–45, 145, 230.
19 Boothman, "Strategic Transformations," 291–311.
20 Chandler, *Strategy and Structure*, introduction; Wrigley, "Divisional Autonomy and Diversification"; Scott, "The Industrial State," 133–48; Greiner, "Evolution and Revolution," 37–46.
21 Dyer and Sicilia, *Labors of a Modern Hercules*, xxi.

22 See Chandler, *Strategy and Structure*, especially the introduction.

23 *Annual Report* (1980), 1.

24 See Dyer and Sicilia, *Labours of a Modern Hercules*; Hounshell and Smith, *Science and Corporate Strategy*; Stobaugh, *Innovation and Competition*; Spitz, *Petrochemicals*; Pettigrew, *The Awakening Giant*.

25 McCraw, *The Essential Alfred Chandler*, 492–4.

CHAPTER ONE

1 Coates, *The Commerce in Rubber*, 3–7.

2 Anderson, *Edinburgh Bee* (1791), 33.

3 See, for example, Innis, *The Fur Trade in Canada*, especially 383–402, and Easterbrook and Aitken, *Canadian Economic History*, 1–350.

4 Bliss, "Rich by Nature," 78–90.

5 Wolf, *Rubber*.

6 The Country Housewife, "The Rubber-band Domesticated," *Chatelaine*, April 1928, 73

7 Ibid.

8 Litchfield, "Rubber's Position in Modern Civilization," 567.

9 Davies, "Rubber Is an Industrial Sinew of Democracy," 10–11.

10 "Rubber Goes to War," *Business Week*, 25 October 1941, 21–2, 25.

11 Babcock, *History*, 319.

12 Wickham, *Rough Notes*.

13 Bickmore, *Travels*, 18.

14 Reso, "Rubber in Brazil." 341–66; see also Coates, *The Commerce in Rubber*, 89–154.

15 Gibb, "The Control of Rubber."

16 Roberts, *From Three Men*, 5–28.

17 Marchildon, *Profits and Politics*, especially 62–96, 143–80.

18 "The Rubber Merger," *Globe and Mail*, 26 June 1907, 6.

19 French, *The U.S. Tire Industry*, 45–56.

20 Marshal et al., *Canadian-American Industry*, 29–33.

21 Canada, House of Commons, *Debates*, 7 March, 1876.

22 *Commercial and Financial Chronicle*, 15 January 1916, 254–5.

23 Dominion Bureau of Statistics, *The Canada Year Book* (Ottawa, 1941), 318–19, 432–3.

24 Sun Life Assurance Company of Canada, *The Canadian Automotive Industry*, table 20, 41

25 McShane, *Down the Asphalt*.

26 Hurley, "History of Natural Rubber," 215–24.

27 Dominion Bureau of Statistics, *Canada Year Book*, 319.

28 Williams, *Proceedings of the Royal Society*, 10 (1860).

29 Landes, *The Unbound Prometheus*, 269–76.

30 The best scholarly account of prewar synthetic-rubber development is Solo, *Across the High Technology Threshold*. See also, Howard, *Buna Rubber*, and Morton, "History of Synthetic Rubber," 225–38.

31 Morton, "History of Synthetic Rubber," 226.

32 Furukawa, *Inventing Polymer Science*, chaps. 1–4.

33 Morton, "History of Synthetic Rubber," 225–38.

34 Warrington and Newbold, *Chemical Canada*, especially 45–69; and Warrington and Nicholls, *A History of Chemistry in Canada*.

35 Whitby, *Synthetic Rubber*. Whitby also made a number of practical contributions to the rubber industry, laying the basis for the general use of fatty acids in rubber manufacturing. See Grace, "The Rubber Industry in Canada," 318.

36 The best accounts are in Hounshell and Smith, *Science and Corporate Strategy*; Reich, *The Making of American Industrial Research*; Wise, *Willis R. Whitney*; and Hodges, "Color It Kodachrome," 46–53.

37 Hounshell and Smith, *Science and Corporate Strategy*, 251–7.

38 "Neoprene," *Canadian Chemistry and Process Industries* (February 1938), 55; and "Neoprene in Chemical Construction," *Canadian Chemistry and Process Industries* (October 1939), 532.

39 Hounshell and Smith, *Science and Corporate Strategy*, 230–57; Smith, "The Ten-Year Invention," 34–55.

40 Herbert and Bisio, *Synthetic Rubber*, 36.

41 See Coates, *The Commerce in Rubber*, 205–300.

42 Quoted in Borkin, *Crime and Punishment*, 79.

43 Howard, *Buna Rubber*, especially 35–46.

44 Herbert and Bisio, *Synthetic Rubber*, table 11.1, 127.

CHAPTER TWO

1 Canada, House of Commons, *Debates*, 23 March 1944, 1775.

2 Williamson, "150,000 Cars off the Road by Next Year," *Ottawa Citizen*, 15 June 1942, 1–2.

3 Ibid.

4 Beland, "The Rubber Problem," *Canadian Chemistry and Process Industries* (August 1942), 457.

5 Williamson, "150,000 Cars off the Road by Next Year," 1–2.

6 See, for example, Veblen, *The Engineers and the Price System*, especially the introduction.

7 McDowall, *Steel at the Sault*, 183.

8 See Campbell, *Global Mission*, chap. 7; Bothwell, *Eldorado*, 79–154; and MacKay, *Empire of Wood*, chap. 7.

9 Kennedy, *Department of Munitions and Supply*, 191.

10 Canada, Privy Council Office, "Rubber 4," *Canadian War Orders and Regulations*, vol. 3 (30 June 1943).

11 "Rubber – for Some," *Business Week*, 31 January 1942, 22.

12 Howe, "Civilians to Help by Curbing Buying," *Globe and Mail*, 8 January 1942, 4.

13 Canada, Privy Council Office, "Rubber 1," *Canadian War Orders and Regulations*, vol. 11 (21 December 1943).

14 W.H. Cook, "Co-operative Work in Progress in Canada in Preparation of Rubber from Native Plants" (8 January 1942), Polysar Papers, vol. 34, file: National Research Council, 1942–48.

15 "Memorandum re Production of Natural Rubber in Canada" (16 January 1943), Department of Agriculture Papers, vol. 3398, file: War files, Russian Dandelion (Re: rubber) and Milk Weed Production in Canada, 1943–1947; and "Development of Natural Rubber Resources," *Canadian Chemistry and Process Industries* (May 1943), 296.

16 Eggleton, *National Research in Canada*, especially 241, 261, 325–6.

17 G.K. Sheils to J.R. Nicholson (2 May 1942), Polysar Papers, vol. 17, file: Plants as a Source of Rubber, 1942–44.

18 J.R. Nicholson, interview with R. Bothwell, Bothwell Papers, B88–0074/022.

19 For a discussion of this broad-based belief see McKillop, *Matters of Mind*, 521–46, and Avery, *The Science of War*, especially chap. 2.

20 J.R. Nicholson to G.K. Sheils (28 March 1942), Polysar Papers, vol. 1, minute book 1; and J.R. Nicholson (25 May 1942), Polysar Papers, vol. 30, file: DMS Canadian Project, part 1.

21 J.R. Nicholson to G.H. Duff (8 May 1942), Polysar Papers, vol. 17, file: Plants as a Source of Rubber, 1942–44.

22 Ibid., 4.

23 Gough, "Man Made Rubber," *Maclean's*, 1 March 1944, 19.

24 Laux and Molot, *State Capitalism*, especially chap. 2.

25 Innis, *The Problems of Staple Production*, 80–1.

26 See, for example, Leacock, "What Is Left of Adam Smith," 41–51.

27 Corry, "The Fusion of Government and Business," 301–16.

28 Peers, *The Politics of Canadian Broadcasting*, chap. 6.

29 Aitken, "Defensive Expansionism," 184.

30 Howe, "Why Crown Firms?" *Financial Post*, 20 December 1958, 23–4.

31 Ibid.

32 J.A. Schultz, "Shell Game," 41.

33 Canada, House of Commons, *Debates*, 21 March 1944, 1715–17.

34 Ibid., 1715.

35 Ibid., 27 March 1944, 1868–9.

36 Ibid., 14 May 1946, 1517.

37 See, respectively, Smith, *It Seems like Only Yesterday*, chaps. 3 and 4; Bothwell, *Nucleus*, chap. 3; Bothwell and Kilbourn, *C.D. Howe*, chaps. 17 and 18.

38 P.C. 2369, 27 March 1942, 1.

39 Herbert and Bisio, *Synthetic Rubber,* 90–1.

40 Shell Oil, *Canadian Petrochemical Industry,* 6.

41 "Notes on the Organization of Polymer Corporation Ltd. for Operations" (3 March 1943), Department of Munitions and Supply (DMS) Papers, vol. 6, folder 7.

42 *Globe and Mail,* 12 January 1942, 3.

43 Bertin, "The Long Chain," 49.

44 Bishop to Howe (18 May 1942), DMS Papers, vol. 5, folder 1.

45 Williamson to Berkinshaw (10 February 1942), ibid.

46 Howe to Nicholson (8 February 1942), ibid.

47 Sheils to Pettigrew (15 February 1942), ibid.

48 There are a number of rich and colourful histories about the dollar-a-year men. Among the best are Granatstein, *The Ottawa Men,* and Owram, *The Government Generation.*

49 Bothwell, *Eldorado.* On the relationship between Howe and G. LaBine, see 99–102, 120–3, and 157.

50 Howe to Crawford (24 April 1942), DMS Papers, vol. 5, folder 1.

51 G.K. Sheils to H. Bordon (20 March 1942), and H. Bordon to A.L. Bishop, (23 March 1942), ibid.

52 Howe to Crawford (24 April 1942), ibid.

53 Crawford to Howe (27 April 1942), ibid.

54 Canada, House of Commons, *Debates,* 16 June 1943, 3715 and 3711, respectively.

55 "General Report" (28 January 1942), Polysar Papers, vol. 30, file: DMS Canadian Project, part 1.

56 C.Y. Hopkins to J.R. Nicholson (7 January 1942), NRC Papers, vol. 129, file: Proposed Manufacture of Synthetic Rubber in Canada, 1941–2.

57 "Memorandum for Polymer Board re Negotiations with Officials of the War Productions Board at Washington" (15 May 1942), Polysar Papers, vol. 12, file: Directors' Reports, 1942–3.

58 For a more detailed description of this complex and ever-changing wartime system of priorities, see James, *Wartime Economic Co-operation,* 67–86.

59 "Minutes of the RRC" (21 March 1942), Reconstruction Finance Corporation (RFC) Papers, vol. 3, 465; ibid., vol. 4, 6.

60 "Minutes of a Meeting of the Committee on the Use of Alcohol in the Synthetic Rubber Programme" (3 June 1942) Polysar Papers, vol. 40, file: Alcohol as base for butadiene and rubber, 1942–4; and T.R. Griffith, "Report re Synthetic Rubber from Alcohol" (27 March 1942), NRC Papers, vol. 128, file 17–13R-21.

61 V. Podoski to C.D. Howe (5 February 1942), C.D. Howe Papers, vol. 27, file: Polymer Corp (10), 1942–3.

62 C.D. Howe to V. Podoski (17 February 1942), ibid.

63 Bothwell and Kilbourn, *C.D. Howe,* especially 104–13, 159–60, 212–14, 265–6.

64 J.R. Nicholson to C.J. McKenzie (16 February 1942), NRC Papers, vol. 128, file: 17–13R-21.

65 Mackenzie to Nicholson (18 February 1942), NRC Papers, vol. 128, file: 17–13R-21.

66 Ibid.

67 "Resolution of the City of North Battlefield" (17 May 1943), C.D. Howe Papers, vol. 46, file: Polymer Corporation, folder 8.

68 E. Birch to C.D. Howe (8 February 1943), ibid.

69 Thompson, *The Harvests of War*, especially chaps. 2, 3, and 7.

70 Canada, House of Commons, *Debates*, 1942, 4752.

71 D. Craven to C.D. Howe (8 June 1943) C.D. Howe Papers, vol. 46, file: Polymer Corporation, folder 8; B.J. O'Connor to W.L.M. King (4 June 1943), ibid.; M.J. Dubois to W.L.M. King (3 June 1943), ibid.; J. Anderson to W.L.M. King (27 May 1943), ibid.; G. Hodgkin to W.L.M. King (3 June 1943), ibid.; P. Hewitt to J. Gardiner (17 May 1943), ibid.; and J.A. McLean to W.L.M. King (21 May 1943), ibid.

72 Sheils to Nicholson (22 May 1942), DMS Papers, vol. 5, folder 3.

73 C.D. Howe to H.B. Speakman (29 May 1942), C.D. Howe Papers, vol. 47, file: Polymer Corporation, 1942.

74 For a more detailed discussion of the role and significance of the Ontario Research Foundation, see Oliver, "Government, Industry and Science," 161–70.

75 Sir Clive Baillieu, "Memorandum on the Measures Adopted in the United Kingdom for the Control and Conservation and Use of Synthetic Rubber" (1 April 1942), C.D. Howe Papers, vol. 43, file: Rubber 1942.

76 H.B. Speakman to C.D. Howe (5 June 1942), C.D. Howe Papers, vol. 47, file: Polymer Corporation, 1942.

77 W.H. Cook, "Agricultural Surpluses as Raw Materials for Manufacture of Rubber and Other War Chemicals" (24 July 1942), Polysar Papers, vol. 34, file: National Research Council, 1942–8.

78 T.R. Griffith, "Report re Synthetic Rubber from Alcohol" (27 March 1942), NRC Papers, vol. 128, file: 17–13R-21; C.Y. Hopkins, "Proposed Production of Alcohol for Manufacture of Synthetic Rubber," (7 January 1942), ibid.

79 "Memorandum" (17 August 1942), C.D. Howe Papers, vol. 47, file: Polymer Corporation, 1942.

80 C.D. Howe to J.R. Nicholson (20 August 1942), ibid.

81 Ibid.

82 Carter, *So That Man May Prosper*, 19.

83 Ibid., 30–2.

84 For a discussion of Howe's continentalist views, see McDowall, *Steel at the Sault*, 169–71 and chap. 8.

85 Canada, House of Commons, *Debates*, 22 June 1943, 3897.

86 Ibid., 23 March 1944, 1775.

87 Howe to Bishop (26 September 1942), DMS Papers, vol. 5, folder 3.

88 Ibid. (22 September 1942).

89 Ibid. (19 May 1942), folder 1.

90 Ibid.

91 Howe to D. Stairs, C.D. Howe Papers, vol. 47, file: Polymer Corporation, 1942.

92 C.D. Howe, quoted in Peter Newman, *The Canadian Establishment*, vol. 1, 375.

93 C.D. Howe to A.L. Bishop (24 September 1942), Polysar Papers, vol. 12, file: Directors' Correspondence, 1942–3.

94 C.D. Howe to A.L. Bishop (26 September 1942), DMS Papers, vol. 5, folder 3.

95 L. Bertin, "The Long Chain," 48–9.

96 C.D. Howe to A.L. Bishop (26 September 1942), DMS Papers, vol. 5, folder 3.

97 R.C. Berkinshaw to G.K. Sheils (15 December 1942), ibid.

98 D.W. Ambridge, "Memorandum regarding Polymer Corporation's Sarnia Project and Its Relation to the United States Synthetic Rubber Program," C.D. Howe Papers, vol. 47, file: Polymer Corporation, 1942.

99 Ibid.

100 D. Ambridge, "Memorandum Re: Priority Situation" (February 3, 1943), C.D. Howe Papers, vol. 47, folder 10.

101 Colonel Dewey to R.C. Berkinshaw (7 July 1943), C.D. Howe Papers, vol. 46, file: Polymer Corporation, folder 9.

102 Gough, "Man-Made Rubber," *Maclean's*, 1 March 1944, 20.

103 *Sarnia Canadian Observer,* 23 February 1944.

104 *Moncton Transcript,* 9 March 1944, 2.

105 Canada, House of Commons, *Debates,* 21 March 1944, 1705.

106 Ibid., 23 March 1944, 1775.

107 C.D. Howe, "Anniversary Address," *Polysphere* (October 1944), 5.

CHAPTER THREE

1 Canada, House of Commons, *Debates,* 16 June 1943, 3707.

2 Howe quoted in *Polysphere,* vol. 1 (October 1944), 1.

3 "Sarnia Synthetic Rubber: General Review of the Process and Plant, " *Canadian Chemistry and Process Industries* (February 1944), 84.

4 Gough, "Man-Made Rubber," *Maclean's*, 1 March 1944, 20.

5 Canada, House of Commons, *Debates,* 27 March 1944, 1906.

6 Ibid., 1868.

7 Ibid., 4 June 1946, 2176.

8 Chandler, "State Enterprise," 711–42.

9 Ibid.

10 Holt, "Long-Term Outlook for Natural Rubber," 49–51.

11 Traves, *The State and Enterprise*, 31, 102–18, 122–3, and 153–4.

12 Smith, "Synthetic vs Natural Rubber after the War," *Saturday Night*, 29 April 1944, 38–9, 47.

13 Canada, House of Commons, *Debates*, 14 May 1946, 1516.

14 Bauer, "Prospects of Rubber," 381–90, and Cook, "Rubber Riddle," 606.

15 I.C. Rush, interview, Sarnia, November 1999.

16 See Chandler, *Strategy and Structure*, especially the introduction.

17 Canada, House of Commons, *Debates*, May 1946, 1909.

18 Ibid., February 1949, 874.

19 Doern and Devlin, "The Farm Credit Corporation," 369–70.

20 Smiley, "Canada and the Quest for a National Policy," 47.

21 Granatstein, *The Ottawa Men*, chap. 6.

22 Norrie and Owram, *History of the Canadian Economy*, 393.

23 See Owram, *The Government Generation*, 221–317; Granatstein, *The Ottawa Men*, 134–88; and Neill, *History of Canadian Economic Thought*, 172–90.

24 Howe, quoted in Bothwell and Kilbourn, *C.D. Howe*, 263.

25 Howe, "Industrial Development in Canada," 209.

26 Laux and Molot, *State Capitalism*, 4.

27 Langford, "Air Canada," 251. There is some debate over the rationale, or lack thereof, for government intervention in aviation. Howe's biographers Bothwell and Kilbourn (*C.D. Howe*) and J. Langford ("Air Canada") argue that Howe was motivated by the pragmatics of the matter rather than any ideological commitment to government intervention. Bliss, on the other hand, sees Howe as ideologically committed, bent on government control of Canada's national aviation industry (*Northern Enterprise*, 442–3). There is, however, a third school of thought. In *Politics and the Airlines*, D. Corbett argues that the establishment of Trans-Canada Air Lines was rooted neither in pragmatics nor ideology. In Corbett's opinion, there seems to have been very little rational thought of any kind behind the establishment of Trans-Canada Air Lines. "Canada seemed to have established a publicly owned monopoly of air service," Corbett writes, "in a fit of absence of mind, as Britain is said to have acquired her Empire"(106).

28 Canada, *White Paper on Employment and Income*, 13.

29 Howe et al., *Canada: Nation on the March*.

30 Howe, "Industrial Development in Canada," 209.

31 Howe, "Canada's New Economic Program," *Industrial Canada* (January 1948), 67–8; "Achievements of Canadian Manufacturers," *Industrial Canada*, (October 1948), 71–3; "Industrial Development in Canada," 207–13; "Canada Expands Industrially," *Industrial Canada* (January 1949), 69–70.

32 *White Paper on Employment and Income*, 1.

33 See Foreman-Peck and Millward, *Public and Private Ownership*, chap. 8, and Chadeau, "The Rise and Decline of State-Owned Industry," 186–90.

34 Bothwell, *Eldorado*, 164–97. Eldorado nonetheless turned out to be a cash cow, generating a good deal of money for the government before the bottom dropped out of the uranium market in the late 1950s. But it was not for the sake of future profit that Howe decided to retain Eldorado; this was an industry with peculiar strategic implications that could not be catered to by pure commercial endeavour.

35 Borins, "World War II Crown Corporations," 463.

36 "War Plants Going, Going, Almost Gone," *Financial Post*, 25 January 1947, 7. The Crown corporations that were still active were Eldorado Mines, Wartime Housing, and Polymer Corporation.

37 Nicholson to Williamson, 22 October 1943, Polysar Papers, vol. 33, file: Rubber Controller Correspondence, 1942–4.

38 Ambridge to Berkinshaw (26 November 1943), C.D. Howe Papers, vol. 46, file: Polymer Corporation, 1943–44, (9). Ambridge to Howe (26 November 1943), ibid.

39 Berkinshaw, "The Future of the Synthetic Rubber Industry," 157.

40 Berkinshaw, "Rubber Production Costs among the Lowest in Industry," 2.

41 Ibid., 156.

42 Howe, "Anniversary Address," reprinted in *Polysphere* (October 1944), 1, 5.

43 Dewey to Howe (20 October 1944), C.D. Howe Papers, vol. 46, file: Polymer Corporation, 1944–1945, (7).

44 Nicholson to Howe (7 October 1944), C.D. Howe Papers, vol. 46, file: Polymer Corporation, 1944–1945, (7).

45 Howe to the Minister of National Revenue (August 1942), C.D. Howe Papers, vol. 47, file: Polymer Corporation, 1942, (11).

46 Canada, House of Commons, *Debates*, 16 June 1943, 3713.

47 Howe to Nicholson (25 November 1944), C.D. Howe Papers, vol. 46, file: Polymer Corporation, 1944–1945, (7).

48 Howe, "Anniversary Address," 1.

49 Howe to Nicholson (25 November 1944), C.D. Howe Papers, vol. 46, file: Polymer Corporation, 1944–5.

50 Ibid.

51 Howe to Nicholson (25 September 1945), C.D. Howe Papers, vol. 46, file: Polymer Corporation, 1944–5, (7).

52 Howe, "Anniversary Address," 1.

53 Rowzee, "Sarnia," 21–7.

54 Elford, "Sarnia," 170–85.

55 Urquhart, *Historical Statistics of Canada*, 474.

56 Davis, "The Canadian Chemical Industry," 157.

57 Ibid., 167.

58 Brendan J. O'Callaghan, "The Government's Rubber Projects," vol. 2, Reconstruction Finance Corporation *Report*, 1948, as revised in 1955 under the supervision of Bertram H. Weimar, Office of Synthetic Rubber, Federal

Facilities Corporation, (u.s.) National Archives, Record Group 234, file no. 26, 607–51.

59 Howe to Campbell, (24 December 1946), C.D. Howe Papers, vol. 45, file: Polymer Corporation, 1945–1946, (6).

60 In a number of important ways, Alcan's history paralleled Polymer's. To meet wartime demand, Alcan had increased its capacity fivefold to five hundred thousand tons of ingots per year. When domestic demand dried up at the end of the war, it reorganized and rebuilt its international sales organization, with a principal object of moving a larger volume of Canadian ingots than ever before in peacetime. See Campbell, *Global Mission*, chap. 8.

61 "Memorandum regarding Technical Division" (12 May 1944), Polysar Papers, vol. 34, file: National Research Council, 1942–8.

62 Chandler, *Strategy and Structure*, especially xi-xiv, 1–17.

63 Ibid., 15.

64 See, Reich, *American Industrial Research*.

65 Berkinshaw to C.J. Mackenzie (12 May 1944), Polysar Papers, vol. 34, file: National Research Council, 1942–8.

66 Canada, Department of Reconstruction and Supply, *Research and Scientific Activity*, especially 6.

67 Ibid.

68 Rowzee to Berkinshaw (26 October 1944), Polysar Papers, vol. 34, file: National Research Council, 1942–8.

69 Berkinshaw to Howe (7 November 1944), Polysar Papers, vol. 34, file: National Research Council, 1942–8.

70 D. Mackenzie to Berkinshaw (3 November 1944), Polysar Papers, vol. 34, file: National Research Council, 1942–8.

71 Rowzee, "Address to the Vancouver, Wellington-Waterloo and Toronto Sections, and the Ontario Rubber Section of the Chemical Institute of Canada," (November 1945), Polysar Papers, vol. 43, file: addresses and articles 1940–1963, part 1.

72 Rowzee, "Synthetic Rubber Industry in Germany," 816.

73 Rowzee, quoted in *Polysphere* (June 1946), 5.

74 See Chandler, *Strategy and Structure*, 374–8; and *Scale and Scope*, 107–8.

75 "Review of Accomplishments" (December 1971), Buckler Papers, vol. 1. During the period 1945–51, Polymer's research and development accomplishments included

1 The first commercial use (1948) of a catalyst for the dehydrogenation of butylenes to butadienes. This development was essential for Sarnia economics and made a significant contribution for many years.

2 The basic improvement (1949) of a polymerization recipe used to manufacture buna-s type rubber. The recipe was later used by producers world-wide.

3 The prevention of buckling of butyl inner tubes at low temperatures concurrent with a 20 percent reduction in tube material costs (1949). This development saved and reestablished the prime market for butyl rubber, namely, automotive tire inner tubes.

4 The first (1949) large-scale production and promotion of a self-reinforced rubber. This was later used universally as a shoe-soling material.

5 The first commercial use (1950) of an improved polymerization recipe for the manufacture of oil-resistant butadiene/acrylonitrile copolymers at low temperature.

6 The first commercial production (1950) of a useful general-purpose synthetic rubber containing 30 percent low-cost oil as an extender.

7 The first commercial production (1950–52) of types of butyl rubber designed for special purposes such as high-voltage cables and curing bags.

76 Solo, "Research and Development in the Synthetic Rubber Industry," 73.

77 Buckler, "Butyl Inner Tubes," 34–48.

78 Annual *Report* (March 1946), 6.

79 "Minutes of the Board of Directors" (November 1945), DMS Papers, vol. 2.

80 I.C. Rush and E.J. Buckler, interviews, Sarnia, November 1999.

81 Canada, House of Commons, *Debates*, 14 May 1946, 1516.

82 Polymer Executive Committee to Howe (5 November 1946), DMS Papers, vol. 7.

83 A.P. Mechin, "Address at the Lions Club of Sarnia, Ontario," (25 October 1946), DMS Papers, vol. 7. Similar statements were made by the other members of the corporation. See Nicholson to Howe (7 October 1944), C.D. Howe Papers, vol. 46, file: Polymer Corporation, 1944–5, (7); Rowzee, "Address at the Kinsmen's Club of London, Ontario," (25 March 1946), DMS Papers, vol. 7; Rowzee, "Address at Kiwanis Club of London, Ontario" (27 August 1946), DMS Papers, vol. 7; L.D. Dougan, "Address to the Canadian Manufacturers' Association," (Toronto, 5 June 1946), DMS Papers, vol. 7.

84 Rae, *Statement of Some New Principles*, especially 119–29.

85 Polymer's Executive Committee to C.D. Howe (5 November 1946), DMS Papers, vol. 7.

86 Neill, *A History of Canadian Economic Thought*, 72–91.

87 Howe to G. Bateman (1 November 1946), C.D. Howe Papers, vol. 46, file: Polymer Corporation, 1945–6, (7).

88 Ibid.

89 Polymer's Executive Committee to C.D. Howe (5 November 1946), DMS Papers, vol. 7.

90 Howe to Nicholson (9 November 1946), DMS Papers, vol. 7.

91 Plumptre, "Synthetic Tires," 6–7.

92 Canada, Dominion Bureau of Statistics, *Consumption, Production and Inventories of Rubber*, vol. 20, no. 1 (January 1966), 4.

93 Ibid.

94 Annual *Report* (March 1947); see schedules C and D.

95 Canada, House of Commons, *Debates*, 19 June 1948, 5526.

96 Canada, House of Commons, *Debates*, 20 November 1945, 2332.

97 Annual *Report* (March 1948), 3.

98 Ibid, 8.

99 Rowzee, "Synthetic Rubber Industry in Germany," 814–16.

100 Nicholson to Howe (28 September 1950), C.D. Howe Papers, vol. 44, file: Polymer Corporation, 1949–1950, (2).

101 There was, however, one exception. After the war Du Pont of the United States resumed exports of its specialized product neoprene to Europe.

102 There is an ongoing historiographical debate over whether the Marshall Plan was actually necessary for European recovery. In *The Reconstruction of Western Europe*, Alan Milward argues that from an economic perspective Marshall Plan aid was not necessary, because economic recovery was already under way by 1948. This conclusion is echoed by Imanuel Wexler in *The Marshall Plan Revisited*. Opposing Milward and Wexler are historians who argue that the Marshall Plan "saved" Western Europe from economic collapse. In *The Marshall Plan*, Michael Hogan argues that had there been no Marshall Plan aid, there would have been "a serious crisis in production that would have come with the collapse of critical dollar imports" (431). In his study *Economic Ideas and Government Policy*, Alec Cairncross similarly argues "that the Marshall Plan prolonged and underpinned European economic recovery when it was in danger of collapsing for lack of the necessary finance" (104). In *The Marshall Plan Days*, Charles Kindleberger makes perhaps the most controversial claim, stating stridently that "Marshall plan dollars did save the world" (247).

103 Granatstein and Hillmer, *For Better or Worse*, 174–5; Cuff and Granatstein, *Ties That Bind*, 142–3; and Cuff and Granatstein, *American Dollars-Canadian Prosperity*, 83–139.

104 Cuff and Granatstein, *American Dollars-Canadian Prosperity*, 138.

105 Annual *Report* (March 1946 and March 1949).

106 Annual *Report* (March 1949). The net profit for the fiscal year 1948 was $430,542,65, after making provision for a depreciation reserve of $2,356,711.91. Gross sales revenue for the year amounted to approximately $21 million, up $4 million from the previous year.

107 Phillips, *Competition*, Table 38, 252.

108 Annual *Report*, (March 1951), 3.

109 W.L. Dack, *Financial Post*, 29 July 1950, 1–3.

110 Howe to E.J. Brunning (6 May 1951), DMS Papers, vol. 3.

111 Annual *Report* (March 1951), 3.

112 C.E. Morrison to R.E. Hatch (16 August 1950), DMS Papers, vol. 7.
113 I.C. Rush, interview (Sarnia, November 1999).
114 Rowzee, "Report on Trip to Europe" (7 December 1951), DMS Papers, vol. 3.
115 Ibid., 26.
116 Hatch, quoted in "The Long Chain," 119.
117 Laux and Molot, *State Capitalism*, 72–8.
118 Doern and Tupper, "Understanding Public Corporations," 33.
119 Boothman, "Strategic Transformations," 299–311.
120 The other Canadian companies "going global" at this time included Alcan and Massey-Ferguson. See Campbell, *Global Mission*, especially 188–207, 397–418; and Neufeld, *A Global Corporation*, 87–91, 187–90, 290–303.

CHAPTER FOUR

1 One of the first to criticize Howe's liberal/continentalist investment policies was fellow Liberal Walter Gordon. In his *Report* (1957) on Canada's economic prospects, Gordon commented that the growing level of American direct investment in Canada was leading to a loss of industrial control (40–2). Later, in such works as *Troubled Canada: The Need for New Domestic Policies* and *Storm Signals: New Economic Policies for Canada*, he criticized Howe's policies more forcefully. In *Storm Signals*, for instance, Gordon argued that "The Right Honourable C.D. Howe ... saw no inherent danger in the continuing sales of Canada's resources and business enterprises to foreigners" (11). Gordon's disciples Libbie Park and Frank Park, in their study *The Anatomy of Big Business*, identify C.D. Howe as one of the "sellers of Canada" (58–60). Likewise, in *The Canadian Corporate Elite: An Analysis of Economic Power* Canadian political economist Wallace Clement argues that Howe was a menace to Canada because he acted as a kind of instrument of the American takeover of Canadian business (88–9). Some commentators on the other end of the ideological spectrum agreed. In *Canada's First Century*, the conservative historian Donald Creighton, for example, blamed Howe's continentalist policies for relegating Canada to neocolonial status (286). Similarly, in *Lament for a Nation*, George Grant censured Howe and the Liberals for reducing Canada to a branch plant of the United States (8–9). On the other hand, Michael Bliss argues that it is not true that Howe acted as a menace to Canada by aiding the takeover of Canadian business after the war. Similarly, the overwhelming message of Bothwell and Kilbourn's *C.D. Howe* is that C.D. Howe was a good Canadian.
2 D. Slater, "Consumption Expenditure in Canada," 4.
3 Owram, *Born at the Right Time*, chap. 4.
4 *Saturday Night*, 27 March 1951, 10-11.
5 Elford, "Canada's Chemical Valley," 179.

6 T. Siew Sin, quoted in *Polysphere* (December 1958), 6.

7 Spitz, *Petrochemicals*, chap. 8; Chapman, *The International Petrochemical Industry*, chap. 5; and Quintella, *The Strategic Management of Technology*, 77–8.

8 Johnson, *The Challenge of Change*, 201.

9 Dedman, *Challenge and Response*, especially chaps. 4–6.

10 Chapman, *The International Petrochemical Industry*, 111–15.

11 Ashley, *Canadian Crown Corporations*, 246.

12 Barrington (September 1953), quoted in *Polysphere*, 25.

13 Bliss, *Northern Enterprise*, 8.

14 Howe, "Department of Defence Production, Press Release" (8 June 1951), DMS Papers, vol. 7.

15 Bertin, "The Long Chain," 120–1.

16 Hatch interview (Toronto, July 2000) and Buckler interview (Sarnia, November 1999).

17 Barrington to Howe (1 June 1951), C.D. Howe Papers, vol. 44. file: Polymer Corporation, 1950–1951, (1).

18 Barrington, quoted in *Polysphere* (July 1951), 1

19 Howe to J.R. Nicholson (28 October 1944), C.D. Howe Papers, vol. 46, file: Polymer Corporation, 1944–5, (7).

20 Canada, House of Commons, Special Committee on War Expenditures, *Fifth Report*, 12 August 1944, 54.

21 Canada, House of Commons, *Debates* (16 June 1943), 3707–8; ibid., (27 March 1944), 1867–71.

22 Howe to A.G. Partridge (18 October 1951), DMS Papers, vol. 7.

23 Howe to J.D. Barrington (5 October 1951), C.D. Howe Papers, vol. 44, file: Polymer Corporation, 1950–1, (1).

24 Ashley, *Canadian Crown Corporations*, table 2, 237.

25 "Minutes of the Board of Directors" (27 September 1951), DMS Papers, vol. 12.

26 Canada, House of Commons, *Debates*, 31 March 1952, 952.

27 Ibid., 952–3.

28 Howe to J.R. Nicholson (25 September 1945), C.D. Howe Papers, vol. 46, file: Polymer Corporation, 1944–1945, (7).

29 "Minutes of the Board of Directors" (8 June 1951), DMS Papers, vol. 12.

30 Bertin, "The Long Chain," 123–4.

31 P.C. 2279. The agreement was retroactive to 1 April 1951.

32 *Report* of the Auditor General, 1951–2, paragraph 107.

33 *Statutes of Canada*, 15-16 Geo. 6, c. 12.

34 Canada, House of Commons, *Debates*, 31 March 1952, 953.

35 Ibid.

36 Ibid., 27 March 1944, 1900.

37 Ibid.

38 Owram, *Born at the Right Time*, chap. 4.

39 McLuhan, *The Mechanical Bride*, v.

40 *Maclean's*, 1 July 1952, 26.

41 Ibid., 18 August 1956, 48.

42 "Minutes of the Meeting of the Board of Directors of Polymer" (7 August 1952), DMS Papers, vol. 12.

43 "Minutes of the Meeting of the Board of Directors of Polymer" (1 May 1952), DMS Papers, vol. 12.

44 *Maclean's*, 1 February 1953, 31.

45 Ibid., 30 April 1955.

46 Ibid., 28 May 1955.

47 See *Maclean's*, 2 March 1957, and 30 April 1955.

48 Ibid., 28 May 1955.

49 See Meikle, *American Plastic*; Handley, *Nylon*; and Clarke, *Tupperware*.

50 *Maclean's*, 1 January 1954, 49.

51 Ibid., 1 June 1954, 98.

52 Ibid., 16 April 1955.

53 Meikle, *American Plastic*, 173.

54 Goldman, *Reading Ads Socially*, 2.

55 Nye, *Image Worlds*, 155.

56 Marchand, *Advertising the American Dream*, 52–87.

57 Rowzee, "Synthetic Rubber Industry in Germany," 316.

58 *Maclean's*, 30 April 1955.

59 Slater, "Consumption Expenditures in Canada," 132.

60 Lower, *Canadians in the Making*, 424.

61 Sun Life Assurance Company of Canada, *Report* to the Royal Commission on Canada's Economic Prospects, "The Canadian Automotive Industry," 115.

62 *Maclean's*, July 1954, 7

63 Ibid., 114

64 Halberstam, *The Fifties*, 127.

65 McLuhan, *The Mechanical Bride*, 84.

66 Laqueur, *Germany Today*, 32

67 Bloomfield, *The World Automotive Industry*, appendix 1, 356.

68 Ibid., table 27, 183.

69 Ibid.

70 Phillips, *Competition*, table 25, 158.

71 Dominion Bureau of Statistics, "Consumption Production and Inventories of Rubber" (Ottawa, April 1966), table 4, 4.

72 *Maclean's*, 3 March 1956, 58.

73 Barrington quoted in *Financial Post*, 9 April 1955, 33.

74 Solo, "Research and Development," table 1, 71.

75 Ibid., 79.
76 See Lucas, "Mechanics of Economic Development," 3–42; Romer, "Idea Gaps," 543–73; and Howitt et al., *The Implication of Knowledge-Based Growth*, passim.
77 Solo, "Research and Development," 79.
78 Buckler, "Canadian Case History," 295–7.
79 Buckler, "Research – an Industrial Operation" (24 November 1953), Polysar Papers, vol. 146, file: E.J. Buckler speeches, 1953, 6.
80 Buckler, "Industrial Research: An Address to School Teachers Visiting Polymer" (October 6, 1955), Polysar Papers, vol. 146, file: E.J. Buckler speeches, 1955–8.
81 Ibid., 3.
82 Buckler, "Research – an Industrial Operation," 4.
83 Ibid., 4.
84 Ibid., 10.
85 Buckler, "Industrial Research."
86 Ibid., 3.
87 Hounshell and Smith, *Science and Corporate Strategy*, 371.
88 Examples include the evolution of the catalyst system for the making of "cold" rubber, the study of the mechanism of bromination of butyl to make bromobutyl polymer (the ultimate inner liner rubber), and the evolution of a rapid and reliable test for measuring the molecular weight of polymer during polymerization (in the production of Krynol).
89 See Herbert and Bisio, *Synthetic Rubber*, 151–6, and Morris, *The American Synthetic Rubber Program*, 32–9.
90 Rowzee, "Address Given by E.R. Rowzee at the Kinsmen's Club of London, Ontario" (25 March 1946), DMS Papers, vol. 7.
91 Buckler and Rush interviews (Sarnia, November 1999).
92 Rowzee, "Synthetic Rubber Industry in Germany," *Canadian Chemistry and Process Industries* (December 1945), 815.
93 See Avery, *The Science of War*; Hartcup, *The Challenge of War*; Mellor, *Australia in the War*; and Zuckerman, *Scientists and War*, especially 103–15.
94 Avery, *The Science of War*, 4.
95 See Farquharson, "Governed or Exploited?" 23–42; Gimbel, *Science, Technology, and Reparations*; Bower, *The Paperclip Conspiracy*; and Krammer, "Technology Transfer," 69–103.
96 Henderson, "Memoirs of a Canadian Engineer," Gordon Henderson Papers, vol. 1, 205.
97 Burchard, *Q.E.D. – M.I.T. in World War II*, 108–12.
98 Henderson, "Memoirs of a Canadian Engineer," 205; Rowzee, "Talk on Trip to England and Germany" (12 February 1945), Polysar Papers, vol. 43, file: Addresses and Articles, 1940–63.
99 J.R. Donald to H.J. Carmichael (10 February 1945), Polysar Papers, vol. 25, file: Research and Development, part 1.

100 Rowzee, "Trip to England and Germany," 7–10.

101 Ibid., 12.

102 Ibid., 13.

103 Rowzee, "Synthetic Rubber Industry in Germany," 815; see also his comments to the board of directors in "Minutes" (13 June 1945), Polysar Papers, vol. 1.

104 Nicholson to Howe (6 September 1949), Polysar Papers, vol. 13, file: Farbenfabriken Bayer Leverkusen Equipment; Nicholson to A.F.W. Plumptre (24 October 1949), ibid.; Nicholson to J.H. Thurrott (14 January 1950), ibid.; Nicholson to D. Wilgress (14 February 1950), ibid.; Nicholson to Plumptre (11 March 1950), ibid.; and Nicholson to Plumptre (21 March 1950), ibid.

105 Howe to L.B. Pearson (7 September 1949), Polysar Papers, vol. 13, file: Farbenfabriken Bayer Leverkusen Equipment, 1949–50.

106 "Analysis of Equipment Released from Farbenfabriken Bayer Leverkusen" (14 February 1950), Polysar Papers, vol. 13, file: correspondence 1949–51; see also G. Henderson's personal account in his "Memoirs of a Canadian Engineer," 205–26.

107 Ivanovszky, "BIOS Trip to Germany, 1946," 37–48; Faragher, "Collecting German Industrial Information," 3817; Kleiderer, "The Pharmaceutical Industry of Germany," 1206–8; Enloe, "The War and the German Drug Industry," 3046–48; Kuhn, "Development in the German Chemical Industry," 1516–22; Weidlein, "Synthetic Rubber Research," 771–4; Goggin, "Advances in Plastic," 339–43, and "New Tanning Agents," 1980–1, 2029.

108 Morris, *American Synthetic Rubber,* 32–9. See also Davis, "The Canadian Chemical Industry," 54.

109 Morris, *American Synthetic Rubber,* 36–7.

110 Solo, "Research and Development," 78.

111 Ibid., 70.

112 Solo, *Across the High Technology Threshold,* 101–3.

113 "Merger," *Chemical and Engineering News* (25 June 1951).

114 *Financial Post,* 7 April 1951, 1.

115 Nicholson would not experience the same success at Brazilian Traction. His business philosophy and approach were at odds with the South American way of doing things. See McDowall, *The Light,* especially 391.

116 Howe, "Department of Defence Production, Press Release" (8 June 1951), DMS Papers, vol. 7.

117 Rowzee, "Trip," 3.

118 Rowzee, "Report to the President" (7 December 1951), DMS Papers, vol. 3, 6–8.

119 Rowzee, "Report to the President," 23.

120 Ibid.

121 Ibid., 24.

122 See "Minutes of the Board of Directors" (September 1951–August 1953), DMS Papers, vol. 12.
123 Annual *Report* (March 1950).
124 For a concise and colourful discussion of the pipeline debate, see Bothwell and Kilbourn, *C.D. Howe*, chap. 18.
125 Ibid., 331.
126 Canada, House of Commons, *Debates*, January 1956, 136.
127 Ibid., 135–7.
128 "Why Crown Firm? C.D. Howe Speaks," *Financial Post*, 20 December 1958, 23–4.

CHAPTER FIVE

1 Rowzee, "Objectives for 1960" (22 January 1960), Gordon Churchill Papers, vol. 37, 2.
2 Chandler, *Scale and Scope*, 8, 18, 39, 408, 464, 606–8, 614; Wilkins, *The Maturing of Multinational Enterprise*, especially chaps. 13–15; Niosi, *Canadian Multinationals*, especially 98–101, 113, 116–20, 125–67; and Vernon, *Sovereignty at Bay*, 86–98.
3 During the 1960s, critics denounced the MNE as an instrument of neowestern imperialism. Academics like Andre Gunder Frank argued that the multinational corporation retarded the development of the underdeveloped world. Through it, Frank argued, the capitalist metropolis expropriated the economic surplus of satellite countries, "suck[ing] capital out of the periphery and dominat[ing] the periphery at all levels (*Latin America*, 227–8). Others argued that the MNE undermined national sovereignty and cultural autonomy (Vernon, *Sovereignty at Bay*, especially chaps. 5, 6, and 7). A similar sentiment was expressed in Canada. See, for example, Lexer, *Canada Ltd.*; Rotstein, *The Precarious Homestead*; Warnock, *Partner to Behemoth*; and Gordon, *Storm Signals*. Partly as a result of C.D. Howe's postwar reconstruction program, U.S. direct investment in Canada reached $17 billion by 1960. The extent of American ownership prompted Walter Gordon – both as a royal commissioner in the 1950s and as a finance minister in the early 1960s – to call for new economic policies that would limit the level of direct foreign investment in Canada (Gordon, *A Choice for Canada*). While the philosopher George Grant "lamented for the nation," the social scientist Kari Levitt told of the "silent surrender" of national sovereignty to the multinational corporation (Grant, *Lament for a Nation*; Levitt, *Silent Surrender*). According to Levitt, Canada's capitalist class had become the willing partners of the MNE, headquartered in the United States. Together, Levitt maintained, they had fashioned a system for holding the Canadian economy in thrall, narrowing its range of opportunities, and eliminating its power of choice.

The multinational corporation, Levitt concluded, had reduced Canada to neocolonial status. Despite these criticisms, the MNE proliferated in the postwar period.

4 McDowall, *Brazilian Traction*, chaps. 2 and 3. See also Armstrong and Nelles, *Southern Exposure*, chap. 2.

5 Chandler, *Scale and Scope*, 117, 122, 171–5, 213–17, 446–52.

6 Ibid., 36–45, 145, 230.

7 Kindleberger, *American Business Abroad*, 6.

8 Chandler, *Scale and Scope*, 594–7.

9 Wilkins, *Multinational Enterprise*, 379–81. Understanding when and why direct investment of this nature has taken place has preoccupied historians and economists for decades. According to the economist Peter Gray, firms sometimes expanded abroad for defensive reasons, either to forestall competition in a new market or to obtain assured sources of supply of some raw material vital to the domestic operation of the parent company (see Gray, *The Economics of Business Investment Abroad*, 8). At other times – as was the case with American industrial expansion into Canada after 1870 – firms invested in distant production facilities to avoid tariffs and other discriminatory legislation that would raise the cost of finished goods shipped across national borders. In such cases, direct investment occurs because of the greater cost-effectiveness and profitability resulting from what economists term "country-specific advantages." The postwar boom in Canada brought a surge of such foreign direct investment.

   A third reason for investing in manufacturing abroad has been identified by Mira Wilkins, among others. According to Wilkins, during the 1950s and 1960s American firms often found it impossible to obtain effective market penetration with exports from the home front, and as a result they set up manufacturing facilities abroad (Wilkins, *Multinational Enterprise*, 379). Thus, while some market-oriented investments were made to defend existing foreign markets, most – according to Wilkins – were aggressive new stakes designed to penetrate new overseas markets. While accepting all these reasons as valid interpretations of why direct investment takes place, Alfred Chandler argues that such investment cannot occur successfully until the firm itself has developed the organizational capabilities – the facilities and skills in production, marketing, and management – to achieve economies of scale and scope at home. The expansionary urge, in Chandler's mind, is thus primordially organizationally driven, not market-driven. Once it has developed the capabilities, the corporation can then expand into foreign markets, first through exports and then by direct foreign investment in manufacturing facilities abroad. According to Chandler, organizational capabilities provide the core dynamic for the continuing evolution of the modern industrial enterprise (Chandler, *Scale and Scope*, 594–7).

10 Barnet and Müller, *Global Reach*, especially 123–147.

11 Taylor and Baskerville, *A Concise History of Business in Canada*, 463–4.

12 Campbell, *Global Mission*, 404–5.

13 MacKay, *Empire of Wood*, 245–75.

14 Neufeld, *A Global Corporation*, 290–302.

15 See, for example, Bliss, *Northern Enterprise*, 479–80.

16 Chapman, *The International Petrochemical Industry*, 101–6.

17 Spitz, *Petrochemicals*, 338–43.

18 Rowzee, "Objectives for 1960" (22 January 1960), Gordon Churchill Papers, vol. 37, 2.

19 Ibid.

20 Ibid., 4.

21 Phillips, *Competition*, table 10, 63–4.

22 "Minutes of the Board of Directors" (17 September 1959), DMS Papers, vol. 12.

23 Rowzee, "Objectives," 4.

24 Ibid.

25 "Minutes of the Board of Directors" (14 September 1960), DMS Papers, vol. 12.

26 Canada, House of Commons, Standing Committee on Public Accounts, *Minutes of Proceedings and Evidence*, no. 11 (9 May 1961), 327.

27 Rowzee, "Objectives for 1960," 3–5.

28 Ibid.

29 *Minutes of Proceedings and Evidence*, no. 11, 336.

30 Ibid.

31 Ibid.

32 Ibid., 323.

33 Rowzee, "Objectives for 1960," 5.

34 Ibid., 5.

35 "Minutes of the Board of Directors" (16 June 1960), DMS Papers, vol. 12.

36 Rowzee, "Objectives for 1960," 5.

37 Ibid., 5.

38 Ibid., 6.

39 Rowzee to O'Hurley (2 August 1960), DMS Papers, vol. 15.

40 Rowzee, "Objectives for 1960," 6.

41 *Financial Post*, 11 June 1960, 3.

42 Ibid., 27 June 1953, 35.

43 *Executive* (September 1960), 21.

44 B. Henderson, "Canada's Polymer," *Monetary Times*, November 1956, 27–9.

45 Annual *Report* (1960), 5, 8–9.

46 Barrington (September 1953), quoted in *Polysphere*, 25.

47 Buckler, "Canadian Case History," 295–301.

48 Canada, Royal Commission on Canada's Economic Prospects, Final *Report* (Ottawa 1957), 445–58.
49 Annual *Report* (1960), 4–5.
50 Hatch, interview, Toronto, May 2000.
51 Annual *Reports* (1944–1961).
52 *Financial Post*, 5 March 1960, 4.
53 Mullington, "The Federal Government," tables 4 and 5, 47 and 57.
54 D. Golden, interview, Ottawa, October 2000.
55 R. O'Hurley to J.G. Diefenbaker (24 September 1958), DMS Papers, vol. 7.
56 Ibid.
57 Canada, House of Commons, *Debates*, 28 July 1960, 7123.
58 Ibid., 3 June 1946, 2128–9; ibid., 4 June 1946, 2156–7.
59 *Financial Post*, 11 June 1960, 3,5; ibid., 5 March 1960, 4; and *Canadian Chemical Processing* (October 1958), 24–8.
60 See Barrington's testimony in Bertin's "The Long Chain," 160. The argument that Howe was sympathetic to privatization is further strengthened by Bothwell's finding that Howe was going to privatize Eldorado if the Liberals had won the 1957 election. See Bothwell, *Eldorado*, 413.
61 P.C. Allen to O'Hurley (27 November 1959), DMS Papers, vol. 7.
62 Mullington, "The Federal Government," 58.
63 W.M. Hall to R. O'Hurley (14 January 1963), DMS Papers, vol. 15; Hall to O'Hurley (12 December 1962), DMS Papers, vol. 15.
64 G.H. Elliot to M.W. McCutcheon (20 December 1962), DMS Papers, vol. 15; J.G. Davoud to G.W. Hunter (13 December 1960), DMS Papers, vol. 15; B.G. Barrow to G.W. Hunter (16 September 1960), DMS Papers, vol. 15; J.W. Murphy to O'Hurley (11 June 1959), DMS Papers, vol. 15.
65 R.A. Wisener to M.W. McCutcheon (25 January 1963), DMS Papers, vol. 15; R.A. Wisener to O'Hurley (8 January 1962), ibid.
66 *Financial Post*, 5 March 1960, 4; Barrington to O'Hurley (15 June 1961), DMS Papers, vol. 15.
67 Fleming, *The Summit Years*, 210.
68 Canada, Privy Council Office, *Cabinet Conclusions*, vol. 2745 (22 July 1959), 4.
69 See Barrington's testimony in Bertin's "The Long Chain," 160.
70 Barrington to O'Hurley (15 June 1961), DMS Papers, vol. 15.
71 For Berkinshaw's opinion of Barrington's offer see the *Financial Post*, 11 June 1960.
72 "Department of Defence Production, Memorandum re Polymer Corporation" (25 February 1963), DMS Papers, vol. 15.
73 J.H. Ferguson to D. Fleming (28 April 1959), DMS Papers, vol. 7.
74 Fleming to Ferguson (30 April 1959), DMS Papers, vol. 7.
75 Canada, House of Commons, *Debates*, 28 July 1960, 7123.

76 "Minutes of the Meeting of the Board of Directors" (16 June 1960), DMS Papers, vol. 12.

77 A. Blair to G. Hees (15 June 1961), DMS Papers, vol. 16.

78 "Resolution Passed at the Ninth Conference of Canadian District Council O.C.A.W." (15 September 1962), DMS Papers, vol. 15.

79 C. Jodoin to O'Hurley (9 June 1961), DMS Papers, vol. 15.

80 "Minutes of the Meeting of the Board of Directors" (16 June 1960), DMS Papers, vol. 12.

81 Canada, House of Commons, *Debates*, 28 July 1960, 7123.

82 Ibid., and "Minutes of the Cabinet Committee on Possible Methods of Disposition of the Polymer Corporation" (15 June 1960), DMS Papers, vol. 15.

83 Privy Council Office, *Cabinet Conclusions*, vol. 2747 (7 September 1960), 3.

84 See Dimma, *The Canada Development Corporation*, vol. 2, 290–2, and Stursberg, *Diefenbaker,* 112.

85 Fleming, "Business and Government" (Toronto, April 1965), Fleming Papers, vol. 156, file 5.

86 Azzi, *Walter Gordon,* 114–5.

87 Ibid., chap. 3, especially 71, 82–4.

88 For the response to Coyne's policy by Keynesians within the world of academe, see Gordon, *Economists versus the Bank of Canada.*

89 Coyne, "Testimony before the Senate Standing Committee on Manpower and Employment"(April 1961), in Neufeld *Money and Banking,* 308–17.

90 Annual *Report of the Governor to the Minister of Finance, Bank of Canada* (Ottawa, 1960), 20–3.

91 For a more extensive account of this episode see Smith, *Rogue Tory,* 393–414.

92 Ibid., 325.

93 Ibid., 320–1.

94 "Report of Committee of Cabinet," DMS Papers, vol. 15.

95 *Cabinet Conclusions* (24 August 1960), 9.

96 Ibid., 10.

97 Ibid.

98 Ibid. (7 September 1960), 3.

99 Ibid. (24 August 1960), 11.

100 Ibid., 12.

101 "Report of Committee of Cabinet," DMS Papers, vol. 15, 6.

102 *Cabinet Conclusions* (7 September 1960), 2.

103 Ibid., 3.

104 Richards and Pratt, *Prairie Capitalism,* 67.

105 *Cabinet Conclusions* (7 September 1960), 3.

106 Ibid.

107 Canada, Royal Commission on Government Organization, *Report*, vol. 2, 349.

108 Ibid.

109 Ibid. "By the very reason of its good management and commercial success in world markets, it has become established as a valuable and unique Canadian asset, possessing highly specialized scientific, production and marketing skills and experience, and providing careers and a livelihood for more than 2,500 men and women. Under these circumstances, general public approval can only be expected if its sale is made on terms which ensure that control of the undertaking will remain in Canadian hands and that its integrity will be preserved by its new owners" (349–50).

110 "Report of Committee of Cabinet," 6.

111 *Cabinet Conclusions* (7 September 1960), 3.

112 See O'Hurley's speech in Canadian Industrial Preparedness Association's *The Bulletin* (28 November 1960), 2–3.

113 *Financial Post*, 5 November 1960.

114 Rowzee, "Objectives for 1960" (22 January 1960), Gordon Churchill Papers, vol. 37, 6.

115 "Minutes of the Board of Directors" (16 June 1960), DMS Papers, vol. 12.

116 Canada, Standing Committee on Public Accounts, *Minutes* (9 May 1961), 336.

117 G.W. Hunter to H.C. Green (14 April 1958), DMS Papers, vol. 7.

118 Phillip, *Competition*, 80.

119 "Minutes of the Board of Directors" (15 June 1961), DMS Papers, 296-8-1, vol. 12.

120 "Report of Trip to Europe" (December 1951), 20–4.

121 *Financial Post*, 17 June 1960, 64.

122 By 1966, the number of countries with SBR technology had risen to twenty-two. In addition to Canada and the United States, France, West Germany, Italy, the Netherlands, Belgium, Australia, South Africa, India, Japan, Russia, East Germany, Rumania, Poland, Czechoslovakia, Communist China, Brazil, Mexico, Spain, and Argentina had SBR plants in operation.

123 "Minutes of the Board of Directors" (15 June 1961), DMS Papers, vol. 12. According to Polymer's figures, a plant in Belgium would return 17 percent on investment, after tax, compared with about 10 percent for Sarnia facilities. Even if prices dropped 15 percent, the estimated return would still be 10 percent for the Belgian plant, while the return on the Sarnia facilities would be no more than 5 percent.

124 Ibid.

125 "Minutes of the Board of Directors" (20 July 1961), DMS Papers, vol. 12.

126 "Minutes of the Board of Directors" (18 April 1962), DMS Papers, 296–8–1, vol. 12.

127 *Cabinet Conclusions* (21 September 1961), 3.

128 Ibid., 4.

129 "Minutes of the Board of Directors" (28 April 1961), DMS Papers, 296–8–1, vol. 12.

130 *Polysphere* (October 1962), 8.

131 McMillan, *The Chain Straighteners*, 27–45.

132 *Financial Post*, 20 June 1959, 53.

133 Ibid.

134 Dyer and Sicilia, *Labours of a Modern Hercules*, 288.

135 Hounshell and Smith, *Science and Corporate Strategy*, 494.

136 McMillan, *The Chain Straighteners*, 144.

137 For more biographical information on Ziegler, see ibid., 27–45.

138 Quoted ibid., 145.

139 Buckler, "Statement to Agents – Review of Polybutadiene Development" (25 June 1962), Polysar Papers, vol. 146, file: Buckler speeches, folder 2.

140 Buckler, "Canadian Contributions," 10.

141 Interview with B. Pursell (Sarnia, July 2000); interview with Buckler (Sarnia, July 2000); and interview with F. Bentley (Sarnia, November 1999).

142 Buckler, Review of Research and Development Program (May 1962), Polysar Papers, vol. 146, file: E.J. Buckler speeches, folder 2.

143 Buckler, "Future Natural/Synthetic Prospects," Polysar Papers, vol. 146, file: E.J. Buckler speeches, 1959–65.

144 Ibid.

145 Buckler, "Polymer Corporation: The Future," Polysar Papers, vol. 146, file: E.J. Buckler speeches, folder 3.

146 While production increased 109 percent during the period, employment levels increased by only 42 percent.

147 Rowzee, "Objectives," 4.

148 W.L. Dack, "Chemicals and Plastics: A Feature Report," *Financial Times* (11 June 1966), C1–C12.

CHAPTER SIX

1 Rowzee, "The Polymer Plan" (6 May 1969), Polysar Papers, vol. 46, file: Minister of Supply and Services – Correspondence and Reports, 1969–70.

2 Chandler, *Scale and Scope*, 617–21; Rumelt, *Strategy, Structure*, especially 50–63; Channon, *Strategy and Structure*, 52–68; Dyas and Thanheiser, *Emerging European Enterprise*, 72; Scott "The Industrial State," 133–145; and Sobel, *The Age of Giant Corporations*, chaps. 8 and 9.

3 Diversification is related if there is some element in the diversifying strategy that entails activities or resources that are common to the existing activities and resources of the firm. Diversification is unrelated if investment projects have nothing in common with other activities of the firm or if the resources of the firm and the experience gained using those resources are not applied to new activities undertaken as a result of an investment strategy. Diversification into unrelated industries thus involves a departure from the firm's existing areas of specialization, and according to the economist Edith Penrose, may be one of three kinds: 1 entry into new markets with new products using the same production base; 2 expansion in the same market with new products but in a different area of technology; and 3 entry into new markets with new products based in a different area of technology. See Penrose, *Growth of the Firm,* 109–11.

4 Chandler, *Scale and Scope,* 622.

5 Rumelt, *Strategy, Structure,* 53–5.

6 Drucker, *The Practice of Management*; Knoontz, "The Management Theory Jungle," 174–88.

7 Katz, "Skills of an Affective Administrator," 33–42.

8 Editors of *Fortune* magazine, *The Conglomerate Commotion.*

9 Hounshell and Smith, *Science and Corporate Strategy,* chap. 22, especially 538–40.

10 Lank and Williams, *The Du Pont Canada History,* chap. 21.

11 Goldenburg, *Canadian Pacific,* chaps. 10 and 13.

12 Porter, "From Competitive Advantage to Corporate Strategy," 43–59; Peters and Waterman, *In Search of Excellence*; Hayes and Abernathy, "Managing Our Way," 67–77.

13 Markides, "Back to Basics," 12–25.

14 Stobaugh, *Innovation and Competition,* 67–78.

15 Rowzee, "Responsibility and Enterprise," *Rubber World* (August 1967), 80–2.

16 Annual *Report* (1967), 4.

17 Rowzee to Drury (16 February 1968), Annual *Report,* 4.

18 Rowzee, "Objectives for 1960" (22 January 1960), Gordon Churchill Papers, vol. 37, 1–6.

19 Annual *Report* (1967), 7.

20 Wood Gundy, "Polymer Corporation Limited: A Valuation for the Department of Supply and Services, Government of Canada" (14 April 1972), especially 9, 32–50, Polysar Papers, vol. 46, file: Report for the Government of Canada.

21 Buckler, Bentley, Dudley, and Rush interviews (Sarnia, November 1999); Bryne and Pursell interviews (Sarnia, July 2000).

22 Hatch interview (Toronto, May 2000).

23 W.F. Ackerman, "General Survey: Polymer Corporation Limited" (February 1969), 9, Polysar Papers, vol. 48. Cited hereafter as the Ackerman *Report.*

24 Ibid., iii.

25 Rowzee, "Address to the Institute of Synthetic Rubber Producers" (24–26 April 1967), Polysar Papers, vol. 44, file: Addresses, Speeches, Articles, 1967–8.

26 Hatch, "Strategy for Growth" (22 September 1969), Polysar Papers, vol. 134, file: Corporate Planning and Diversification, 1968–70.

27 Rowzee to Richardson (9 December 1969), Polysar Papers, vol. 46, file: Correspondences, 1969–70.

28 Ibid.

29 *Cabinet Conclusions* (19 December 1969), 4.

30 Ackerman *Report*, iv.

31 Ibid., vi.

32 Ibid., x.

33 Ibid., 6.

34 Ibid., vi.

35 Ibid.

36 Ibid.

37 Hatch interview (Toronto, March 2000).

38 *Financial Times*, 1 June 1964.

39 Ackerman *Report*, iv.

40 Ibid., xi.

41 Ibid., 23–5.

42 Chandler, "Development, Diversification and Decentralization," 107–9; *Scale and Scope*, 175–8.

43 Chandler, *Scale and Scope*, 188.

44 Ibid., xi.

45 Rowzee, "Memorandum re Polymer Plan" (6 May 1969), Polysar Papers, vol. 46, file: Minister of Supply and Services – Correspondence and Reports, 1969–70.

46 Ibid.

47 Ackerman *Report*, xi.

48 "Canadian Firm Seeks Expanded u.s. Market," *Chemical and Engineering News*, vol. 48 (5 October 1970), 15.

49 *Financial Post*, 10 May 1969, 45.

50 B. Pursell interview (Sarnia, November 1999); F. Bentley interview (Sarnia, November 1999); Hatch interview (Toronto, July 2000); W. Petryschuk interview (Sarnia, July 2000).

51 Forrestal, *The Story of Monsanto*, 187–91, 210.

52 Dyer and Sicilia, *Labors of a Modern Hercules*, 363–73.

53 Hatch, "Philosophy for Growth" (22 September 1969), Polysar Papers, vol. 134, file: Corporate Planning and Diversification, 1968–70.

54 Hatch to Rowzee (22 September 1969), ibid.

55 Ibid.

56 Hatch, "Philosophy for Growth" (22 September 1969), ibid.

57 Hatch, "Strategy for Growth" (22 September 1969), ibid.

58 Ibid.

59 Hatch interview (Toronto, July 2000).

60 Hatch to Rowzee (22 September 1969), Polysar Papers, vol. 134, file: Corporate Planning and Diversification, 1968–70.

61 Ibid.

62 Hatch, "Strategy for Growth," 3.

63 "News Release" (4 February 1970), DMS Papers, vol. 16, file: ERD-4560–2.

64 G. Bracewell, "The Future," *Polysphere* (April 1972), 8.

65 "Minutes," (25 September 1969), Polysar Papers, vol. 4, bk 11, 6.

66 "News Release" (4 February 1970), DMS Papers, vol. 16, file ERO.4560–2.

67 Buckler interview (Sarnia, March 2001).

68 Annual *Report* (1973), 9.

69 Statistics Canada, *Housing Starts and Completions*, vol. 28, no. 12 (December 1975), 15.

70 Annual *Report* (1971), 10.

71 Hatch to Rowzee (22 September 1969), Polysar Papers, vol. 134, file: Corporate Planning and Diversification, 1968–70.

72 Hatch, quoted in Polysphere (May-June 1970), 8.

73 "Minutes of the Board of Directors" (December 4 1969), Polysar Papers, vol. 4, bk 11, 6.

74 Penrose, *Growth of the Firm*, 127–32, 156–8. Penrose argued that there are benefits to acquisition. A valuable market position can often be obtained that might otherwise have taken years to build up. And immediate pressure from competition is often substantially reduced. Of especial importance is the fact that a firm could also acquire an experienced management "team" and an experienced technical and labour force. Hence, acquisition could be used as a means of obtaining the productive services and knowledge that are necessary for a firm to establish itself in the new field.

75 Hatch to Rowzee (22 September 1969), Polysar Papers, vol. 134, file: Corporate Planning and Diversification, 1968–70.

76 Annual *Report* (1973), 9.

77 Hatch to the Board of Directors (19 September 1972), Polysar Papers, vol. 135, file: Development/Diversification, 1963–72.

78 Annual *Report* (1977), 9.

79 Annual *Report* (1971), 11.

80 Buckler, "Nostalgia," 7.

81 Buckler to Bellamy (14 July 2001).

82 See Gratwick, "Canadian National: Diversification and Public Responsibilities in Canada's Largest Crown Corporation," 244–5.

83 Smith, *It Seems like Only Yesterday*, chaps. 25–7.

84 Boothman, "Strategic Transformations among Canadian Crown Corporations," 309.

85 Ackerman *Report,* xi.

86 Annual *Report* (1971), 2.

87 "Notes – Board of Directors' Dinner in Montreal" (February 26, 1969), Polysar Papers, vol. 44. file: Directors' Correspondence, 1968–70.

88 "The Waffle Resolution 133," in Godfrey and Watkins, *Gordon to Watkins to You,* 103.

89 Canada, Privy Council Office, Task Force on the Structure of Canadian Industry, *Report,* especially 273–5.

90 Rohmer, *Ultimatum,* and Purdy, *The New Romans.*

91 Creighton, *Takeover.*

92 See Levitt, *Silent Surrender;* Lexer, *Canada Ltd;* Naylor, *History of Canadian Business;* and Clement, *Canadian Corporate Elite.*

93 See I. Macdonald, "Foreign Ownership," 187–90, and Watkins, "Economics in Canada," 197–208.

94 Canada, Privy Council Office, *Report: Foreign Direct Investment in Canada.*

95 "u.s. Investment Not Needed," *Ottawa Citizen,* 12 February 1972.

96 Guillet, "Nationalism and Canadian Science," 221–31.

97 Interviews with Rush (Sarnia, November 1999), Buckler (Sarnia, July 2000), and Hatch (Toronto, July 2000).

98 Rowzee, "In Pursuit of a Global Market," *Industry Canada* (July 1971), 29–31.

99 *Globe and Mail,* 8 June 1971.

100 Rowzee, "In Pursuit of a Global Market," 31.

101 Ibid.

102 Two of the best books on the NEP are Doern and Toner, *The Politics of Energy,* and Fossum, *Oil, the State and Federalism.*

103 Graham, *Canada Development Corporation: A Corporate Background Report,* 1.

104 *Globe and Mail,* 25 April 1969, and *Canadian Dimension,* May-June, 7, 22.

105 Fleming, *So Very Near,* 653; Meyer, "Will the CDC Lead to the Total Socialization of the Economy," *Executive* (March 1971), 13.

106 N.J. McKinnon, "An Address Delivered to the Canadian Club of Toronto" (17 January 1966), 8. Walter Gordon Papers, vol. 4.

107 Ibid., 11.

108 *Canadian Dimension,* May-June, 1965, 7, 22.

109 For a more through analysis of the nature of mixed enterprises, see Musolf, *Mixed Enterprise,* especially 3–7.

110 W.L. Gordon, "Discussion regarding the Canada Development Corporation (23 March 1964), Walter Gordon Papers, vol. 4, file: CDC.

111 Gordon, "Address to the Canadian Club, Sarnia: Polymer and the Canada Development Corporation" (7 October 1965), Walter Gordon Papers, vol. 37, file: Speeches, 1965.

112 Ibid.

113 Gordon, "Discussion" (23 March 1964), Walter Gordon Papers, vol. 4, file: CDC.

114 Gordon, "Address" (7 October 1965), Walter Gordon Papers, vol. 37, file: Speeches, 1965.

115 "The Canadian Development Corporation," *Canadian Dimension*, May-June 1965, 7, 22.

116 Canada, House of Commons, *Debates*, 7 June 1971, 6431.

117 Underhill, "Oh Canada," 227–9.

118 Hardin, *A Nation Unaware*, 133–4.

119 Watkins, "Will We Have to Nationalize?" *Canadian Dimension*, July 1969, 4–5; D. Godfrey and Watkins, *Gordon to Watkins to You*, 104–5.

120 Ibid.

121 Hardin, *A Nation Unaware*, 242–4; The Editors, "The Canadian Development Corporation," *Canadian Dimension*, 22.

122 Canada, House of Commons, *Debates*, 7 June 1971, 6433.

123 Rowzee, "Objectives for 1960" (22 January 1960), Gordon Churchill Papers, vol. 37, file: Polymer Corp. Ltd; "Minutes of the Board of Directors" (16 June 1960), Polymer Papers, vol. 12; "Minutes of the Board of Directors" (1 February 1963), Polysar Papers, vol. 4; and "Minutes of the Board of Directors" (16 October 1969), Polysar Papers, vol. 4.

124 Rowzee, "Memorandum on Growth and Diversification," (9 December 1969), Polysar Papers, vol. 134, file: Corporate Planning, Diversification 1968–70.

125 Rowzee to the Board of Directors (21 May 1965), Polysar Papers, vol. 4.

126 "Minutes of the Board of Directors" (25 March 1965), Polysar Papers, vol. 4.

127 Azzi, *Walter Gordon*, especially 114–17, 139–40, and 148–9. See also Azzi, "Intuitive Nationalist," 121–35.

128 Gordon, "Polymer and the Canada Development Corporation," speech to the Canadian Club of Sarnia (7 October 1965), Walter Gordon Papers, vol. 37, file: Speeches (part 6).

129 Rowzee to the Board of Directors (21 May 1965), Polysar Papers, vol. 46, file: Correspondence, 1965.

130 Canadian Trade Committee, *The Canada Development Corporation – An Assessment of the Proposal* (Toronto 1966), especially 7. The Canadian Trade Committee, which was made up of such industrial dignitaries as J.D. Barrington, Earle McLaughlin, the president of the Royal Bank of Canada and W.O. Twaits, the president of Imperial Oil Limited, condemned Gordon's proposal to sell Polymer to the CDC, calling the idea "indefensible." According to the committee's report, which was prepared by the economist E.P. Neufeld, the sale to the CDC would do little, if anything, to benefit Polymer. If it was to benefit anyone, the committee maintained, it

would be the CDC, bolstering its earnings and assisting in the marketing of its shares.

131 "Memorandum" (21 May 1965), Polysar Papers, vol. 46, file: Department of Defense Production (part 2).

132 Rowzee to the Board of Directors (21 May 1965), vol. 46, file: Correspondence, 1965.

133 Ibid., 6.

134 Rowzee to Richardson (8 March 1972), Polysar Papers, vol. 46, file: Correspondence, 1971–2.

135 "Minutes of the Board of Directors' Meeting" (27 January 1972), Polysar Papers, vol. 4, book 12.

136 *Polysar Progress* (September–October 1972), 1.

137 Ibid.

138 Privy Council Office, *Cabinet Minutes* (13 July 1972), 11.

139 Wood Gundy, "Polymer Corporation Limited: A Valuation for the Department of Supply and Services, Government of Canada" (14 April 1972), Polysar Papers, vol. 46; "Inter Department Memo re: Valuation of Polymer Corp. Ltd. and its subsidiaries." (17 January 1972), Polysar Papers, vol. 44; Rowzee's "preferred number" – as he put it – was $60 million. See Rowzee to Richardson (18 January 1972), Polysar Papers, vol. 44.

140 Ackerman *Report*, iv.

141 "Minutes of the Board of Directors" (26 October 1972), Polysar Papers, vol. 4, bk 12.

142 Hatch interview (Toronto, July 2000).

143 To avoid confusion, I will continue to refer to the company by its original name, Polymer.

144 Annual *Report* (1978), 7.

145 Henderson, *Plain Talk!* 323.

146 Ibid., 329.

147 Ibid.

148 Henderson to P.E. Trudeau (23 March 1973). A copy of the letter in its entirety can be found in Standing Committee on Public Accounts, *Minutes of Proceedings and Evidence*, issue 19 (1 March 1977), appendix PA-88.

149 Henderson, *Plain Talk!* 323.

150 Trudeau to C.M. Drury (27 March 1973). A copy of the letter can be found in Standing Committee on Public Accounts, *Minutes of Proceedings and Evidence*, issue 19 (1 March 1977), appendix PA-90.

151 Ibid.

152 Ibid.

153 Henderson, *Plain Talk!* 334.

154 Polymer's internal investigation, which was undertaken by David Stanley and John B. Ayleworth, concluded that the "great bulk" (i.e., 80 to 95 percent) of PISA's business was neither illegal nor immoral. In total,

there were sales to some thirteen direct customers and to fourteen of PISA's distributors that involved "objectionable or questionable practices." See J.B. Aylesworth and D.A. Stanley, *Report* to the Board of Directors of Polysar Limited on Certain Invoicing and Payment Practices of Polysar International S.A. (31 January 1977), 3–4.

155 Henderson, *Plain Talk!* 334.

156 *Globe and Mail,* 27 November 1976, 1, 10–11.

157 W. Dimma, interview (Toronto, March 2001).

158 E. Homburger to W.J Dyke (14 February 1973), Polysar Papers, vol. 54, file: Public Accounts Committee, 1973–7; Russell Baker to W.J Dyke (1 March 1973), Polysar Papers, vol. 54, file: Public Accounts Committee, 1973–77.

159 I.C. Rush, "Press Release: Information from Polysar Ltd." (28 November 1976), Polysar Papers, vol. 54, file: Public Accounts Committee 1973–77.

160 Ibid.

161 Canada, House of Commons, *Debates,* 30 November 1976, 1499.

162 Ibid., 1500.

163 Canada, House of Commons, Standing Committee on Public Accounts, *Minutes of Proceedings and Evidence,* issue 20 (3 March 1977), 35.

164 See J.B. Aylesworth and D.A. Stanley, *Report* to the Board of Directors of Polysar Limited on Certain Invoicing and Payment Practices of Polysar International S.A. (31 January 1977), 6–7.

165 Canada, House of Commons, Standing Committee on Public Accounts, *Minutes of Proceedings and Evidence* 39 (5 July 1977), 3–18.

166 See the series of articles by L. Watkins in the *Globe and Mail,* 21 September 1982, B12; 30 October 1982, B16; 5 November 1982, B11; 23 November 1982, B9.

167 Laux and Molot, *State Capitalism,* 7.

168 A. Whittingham, "The Seedy Assault on the CDC," *Maclean's,* (1 June 1981), vol. 94, no. 22, 46–7.

169 Canada, House of Commons, *Debates* (30 November 1976), 1500.

170 Canada. Privy Council Office, *Crown Corporations.*

171 Ibid., 21.

172 "Canadian Firm Seeks Expanded U.S. Market," *Chemical and Engineering News,* vol. 48 (5 October 1970), 15.

173 Ibid., xi.

174 Annual *Report* (1977), 20.

175 Ibid.

176 Ibid.

177 Wood Gundy, *Report,* 35.

178 Prahalad and Hamel, "Core Competence," 79–91.

179 In "Innovation in a Cold Climate: The Dilemma of Canadian Manufacturing," *Report* 15 (October 1971), The Science Council of Canada identified

eight impediments to innovation in Canada: 1 an inadequate technology base, 2 limited market size and market access, 3 poor climate for investment, 4 inadequate management skills, 5 improper location of industry, 6 tariff and nontariff barriers, 7 the lack of size and stability in Canadian industrial laboratories, and 8 the multinational corporation.

CHAPTER SEVEN

1　R. Dudley, quoted in *Polysphere Fifty*, 93.
2　Biggadike, "The Risky Business of Diversification," 111.
3　Hayes and Abernathy, "Managing Our Way," 69–77.
4　Goldenburg, *Canadian Pacific*, especially chaps. 11 and 14.
5　Markides, "Back to Basics," 12.
6　Colvin, "The De-Geneening of ITT," 36.
7　Peters and Waterman, *In Search of Excellence*, chap. 10.
8　Markides, "Back to Basics," 12–24.
9　Bliss, *Northern Enterprise*, 551.
10　"Companies to Watch: Easton Aluminum Inc.," *Fortune*, 12 October 1987, 97; "Companies to Watch: Tyco Toys," ibid., 14 March 1988, 96.
11　"Management Brief," *The Economist*, vol. 313, 28 October 1989, 78.
12　Mullington, "The Federal Government," especially 54–63.
13　Chandler, *Scale and Scope*, 227–9.
14　Ibid., 36–45, 145, 230.
15　Ibid., 58.
16　Hardin, *A Nation Unaware*, 242–4.
17　"Polymer Ponders Its Future," *Executive* (March 1971), 52.
18　Rush interview (Sarnia, November 1999).
19　Pursell interview (Sarnia, November 1999) and Bentley interview (Sarnia, November 1999).
20　Annual *Report* (1980), 1.
21　Quintella, *The Strategic Management of Technology*, 78–9.
22　Spitz, *Petrochemicals*, 486–91.
23　Richards and Pratt, *Prairie Capitalism*, especially chap. 9.
24　Alberta Research Council, *Papers Presented at Symposium on the Occurrence and Chemical Utilization of Light Hydrocarbons*, Circular 23 (1957).
25　Foster, *The Blue-Eyed Sheiks*, 301.
26　Annual *Report*, 15.
27　"It's High Noon for High Technology," *Financial Post*, 25 October 1990, s1.
28　C. McMillan, "From Quality Control to Quality Management," 31–40; "How Japan Uses Technology for Competitive Success," 34–8.
29　"It's High Noon for High Technology," s1.
30　"Financing R&D: Tax Breaks Would Help," *Financial Post*, 25 October 1980, s6.

31 Buckler, "Canadian Contributions," 3–12.
32 Buckler to Hatch (19 March 1969), Polysar Papers, vol. 133, file: Canada General.
33 Ibid., 11.
34 Dudley interview (Sarnia, November 1999).
35 French, *The u.s. Tire Industry*, 102.
36 Buckler interview (Sarnia, November 1999).
37 Ibid.
38 Annual *Report* (1982), 1.
39 Ibid., 29.
40 Graham, "Canada Development Corporation," 51.
41 Chapman, *The International Petrochemical Industry*, 194–9.
42 Doern and Toner, *The Politics of Energy*, 222–6.
43 Dudley interview (Sarnia, November 1999).
44 Rush interview (Sarnia, November 1999).
45 *Report of the Petrochemical Industry Task Force.*
46 Annual *Report* (1985), 1.
47 Annual *Reports* (1983, 1984, 1985).
48 Tarasofsky, "Something Ventured: The Canada Development Corporation, 1972–1985," 40.
49 McFetridge, "Commercial and Political Efficiency," table 6–1, 223.
50 Boardman "An Evaluation of Canada Development Corporation"; Brady and Vining, "An Evaluation of Canada Development Corporation"; Tarasofsky, "The Canada Development Corporation."
51 McFetridge, "Commercial and Political Efficiency," 226.
52 Ibid.
53 P. Foster, "cdc's Hampson Bids Farewell," *Financial Post*, 18 May 1987, 14.
54 *Financial Post*, 18 April 1988, 4.
55 Ibid., 6 February 1988, 1.
56 Annual *Report* 1987, 1.
57 Ibid., 7.
58 Ibid., 4.
59 Borins and Brown, *Investments in Failure*, introduction.
60 Ibid., especially 58–67, 143–5.
61 I. Austen, "Canadair Enters a Swift, Steep Nosedive," *Maclean's*, 20 June 1983, 37.
62 Canada, House of Commons, *Debates*, 26 April 1977, 4984–5.
63 Doern and Atherton, "The Tories and the Crowns," 146–50.
64 *Annual Report to Parliament on Crown Corporations*, iv.
65 See, for example, Bliss, *Right Honourable Men*, chap. 10; Doern and Atherton, "The Tories and the Crowns," chap. 3.
66 The term "privatization" is used here in its narrowest sense to refer to the whole or partial sale of state-owned enterprise. In a broader sense, it has

been used to describe those measures (e.g., deregulation, trade liberalization, and increased contracting out of services) that aim at reducing the role of government and enhancing market forces to produce a more competitive economy. See Veljanovski, *Selling the State.*

67 Tupper and Doern, *Privatization, Public Policy and Public Corporations in Canada*, especially chap. 1.

68 Laux and Molot, *State Capitalism*, table 4, 193.

69 Department of Finance, *Budget Papers*, Ottawa, Minister of Finance, 23 May 1985, 26–8.

70 Canada, House of Commons, *Minutes of Proceedings and Evidence of the Legislative Committee on Bill C-66, An Act respecting the reorganization of the Canada Development Corporation*, issue no. 2 (1 October 1985), 4.

71 Dimma interview (Toronto, March 2001).

72 Lyon, *Dome*, chap. 14.

73 A. Whittingham, "The Seedy Assault on the CDC," *Maclean's*, 1 June 1981, 46–7.

74 *Minutes of Proceedings and Evidence of the Legislative Committee on Bill C-66*, 4.

75 Ibid., 4.

76 Ibid.

77 Canada, House of Commons, Bill C-66, An Act respecting the Reorganization of the Canada Development Corporation, 25 November 1985.

78 Quoted in *Financial Times of Canada*, 12 October 1987, 9.

79 Doern and Atherton, "The Tories and the Crowns," 169.

80 D. McGillvary, "Final CDC sale Marks the Death of an Old Dream," *Financial Times of Canada*, 12 October 1987.

81 Canada, House of Commons, *Debates*, 22 November 1985, 8729.

82 Ibid., 10.

83 Ibid.

84 Richards and Pratt, *Prairie Capitalism*, 66.

85 Foster, *The Blue-Eyed Sheiks*, 107–9.

86 Blair quoted in Peter Newman, "The Thinking Man's Energy Baron," *Maclean's*, 26 February 1990, 36.

87 Foster, *The Blue-Eyed Sheiks*, chap. 9.

88 Ibid., chap. 8.

89 Gray, *Wildcatters*, 282–9.

90 Blair, quoted in *Maclean's*, 26 February 1990, 36.

91 Dimma interview (Toronto, March 2001).

92 *Financial Post*, 6 February 1988, 2.

93 Ibid., 12 March 1988, 23.

94 Ibid., 22 February 1988, 30.

95 Dudley interview (Sarnia, November 1999).

96 Peter Newman, "The Bitter Nova-Polysar Slugfest," *Maclean's*, 9 May, 1988, 46.

97 Isautier quote, in *Maclean's*, 9 May 1988, 46.

98 T. Phillips, "Aspirin for Bob Blair: Nova Slashes Debt with the Bayer Deal," *Alberta Report*, 4 June 1990, 15, 17; L. Grogan, "Nova's Numbers Slide but Investor Optimistic," *Financial Post*, 23 July 1990, 10; B. Wickens, "Postponing Nova's Dream: A Crushing Debt Has Forced Nova Corp. to Join the Oil-and-Gas Industry's Great Asset Sell Off," *Maclean's*, 4 June 1990, 52–3; B. Dargie, "Preparing to Peddle Husky: Nova Plummeting Income Fuels Rumours That It Will Sell Husky to Cut Debt," *Alberta Report*, 12 February 1990, 17; and D. Hogarth, "Debt, Streamlining Send Assets Sales Up," *Financial Post*, 28 May 1990, 17.

99 Blair, quoted in *Maclean's*, 4 June 1990, 53.

100 J. Stanford, quoted ibid.

101 Blair quoted ibid.

102 Isautier quoted ibid.

103 Canada, House of Commons, *Debates*, 23 May 1990, 11714.

104 *Sarnia Observer*, 25 April 2002, A1.

105 *Maclean's*, 4 June 1990, 53.

106 Annual *Report* (1987), 10.

CONCLUSION

1 Bliss, " 'Rich by Nature, Poor By Policy' " 78–90.

2 Dales, *The Protective Tariff.*

3 George, "Rates of Return in Railway Investment."

4 Mullington, "The Federal Government as Entrepreneur," 82–3.

5 Stevenson, "Canadian National Railways," 325. While various scholars have expressed doubts whether CN and the CPR can be historically compared, they have not stopped others from trying. Hugh Mullington, for example, has concluded that CN's "financial results have not approached those of Canadian Pacific" ("The Federal Government as Entrepreneur," 87).

6 Nelles, *The Politics of Development*, 413.

7 Borins and Brown, *Investments in Failure*, especially chap. 3.

8 *Globe and Mail*, 1 September, 2001.

9 Mullington, "The Federal Government as Entrepreneur," 93–7.

10 Laux and Molot, *State Capitalism*, chap. 4.

11 Polymer Corporation, Canadian Industries Ltd., and Du Pont of Canada, Annual *Reports* (1960).

12 Doern and Tupper, "Understanding Public Corporations," 33.

13 Interview with Buckler (Sarnia, July 2000).

14 Boothman, "Strategic Transformations," 301–3.

15 Canada, House of Commons, *Debates*, 14 May 1946, 1516.

16 Boothman, "Strategic Transformations," 301–2.

17 Pratt, "Petro-Canada," especially 119–27.

18 Langford, "Air Canada," especially 263.

19 Mullington, "The Federal Government as Entrepreneur," 114.

20 Nelles, *The Politics of Development*, 472–88.

21 Doern and Sims, "Atomic Energy of Canada Limited," especially 63–84.

22 Ibid.

23 B. Henderson, "Canada's Polymer," *Monetary Times*, November 1956, 27–9.

24 Bliss, *Northern Enterprise*, 8.

25 Canada, House of Commons, *Debates*, 16 June 1943, 3715.

26 Schumpeter, *The Theory of Economic Development*, especially 68, 75, 137; and *History of Economic Analysis*, 556.

27 See Dyer and Sicilia, *Labors of a Modern Hercules*; Hounshell and Smith, *Science and Corporate Strategy*; Stobaugh, *Innovation and Competition*; Spitz, *Petrochemicals*.

Bibliography

The Polysar Papers at the National Archives of Canada were the main source of information for this book. The close to two hundred volumes of material cover various aspects of corporate activity from the wartime formation of Polymer in 1942 to the purchase of Polysar by Nova Corporation in 1988. The documentation for the period 1942 to 1970 is particularly extensive and, when examined in conjunction with the Department of Munitions and Supply Papers (RG 28), provides a detailed portrait of the company's operations and performance. Emerging from the documentation is the important role that management played in the development and growth of the firm. Each of the principals – Rowzee, Buckler, Wilk, Hatch, Dougan, and Rush – generated a great deal of documentation. These were thoughtful and deliberate individuals. While there is very little of a personal nature, the student interested in business history can easily trace the evolution of the firm's financing, marketing, new business development, operations, research and development, corporate planning, and production and distribution from their correspondence. It also gives a glimpse into the early diversification effort and the rapid expansion of the company's core petrochemical operations in the early 1970s. Fortunately, Polymer's managers did not limit their discussions to day-to-day operations. They were often reflecting on the role of science and technology in the growth of their firm and the industry in general. Buckler and Rowzee were particularly contemplative. Their papers contain a number of speeches and articles addressing broader or more philosophical questions.

The importance of the Polysar Papers, however, lies in what they tell us not only about the growth of the firm but also about the birth and development of the Canadian synthetic rubber industry. As the documentation relating to patent-sharing arrangements clearly demonstrates, the Polymer project would not have been possible without the assistance of private industry and the U.S. government. The Canadian government – and specifically, C.D. Howe – was instrumental in obtaining this support. The C.D. Howe Papers at the National

Archives in Ottawa are an important additional source of information for anyone interested in government-industry relations. They contain five volumes that deal directly with Polymer Corporation and provide a window into the activities of one of Canada's most successful economic planners. While much of the information located here can be found in the Polysar Papers, there is fresh information on Howe's relationship with officials at the U.S. government's Rubber Reserve Corporation and his postwar plans for the Crown corporation. For those interested in the politics of development, there is a large file relating to the 1942–44 feedstock debate. Howe's continentalist perspective is colourfully countered by the regional/nationalist view of such people as T.C. Douglas.

On some important matters, however, the Howe Papers are silent. There are perhaps several reasons for this. We know from his biographers that Howe often delegated responsibility. The extant documentation depicts a man who surrounded himself with the best and the brightest people. It was their task to "get the job done." Thus, the correspondence, proposals, and reports that crossed Howe's desk were often final or complete. Ideas were often fully developed. Positions were established. All that the proposals needed was Howe's ultimate approval and support: he rarely got involved in the developmental stage, and thus it is difficult at times to trace the evolution in his thought. Adding to these difficulties is the fact that Howe was a man of few words – written or spoken. He accomplished so much, yet said so little. He disliked drawn-out discussions and never talked around an issue. He was always direct and to the point; he was clear and concise. Often he would respond to a written correspondence over the telephone or in person. This was Howe's way. When he did respond in writing, his messages were most often less than a page in length and sometimes only a sentence or two. The war and Howe's management-on-the-run style demanded this. That said, Howe's managerial style does not always make it easy to discern the rationale for some of his public-policy decisions. We do not know, or cannot state for sure, for example, what Howe's precise rationale was for embarking upon the synthetic rubber program in the first place. There is a good deal of circumstantial evidence to suggest that Howe seized the opportunity of war to modernize the Canadian economy and bring new (American) science and technology to Canada. But there is no documentation in the Howe Papers directly stating this. We do have the confirmation of some of Howe's "boys," but no words from Howe himself. In addition, the Howe Papers go silent after 1951. While Howe remained in office and responsible for Polymer until 1957, he had next to nothing to say – at least in an archival sense – about the corporation after 1951. The five volumes relating to Polymer Corporation in the Howe Papers cover the period 1942–51. There is no documentation relating to the period 1951–57. Perhaps this was a result of the success of the firm. Once Polymer was up and running and generating a profit, Howe was willing to fade into the background. His job was done, and he had faith in the capabilities of Polymer's managers.

Howe's hands-off approach to Polymer was emulated by successive ministers of the Crown, and thus there is not a lot of information generated in bureaucratic circles in Ottawa. Indeed, a good deal of government discussion about the affairs of the firm was generated only during the Diefenbaker years (1957–62) over the issue of privatization. By far the best source of information relating to the government's limited position on this matter is found in the Cabinet Conclusions (RG2). The documentation makes it clear that there was nothing close to unanimity within the Cabinet. Opposing positions are clearly outlined, although the advocates of each position are rarely identified. On the issue of privatization, the Polysar Papers provide insights into the views of management and the board of directors, as well as the attitudes and ambitions of Polymer's suitors.

From a broader perspective still, the Polysar Papers are important for what they reveal about the growth of the petrochemical industry in general. The board of directors' minute books (1942–87) contain insightful descriptions of the domestic and international developments in the petrochemical industry. There is information on the nature and sources of growth, the diffusion of technology, the proliferation of producers, patterns of development, corporate strategies, and international locations. The minute books also contain shareholders' minutes and bylaws. The documentation generated by Polymer's managers reflects the extent to which the firm was integrated into the larger international community of petrochemical producers.

Unfortunately, the post-1972 records are not complete. There is very little relating to government-business relations during this period and a limited amount on the diversification effort of the 1970s. For example, the Comshare file is limited to less than twenty pages of documentation. It was during this later period that Polymer/Polysar became a subsidiary of the Canada Development Corporation. The CDC Papers, if they still exist, could not be found and are not in the public domain. It was my intention therefore to fill in some of the historiographical gaps by way of oral interviews. These interviews, as well as the other sources used, are listed below.

ARCHIVAL SOURCES

Manuscript Collections

NATIONAL ARCHIVES OF CANADA
John Bruce Papers
Gordon Churchill Papers
Donald Fleming Papers
Walter Gordon Papers
Gordon Henderson Papers
C.D. Howe Papers

W.L.M. King Papers
Archibald Newman Papers
Polysar Papers

UNIVERSITY OF TORONTO ARCHIVES
Bayer Corporation Ltd (Sarnia): Polymer Historical Files
Bothwell Papers

Public Records

NATIONAL ARCHIVES OF CANADA
RG 2   Privy Council Office
RG 17   Department of Agriculture
RG 19   Department of Finance
RG 20   Department of Industry, Trade and Commerce
RG 24   Department of National Defence
RG 25   Department of External Affairs
RG 27   Department of Labour
RG 28   Department of Munitions and Supply
RG 58   Auditor General
RG 77   National Research Council
RG 98   Department of Supply and Services
RG 117   Office of Custodian of Enemy Property

NATIONAL ARCHIVES OF THE UNITED STATES
RG 234   Reconstruction Finance Corporation

Interviews

Robert Adams
Firm Bentley
Bill Buckler
Phillip Byrne
John Carson
Bill Dimma
Robert Dudley
George Evans
Roger Hatch
David Golden
Russell Gillespie
Bill Pursell
Walter Petryschuk

Ian Rush
Mitchell Sharp
David Stanley
Stan Wilk

Printed Sources

Aharoni, Y. *The Evolution and Management of State-Owned Enterprises.* Cambridge, MA: Ballinger 1986.

Aitken, H.G.J. "Defensive Expansionism: The State and Economic Growth in Canada." In Easterbrook and Watkins, eds., *Approaches to Canadian Economic History,* 183–221. Toronto: McClelland and Stewart 1967.

– *The Welland Canal Company: A Study in Canadian Enterprise.* Cambridge, MA: Harvard University Press 1954.

Aitken, H.G.J., and W.T. Easterbrook, eds. *Canadian Economic History.* Toronto: Macmillan 1956.

Annual Report to Parliament on Crown Corporations and Other Corporate Interests of Canada, 1983-1984. Ottawa: Ministry of Supply and Services Canada 1985.

Armstrong, C., and H.V. Nelles. *Southern Exposure: Canadian Promoters in Latin America and the Caribbean, 1896–1930.* Toronto: University of Toronto Press 1988.

Ashley, C.A. *Canadian Crown Corporations.* Toronto: Macmillan 1965.

Avery, D.H. *The Science of War: Canadian Scientists and Allied Military Technology during the Second World War.* Toronto: University of Toronto Press 1998.

Azzi, S. *Walter Gordon and the Rise of Canadian Nationalism.* Montreal: McGill-Queen's University Press 1999.

– "Intuitive Nationalist: Walter Gordon as Thinker." *Journal of Canadian Studies* 34, no. 1 (winter 2000): 121–35.

Barnet R.J., and R.E. Müller. *Global Reach: The Power of the Multinational Corporations.* New York: Simon and Schuster 1974.

Bauer, P.T. "Prospects of Rubber." *Pacific Affairs* 20 (December 1947): 381–90.

Beland, C.E. "The Rubber Problem." *Canadian Chemistry and Process Industries* (August 1942): 457.

Berkinshaw, R.C. "The Future of the Synthetic Rubber Industry." *Canadian Banker* 52 (1945): 157.

Bickmore, A.S. *Travels in the East Indian Archipelago.* London: Murray 1868.

Bertin, L. "The Long Chain: The Story of Canada's Synthetic Rubber Industry." Unpublished manuscript, 1967.

Biggadike, R. "The Risky Business of Diversification." *Harvard Business Review* (May-June 1979): 101–17.

Bliss, M. "'Rich by Nature, Poor by Policy': The State and Economic Life in Canada." In K.R. Carty and P.W. Ward, eds., *Entering the Eighties: Canada in Crisis,* 78–90. Toronto: Oxford University Press 1980.

- *Northern Enterprise: Five Centuries of Canadian Business.* Toronto: McClelland and Stewart 1987.
- *Right Honourable Men: The Descent of Canadian Politics from Macdonald to Mulroney.* Toronto: Harper Collins 1994.

Bloomfield, G. *The World Automotive Industry.* London: David and Charles 1978.

Boardman, A. "An Evaluation of Canada Development Corporation." Paper presented to the Royal Commission Symposium on Crown Corporations, Ottawa, June 1984.

Boardman, A., and A. Vining. "An Evaluation of Canada Development Corporation." University of British Columbia, Faculty of Commerce and Business Administration, 1984. Mimeographed.

Boothman, B.E. "Strategic Transformations among Canadian Crown Corporations." *Australian Journal of Public Administration* 48, no. 3 (September 1989): 291–311.

Borins, S.F. "World War II Crown Corporations: Their Functions and Their Fate." In J.R. Prichard, ed., *Crown Corporations in Canada: The Calculus of Instrument Choice,* 437–75. Toronto: Butterworth and the Ontario Economic Council 1983.

Borins, S., and L. Brown. *Investments in Failure: Five Government Corporations That Cost Canadian Taxpayers Billions.* Toronto: Methuen 1986.

Borkin, J. *The Crime and Punishment of IG Farben.* New York: Pocket Books 1979.

Bothwell, R. *Eldorado: Canada's National Uranium Company.* Toronto: University of Toronto Press 1984.

- *Nucleus: The History of Atomic Energy of Canada Limited.* Toronto: University of Toronto Press 1988.
- *Canada and the United States: The Politics of Partnership.* Toronto: University of Toronto Press 1992.

Bothwell, R., and J.L. Granatstein. *American Dollars, Canadian Prosperity: Canadian American Economic Relations, 1945–1950.* Toronto: Samuel-Stevens 1978.

Bothwell, R., and W. Kilbourn. *C.D. Howe: A Biography.* Toronto: McClelland and Stewart 1979.

Bower, T. *The Paperclip Conspiracy.* London: Paladin 1987.

Brady, A. "The State and Economic Life In Canada." In K.J. Rea and J.T. McLeod, eds., *Business and Government in Canada:* Selected Readings, 28–42. Toronto: Methuen 1969.

Buckler, E.J. "Low Temperature Performance of Butyl Inner Tubes." In *Proceedings of the Second Rubber Technology Conference,* 34–48. Cambridge, England: W. Heffer & Sons 1948.

- "Canadian Case History: Polymer Corporation Limited." *Research Management* 6 (July 1963): 289–304.
- "Canadian Contributions to Synthetic Rubber Technology." *Canadian Journal of Chemical Engineering* 62 (1984): 3–12.

Burchard, J. *Q.E.D. – M.I.T. in World War II*. New York: John Wiley 1948.

Cairncross, A. *The Price of War*. Oxford: Basil Blackwell 1986.

– *Economic Ideas and Government Policy*. New York: Routledge 1996.

Campbell, D. *Global Mission: The Alcan Story*. Toronto: Ontario Publishing Company 1985.

Campbell, R.M. *Grand Illusions: The Politics of the Keynesian Experience in Canada, 1945–1975*. Peterborough, ON: Broadview Press 1987.

Canada. Department of Reconstruction. *Reconstruction*. Ottawa 1945.

– *White Paper on Employment and Income*. Ottawa 1945.

– Department of Reconstruction and Supply. *Research and Scientific Activity: Canadian Federal Expenditures, 1938–1946*. Ottawa: King's Printer 1947.

– Dominion Bureau of Statistics. *Consumption, Production and Inventories of Rubber* 20, no. 1. (January 1966).

– House of Commons. Special Committee on War Expenditures. Fifth *Report*. Ottawa: King's Printer, August 1944.

– Standing Committee on Public Accounts. *Minutes of Proceedings and Evidence*, no. 11, 9 May 1961; nos. 19 and 20 (1–3), March 1977; no. 39, 5 July 1977.

– *Proceedings*. Ottawa 1958.

Canada. Privy Council Office. *Crown Corporations: Direction, Control, Accountability*. Ottawa: Minister of Supply and Services 1977.

– *Report: Foreign Direct Investment in Canada*. Ottawa: Queen's Printer 1972.

– *Report: Task Force on the Structure of Canadian Industry*. Ottawa: Queen's Printer 1972.

Canada. Royal Commission on Canada's Economic Prospects. Final *Report*. Ottawa: November 1957.

– Royal Commission on Corporate Concentration. *Report*. Ottawa: January 1976.

– Royal Commission on Government Organization. *Report*. 2 vols. Ottawa: Queen's Printer 1962.

– Supply and Services Canada. Petrochemical Industry Task Force. *Report*. Ottawa: Supply and Services Canada, February 1984.

Carter, D. *So That Man May Prosper*. Winnipeg: Contemporary Publishers 1943.

Carty, K.R., and P.W. Ward, eds. *Entering the Eighties: Canada in Crisis*. Toronto: Oxford University Press 1980.

Chadeau, E. "The Rise and Decline of State-Owned Industry in Twentieth-Century France." In P.A. Toninelli, ed., *The Rise and Fall of State-Owned Enterprise in the Western World*, chap. 8. Cambridge: Cambridge University Press 2000.

Chandler, A. *Strategy and Structure: Chapters in the History of the Industrial Enterprise*. Cambridge, MA: MIT Press 1962.

– *The Invisible Hand: The Managerial Revolution in American Business*. Cambridge, MA: Harvard University Press 1977.

– "Development, Diversification and Decentralization." In T.K. McCraw, ed., *The Essential Alfred Chandler: Essays Toward a Historical Theory of Big Business,* 174–216. Boston: Harvard Business Scholl 1988.

– *Scale and Scope: The Dynamics of Industrial Capitalism.* Cambridge, MA: Harvard University Press 1990.

Chandler, M. "State Enterprise and Partisanship in Provincial Politics." *Canadian Journal of Political Science* 15 (1982): 711–42.

Channon, D.F. *The Strategy and Structure of British Enterprise.* Cambridge, MA: Harvard University Press 1973.

Chapman, K. *The International Petrochemical Industry: Evolution and Location.* Oxford: Blackwell 1991.

Clarke, A.J. *Tupperware: The Promise of Plastic in 1950s America.* New York: Smithsonian Institution Press 1999.

Clarke, E.R. *The IDB: A History of Canada's Industrial Development Bank.* Toronto: University of Toronto Press 1985.

Clement, W. *The Canadian Corporate Elite: An Analysis of Economic Power.* Toronto: McClelland and Stewart 1975.

Coates, A. *The Commerce in Rubber: The First 250 Years.* Singapore: Oxford University Press 1987.

Colvin, G. "The De-Geneening of ITT: The Most Famous Conglomerate Around Has Made a U-turn." *Fortune,* 11 January 1982, 34–9.

Cook, J.G. "Rubber Riddle." *The Spectator,* 6 December 1946, 606.

Corbett, D. *Politics and the Airlines.* Toronto: University of Toronto Press 1965.

Corry, J.A. "The Fusion of Government and Business." *Canadian Journal of Economics and Political Science* 11 (1936): 301–16.

Courchene, T.J. "Privatization: Palliative or Panacea," in Kierans and Stanbury, eds., *Papers on Privatization,* 1–36.

Creighton, D. *The Commercial Empire of the St Lawrence, 1760–1850.* Toronto: Ryerson Press 1937.

– *Canada's First Century.* Toronto: Macmillan 1970.

– *Takeover.* Toronto: McClelland and Stewart 1978.

Cuff, R.D., and J.L. Granatstein. *Ties That Bind: Canadian-American Relations in Wartime: From the Great War to the Cold War.* Toronto: Samuel Stevens Hakkert 1977.

– *American Dollars, Canadian Prosperity: Canadian-American Economic Relations, 1945–1950.* Toronto: Samuel Stevens 1978.

Dales, J.H. *The Protective Tariff in Canada's Development: Eight Essays on Trade and Tariffs When Factors Move, with Special Reference to Canadian Protectionism, 1870–1955.* Toronto: University of Toronto Press 1966.

Davies, R.A. "Rubber Is an Industrial Sinew of Democracy." *Saturday Night,* 6 June 1942, 10–11.

Davis, J. "The Canadian Chemical Industry." In Royal Commission on Canada's Economic Prospects, *Final Report.* March 1957.

Dedman, E. *Challenge and Response: A Modern History of Standard Oil Company.* Chicago: Mobium Press 1984.

Dimma, W.A. *The Canada Development Corporation: Diffident Experiment of a Large Scale.* Boston: Harvard Graduate School of Business Administration 1976.

Doern, B. *Privatization, Public Policy, and Public Corporations in Canada.* Halifax, NS: Institute for Research on Public Policy 1988.

Doern, B., and J. Atherton. "The Tories and the Crowns: Restraining and Privatizing in a Political Minefield." In *How Ottawa Spends: Restraining the State,* 129–75. Ottawa: Methuen 1987.

Doern, B., and J.A. Brothers. "Telesat Canada." In B. Doern and A. Tupper, eds., *Public Corporations and Public Policy in Canada,* 221–50. Montreal: The Institute for Research on Public Policy 1981.

Doern, B., and J.F. Devlin. "The Farm Credit Corporation and the Federal Business Development Bank." in A. Tupper and B. Doern, eds., *Privatization, Public Policy and Public Corporations,* 363–97.

Doern, B., and G. Sims. "Atomic Energy of Canada Limited." In B. Doern and J.A. Tupper, eds. *Public Corporations and Public Policy in Canada,* 51–94. Montreal: The Institute for Research on Public Policy 1981.

Doern, B., and G. Toner. *The Politics of Energy: The Development and Implementation of the NEP.* Toronto: Methuen 1985.

Doern, B., and A. Tupper. "Understanding Public Corporations." *Canadian Business Review* 9 (autumn 1982), 33–9.

– eds. *Public Corporations and Public Policy in Canada.* Montreal: The Institute for Research on Public Policy, 1981.

Drucker, P. *The Practice of Management.* London: William Heinemann 1955.

Dyas, G.P., and H.T. Thanheiser. *Emerging European Enterprise: Strategy and Structure in French and German Industry.* London: Macmillan 1976.

Dyer, D., and D. Sicilia. *Labors of a Modern Hercules: Evolution of a Modern Chemical Company.* Boston: Harvard Business School Press 1990.

Easterbrook, W.T., ed. *Approaches to Canadian Economic History.* Toronto: McClelland 1967.

Eggleton, W.E. *National Research in Canada: The NRC, 1916–1966.* Toronto: Clarke, Irwin and Company 1978.

Elford, J. "Sarnia, Canada's Chemical Valley," *Canadian Geographical Journal* 55 (November 1957): 170–85.

Enloe, C.F. "The War and the German Drug Industry." *Chemical and Engineering News* 24 (25 November 1946): 3046–8.

Faragher, W.F. "Collecting German Industrial Information." *Chemical and Engineering News* 26 (December 1948): 3817.

Farquharson, J. "Governed or Exploited? The British Acquisition of German Technology, 1945–1948." *Journal of Contemporary History* 32, no. 1 (January 1997): 23–42.

Fleming, D.M. *So Very Near: The Political Memoirs of the Honourable Donald M. Fleming*. vol. 2, *The Summit Years*. Toronto: McClelland and Stewart 1985.

Forbes, H.D., ed. *Canadian Political Thought*. Toronto: Oxford University Press 1985.

Foreman-Peck, J., and R. Millward. *Public and Private Ownership of British Industry, 1820–1990*. Oxford: Clarendon Press 1994.

Forrestal, D.J. *The Story of Monsanto: Faith, Hope and Five Thousand Dollars: The Trials and Triumphs of the First 75 years*. New York: Schuster 1975.

Fortune Magazine. *The Conglomerate Commotion*. New York: Viking Press 1970.

Fossum, J.E. *Oil, the State, and Federalism: The Rise and Demise of Petro-Canada as a Statist Impulse*. Toronto: University of Toronto Press 1997.

Foster, P. *The Blue-Eyed Sheiks: The Canadian Oil Establishment*. Don Mills, ON: Collins 1979.

Frank, A.G. *Latin America: Underdevelopment of Revolution*. New York: M.R.P. 1969.

French, M.J. *The U.S. Tire Industry: A History*. Boston, MA: G.K. Hall 1990.

Frese, J., and S.J. Judd, eds. *Business and Government*. New York: Sleepy Hollow Press 1985.

Furukawa, Y. *Inventing Polymer Science*. Philadelphia: University of Pennsylvania Press 1998.

George, P.J. "Rates of Return in Railway Investment and Implications for Government Subsidization of the CPR: Some Preliminary Results." *Canadian Journal of Economics* 1, no. 4 (November 1968): 740–62.

Gibb, W.K. "The Control of Rubber." *Canadian Forum*, May 1928, 662–3.

Gimbel, J. *Science, Technology, and Reparations: Exploitation and Plunder in Postwar Germany*. Stanford: Stanford University Press 1990.

Godfrey, D., and M. Watkins. *Gordon to Watkins to You: A Documentary – the Battle for Control of Our Economy*. Toronto: New Press 1970.

Goggin, W.C. "Advances in Plastic in the United States and Germany." *Chemical and Engineering News* 24 (10 February 1946): 339–43.

– "New Tanning Agents Based on German Technology." *Chemical and Engineering News* 26 (5 July 1948): 1980–1, 2029.

Goldenburg, S. *Canadian Pacific: Portrait of a Conglomerate*. Toronto: John Deyell Company 1983.

Goldman, R. *Reading Ads Socially*. New York: Routledge 1992.

Gordon, W. *Troubled Canada: The Need for New Domestic Policies*. Toronto: McClelland and Stewart 1961.

– *A Choice for Canada: Independence or Colonial Status*. Toronto: McClelland and Stewart 1966.

– *Storm Signals: New Economic Policies for Canada*. Toronto: McClelland and Stewart 1975.

Grace, N.S. "The Rubber Industry in Canada: Progress from 1935." In L.W. Shemilt, ed., *Chemical Engineering in Canada: An Historical Perspective*, 316–21. Ottawa: The Canadian Society of Chemical Engineering 1991.

Graham, M.R. *Canada Development Corporation: A Corporate Background Report.* Ottawa: Supply and Services Canada 1977.

Granatstein, J.L. *The Ottawa Men: The Civil Service Mandarins 1935–1957.* Toronto: Oxford University Press 1982.

Granatstein, J.L., and N. Hillmer. *For Better or Worse: Canada and the United States to the 1990s.* Mississauga, ON: Copp Clark Pitman 1991.

Grant, G. *Lament for a Nation.* Toronto: Macmillan 1965.

Gratwick, J. "Canadian National: Diversification and Public Responsibilities in Canada's Largest Crown Corporation." In W.T. Stanbury and F. Thompson, eds., *Managing Public Enterprises,* 237–49. New York: Praeger 1982.

Gray, E. *Wildcatters: The Story of Pacific Petroleum and Westcoast Transmission.* Toronto: McLelland and Stewart 1982.

Gray, H.P. *The Economics of Business Investment Abroad.* New York: Crane, Russak 1972.

Greiner, L.E. "Evolution and Revolution as Organizations Grow." *Harvard Business Review* 50 (1972): 37–46.

Guillet, J. "Nationalism and Canadian Science." In P. Russell, ed., *Nationalism in Canada,* 221–31. Toronto: McGraw-Hill 1966.

Halberstam, D. *The Fifties.* New York: Villard Books 1993.

Handley, S. *Nylon: The Story of a Fashion Revolution.* Baltimore, MD: Johns Hopkins University Press 1999.

Hardin, H. *A Nation Unaware: The Canadian Economic Culture.* Vancouver: J.J. Douglas 1974.

Hartcup, G. *The Challenge of War: Britain's Scientific and Engineering Contributions to World War Two.* New York: Taplinger 1970.

Hayes, B., and B. Abernathy. "Managing Our Way to Economic Decline." *Harvard Business Review* (July-August 1980): 67–77.

Herbert, V. and A. Bisio. *Synthetic Rubber: A Project That Had to Succeed.* Westport, CT: Greenwood Press 1985.

Hodges, L. "Color it Kodachrome." *American Heritage of Invention and Technology* 3, (1987): 46–53.

Hogan, M. *The Marshall Plan: America, Britain, and the Reconstruction of Western Europe 1947–1952.* Cambridge: Cambridge University Press 1987.

Holt, E.G. "Long-Term Outlook for Natural Rubber." *Canadian Chemistry and Process Industries* (June 1946): 49–51.

Hounshell, D. and J. Smith Jr. *Science and Corporate Strategy: Du Pont R&D, 1902–1980.* New York: Cambridge University Press 1988.

Howard, F. *Buna Rubber: The Birth of an Industry.* New York: Van Nostrand 1947.

Howe, C.D., et al. "Industrial Development in Canada." *Public Affairs* (December 1948), 209.

– *Canada: Nation on the March.* Toronto: Clarke, Irwin 1953.

Howitt, P. et al. *The Implication of Knowledge-Based Growth for Micro-Economic Policies.* Calgary: University of Calgary Press 1996.

Hurley, P.E. "History of Natural Rubber." In R. Seymour, ed., *History of Polymer Science and Technology*, 215–24. New York: Marcel Dekker 1982.

Hutcheson, J. "The Capitalist State in Canada." In K.J. Rea and J.T. McLeod, eds., *Business and Government in Canada: Selected Readings*, 43–61. Toronto: Methuen 1969.

Innis, H.A. *A History of Canadian Pacific Railway*. London: McClelland 1923.

– *The Fur Trade in Canada: An Introduction to Canadian Economic History*. New Haven, CT: Yale University Press 1930.

– *The Problems of Staple Production*. Toronto: Ryerson Press 1933.

– *The Cod Fisheries: The History of an International Economy*. New Haven, CT: Yale University Press 1940.

– "Government Ownership and the Canadian Scene." In M.Q. Innis, ed., *Essays in Canadian Economic History*, 78–96. Toronto: University of Toronto Press 1956.

Innis, M.Q., ed. *Essays in Canadian Economic History*. Toronto: University of Toronto Press 1956.

Ivanovszky, L. "BIOS Trip to Germany, 1946." *Petroleum* 10 (12 February 1947): 37–48.

James, R.W. *Wartime Economic Cooperation: A Study of Relations between Canada and the United States*. Toronto: Ryerson Press 1949.

– *John Rae: Political Economist*. Toronto: University of Toronto Press 1965.

Johnson, A.M. *The Challenge of Change: The Sun Oil Company, 1945–1977*. Columbus, OH: Ohio State University Press 1983.

Katz, R. "Skills of an Affective Administrator." *Harvard Business Review* 33, no. 1 (January-February 1955): 33–42.

Kennedy, J. *History of the Department of Munitions and Supply*. 2 vols. Ottawa: E. Cloutier, King's Printer and Controller of Stationery 1950.

Keynes, J.M. *The General Theory of Employment, Interest and Money*. Cambridge: Cambridge University Press 1936.

Kindleberger, C. *American Business Abroad: Six Lectures on Direct Investment*. New Haven, CT: Yale University Press 1969.

– *The Marshall Plan Days*. Boston, MA: Allen 1987.

Kleiderer, E.C. "The Pharmaceutical Industry of Germany." *Chemical and Engineering News* 27 (25 April 1949): 1206–8.

Klien, L. *A Social Scientist in Industry*. Epping, England: Gower Press 1976.

Knoontz, H. "The Management Theory Jungle." *Academy of Management Journal* (December 1961): 174–88.

Koerner, S. "Canada and the Post-War Reparations Programme." Edmonton, May 2000. Unpublished.

Krammer, A. "Technology Transfer as War Booty: The U.S. Technical Oil Mission to Europe, 1945." *Technology and Culture* 22, no. 1 (January 1981): 68–103.

Kuhn, H.A. "Development in the German Chemical Industry." *Chemical and Engineering News* 23 (September 1945): 1516–22.

Landes, D.S. *The Unbound Prometheus: Technological Change and Industrial Development in Western Europe from 1750 to the Present.* Toronto: McGraw Hill 1993.

Langford, J.W. "Air Canada." In B. Doern and A. Tupper, eds., *Public Corporations and Public Policy in Canada,* 251–84. Montreal: Institute for Research on Public Policy 1981.

Lank, H.H., and E.L. Williams. *The Du Pont Canada History.* Toronto: Du Pont Canada 1980.

Laqueur, W. *Germany Today.* London: Weidenfeld and Nicolson 1985.

Larratt-Smith, M.H. "C.D. Howe's Role in the Creation and Early Development of Polymer Corporation Ltd., 1942–1946." MA thesis, University of Toronto 1968.

Laux, J.K., and M.A. Molot. "Potash Corporation of Saskatchewan." In B. Doern and A. Tupper, eds., *Public Corporations and Public Policy,* 189–220. Montreal: Institute for Research on Public Policy 1981.

– *State Capitalism: Public Enterprise in Canada.* Ithaca, NY: Cornell University Press 1988.

Lazonick, W. *Business Organization and the Myth of the Market Economy.* Cambridge: Cambridge University Press 1991.

Leacock, S. "What Is Left of Adam Smith?" *Canadian Journal of Economics and Political Science* 1 (1935): 41–51.

Levitt, K. *Silent Surrender: The Multinational Corporation in Canada.* Toronto: Macmillan 1970.

Lexer, R. *Canada Ltd.* Toronto: McClelland and Stewart 1971.

Litchfield, P.W. "Rubber's Position in Modern Civilization." *Scientific Monthly* 49 (December 1939): 566–7.

Lower, A. *Canadians in the Making.* Toronto: Longmans 1958.

Lucas, R. "On the Mechanics of Economic Development." *Journal of Monetary Economics* 22 (1988): 3–42.

Lumsden, I., ed. *Close the 49th Parallel etc.: The Americanization of Canada.* Toronto: University of Toronto Press 1970.

Lyon, J. *Dome: The Rise and Fall of the House That Jack Built.* Toronto: Macmillan 1983.

Macdonald, I. "Foreign Ownership: Villain or Scapegoat?" In P. Russell, ed., *Nationalism in Canada,* 178–202. Toronto: McGraw-Hill 1966.

MacKay, D. *Empire of Wood: The MacMillan Bloedel Story.* Toronto: Douglas & McIntyre 1982.

Marchand, R. *Advertising the American Dream: Making Way for Modernity, 1920–1940.* Berkley, CA: University of California Press 1985.

Marchildon, G.P. *Profits and Politics: Beaverbrook and the Gilded Age of Canadian Finance.* Toronto: University of Toronto Press 1996.

Markides, C. "Back to Basics: Reversing Corporate Diversification." *Multinational Business* 4 (1991): 12–25.

Marshal, H. et al. *Canadian-American Industry: A Study in International Investment.* Toronto: McClelland and Stewart 1976.

McCraw, T.K., ed. *The Essential Alfred Chandler: Essays toward a Historical Theory of Big Business.* Boston: Harvard Business School 1988.

McDowall, D. *Steel at the Sault: Francis H. Clergue, Sir James Dunn, and the Algoma Steel Corporation, 1901–1956.* Toronto: University of Toronto Press 1984.

– *The Light: Brazilian Traction, Light and Power Company, 1899–1945.* Toronto: Toronto University Press 1988.

McFetridge, D.F. "Commercial and Political Efficiency: A Comparison of Government, Mixed, and Private Enterprises." In D.F. McFetridge, ed., *Canadian Industrial Policy in Action*, 195–230. Toronto: University of Toronto Press and the Royal Commission on the Economic Union and Development Prospects for Canada 1985.

– ed. *Canadian Industrial Policy in Action.* Toronto: University of Toronto Press and the Royal Commission on the Economic Union and Development Prospects for Canada 1985.

McKillop, A.B. *Matters of Mind: The University in Ontario.* Toronto: University of Toronto Press 1994.

McLuhan, M. *The Mechanical Bride: Folklore of Industrial Man.* New York: Vanguard Press 1951.

McMillan, C. "From Quality Control to Quality Management: Lessons from Japan." *Business Quarterly* 47 (May 1982): 31–40.

– "How Japan Uses Technology for Competitive Success: Lessons for Canadian Management." *Business Quarterly* 54 (summer 1988): 34–8.

McMillan, F. *The Chain Straighteners – Fruitful Innovation: The Discovery of Linear and Stereoregular Polymers.* London: Macmillan Press 1979.

McShane, Clay. *Down the Asphalt Path: The Automobile and the American City.* New York: Columbia University Press 1994.

Meikle, J. *American Plastic: A Cultural History.* New Brunswick, NJ: Rutgers 1995.

Mellor, D.P. *Australia in the War of 1939–45: The Role of Science and Industry.* Canberra: Australian War Memorial 1958.

Milward, A. *The Reconstruction of Western Europe, 1945–1951.* London: Methuen 1984.

Mintzberg, H. *The Structuring of Organizations.* Englewood Cliffs, NJ: Prentice-Hall 1978.

Morris, P.J. *The American Synthetic Rubber Research Program.* Philadelphia: University of Pennsylvania Press 1989.

Morton, M. "History of Synthetic Rubber." In R. Seymour, ed., *History of Polymer Science and Technology*, 225–38. New York: Marcel Dekker 1982.

Mullington, H.J. "The Federal Government as an Entrepreneur: The Canadian Experience." MA thesis, Carleton University 1969.

Mulvale, J.P. "Dependency, Nationalism, and Imperialism in the Canadian Petrochemical Industry: A Case Study of Polymer Corporation of Sarnia, Ontario." MA thesis, University of Windsor 1985.

Musolf, L.D. *Mixed Enterprise: A Developmental Perspective.* Lexington, MA: Lexington Books 1972.

Naylor, R.T. *The History of Canadian Business, 1867–1914.* 2 vols. Toronto: Lorimer 1975.

Neill, R.F. *A History of Canadian Economic Thought.* London: Routledge 1991.

Nelles, H.V. *The Politics of Development: Forests, Mines and Hydro-Electric Power in Ontario, 1849–1941.* Toronto: Macmillan of Canada 1974.

Neufeld, E.P. *A Global Corporation: A History of the International Development of Massey Ferguson Limited.* Toronto: University of Toronto Press 1969.

– ed. *Money and Banking in Canada: Historical Documents and Commentary.* Toronto: Stewart 1964.

Newman, P.C. *The Canadian Establishment.* Toronto: Seal Books 1975.

Nicholls, R.V., and C.J. Warrington. *A History of Chemistry in Canada.* Toronto: Pitman and Sons 1949.

Niosi, J. *Canadian Multinationals.* Toronto: Between the Lines 1985.

Norrie, K., and D. Owram. *A History of the Canadian Economy.* Toronto: Harcourt Brace 1996.

Nye, D.E. *Image Worlds: Corporate Identities at General Electric, 1890–1930.* Cambridge, MA: MIT Press 1985.

O'Callaghan, B.J. "The Government's Rubber Projects." vol. 2, Reconstruction Finance Corporation Report, 1948, as revised in 1955 under the supervision of Bertram H. Weimar, Office of Synthetic Rubber, Federal Facilities Corporation (U.S.) National Archives, Record Group 234, file no. 26.

Oliver, P. "Government, Industry and Science in Ontario: The Case of the Ontario Research Foundation." In P. Oliver, ed., *Public Persons: The Ontario Political Culture,* 1914–1934, 161–70. Toronto: Clarke 1975.

– ed. *Public Persons: The Ontario Political Culture, 1914–1934.* Toronto: Clarke 1975.

Owram, D. *The Government Generation: Canadian Intellectuals and the State, 1900–1945.* Toronto: University of Toronto Press 1986.

– *Born at the Right Time: A History of the Baby Boom Generation.* Toronto: University of Toronto Press 1996.

Panitch, L., ed. *The Canadian State: Political Economy and Political Power.* Toronto: University of Toronto Press 1977.

Park, L., and F. Park. *The Anatomy of Big Business.* Toronto: Lewis and Samuel 1962.

Peers, F.W. *The Politics of Canadian Broadcasting, 1920–1951.* Toronto: University of Toronto Press 1969.

Penrose, E. *The Theory of the Growth of the Firm.* Oxford: Blackwell 1959.

Peters, T., and R. Waterman. *In Search of Excellence: Lessons from America's Best-Run Companies.* New York: Harper and Row 1982.

Pettigrew, A. *The Awakening Giant: Continuity and Change in ICI.* Oxford: Blackwell 1985.

Phillips, C.F. *Competition in the Synthetic Rubber Industry.* Chapel Hill, NC: University of North Carolina Press 1962.

Plumptre, A.F.W. "Synthetic Tires a Problem for Ottawa, Not Industry." *Saturday Night,* vol. 62, 28 June 1947, 6–7.

Polysar Rubber Corporation. *Polysphere Fifty: A Special Issue to Commemorate Polysar Rubber Corporation's 50 Years, 1942–1992.* Sarnia: Agfa Imaging Systems and Supplies 1992.

Porter, M. "From Competitive Advantage to Corporate Strategy." *Harvard Business Review* 65, no. 3 (May-June 1987): 43–59.

Prahalad, C.K., and G. Hamel. "The Core Competence of the Corporation." *Harvard Business Review* 68 (May-June 1990): 79–91.

Pratt, L. "Petro-Canada." In B. Doern and A. Tupper, eds., *Public Corporations and Public Policy in Canada,* 95–148. Montreal: The Institute for Research on Public Policy 1981.

Prichard, J.R., ed. *Crown Corporations in Canada: The Calculus of Instrument Choice.* Toronto: Butterworth and the Ontario Economic Council 1983.

Pryke, R. *The Nationalized Industries: Policies and Performance since 1968.* Oxford: Martin Robertson 1981.

Purdy, A., ed. *The New Romans: Candid Canadian Opinions of the U.S.* Edmonton: Hurtig 1968.

Quintella, R.H., *The Strategic Management of Technology in the Chemical and Petrochemical Industries.* London: Printer Publishers 1993.

Rae, J. *Statement of Some New Principles on the Subject of Political Economy.* In R.W. James, ed., *John Rae: Political Economist.* Toronto: University of Toronto Press 1965.

Rea, K.J., and J.T. McLeod, eds. *Business and Government in Canada: Selected Readings.* Toronto: Methuen 1969.

Reich, L. *The Making of American Industrial Research: Science and Business at GE and Bell, 1876–1926.* New York: Cambridge University Press 1985.

Report of the Petrochemical Industry Task Force. Report to the Minister of Energy Mines and Resources and to the Minister of Regional Industrial Expansion. Ottawa: Supply and Services Canada 1984.

Reso, R.A. "Rubber in Brazil: Dominance and Collapse, 1876–1945." *Business History Review* 51 (1977): 341–66.

Richards, J., and L. Pratt. *Prairie Capitalism: Power and Influence in the New West.* Toronto: McClelland and Stewart 1979.

Rohmer, R. *Ultimatum.* Toronto: Clarke Irwin 1973.

Romer, P. "Idea Gaps and Object Gaps in Economic Development." *Journal of Monetary Economics* 32 (1993): 543–73.

Ross, D. "Patents and Bureaucrats: U.S. Synthetic Rubber Development before Pearl Harbor." In J. Frese and S.J. Judd, eds., *Business and Government,* 119–55. New York: Sleepy Hollow Press 1985.

Rotstein, A. *The Precarious Homestead.* Toronto: New Press 1971.

Rowzee, E.R. "Sarnia, the Birthplace of Canada's Petrochemical Industry." *Chemistry in Canada* (February 1950): 21–27.

Rumelt, R.P. *Strategy, Structure, and Economic Performance.* Boston: Harvard University Press 1974.

Russell, P., ed. *Nationalism in Canada.* Toronto: McGraw-Hill 1966.

Schultz, J.A. "Shell Game: The Politics of Defense Production, 1939–1942." *American Review of Canadian Studies* 16 (spring 1986): 41–57.

Schumpeter, J. *The Theory of Economic Development.* Cambridge, MA: Harvard University Press 1934.

– *History of Economic Analysis.* New York: Oxford University Press 1954.

Scott, B.R. "The Industrial State: Old Myths and New Realities." *Harvard Business Review* (March-April 1973): 133–45.

Seymour, R. *History of Polymer Science and Technology.* New York: Marcel Dekker 1982.

Shell Oil Company of Canada. *The Canadian Petrochemical Industry.* Toronto: Ryerson Press 1956.

Shemilt, L.W., ed. *Chemical Engineering in Canada: An Historical Perspective.* Ottawa: The Canadian Society for Chemical Engineering 1991.

Slater, D. "Consumption Expenditure in Canada." In Royal Commission on Canada's Economic Prospects, Final *Report.* Ottawa: November 1957.

Smiley, D. "Canada and the Quest for a National Policy." *Canadian Journal of Political Science* 8 (March 1975): 40–62.

Smith, D. *Rogue Tory: The Life and Legend of John G. Diefenbaker.* Toronto: Macfarlane, Walter & Ross 1998.

Smith, J.K. "The Ten-Year Invention: Neoprene and Du Pont Research, 1930–1939." *Technology and Culture* 26, no. 1 (January 1985): 34–55.

Smith, P. *It Seems like Only Yesterday: Air Canada, The First Fifty Years.* Toronto: McClelland and Stewart 1986.

Sobel, R. *The Age of Giant Corporations: A Microeconomic History of American Business, 1914–1984.* Westport, CT: Greenwood Press 1984.

Solo, R. "Research and Development in the Synthetic Rubber Industry." *Quarterly Journal of Economics* 63 (1954): 61–82.

– *Across the High Technology Threshold: The Case of Synthetic Rubber.* Norwood: Norwood Editions 1980.

Spitz, P.H. *Petrochemicals: The Rise of an Industry.* New York: Wiley 1988.

St Clair Processing Corporation. *Synthetic Rubber: A Process Digest.* Toronto: St Clair Processing 1943.

Stanbury, W.T., and F. Thompson. *Managing Public Enterprises.* New York: Praeger 1982.

Stevenson, G. "Canadian National Railways and Via Rail." In A. Tupper and B. Doern, eds., *Privatization, Public Policy and Public Corporations in Canada,* 45–92.

Stewart, W. *Uneasy Lies the Head: The Truth about Canada's Crown Corporations.* Toronto: Shrup 1987.

Stobaugh, R.B. *Innovation and Competition: The Global Management of Petrochemical Products.* Boston, MA: Harvard Business School Press 1988.

Stursberg, P. *Diefenbaker: Leadership Gained.* Toronto: University of Toronto Press 1975.

Sun Life Assurance Company of Canada. *The Canadian Automotive Industry.* Hull: Royal Commission on Canada's Economic Prospects 1956.

Tarasofsky, A. "The Canada Development Corporation, 1973–1983." Paper Presented to the Economic Council of Canada's Conference on Government Enterprise, Toronto: November 1984.

Taylor G.D., and P.A. Baskerville. *A Concise History of Business in Canada.* Toronto: Oxford University Press 1994.

Thompson, J.H. *The Harvests of War: The Prairie West, 1914–1918.* Toronto: McClelland and Stewart 1978.

Toninelli, P.A., ed. *The Rise and Fall of State-Owned Enterprise in the Western World.* Cambridge: Cambridge University Press 2000.

Traves, T. *The State and Enterprise: Canadian Manufacturers and the Federal Government, 1917–1931.* Toronto: University of Toronto Press 1979.

Tuttle Jr., W. "The Birth of an Industry: The Synthetic Rubber 'Mess' in World War II." *Technology and Culture* 22, no. 1 (January 1981): 35–67.

Underhill, F. "Oh Canada, Our Land of Crown Corporations." In H.D. Forbes, ed. *Canadian Political Thought,* 227–9. Toronto: Oxford University Press 1985.

Urquhart, M.C., ed., *Historical Statistics of Canada.* Toronto: MacMillan 1965.

Veljanovski, C.G. *Selling the State: Privatisation in Britain.* London: Weidenfeld and Nicolson 1987.

Vernon, R. *Sovereignty at Bay: The Multinational Spread of U.S. Enterprises.* New York: Basic Books 1971.

Waddell, C.R. "The Wartime Price and Trade Board: Price Control in Canada in World War II." PHD diss., York University 1981.

Warmington, A., T. Lupton, and C. Gribbin. *Organization Behaviour and Performance: An Open Systems Approach to Change.* London: Macmillan 1977.

Warnock, J. *Partner to Behemoth.* Toronto: New Press 1970.

Warrington, C.J. *A History of Chemistry in Canada.* Toronto: Pitman 1949.

Warrington, C.J., and B.T. Newbold. *Chemical Canada, Past and Present.* Ottawa: The Chemical Institute of Canada 1970.

Watkins, M. "The Dismal State of Economics in Canada." In I. Lumsden, ed., *Close the 49th Parallel: The Americanization of Canada,* 197–208. Toronto: University of Toronto Press.

Weidlein, E.R. "Synthetic Rubber Research in Germany." In *Chemical and Engineering News* (25 March 1946): 771–4.

Wexler, I. *The Marshall Plan Revisited: The European Recovery Program in Economic Perspective.* Westport, CT: Greenwood 1983.

Whitby, G.S., ed. *Synthetic Rubber.* New York: John Wiley & Sons 1954.

Wilbur, J.R.H., ed. *The Bennett New Deal: Fraud or Portent?* Toronto: Copp Clark 1968.

Wilkins, M. *The Maturing of Multinational Enterprise.* Cambridge, MA: Harvard University Press 1974.

Wilkins, M., and F. Hill. *American Business Abroad: Ford on Six Continents.* Detroit: Wayne State University Press 1964.

Wise, G. *Willis R. Whitney, General Electric, and the Origin of U.S. Industrial Research.* New York: Columbia University Press 1985.

Wolf, Howard, and Ralph Wolf. *Rubber: A Story of Glory and Greed.* New York: Covici, Friede 1936.

Wrigley, L. "Divisional Autonomy and Diversification." Unpublished DBA diss. Harvard Business School 1970.

Zuckerman, S. *Scientists and War: The Impact of Science on Military and Civil Affairs.* New York: Hamilton 1967.

Index